INTRODUCTION POLICING IN CANADA

Jayne Seagrave
Simon Fraser University

Prentice Hall Canada Inc.
Scarborough, Ontario

Canadian Cataloguing in Publication Data

Seagrave, Jayne, 1961–   .
    Introduction to policing in Canada.

ISBN 0-13-263997-1

1. Police – Canada. I. Title.

HV8157.S43 1997 363.2'0971 C96-931190-7

Prentice-Hall, Inc., Englewood Cliffs, New Jersey
Prentice-Hall International (UK) Limited, London
Prentice-Hall of Australia, Pty. Limited, Sydney
Prentice-Hall Hispanoamericana, S.A., Mexico City
Prentice-Hall of India Private Limited, New Delhi
Prentice-Hall of Japan, Inc., Tokyo
Simon & Schuster Asia Private Limited, Singapore
Editora Prentice-Hall do Brasil, Ltda., Rio de Janeiro

ISBN 0-13-263997-1

Acquisitions Editor: Rebecca Bersagel
Production Editor: Kelly Dickson
Copy Editor: Linda Cahill
Editorial Assistant: Shoshana Goldberg
Production Coordinator: Jane Schell
Cover Design: Ignition Design & Communication/Kyle Gell
Page Layout: Arlene Edgar

24 25 26 DPC 09 08 07

Printed in Canada

Every reasonable effort has been made to obtain permissions for all articles
and data used in this edition. If errors or omissions have occurred, they
will be corrected in future editions provided written notification has been
received by the publisher.

We welcome readers' comments, which can be sent by e-mail to
    collegeinfo_pubcanada@prenhall.com

Table of Contents

8 Stress and the Hazards of Police Work 162

Preface

Introduction to Policing in Canada is a sociologically-based, introductory-level textbook providing information on the key issues and debates that characterize policing. The text has been written to provide students of policing with a comprehensive collection of the ideas and issues that have influenced the historical development of policing in Canada and which continue to affect its development today. Unlike many of the existing texts on Canadian policing, *Introduction to Policing in Canada* is not an edited book containing a series of original and previously published articles, but rather an extensive, logically structured, referenced review of the policing process, police behavior, operations and organization. It offers both a descriptive and an analytical account of policing from its inception to date within a Canadian context.

To encourage students to understand how the concept of policing fits within Canadian society, the book utilizes theoretical perspectives, research findings, policy developments and organizational initiatives to inform its discussion in the belief that to explore and understand the diverse nature of police operations it is necessary to marry theory, empirical research, policy initiatives and policing practices. By integrating these elements, *Introduction to Policing in Canada* provides an extensively-referenced analysis and account not only of how the police currently function but of how they existed in the past, how they are changing and how they may exist in the future.

The text is targeted at undergraduate university and college students taking their first course on the police and includes issues most appropriate to an understanding of policing in Canada. It is hoped the book will also be of interest to a broader audience including police practitioners and policy makers many of whom may be familiar with the practice of policing but not the theory and research. The text also provides a useful supplement to courses on police management, community policing and Canadian criminal justice.

Throughout the book, attempts have been made to utilize Canadian data. While this has been possible for certain subjects, for others it has been necessary to draw on literature from other countries, most notably the United States. There is a tremendous need for research to be conducted on the unique organizational processes that characterize Canadian policing. By taking courses on policing, future academics may recognize this gap and go on to conduct much-needed research. One of the aims of this book is to encourage ongoing interest in the issue of policing in Canada and to stimulate further research.

ORGANIZATION

The book is divided into twelve chapters. The first four chapters serve to contextualize policing in Canadian society. Chapter 1 introduces students to the concept of policing and illustrates the interrelationships police agencies have with other agents of the criminal justice system and the public. The second chapter discusses the development of modern-day police agencies and provides an historical account of how the three levels of Canadian policing—federal, provincial and municipal—developed. As it is this tripartite system that characterizes Canadian policing, making it unique from policing systems in other western democracies, it is important for students to understand the historical antecedents. The third chapter illustrates how these three levels exist and coexist today. The subject matter presented in Chapters 2 and 3 is primarily descriptive, presenting a conceptual framework. Chapter 4 supplements this descriptive account by providing a theoretical discussion of the police role and its evolution. The first four chapters, therefore, provide the descriptive, theoretical and structural foundations on which the material presented in the following chapters can be placed.

Chapters 5 and 6 are concerned with police organization and management. Chapter 5 discusses personnel. The first part of the chapter looks at the recruitment and selection process while the second part focuses on a recent concern for police organizations: the ongoing attempts to recruit women, ethnic minorities and homosexuals to policing. The success of these developments to date and their future potential are reviewed. Chapter 6 addresses one of the key aims of the text by integrating theories of police organizations with research findings and includes details of many seminal academic works on policing, thereby introducing the student to the works of a number of renowned police scholars. This chapter also highlights organizational change—a key issue in many police agencies—and the factors which influence it.

Chapter 7 grounds an analysis of police behavior in both theoretical and empirical perspectives as do the following two chapters on stress and deviance and accountability. Each of these chapters presents theoretical perspectives, research findings and current policies and practices to address comprehensively the topic under review and to acquaint the student not only with the academic literature but also with police policies and practices.

The final three chapters discuss issues that are currently being debated in the police environment and will continue to be of considerable interest in the future. The growth and development of community policing was felt to be significant enough to justify two chapters. Chapter 10 describes how community policing is being interpreted and the various theories behind its acceptance and then moves on to review more pragmatic concerns, such as how it is being introduced in police organizations. Chapter 11, by drawing again on the tripartite structure of policing, reviews how community policing is being implemented. The final chapter discusses policing Aboriginal peoples. This issue, like that of community policing, has been and will continue to be of primary interest to police organizations across the country for the foreseeable future.

FEATURES

In order to make *Introduction to Policing in Canada* an effective learning instrument for students, the book contains a number of features.

Canadian content. The book has been designed to focus on policing within a Canadian context and so wherever possible examples of Canadian research, policies and practices have been included.

Academic research. Many chapters utilize studies from both Canada and other western democracies to inform the discussion. A conscious attempt has been made to include the seminal works by internationally-known police scholars to acquaint the student with those individuals who have influenced and guided our understanding of policing.

Headings and subheadings. These are used extensively throughout to break up the text and to detail the content of each section.

Introductions and summaries. Each chapter begins with an introduction, providing the reader with a synopsis of the issues to be covered, and ends with a summary detailing the most important ideas presented in each chapter.

Questions for discussion. At the end of each chapter, ten questions for classroom discussion are included. These often contain some of the more controversial issues, draw on the information presented in the chapter and are designed to assess the students' ability to grasp the topics under review.

Further reading. Abstracts of other texts pertinent to the chapter subject are contained at the end of each chapter. These citations include not only Canadian literature but also references to internationally-known works on policing and are intended to familiarize the student with the respected literature.

References. Each chapter is extensively referenced, enabling the student to find additional works which may be of interest.

Appendices. The RCMP Act and Ontario Police Services Act provide examples of Canadian police acts.

Bibliography. A comprehensive bibliography listing all the works cited appears at the end of the text.

SUPPLEMENTS

Instructor's manual. An instructor's manual outlines and summarizes the basic structure of each chapter and suggests ways in which material can be presented. The manual contains over 200 multiple choice questions and 60 short answer essay questions.

ACKNOWLEDGMENTS

I would like to thank numerous colleagues and friends at Simon Fraser University for their helpful comments and assistance on earlier versions of various chapters in this book; the reviewers, especially Barry Leighton; the editorial staff at Prentice Hall for their enthusiasm and guidance; and Andrew Dewberry who made me put pen to paper (or more aptly, fingers to keyboard).

JS, August, 1996

CHAPTER 1

THE CONCEPT OF POLICING

INTRODUCTION

There can be little doubt that the police occupy a pivotal position in Canadian society where concern for effective and equal law enforcement is a primary consideration. Compared to policing systems in other western democracies, the organization and administration of policing in Canada is unique. It is characterized by three different policing systems: federal, provincial and municipal, each serving different populations. These systems have developed independently of each other with differing purposes. This particular organizational composition, coupled with profound social and economic changes taking place in Canadian society, challenges all police forces and leads to debate over the structure, role and process of policing. This text has been written to contextualize and give an understanding of the distinctive nature of policing in Canada.

The aim of this initial chapter is to provide a discussion of the concept of policing. After defining the term, the chapter explores what the term implies for both totalitarian and democratic governments. The relationship between the police and the rule of law is then discussed as is the relationship between the police and the criminal justice system. The chapter concludes with a discussion of the public's perception of policing and an acknowledgment that there is a lack of Canadian data on the police, which requires us to draw on works from other western democracies to inform our understanding of the concept.

DEFINING THE POLICE

The word 'police' derives from two Greek words: *politeuein*—which means to engage in political activity or to be a citizen—and *polis* which means city or state (Roberg and Kuykendall, 1993). The origins of the word illustrate the link between the individual and the political process, as police organizations stand between the citizen and the state.

Both Bittner (1970) and Klockars (1985) define the police by examining what makes them distinctive from other government agencies. In this analysis they suggest that the use of coercive force is their defining characteristic. The police are granted the authority to compel individuals to comply with the requirements of the law. The police can be defined as non-military individuals or organizations who are given the general right by government to use coercive force to enforce the law and whose primary purpose is to respond to problems of individual and group conflict that involves illegal behavior (Roberg and Kuykendall, 1993). The police are, therefore, differentiated from others in their right to use force (Shearing and Leon, 1992).

Our concept of policing has changed as societies have developed. Once, decisions were made at the community level, but societies have become increasingly dependent on government, the law and the legal system not only to control deviant behavior but to provide a range of social services. Historically, citizens were involved in policing to a far greater extent than they are now. Prior to the mid-nineteenth century, communities were to an extent self-policing, a trait which still remains today when citizens function as police officers by exercising their civic responsibility in reporting crimes and assisting police organizations.

In defining the police, it is important to acknowledge distinctions among the citizen's role in policing (the citizen police officer), the public police and private police. Public police are police officers employed, trained and paid for by government whose objective is to enforce government laws. They are the ones most people recognize as police officers. Their origins date back to the first public police force introduced in London, England in 1829. In contrast, private police are police employed by an individual or organization, for example by a bank, department store or university (see Chapter 3), to serve a specific purpose. The number of these officers has grown considerably over the last thirty years. Private police are often referred to as security guards. There are, therefore, three types of police: citizen, public and private. This book is concerned with public policing.

The police do far more than enforce the law. As will be shown in Chapter 4, their functions include the maintenance of order and a wide array of government and social services (Marquis, 1994; Shearing and Leon; 1992). It is frequently noted that one of the defining characteristics of the police is their provision of a 24-hour service 365 days a year. Canadian society has tended to view police predominantly as law enforcers—the guardians of society whose functions are writ in law and whose policies and procedures are legal and overseen by the courts (Martin, 1995). As this text will illustrate, any definitions which position the police primarily as law enforcers are substantially flawed. Analysis of the daily activities of police officers in Canada and elsewhere has shown their role and function to be far broader than law enforcement (Ericson, 1982; Shearing and Leon, 1992). Although the public tends to see this as their defining characteristic, their scope is much larger and incorporates a vast array of social order and public service functions.

THE POLICE IN A DEMOCRATIC SOCIETY

There are two forms of government a society can chose to adopt: totalitarian or democratic. Totalitarian governments are characterized by a power centre represented by a dictator, a small number of people or one political party. Laws and policies are introduced and enforced for the benefit of those in power and social order is maintained at the expense of individual freedoms. The police in totalitarian societies enforce the laws of a powerful minority group. In contrast, democratic governments enact and enforce laws through elected representatives who have been chosen to represent the majority through the democratic process of elections. Democratic governments are usually committed to the idea of majority rule and minority rights (Roberg and Kuykendall, 1993). Majority rule is where the will of the majority (those who have voted for their representative) determines how resources are used and what laws should prevail, but these should not be at the expense of minority rights. Democratic governments acknowledge that all people have certain rights regardless of what the majority may prefer. For example, while the majority may be against a demonstration by a fascist political party this (minority) organization has the right to free expression.

Police organizations as agents of government walk a delicate tightrope in enforcing both majority rule and minority rights (Shiner, 1994). They form an important link between citizens and government in carrying out the police power of government as it relates to crime and order maintenance. Police act for government and the state and thereby act for the general populace; they are not independent of but responsible and accountable to the public.

The police represent the legitimate use of force governments have to control citizens and so they exist, in concept and in practice, at odds with many of the most important characteristics of a democratic society. In this regard, they have been seen as an anomaly in a free society (Goldstein, 1977). Democratic society is characterized by freedom, equality and participation; the police represent the authority government has over an individual, which is why they may be treated with suspicion and even hostility by some.

THE POLICE AND THE RULE OF LAW

The formulation and development of the law and its enforcement can be seen from two conflicting positions: consensus and critical. The consensus view sees legislation and the law as reflecting the needs and values of society and as protecting the interests of that society. In this interpretation, the police act to carry out the demands of the majority. For a balanced relationship to exist between individuals in a society, government rules and laws must be introduced and enforced. Governments require citizens to do certain things (for example, obtain a driver's licence prior to driving a car) and prohibit certain things (theft, murder, arson). The police acting as government agents ensure there is adherence to laws, and these laws must reflect the values and purposes of society (Roberg and Kuykendall, 1993). This is the consensus interpretation.

In contrast, critical interpretations consider legislation and its consequences to be in the interests of specific powerful groups who use it as a means of social control. The law is an instrument of social control used by the powerful to protect their interests; the police act as agents of social control ensuring the interests of the powerful are protected. Critical interpretations see the law and the police as being controlled by a few, serving the interests of the minority and contrast with the consensus view that contends the law and the police undertake the will of the majority.

The law is both a body of statements that defines what is to be considered a breach of the peace (substantive law) and a collection of statements providing authorization or instructions for how the police should deal with breaches of the peace (procedural law) (Shearing and Leon, 1992). The laws developed by the government in Canada can be placed into two categories: substantive law, which contains public and private law, and procedural law, which incorporates civil and criminal procedure.

Substantive law

Substantive law identifies prohibited or required behaviour and sets out sanctions for failing to observe the law. It incorporates the rules and principles that define the standards of two subcategories: private law and public law.

Private law (for example, contracts, property, real estate, family, estate law).   Private law is primarily concerned with conflicts between two independent parties.

Public law (for example, criminal law, taxation, constitutional law).
Public law is characterized by serving some public interest, which is why criminal law is found here.

Procedural law

Procedural laws articulate how legal matters travel through the legal system. They can be broken down into two categories: civil procedure and criminal procedure.

Civil procedure.   Civil procedure includes the rules of court (various statutes apply depending upon the level of court) which outline how civil matters such as contracts or property law will be pursued by the parties in the case.

Criminal procedure. Criminal procedure outlines specific rules defining how a criminal charge will be prosecuted. Criminal procedure is concerned with the relationship between individuals and government and provides rules which govern the conduct of individuals in society.

Procedural laws clarify how the police enforce substantive laws. The Canadian Charter of Rights and Freedoms entrenches a number of constitutional rights on behalf of the accused person and provides remedies for the infringement of these rights. In substantive law, police officers must follow procedural laws. Procedural laws exist to ensure police power is not abused and to reduce the possibility the police, as agents of government, will exceed their terms of reference.

The police are primarily concerned with criminal law. When issues are brought to court, the crime is seen to have been perpetrated by the citizen or citizens against the state. Unlike private law, which is primarily concerned with arguments between two opposing independent parties, criminal law recognizes that crimes are committed against the state, and the state prosecutes in the interest of society.

In order to ensure that laws are developed, introduced and enforced in a non-discriminatory fashion, three branches of government within a democracy oversee the process. All three are found at both the federal and provincial levels of government in Canada. The first is the legislative branch, which has elected officers who make laws (politicians); the second is the executive branch, which enforces the laws (police, government officials); while the third, judicial branch (judges, courts, lawyers) interprets the law and applies it within the context of a changing society. The Canadian police act in the executive branch of government, enforcing laws made by the legislative branch and interpreted by the judicial branch. All three arms of government oversee one another and provide a regulatory mechanism to control governmental power. As laws and interpretations of them are constantly being reviewed, reformed and introduced, police officers work in a dynamic, ever-changing environment. Because of this, they are faced with a number of stresses and challenges as they seek to perform their mandate. (These stresses will be discussed in Chapter 8.)

THE POLICE AND POLITICS

Although the police are accountable to various levels of government, they must be politically neutral:

> ...the tradition of political neutrality imposes that the police apply the law equally to all individuals without regard to personal biases or ideologies and that the police be immune from political interference designed to advance the interests of a particular party or ideology (Hatherly, 1991, p. 29).

The concept of political neutrality includes two related principles: firstly that law enforcement should be conducted in a fair and impartial manner affecting all citizens in an equal way, and secondly that police organizations should not be subject to political interference or intervention by governments. In examining further these principles, it is evident that a total separation of policing from politics is impossible. Policing is an inherently political activity because of both its institutional mandate awarded by the state and the way in which such a mandate is released (Hatherly, 1991). The fact that police officers enforce the law and uphold the peace means they are acting on the premise that social order needs to exist; police organizations have been created by governments so that this order can be maintained. Moreover, they are accountable to government officials, the elected representatives of the community. The police are, therefore, integrally related to governments who are in turn politically accountable to their communities for the actions of the police. This close association means it is not possible to isolate policing from the political context in which it takes place, and leads to debate over political neutrality.

THE POLICE AND THE CRIMINAL JUSTICE SYSTEM

Examinations of the criminal justice system centre on three components: police, courts and corrections. The police function as the 'gatekeepers' of this system by initially processing individuals who violate the law. Some commentators regard these three components as related yet independent, while others regard them as a 'system.'

A system may be defined as a set of interrelated components working separately or together toward a specific goal in a complex setting (Luthans, 1979). To further complicate this analogy, the police can be regarded as a subsystem of the criminal justice system. The police subsystem can be viewed as a system on its own, consisting of federal, provincial and municipal police subsystems characterized by three types of police organizations: the Royal Canadian Mounted Police (RCMP), provincial police forces and municipal police agencies.

In analyzing the Canadian criminal justice system, Griffiths and Verdun Jones (1994) list reasons why it qualifies as a system:

- All criminal justice agencies (police, courts and corrections) operate under the Constitution Act of 1867, process offenders under the auspices of the Criminal Code and in accordance with the regulations for procedure and evidence articulated in the Canadian Charter of Rights and Freedoms.

- There is an interdependence between criminal justice agencies, for example, the enforcement practices of the police affect the number and nature of cases that appear in the courts.

- Unlike the practice in the United States, where each state is responsible for enacting criminal statutes and establishing a system of criminal justice, in Canada the legislative and judicial arrangements show a degree of uniformity across the country by operating under the Criminal Code. The RCMP polices federal, provincial and municipal levels, making it a national police force in that it is given responsibility by three levels of government across the country. National police forces are not found in the United States where there is a clear demarkation between federal (FBI) and state jurisdiction.

While there are obvious merits in seeing the police as part of the wider criminal justice system, it is also important to recognize that the police agency as an institution "...has a life and an importance of its own independent of the systems to which it relates" (Goldstein, 1977, p. 33). Police officers clearly have a different mandate from those officials employed in courts and corrections; their activities and decision-making processes vary considerably from other criminal justice personnel and their operational goals may not accord with other components of the system. Furthermore, the volume of work handled by the police is far greater than the rest of the criminal justice system. In all these respects they form a distinctive body. Despite these individual characteristics, police functioning "...relies heavily upon and is almost inextricably interrelated with the operations of the criminal justice system—the process of arrest, prosecution, trial, sentencing, imprisonment or probation and parole" (Goldstein, 1977, p. 21). According to Goldstein, this reliance on the criminal justice system has made all police functions, even those of a non-criminal nature, almost synonymous with it, leading to the belief in the public's mind that all police work includes crime. As mentioned above, this point is explored at length in Chapter 4 where it is shown that the police role incorporates considerably more than crime control, and that many clients of the police have no contact with the other two components of the system.

THE POLICE AND THE PUBLIC

Generally, Canadians hold their police officers and police forces in high esteem. An understanding of the extent and nature of this support is important because it provides insights into why police-community relations policies succeed or fail and helps in comprehending the background to police initiatives.

In an international survey, Canadians were found to be most supportive of their police forces, with nine out of ten being satisfied by the performance of their police officers (Normandeau and Leighton, 1990). This overall support is reflected in regional findings. In Nova Scotia, 80% of residents described police-community relations as excellent (Murphy and Clairmont, 1990); these figures have been mirrored in Ontario (Yarmey, 1991) and New Brunswick (Baseline, 1991). Overall, Canadians have positive perceptions of the police, particularly on measures of approachability and enforcing the law (Statistics Canada, 1991).

Although the level of overall support is high, it is important to recognize that certain groups in society are more supportive than others. Older Canadians tend to be more appreciative of the police than do younger people, particularly males, who are more likely to have had direct contact with the police. This factor was identified in the *Canadian Urban Victimization Survey* (Canada, 1985) and recognized by others (Brillion et al., 1984; Murphy and Lithopoulos, 1988, Statistics Canada, 1991).

Aboriginal peoples and members of cultural and ethnic minorities are more prone to hold negative perceptions of the police. Griffiths and Verdun Jones (1994) state this to be a virtually unresearched area; however, Forcese (1991) contends that variations in evaluations of police performance by members of ethnic groups is regularly identified in research. Murphy and Lithopoulos (1988) undertook research in Metropolitan Toronto to find European and Anglo-Celtic residents had high evaluations of the police whereas Italians and East Indians had low evaluations. Research undertaken on the relationships between the police and Aboriginal peoples has shown these to be poor, often characterized by mistrust and hostility (Hamilton and Sinclair, 1991; Sunahara, 1992).

Studies have suggested that direct personal contact with a police officer or police agency determines attitudes and shapes the opinion an individual has of the police. Negative attitudes may be fostered if people experience or witness police misconduct, or even receive anecdotal information about such occurrences (Forcese, 1992). Victims of crime also tend to be more disenchanted with the police (Yarmey, 1991). Personal contact therefore influences public perception.

Public satisfaction with police services is not uniform across Canada, but varies between provinces and even between adjacent areas. A 1981 survey of Quebec, Ontario and Manitoba found overall that 86% of respondents were satisfied with police services, but dissatisfaction was higher in Quebec at 26% compared to 8% in Manitoba and 7% in Ontario (Brillion et al., 1984). In Toronto, a study of attitudes towards the police found considerable variations not only across different neighborhoods but among groups within neighborhoods (Murphy and Lithopoulos, 1988). In discussing public satisfaction, it is important to acknowledge regional variations.

It would, therefore, appear that, while certain groups within Canadian society do not hold positive views about the police, overall the police receive considerable public support.

STUDIES OF CANADIAN POLICING

The police occupy a fundamental position in Canadian society and yet the perceptions that many Canadians have of their police service are frequently based on unrealistic and sensational media accounts. Even in the academic community, the knowledge and comprehension of *Canadian* policing is limited as sociological, criminological and organizational studies of police agencies are rare. Consequently, in understanding the concept of policing in Canadian society, much of our insight is gleaned from studies undertaken in other countries, most notably the United States, and to a lesser extent Britain, each of which has a longer more prolific tradition of police research and whose cultures resemble Canada's, enabling comparisons to be made.

The dearth of literature on policing from a Canadian perspective necessitates the inclusion of American and British literature in this book to a degree that is almost embarrassing to one who has striven to include Canadian material. This failing is less extreme for chapters on, for example, community policing and police personnel, but in chapters that address issues such as police stress and the police role and function, reliance on foreign material is heavy.

Although a number of books are available on the historical development of the RCMP (Brown and Brown, 1978; Kelly and Kelly, 1976; Waldon, 1982) and other police agencies (Fox, 1971; Higley, 1984; Stonier-Newman, 1991; Talbot et al., 1986), the amount of empirical research is small compared to that from the US and Britain. This has resulted in Canadian academics and police commentators applying the findings of research undertaken in the United States (and elsewhere) to Canada (Murphy, 1988). Some of this research is clearly applicable, for example, it has been found that the characteristics of the police subculture are similar in many countries (Bayley, 1985) and, therefore, one can apply the findings of the subcultural studies undertaken in the UK and US to Canada. When Canadian studies of police work have been undertaken, they have shown similarities with studies undertaken in other countries. Previous studies conducted elsewhere have acted as 'methodological springboards' in which to ground research questions and assess methodologies. For example, in conceptualizing his study of patrol work in a Canadian city, Ericson (1982) draws heavily on literature from other countries.

While there are obvious advantages in drawing on research from other countries, the practice has severe limitations. The administrative and bureaucratic structure of Canadian policing, which includes the RCMP, provincial police departments and independent municipal police agencies, has no parallel in Britain, which has larger police forces, nor the US, which has a greater number of smaller police agencies. The structure of policing in Canada falls somewhere between these two extremes and justifies its own research agenda. In addition, the historical antecedents, demographic, socio-economic and ethnic composition of the Canadian population are difficult to equate to either the United States or Britain. There are many policing issues unique to Canada, for example, the role of the RCMP in undertaking national, provincial and local police duties, the need to police vast areas of sparsely-populated land and the problems of policing rapidly-growing urban communities. Such uniquely Canadian issues cannot be informed by studies from other jurisdictions.

Police practitioners and academics in Canada have drawn on studies from other countries to inform their policies on policing but there is clearly a need to initiate Canadian research. Unlike Britain, which has the Police Foundation and the Home Office Research and Planning Unit, and the United States, which has the Police Executive Research Forum and the Police Foundation, Canada does not have a national facility for promoting and initiating policing research. Since the April 1993 demise of the *Canadian Police College Journal*, it does not have a vehicle for the dissemination of the results of projects conducted in Canada.

Although the comparative lack of research can be attributed in part to Canada's smaller population, without an autonomous institute for Canadian police research similar to those in other western democracies, police research will remain fragmented and peripheral, being primarily conducted in university departments, the Canadian Police College and under contract to federal and provincial governments, subject to haphazard funding.

Although criminological theories about the police have been used to explore policing in Canada and have led researchers to argue that there are more similarities in 'Anglo-American' policing than differences, this point is "clearly open to challenge" (Fielding, 1988, p. 62). In testing theory, the research techniques employed must account for local conditions; more topic-specific treatment of Canadian policing is needed. Theories of policing may be taken from other jurisdictions and applied in Canada but empirical analysis must be located here. There exists a need for research on law enforcement in Canada in order to enhance our currently limited understanding of it.

SUMMARY

This chapter has sought to provide an introduction to the concept of police. The term derives from Greek origins linking the citizen with the state. The type of police system a society develops is dependent upon the system of government: totalitarian or democratic. The laws which govern police and society are also dependent on the political system. The police form part of the criminal justice system and, in Canada overall, receive considerable public support. The lack of literature on Canadian policing necessitates drawing on empirical research from other western democracies to inform our analysis.

QUESTIONS FOR DISCUSSION

1. What are the defining characteristics of the police?
2. Define the three types of police officer.
3. Describe the types of policing systems that exist in democratic and totalitarian societies.
4. In what ways may the concept of policing be at odds with the concept of a democratic society?
5. Provide examples of the conflict between majority rule and minority rights.
6. Describe the difference between civil and criminal law.
7. To what extent should the police be treated as an integral part of the criminal justice system and to what extent an autonomous agency?
8. Why do you think public satisfaction with police services varies among provinces?
9. Why do you think the Canadian population is broadly supportive of the police?
10. Why are there comparably fewer studies on policing conducted in Canada than there are in Britain or the United States?

FURTHER READING

Bittner, E. (1970). *The Functions of Police in Modern Society.* Washington D.C.: Center for Studies of Crime and Delinquency, National Institute of Mental Health. This text is somewhat of a classic and examines the function and role of policing within the wider context of the criminal justice system. It explains and interprets the police officers' role and the influence organizational structure, coupled with considerable occupational independence, has upon it.

McDougall, Allan K. (1988). *Policing: The Evolution of a Mandate.* Ottawa: Canadian Police College. This text examines the police in light of the changing, heterogeneous composition of Canadian society and in relation to government.

Stenning, Philip C. (1982). *Legal Status of the Police.* Ottawa: Law Reform Commission of Canada. This work provides a factual review of the origins of police constables in England and Canada to contextualize their legal status. From this point, the author examines how their status relates to their independence and government control.

The Canadian Police College Journal. Although this journal ceased publication in 1993, over the course of its 14-year life it included a number of academic and practitioner-oriented articles, authored by police officers, policy makers and academics. The existing copies provide diverse opinion on a broad range of policing issues from a Canadian perspective.

REFERENCES

Baseline Market Research Ltd. (1991). *Public Attitude Survey: Crime, Safety and Policing Services in New Brunswick.* New Brunswick: Department of the Solicitor General.

Bayley, D.H. (1985). *Patterns of Policing: A Comparative International Analysis.* New Jersey: Rutgers University Press.

Bittner, E. (1970). *The Functions of Police in Modern Society.* Cevy Chase, Md.: National Institute of Mental Health.

Brillion, Yves, Louis-Guerin, Christian and Lamarche, Marie Christine (1984). *Attitudes of the Canadian Public Toward Crime Policies.* Montreal: International Centre for Comparative Criminology, University of Montreal.

Brown, Lorne and Brown, Caroline (1978). *The Unauthorized History of the RCMP.* Toronto: Lewis and Samuel.

Canada (1985). "Criminal victimization of elderly Canadians." *Canadian Urban Victimization Survey Bulletin 6:1.*

Ericson, R. (1982). *Reproducing Order: A Study of Police Patrol Work.* Toronto: University of Toronto Press.

Fielding, N. (1988). "Competence and Culture in the Police." *Sociology, 22*(1).

Forcese, Dennis P. (1992). *Policing Canadian Society.* Scarborough: Prentice Hall.

Fox, A. (1971). *The Newfoundland Constabulary.* St. John's: Robinson Blackmore Printing and Publishing Ltd.

Goldstein, H. (1977). *Policing a Free Society.* Cambridge Mass.: Ballinger.

Griffiths, Curt T. and Verdun Jones, Simon N. (1994). *Canadian Criminal Justice.* Toronto: Harcourt Brace.

Hatherly, Mary E. (1991). *The Legal Status of the Police.* Fredericton: Department of the Solicitor General New Brunswick.

Hamilton, Associate Chief Justice A.C. and Sinclair, Associate Chief Judge C.M. (1991). *Report of the Aboriginal Justice Inquiry of Manitoba. The Justice System and Aboriginal People.* Vol. 1. Winnipeg: Queen's Printer.

Higley, Dan D. (1984). *OPP: The History of the Ontario Provincial Police Force.* Toronto: The Queen's Printer.

Kelly, W. and Kelly, N. (1976). *Policing in Canada.* Toronto: MacMillan.

Klockars, C.B. (1985). *The Idea of Police.* Newbury Park, California: Sage.

Luthans, F. (1985). *Organizational Behaviour.* New York: McGraw-Hill.

Marquis, Greg (1994). "Power from the street: The Canadian municipal police." In R.C. Macleod and David Schneiderman (Eds.) *Police Powers in Canada: The Evolution and Practice of Authority.* Toronto: University of Toronto Press.

Martin, Maurice A. (1995). *Urban Policing in Canada: Anatomy of an Aging Craft.* Montreal: McGill Queens University Press.

Murphy, C. (1988). "Community problems, problem communities and community policing in Toronto." *Journal of Research in Crime and Delinquency, 24*(4).

Murphy, C. and Clairmont, D. (1990). *Rural Attitudes and Perceptions of Crime, Policing and Victimization: Preliminary Findings from a Survey of Rural Nova Scotians.* Halifax: Atlantic Institute of Criminology, Dalhousie University.

Murphy, C. and Lithopoulos, S. (1988). *Social Determinants of Attitudes Towards the Police: Findings from the Toronto Community Policing Survey.* Ottawa: Solicitor General of Canada.

Normandeau, A. and Leighton, B. (1990). *A Vision of the Future of Policing in Canada: Police Challenge 2000—Background Document.* Ottawa: Police and Security Branch, Ministry Secretariat, Solicitor General.

Roberg, Roy R. and Kuykendall, Jack (1993). *Police and Society.* Belmont California: Wadsworth Publishing Company.

Shearing, Clifford D. and Leon, Jeffrey S. (1992). "Reconsidering the police role: A challenge to a challenge of a popular conception." In K.R.E. McCormick and L.A. Visano (Eds.) *Understanding Policing.* Toronto: Canadian Scholars Press.

Shiner, Roger A. (1994). "Citizens' rights and police powers." In R.C. Macleod and David Schneiderman (Eds.) *Police Powers in Canada: The Evolution and Practice of Authority.* Toronto: University of Toronto Press.

Statistics Canada (1991). "Public perceptions of crime and criminal justice." *Juristat 11*(1). Ottawa: Statistics Canada.

Stonier-Newman, Lynne (1991). *Policing A Pioneer Province: The B.C. Provincial Police 1858-1950*. Madeira Park B.C.: Harbour Publishing.

Sunahara, D.F. (1992). "Public inquiries into policing." *Canadian Police College Journal, 16*(3).

Talbot, C.K., Jayewardene, C.H.S. and Juliani, T.J. (1986). *Canada's Constables: The Historical Development of Policing in Canada*. Ottawa: Crimcare Inc.

Waldon, K. (1982). *Visions of Order: The Canadian Mounties in Symbol and Myth*. Toronto: Butterworths.

Yarmey, A.D. (1991). "Retrospective perceptions of police following victimization." *Canadian Police College Journal, 15*(2).

THE ORIGINS AND DEVELOPMENT OF POLICING IN CANADA

INTRODUCTION

Much of the structure, operation and organization of policing in Canada was taken from policing systems in England and France. Therefore, before an examination of the historical development of policing in Canada can be conducted, attention needs to be given to the origins of policing in the western world as these early policing systems influenced the structure, formulation and philosophy of Canadian policing. The first part of this chapter, therefore, outlines the development of early police systems, focusing on the first modern police system which was established in nineteenth-century England. This is followed by a discussion of the origins and development of the federal, provincial and municipal policing systems which currently exist in this country.

THE HISTORICAL DEVELOPMENT OF POLICING

It has been argued that the modern systems of law enforcement established in Canada have experienced only minimal transformation since the inception of their predecessors in England (Hatherly, 1991) and that the structure and operation of police forces in Canada can be related to those in London (Sewell, 1985). In order to contextualize a discussion about the development of policing in Canada, an analysis of the first contemporary police force in the western world is required. The creation of the first modern police force is attributed to Sir Robert Peel who, in 1829 while Home Secretary (the person responsible for internal security in England), established the first recognized police force, the Metropolitan Police in London, England.

Although the Metropolitan Police sowed the seeds for the development of the system of policing we recognize today, early systems of policing can be traced back to medieval Europe where a nobleman or monarch would employ a sheriff and men to collect taxes, enforce laws relating to property and protect the peace (Cooper, 1981; Forcese, 1992; McDowell, 1993).

The watch system

The Statute of Westminster of 1285 affirmed an early system of policing by developing the 'watch and ward' approach. A 'watch,' or group of watchmen, of a size dependent upon the size of the town, was introduced under the auspices of a constable (Cooper, 1981). One man from each parish served for one year as the constable responsible for organizing the watch, managing the watchmen, guarding the gates of the town and for bringing offenders to court (Sewell, 1985). No payment was received for the work. Men were recruited to watch over neighborhoods, primarily at night, and had powers of arrest during the hours of darkness. All the men of a town had to serve on the watch on a rotating basis and there was punishment for those who did not serve (Cooper, 1981). In the mid 1300s the office of the justice of the peace was created. The local constables became assistants to the justices of the peace and their role was extended to include serving warrants and delivering prisoners into custody (Uchida, 1993).

The watch system continued as the primary system of policing for hundreds of years. However, with the advent of urbanization, a more affluent middle class developed, the more wealthy members of which hired others to substitute for them on the watch. It was this practice, together with the perception that crime was increasing, that led to the introduction of a full-time paid police force.

The Bow Street Runners

In 1750, police reformer and magistrate Henry Fielding secured funds to hire people to catch criminals. These individuals became known as the Bow Street Runners as they operated primarily around the Bow Street area of London. They were concerned with the apprehension of criminals, not crime prevention (Sewell, 1985). The initiative was expanded over the course of the next seventy years to include foot and horse patrols, and by the 1800s, nine such organizations existed in London (Roberg and Kuykendall, 1993).

The first police bill

In the late eighteenth century, street crime and rowdiness, much of it attributed to the widespread availability of gin, prompted the authorities in England to seek ways to control unruly people. The Gordon riots of 1780, when for nearly a week London experienced mob violence which was eventually quelled by the army (Critchley, 1978), succeeded in adding more fuel to the debate. In 1785, William Pitt introduced a Police Bill in Parliament to establish a police force in London which would be responsible for apprehending criminals and preventing crime.

Pitt's 1785 bill met with intense opposition and severe criticism for a number of reasons. It was felt that a new police force would be a secret organization similar to the French gendarmes, with spies and informers (Sewell, 1985). France had formed a Sûreté in 1810 that included many former criminals and was regarded by many as a corrupt force (Forcese, 1992). The English were therefore reluctant to embrace what was regarded as a French initiative. In addition, the City of London strongly opposed the bill seeing it as a violation of its corporate dignity and right to self government (Critchley, 1978). Many argued the bill was a threat to personal liberty and an invasion of privacy. It was subsequently defeated.

Although Pitt's bill of 1785 did not reach fruition in the English Parliament, in 1786 a similar bill was enacted in the Irish Parliament which laid the foundations of the Royal Irish Constabulary (Cooper, 1981).

The need for reform

Despite opposition to the 1785 Police Bill, during the next forty years a number of factors led people to recognize the need for an organized system of policing. At the end of the 1700s hundreds of individuals started to move off the land to the newly-developing towns to find work. The Industrial Revolution brought massive social and economic change; the population of London doubled between 1750 and 1820. With industrial growth came social disorganization as crime, riots and public health issues developed, illustrating the inadequacies of the existing systems of law enforcement. Social, economic and demographic changes therefore resulted in demands for an organized system of law enforcement. The constable system could no longer deal with the pressures of industrialization and alternative solutions were sought.

Reasons for the pressure to introduce a police service can be listed as follows:

- As the Industrial Revolution progressed, providing more wealth, an increasingly vocal middle class complained about the problems of walking safely in the streets, which were populated by thieves, beggars and prostitutes, and began to recognize the need for a system of law enforcement (Sewell, 1985; Uchida, 1993).

- Companies were increasingly looking for ways to protect their property and starting to establish their own private forces, the most notable being the Marine Police, established in 1798 to protect the interests of the Port of London. Recognizing the need for such a provision, the government introduced the Thames River Police Act in 1800 and converted this private venture to a public concern (Critchley, 1978).

- Philosophers such as Jeremy Bentham successfully argued for prevention over punishment. As Bentham's views received more credibility, the establishment of a police force that aimed to prevent crime by deterring criminals with fear of apprehension was given more credibility and counteracted concerns about the French system.

- In the year prior to the creation of the Metropolitan Police, there were 4500 watchmen employed by the City of London, the Metropolitan District and local parishes, in addition to 450 Thames River Police and the Bow Street Patrols, resulting in the expenditure of a quarter of a million pounds (Critchley, 1978). Economic and rational considerations therefore came into play as the benefits of establishing one integrated system were realized.

Sir Robert Peel and the principles of policing

Robert Peel introduced legislation in the English Parliament to establish a police force in London. The Metropolitan Police Act, passed by the British Parliament in 1829, established the police office at Scotland Yard from which a new force of police officers were to be supervised. Initially, Charles Rowan, who had a military background, and Richard Mayne, who was a barrister, were appointed to develop the force. They adopted a military approach still evident in policing systems today. One hundred men started policing London on 29 September 1829; the following year the force had grown to over 3,000. By the 1850s, every borough and county in England was required to develop its own police force.

Rowan and Mayne suggested nine principles which were to guide the new force:

1. To prevent crime and disorder as an alternative to their repression by military force and by severity of legal punishment.

2. To recognize always that the power of the police to fulfill their functions and duties is dependent on public approval of their existence, actions and behavior, and on their ability to secure and maintain public respect.

3. To recognize always that to secure and maintain the respect and approval of the public means also the securing of the willing cooperation of the public in the task of securing observance of laws.

4. To recognize always that the extent to which the cooperation of the public can be secured diminishes, proportionately, the necessity of the use of physical force and compulsion for achieving police objectives.

5. To seek and preserve public favor, not by pandering to public opinion, but by constantly demonstrating absolutely impartial service to law, in complete independence of policy and with regard to justice and injustices of the substance of individual laws; by readily offering individual service and friendship to all members of the public without regard to their wealth or social standing; by ready exercise of courtesy and friendly good humor; and by ready offering of sacrifice in protecting and preserving life.

6. To use physical force only when the exercise of persuasion, advice and warning is found to be insufficient to obtain public cooperation to an extent necessary to secure observance of law to restore order; and to use only the minimum degree of physical force which is necessary on any particular occasion for achieving a police objective.

7. To maintain at all times a relationship with the public that gives reality to the historic tradition that the police are the public and the public are the police; the police being only members of the public who are paid to give full-time attention to duties which are incumbent on every citizen, in the interests of community welfare and existence.

8. To recognize always the need for strict adherence to public executive functions, and to refrain from even seeming to usurp the powers of the judiciary or avenging individuals or the state, and from authoritatively judging guilt or punishing the guilty.

9. To recognize always that the test of police efficiency is the absence of crime and disorder and not the visible evidence of police action in dealing with them.

These principles primarily concerned police behavior. What remained unclear in 1829, and still remains ill defined today, is the real role and function of police in society, an issue which will be discussed in Chapter 4.

Despite the passage of the 1829 Act, the British populace continued to show considerable resistance to the new police (Roberg and Kuykendall, 1993). This opposition centred on a fear the police would be a means of government control and intervention in private lives (Martin, 1995). However, during the course of the nineteenth century, these fears dissolved as the police became accepted and supported by the population. Reiner (1985) has identified several policies that were instrumental in facilitating the acceptance of the police by the public:

- The police established a bureaucratic and hierarchical chain of command. Police officers were recognized as operating under tight, internal organizational controls.

- The police were seen to be administered under well-articulated legal constraints. The rule of law was a prime characteristic of police operations.

- The police were established to be nonpartisan and insulated from direct political control.

- The strategy of minimum force and the absence of weapons other than the 'truncheon' (baton) helped officers gain credibility.

- The image of the police as a 24-hour *service* did much to promote legitimacy and acceptance.

- The preventative role of policing was stressed over the law enforcement one.

In addition to the factors identified by Reiner, it can be seen that Peel and his associates carefully orchestrated the introduction of the police. They selected men who were even-tempered and reserved, chose an unassuming uniform of blue—not the military red of the day—insisted that officers be polite and restrained and stressed prevention over law enforcement (Uchida, 1993). During the course of the nineteenth century, the 'bobbies' or 'peelers' as they were known became accepted as an integral part of society.

TABLE 2.1 Significant Dates in the Development of Modern Policing

1285	The Statute of Westminster established the 'Watch and Ward' approach
1750	Henry Fielding established the Bow Street Runners
1780	Gordon Street Riots
1785	William Pitt introduced the first Police Bill to create a police force; it was defeated
1786	Royal Irish Constabulary established
1798	Marine Police created
1800	Thames River Police Act
1829	Passage of the Metropolitan Police Act introduced by Robert Peel created the first modern police force

Table 2.1 lists the main events which led to the creation of a comprehensive police service.

INFLUENCES ON CANADIAN POLICING

The historical review of policing in England has considerable bearing on the development of Canadian policing as many of the philosophies and ideologies developed there were transported and introduced here. McDougall (1988) demonstrates the influence of English reformers and developments on the system of municipal government in Ontario and Ericson (1982) notes Canada inherited a tradition of public police that began with Peel's London police. As in Britain, early police systems in Canada were characterized by the watch system but as the population increased and moved to towns and cities, this system of policing was no longer viable (Cooper, 1981). Canada at first adopted the policing system that had developed in England but later developed its own, parallel system. However, not all Canadian police agencies can be easily likened to those in England, as noted by Mawby (1990). Events such as the Yukon gold rush of 1897, the exploration of the MacKenzie delta and the Arctic archipelago resulted in the North West Mounted Police engaging in a far wider range of roles than those performed by their English counterparts or those employed by Canadian municipalities.

While colonial influences have undoubtedly affected the development of policing, a number of other issues have also contributed to the unique character of the police system in Canada. In attempting to understand the development of policing in Canada, these other factors should also be borne in mind.

Demographic influences

The growth of immigration and settlement patterns from east to west in the late nineteenth and early twentieth centuries, coupled with increasing urbanization, affected the growth and development of police agencies. These influences continue to be felt today when disproportionate numbers of culturally diverse visible minorities who hold different expectations than the resident population settle in Canadian urban centres such as Toronto, Montreal and Vancouver. These groups exert pressure on the police to improve, and in some instances, reassess and alter their delivery of service.

Political influences

The involvement of the federal, provincial and municipal governments in policing has undoubtedly influenced its development. For example, early legislation created and extended the auspices of the RCMP while more recent acts, including the Multiculturalism Act (1988), the Employment Equity Act (1986) and the Canadian Charter of Rights and Freedoms (1982), have affected the delivery of police services.

Geographical influences

The size of the country and the challenges this creates for establishing and developing police services is an issue unique to Canada. The diversity of environments in which Canadians live, from remote, Arctic, sparsely-populated settlements to large, urban metropolises, poses ongoing challenges to police organizations providing services to these diverse communities. This was a challenge faced by early police organizations and continues today.

Social and cultural influences

These influences relate to policing a heterogeneous country in a multicultural environment characterized by an indigenous Aboriginal population, early French and English pioneers and influxes throughout the twentieth century of a wide variety of ethnic and cultural groups. Traditionally, Canada's social order emphasized the assimilation of new immigrants (and the indigenous population). From the 1960s onward, this notion has been challenged and now stress is placed on ethnic and racial diversity as an integral component of Canadian society. The promotion of ethnic and cultural diversity as a national resource places challenges on police agencies, which see themselves caught between a professional crime-fighting model of policing and one advocating policing methods sensitive to the diverse ethnic and cultural composition of the population.

Historical influences

Canadian policing has been strongly affected by the system of policing which developed in England in the 1800s. More recently, the legacy of policies and initiatives developed with the best intentions in the past have been fundamentally challenged, especially with respect to policing Aboriginal people (see Chapter 12). In attempting to understand the problems police agencies have in implementing change, one needs to be cognizant of these antecedents.

THE HISTORICAL DEVELOPMENT OF POLICING IN CANADA

As previously mentioned, one of the unique aspects of Canadian policing is its three distinctive policing systems: municipal, federal and provincial. In order to understand how this singularly distinctive tripartite system came into being, it is necessary to review the historical development of policing in Canada.

Early municipal policing

Early police systems in Canada were diverse and multifaceted. Each area of the country had its own policing arrangements, depending upon the settlement and the origin of the settlers. In Upper Canada, now Ontario, English settlers developed laws and a system of policing similar to that in England. In French Canada, a French system developed. The towns of Quebec and Montreal were among the first areas to develop an identifiable policing system. Responsibility for these early forms of police was taken by the richest landlords, who acted as magistrates, and who formed the town's night watchmen to guard against crime and prevent fires. Police regulations for New France were drafted as early as 1673 (Mawby, 1990). This system existed until the conquest of New France by the British in 1759, when the French system was altered and a more British approach adopted.

There is some debate as to when the first police officer appeared in Canada. Kelly and Kelly (1976) argue that it was in Quebec City in 1651, although Fox (1971) asserts it was in St. John's Newfoundland in 1729. These early police officers served primarily as night watchmen. It was not until the imposition of British laws and the creation of Justices of the Peace in 1673 that their role expanded to include law enforcement (Griffiths and Verdun Jones, 1994).

In 1793, the Parish and Town Officers Act was passed. This provided for the appointment of high constables for each provincial district in Upper Canada. These individuals were required to appoint citizens to act as unpaid constables in each of the parishes or townships (Griffiths and Verdun Jones, 1994; Mawby, 1990). Problems were encountered with this early system of policing as citizens were reluctant to get involved. Constables were not full-time, paid persons and did not constitute police officers in the modern sense, but they were the forerunners of the policing system we have today (Forcese, 1992).

During the nineteenth century, there was growing concern that crime and the criminal classes were increasing and, consequently, there was pressure for Canada to develop a system of crime control. In 1835, Toronto became the first town to introduce a full-time, paid constable, creating the first police force in Canada (Cooper, 1981). By 1859, it had a staff of 32 (Parizeau and Szabo, 1977) and by 1890, almost nine hundred officers (Sewell, 1985). Other areas were then quick to follow Toronto's lead, and police forces were established in Quebec City (1838), Hamilton (1840), Montreal (1843) and Ottawa (1855) (Cooper, 1981).

By 1859, each city and incorporated town in Canada was required to have a chief constable and at least one constable paid by the municipality (Higley, 1984). While in the early years police forces were under the control of the municipal council, in 1859 the Municipal Institutions of Upper Canada Act created boards and commissions of police in order to ensure public control and accountability (Griffiths and Verdun Jones, 1994).

As migration and movement to the west increased, more police forces were established. Calgary hired its first police officer in 1885, while smaller pioneer settlements maintained a system of self policing until they became large enough to warrant a police service. Interestingly, it was often the agents of the Hudson's Bay Company who performed policing roles and functions within the smaller, developing communities. Before Confederation in 1867, western Canada—known as Ruperts Land—was a fiefdom of the Hudson's Bay Company, and law enforcement was provided by the Company (Cooper, 1981). In purchasing Ruperts Land, the federal government gained the responsibility for policing as, with the exception of Manitoba, it was now all federal property.

It was not unusual for early municipal police officers to undertake a variety of functions such as jailer, fireman, tax collector, truancy officer and bailiff. Griffiths and Verdun Jones (1994) have identified three major functions undertaken by early municipal police forces:

• Preventing conflict between ethnic groups, labor groups and industry.
• Maintaining the moral order through the enforcement of puritanical laws often relating to drinking and prostitution.
• Apprehending those involved in criminal activity.

Marquis (1994) argues that municipal autonomy was the primary structural characteristic of urban policing until after the second world war. Changes in the development, structure and operation of municipal governments were promoted by citizens' desire for responsible government. This in turn led to the need for permanent police forces.

The post-war years have seen a trend towards the amalgamation of smaller police departments as urbanization has incorporated towns into metropolitan areas, blurring district boundaries. Between 1963 and 1976, the number of municipal police departments dropped from 710 to 466 (Marquis, 1994) as police forces were amalgamated, resulting in centralized command and communication structures, and promoting resistance by those who felt a loss of local control. This point will be picked up again in Chapter 3.

Early federal policing

The origins of Canada's federal police force, the RCMP, can be traced to the 1845 'Act for the Better Preservation of the Peace and the Prevention of Riots and Violent Outrages at the Near Public Works while in Progress of Construction.' Under this Act, a police force was formed and deployed to maintain order among the laborers employed in the construction of the Welland and Saint Lawrence canals (Kelly and Kelly, 1976; Mawby, 1990). This force formed the model for the North West Mounted Police (NWMP).

In 1868, Parliament passed The Act Respecting Police of Canada which established the Dominion Police Force. This force was to be closely regulated by central government and involved in the enforcement of federal statutes. Its primary responsibility was the protection of federal buildings, but later the force became involved in enforcing laws related to counterfeiting. The Dominion Police was the first authority created with jurisdiction beyond the municipal level (Griffiths and Verdun Jones, 1994). Although the force theoretically had responsibility for all of Canada, in practice its activities were confined to eastern Canada (Cooper, 1981). Policing for the rapidly-developing west was introduced six years later.

In 1873, Parliament passed the Act Respecting the Administration of Justice and for the Establishment of a Police Force in the Northwest Territories, to create Canada's first federal police force, the North West Mounted Police. The NWMP was modeled on the Royal Irish Constabulary and in its first year had an authorized strength of 300 men, many of whom had a military background (Forcese, 1992). The need to create such a body was recognized following the purchase of Ruperts Land in 1869. Although the impetus behind the creation of the force has been the subject of considerable debate (Griffiths and Verdun Jones, 1994), a number of reasons have been advanced:

- It was felt that the Mounted Police would create a federal presence in an area where Native people were often exploited by American traders (Sewell, 1985).

- There was recognition that actual ownership of the area depended upon its occupation, so the force was established in order to assert control, thereby ensuring political and economic sovereignty (Talbot et al., 1986).

- The NWMP assisted with the orderly settlement of indigenous lands by white settlers. The Mounted police took part in negotiations between white settlers and natives over the surrender of lands and the creation of reserves. In contrast to events south of the border, the police were sent to establish order so liberty and freedom could then be enjoyed (Sewell, 1985). The Americans adopted a different approach, believing freedom and liberty came first, with order following far behind.

- The force was also responsible for patrolling the border between the US and Canada, collecting taxes on lands and mines as well as customs and excise duties, protecting banks and distributing mail (Parizeau and Szabo, 1977).

- The maintenance of order on the construction sites of the trans-Canada railway and among prospectors drawn to the Yukon during the Klondike gold rush was a task undertaken by the NWMP (Parizeau and Szabo, 1977).

In its own retrospective analysis, the RCMP (1990) provides a more limited interpretation and states that its early role consisted of three things:

- Preventing crime.
- Establishing friendly relations with Indian peoples by protecting them from unscrupulous whisky traders, preventing inter-tribal violence, the confrontation of potentially troublesome groups such as the American Sioux and the supervision of treaties between Indian tribes and the Canadian government.
- Easing the hardship (e.g. destitution, disease and prairie fires) for immigrants.

Mawby (1990) argues that members of the NWMP had a pivotal role in enforcing the law, interpreting the law, reinterpreting the law and in formulating the law where no law existed. In imposing their own version of Canadian law and order, they achieved two goals. Firstly, they denied any alternative interpretations of the law by Aboriginal peoples, by foreign prospectors or whaling crews or by private organizations like the Hudson's Bay Company. Secondly, they asserted Canadian sovereignty against possible incursions by the United States in the Yukon and Denmark in the North. In this respect, the Mounted Police were the Canadian equivalent to the British forces of imperialism, which introduced law and civil administration to the undeveloped areas of the empire. Officers of the NWMP were agents of a central power created in Ottawa. They imposed a system of control on the North alien to its culture in an attempt to regulate and control it.

There is little doubt that the Mounties are the most widely recognized symbol associated with Canada. Their historical development and exploits have been documented in a number of texts (e.g. Brown and Brown, 1978; Kelly and Kelly, 1976; Stonier Newman, 1984). While their public image is a positive one, research by Waldon (1982) illustrates that, in the early days, the force experienced considerable difficulties. Citizens were critical of their extensive legal powers because they acted as both police officers and magistrates. Internal organizational problems were also evident as the Mounties experienced high rates of desertion and improper behavior, including drunkenness, in their early days (Morgan, 1973). While some of these problems can be attributed to the logistics of introducing and developing a new organization and are difficulties associated with policing largely undeveloped, huge areas of land, questions concerning the Mounties' role continued into the twentieth century when their involvement in quelling and controlling labor disputes at the Canadian Pacific Railway and during the Winnipeg General Strike of 1919 were queried (Brown and Brown, 1978). Their role in breaking the Winnipeg General Strike lost them considerable national support but did prove their worth to government (Mawby, 1990).

At the beginning of the twentieth century, the NWMP had 750 officers; by 1920 the force had grown to a strength of 1,600 (Sewell, 1985). In 1904, King Edward VII proclaimed that the force be known as the Royal North West Mounted Police (RNWMP).

In 1905, the provinces of Saskatchewan and Alberta were created. Instead of establishing their own police forces, they contracted with the federal government for the RNWMP to provide provincial police services, thereby expanding the RNWMP role. In 1920, the federal government changed the name to the Royal Canadian Mounted Police (RCMP) and amalgamated the RNWMP with the Dominion Police by passing the North West Mounted Police Act Amendment Act.

From the 1930s to 1950s the RCMP continued to expand its role in provincial policing with no opposition from the provinces (Macleod, 1994). Its involvement in providing provincial police services had been suspended in Alberta and Saskatchewan in 1917 but was later restored in Alberta in 1928 and in Saskatchewan in 1932. In the same year, the RCMP gained responsibility for provincial policing in Manitoba, New Brunswick, Nova Scotia and Prince Edward Island. In 1950, Newfoundland and British Columbia were added.

The inter-war years saw the RCMP continue to expand its role by obtaining responsibility for customs and excise work in 1932 and by forming a marine and aviation section in 1937 (Kelly and Kelly, 1976). Its jurisdiction also grew as it began providing municipal police services to some communities under contract. The first municipal contract was signed in Flin Flon Manitoba in 1935. This municipal function has continued to expand so that by 1994, the RCMP was responsible for providing police services for 201 municipalities (Statistics Canada, 1996) in addition to 10 provinces and 2 territories.

Early provincial policing

Provincial police are responsible for policing areas outside municipalities. The evolution of provincial police forces is closely linked to the development of the RCMP. The Constitution Act of 1867 gave the federal government responsibility to enact criminal law and procedure while the enforcement of laws and justice administration was under the auspices of the provinces. The Act stated that upon entry to Confederation provinces would enact legislation for the creation of provincial police services. Such legislation was passed in 1870 in Manitoba and Quebec, 1871 in British Columbia, 1901 in Ontario, 1927 in New Brunswick, 1928 in Nova Scotia and 1930 in Prince Edward Island. Newfoundland had established the Royal Newfoundland Constabulary in 1872 and in 1935 introduced a second provincial police force—the Newfoundland Company of Rangers (Talbot et al., 1986).

As illustrated above, the RCMP gradually assumed responsibility for provincial policing during the 1930s when the economic depression made it difficult for provinces to maintain police services (Forcese, 1992). By 1950, all but two provinces—Ontario and Quebec—had the RCMP as their provincial police, a situation which continues to the present day.

The Ontario Provincial Police (OPP) was born in 1909; by 1913, three divisions had been formed and by 1920, these had been expanded and reorganized to include nine districts operating under district inspectors. The founding of the force was in response to the Ontario northwest frontier and the developing mining towns. Forcese (1992) illustrates similarities between the OPP and the RCMP as both were formed to protect frontier expansion and both recruited leaders from a military background. In 1944, the Ontario Police Act was passed allowing the OPP to provide police services under contract with communities in Ontario. The OPP is one of the largest police forces in North America, as is the RCMP.

Provincial policing in Quebec developed in a very similar way to that of Ontario. A rudimentary force was in place at the end of the nineteenth century, with formal organization being introduced much later (Sewell, 1985). The Sûreté de Québec, or Quebec Provincial Police (QPP), was Canada's first provincial police force, founded in 1870; however, its role in those early days was limited. Today it has over 4,000 sworn officers and is one of the most powerful police forces in Canada (Forcese, 1992). Unlike the RCMP and the OPP, it does not operate in Quebec towns on a contract basis but rather as an agency of the Quebec government. The Police Act of 1968 ensured that the QPP had responsibility not only for small towns and rural communities but for the entire territory of Quebec (Stenning, 1981).

The only other provincial police force is the Royal Newfoundland Constabulary, formally the Newfoundland Rangers, which was established in 1872 and which today only polices the city of St. John's. It is the only North American police force in which the members are unarmed.

Table 2.2 details the significant dates in the history of Canadian policing.

SUMMARY

This chapter initially described the historical development of policing in England as this influenced the Canadian policing system and the philosophy on which it is based. The development of Canadian policing was then discussed. It was shown to be influenced by a variety of demographic, social, cultural, geographical, political and historical factors, having grown and developed primarily over the course of the last one hundred years as the country and its population have evolved. It is currently characterized by three administrative and operational levels: federal, provincial and municipal, and in this respect is distinct from policing systems that exist in other western democracies.

TABLE 2.2 Significant Dates in the Development of Canadian Policing

1651	First police officer introduced in Quebec City.
1673	Justices of the Peace introduced.
1793	Parish and Town Officers Act passed requiring the appointment of high constables in each provincial district in Upper Canada.
1835	Toronto establishes first police force in Canada.
1845	Act for the Better Preservation of the Peace and the Prevention of Riots and Violent Outrages at the Near Public Works while in Progress of Construction creates police force to maintain order among laborers on the Welland and Saint Lawrence Canal projects.
1859	Municipal Institutions of Upper Canada Act requires each city and incorporated town to have a chief constable and at least one police officer.
1867	Confederation
1868	The Act Respecting the Police of Canada establishes the Dominion Police Force.
1869	Federal government purchases Ruperts Land from the Hudson's Bay Company.
1870	Quebec Provincial Police formed. First provincial police force.
1872	Royal Newfoundland Constabulary established.
1873	The Act Respecting the Administration of Justice and for the Establishment of a Police Force in the Northwest Territories creates the North West Mounted Police.
1904	North West Mounted Police change name to Royal North West Mounted Police.
1905	Royal North West Mounted Police undertake first provincial police duties in Alberta and Saskatchewan.
1909	Ontario Provincial Police created.
1920	North West Mounted Police Act Amendment Act creates the Royal Canadian Mounted Police and amalgamates the Dominion Police and the Royal North West Mounted Police.
1935	First RCMP municipal contract signed with Flin Flon, Manitoba.
1944	Ontario Police Act allows for the Ontario Provincial Police to supply municipal police services under contract.

QUESTIONS FOR DISCUSSION

1. Describe briefly the watch system.
2. How relevant are Peel's Principles of Policing to the operation of police forces in Canada today?
3. What were the main reasons behind the establishment of a police force in London?
4. What factors led to the public's acceptance of the London police?
5. What 'non-policing' roles did the early members of the RCMP undertake?
6. What were the main reasons for establishing the NWMP?
7. Discuss the influences on the development of Canadian policing.
8. Why has it been argued that there are similarities between the RCMP and OPP?
9. What were the early functions of a municipal police officer?
10. When did the first police officer appear on the streets of Canada?

FURTHER READING

Kelly, Nora and Kelly, William (1973). *The Royal Canadian Mounted Police: A Century of History*. Edmonton: Hurtig Publishers. This work is a factual account of the historical growth and development of the RCMP.

Kelly, William and Kelly, Nora (1976). *Policing in Canada*. Toronto: The Macmillan Company. This extensive, although essentially uncritical, descriptive work reviews the history and development of policing in Canada from its inception until the 1970s.

Talbot, J., Jayewardene, C.H.S. and Juliani, T.J. (1985). *Canada's Constables: The Historical Development of Policing in Canada*. Ottawa: Crimcare Inc. This study looks at federal, provincial and municipal policing. It traces the early development of these forms of policing through three distinct time periods: 1900-20, 1921-45, 1946-84 and argues the three branches of policing have developed in distinctive ways.

REFERENCES

Brown, Lorne and Brown, Caroline (1978). *The Unauthorized History of the RCMP*. Toronto: Lewis and Samuel.

Cooper, H.S. (1981). "The evolution of Canadian policing." In W.T. McGrath and M.P. Mitchell (Eds.) *Police Function in Canada*. Toronto: Methuen.

Critchley, T.A. (1978). *The History of the Police in England and Wales*. London: Constable Publishers.

Ericson, R. (1982). *Reproducing Order: A Study of Police Patrol Work*. Toronto: University of Toronto Press.

Forcese, Dennis P. (1992). *Policing Canadian Society.* Scarborough: Prentice Hall.

Fox, A. (1971). *The Newfoundland Constabulary.* St. John's: Robinson Blackmore Printing and Publishing Ltd.

Griffiths, Curt T. and Verdun Jones, Simon N. (1994). *Canadian Criminal Justice.* Toronto: Harcourt Brace.

Hatherly, Mary E. (1991). *The Legal Status of the Police.* Fredericton: Department of Solicitor General New Brunswick.

Higley, Dan D. (1984). *OPP: The History of the Ontario Provincial Police Force.* Toronto: The Queen's Printer.

Kelly, W. and Kelly, N. (1976). *Policing in Canada.* Toronto: MacMillan.

Macleod, R.C. (1994). "The RCMP and the evolution of provincial policing." In R.C. Macleod and David Schneiderman (Eds.). *Police Powers in Canada: The Evolution and Practice of Authority.* Toronto: University of Toronto Press.

Martin, Maurice A. (1995). *Urban Policing in Canada: Anatomy of an Aging Craft.* Montreal: McGill Queens University Press.

Marquis, Greg (1994). "Power from the street: The Canadian municipal police." In R.C. Macleod and David Schneiderman (Eds.). *Police Powers in Canada: The Evolution and Practice of Authority.* Toronto: University of Toronto Press.

Mawby, R.I. (1990). *Comparative Policing Issues: The British and American System in International Perspective.* London: Unwin Hyman.

McDougall, Allan K. (1988). *Policing: The Evolution of a Mandate.* Ottawa: Canadian Police College.

McDowell, Charles P. (1993). *Criminal Justice in the Community.* Cincinnati: Anderson Publishing.

Morgan, E.C. (1973). "The North West Mounted Police: Internal problems and public criticism, 1874-1925." *Saskatchewan History 26.*

Parizeau, Alice and Szabo, Denis (1977). *The Canadian Criminal Justice System.* Lexington Mass.: Lexington Books.

Reiner, R. (1985). *The Politics of the Police.* Brighton: Wheatshef Books.

Roberg, Roy R. and Kuykendall, Jack (1993). *Police and Society.* Belmont California: Wadsworth Publishing Company.

Royal Canadian Mounted Police (1990). *Fact Sheets.* Ottawa: Ministry of Supply and Services.

Sewell, John (1985). *Police: Urban Policing in Canada.* Toronto: James Lorimer.

Statistics Canada (1996). "Police personnel and expenditure in Canada 1994." *Juristat 16*(1). Ottawa: Statistics Canada.

Stenning, Philip C. (1981). *Police Commissions and Boards in Canada.* Toronto: Centre for Criminology, University of Toronto.

Stonier-Newman, Lynne (1991). *Policing A Pioneer Province: The B.C. Provincial Police 1858-1950.* Madeira Park B.C.: Harbour Publishing.

Talbot, C.K., Jayewardene, C.H.S. and Juliani, T.J. (1986). *Canada's Constables: The Historical Development of Policing in Canada.* Ottawa: Crimcare Inc.

Uchida, Craig D. (1993). "The development of the American Police: An historical overview." In Roger G. Dunham and Geoffrey P. Alpert (Eds.) *Critical Issues in Policing.* Prospect Heights, Illinois: Waveland Press.

Waldon, K. (1982). *Visions of Order: The Canadian Mounties in Symbol and Myth.* Toronto: Butterworths.

THE ORGANIZATION AND ADMINISTRATION OF CANADIAN POLICING

INTRODUCTION

The Canadian Constitution provides for a system whereby policing responsibilities are divided among three levels of government: federal, provincial/territorial and municipal. The Solicitor General in Ottawa is the minister responsible for federal policing while in the provinces the administration of justice falls under the direction of provincial and territorial ministers of justice, attorney generals and solicitor generals. The jurisdiction and structure of policing in Canada among national, provincial and local administrations has been recognized as fragmented and diversified (Stenning, 1981) and as "far from clear" (Taylor, 1981, p. 68). These three policing systems have developed independently of each other, serving different populations. Consequently, in comparison to policing agencies in other western democracies, Canadian policing is unique. This chapter describes the three levels of policing as they currently exist in Canada. It then examines the other agencies that deliver police services and provides statistics on police numbers and expenditures.

MUNICIPAL POLICING TODAY

Municipal police agencies comprise the largest body of police personnel in Canada accounting for 62% of police officers and 55% of police expenditure (Statistics Canada, 1996). There are currently 578 municipal police forces in Canada: 201 are contracted RCMP detachments, 364 are independent police forces and 13 are OPP contract forces. The 364 independent forces employed 31,277 officers, 90% of the municipal police in Canada, with the RCMP employing 3,430 officers on municipal contract (Statistics Canada, 1996). Independent municipal police departments are led by a chief constable, while RCMP contract detachments are headed by an Officer in Charge whose rank depends on the detachment size.

Municipal police forces vary considerably in size. The larger municipal forces include The Montreal Urban Community Police Force with 4,420 members and The Metropolitan Toronto Police Force with 5,057 members (Statistics Canada, 1995); smaller RCMP detachments may consist of only a few members. Municipal police officers enforce laws relating to the Criminal Code, provincial statutes, municipal by-laws and certain federal statutes such as the Narcotics Control Act (Griffiths and Verdun Jones, 1994).

In most provinces, legislation makes it compulsory for cities and towns to maintain their own police force once they reach a certain population size. This size can vary from 500 to 5,000 people depending on the province. Municipalities then have the option of creating their own municipal police department, contracting with the RCMP or provincial police to supply police services or entering into an agreement with a neighboring community to create a regional police force (Statistics Canada, 1990).

A number of municipalities have chosen not to establish their own police force but to contract with a provincial police agency. In Ontario, municipal policing is provided to 13 communities by the OPP under contract; in all other provinces except Quebec, the RCMP as the provincial force contracts to provide municipal policing. Municipal RCMP contracts only occur in provinces already policed by the RCMP. In many cases, provincial RCMP detachments share the same physical location as municipal detachments.

All of the provinces except Newfoundland, Prince Edward Island and Manitoba enacted Police Acts during the 1970s governing policing at both the provincial and municipal levels. These acts vary from province to province but basically set uniform standards for municipal police forces, provide for the creation of police commissions (discussed in Chapter 9) and establish criteria to monitor performance (see Appendix B). Figure 3.1 gives details of a typical organizational chart for a mid-sized municipal police force.

Regionalization

As mentioned in Chapter 2, during the 1960s many smaller police agencies in eastern Canada were amalgamated to form larger police forces. This system of regionalization developed at a brisk pace in Ontario and Quebec. Between 1962 and 1977, 150 police forces in Ontario were amalgamated into ten regional forces which today provide policing for over 50% of Ontario's population. A regional police force was also established in Quebec to serve Montreal and the surrounding area—the Montreal Urban Community Police Force (Griffiths and Verdun Jones, 1994)—and Winnipeg has also amalgamated 13 municipal police forces (Oppal, 1994).

Regionalization is justified for a number of reasons:

• It reduces police costs. The economies of scale suggest it is more reasonable to operate one large police agency than a number of independent small ones.

FIGURE 3.1 Organizational Chart of a Mid-Sized Municipal Police Force

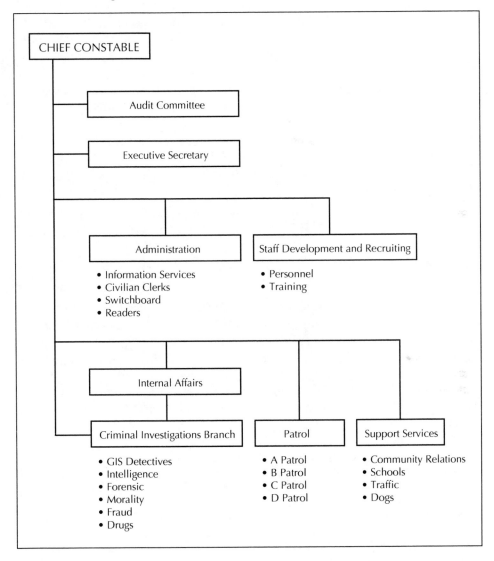

- It eliminates the duplication and inefficiencies in police service that exist when many small police agencies deliver services in one area.
- It promotes a more egalitarian administration of justice and a more equitable delivery of service. Different police forces often have varying policies and practices for responding to calls, enforcing laws and by-laws and providing services to victims; regionalization ensures equality of provision.

- It increases cooperation between law enforcers in neighboring jurisdictions. Criminals are not conscious of police boundaries; they tend to operate not in neighborhoods but in regions. When an area has a number of small forces, there may be little cooperation and exchange of information among independent police organizations. Regionalization improves cooperation and coordination of police services.

- It increases police capacity to deliver specialized services, such as emergency response teams, forensic laboratories and specialized investigation, which smaller police agencies cannot otherwise afford.

- It enhances personnel development. Proponents of regionalization state that it ensures consistency in the recruitment and training of personnel, provides enhanced career opportunities and establishes equity in wages, benefits and working conditions.

Although advocated by a number of politicians and police personnel, regionalization is also resisted. Typically, it is the larger police organizations and their local governments that favor regionalization, whereas the smaller ones tend to raise the following concerns:

- There is a loss of control of policing services if these are handed over to a regional governing body, resulting in less say in how resources are allocated and spent.

- Local police agencies are felt to be part of the local identity and regionalization contributes to a loss of identity.

- Regionalization is thought to be detrimental to the development of community policing, which is a recent policing philosophy advocating closer contacts between the police and the community. If policing resources and policy decisions are removed from the local community, the objectives of community policing cannot be obtained.

- Police personnel also resist regionalization as it may result in the loss of jobs, reallocation of duties, different wage scales and working conditions, different command structures and relocation.

- Regional forces are costly to establish.

> The bottom line is that both police personnel and politicians are likely to have strong reactions to regionalization, but the direction of these reactions depends upon their perceptions of the gains and losses to be incurred through regionalization (Oppal, 1994, p. D6).

Regionalization continues to be an issue of debate in urban areas that have a number of police departments. During the 1990s, the issue has been reviewed in British Columbia, Nova Scotia and Saskatchewan (Oppal, 1994).

Murphy (1991) argues that regionalization is the result of a number of social, economic, political and occupational factors which appear to be moving municipal policing towards a more centralized, bureaucratic and provincially-administered model. He states that regionalization is the second of three phases, the first of which is modernization whereby policing standards, procedures and technology are upgraded in order to introduce some uniformity to municipal police services. The second phase is regionalization, which is seen as a cost-effective way to administer municipal policing. At this stage, municipal governments may choose to terminate contracts with the RCMP and opt for a regional force. The third phase is provincialization, which follows the successful introduction of regionalization and results in provinces developing their own police forces. Murphy believes that non-urban municipal policing in provinces other than Ontario and Quebec is in the process of modernization and regionalization which will eventually lead to a provincially-based, centralized system and may force the RCMP to become an exclusively federal force.

FEDERAL POLICING TODAY

The RCMP provides police services in Canada on three levels: municipal, provincial and federal. Its federal responsibilities are organized under the authority of the Royal Canadian Mounted Police Act of 1959. Expenditure in 1994-95 on federal policing totaled $688.7 million (Statistics Canada, 1996). In all provinces and territories, the RCMP has responsibility to enforce federal statutes such as the Narcotics Control Act and the Indian Act. In all regions of the country where federal statutes must be enforced, including customs and excise, and where federal property is to be protected (for example the Parliament buildings in Ottawa), the RCMP has authority. It therefore has jurisdiction in all ten provinces and two territories of the country. Only in the provinces of Quebec and Ontario does the RCMP have no provincial or municipal responsibilities.

The RCMP is headed by a commissioner under the direction of the Solicitor General of Canada. The authority and accountability for executing the requirements of the RCMP Act rests with the commissioner, who is supported by four deputy commissioners and divisional commanding officers. Thirteen regional divisions, usually located in the provincial or territorial capitals, oversee the localized RCMP administration. In addition, there are 52 subdivisions and 723 detachments across the country. Figure 3.2 shows the organizational chart of the RCMP.

The mandate of the RCMP is to enforce Canadian laws, prevent crime and maintain peace, order and security. Specifically this mandate requires:

- the prevention and detection of offenses against federal statutes.
- the prevention, detection and investigation of crimes and the maintenance of law and order in the provinces, territories and municipalities under contract.
- the provision of investigative and protective services to protected persons and other federal departments and agencies (RCMP, 1995).

The RCMP does not act in isolation, but frequently works in conjunction with other police agencies. It operates and administers several branches, such as the National Crime Intelligence Branch and the Economic Crime Branch, which provide an information resource to other police departments.

FIGURE 3.2 Organizational Chart of the RCMP

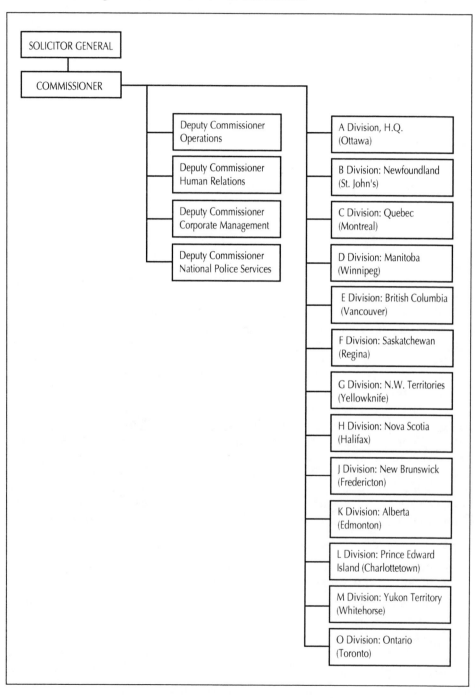

PROVINCIAL POLICING TODAY

As detailed above, there are only three provincial police forces operating in Canada: the OPP, the QPP and the Royal Newfoundland Constabulary (RNC). Newfoundland retains two police forces. The RNC is a provincial force which supplies policing services to the three largest municipalities: St. John's, Corner Brook and Labrador City. The RCMP in Newfoundland provides policing under contract to the other municipalities and rural areas. Provincial forces are responsible for policing areas outside of municipalities and for enforcing provincial laws and the Criminal Code.

Table 3.1 summarizes the policing arrangements for the provinces and territories of Canada.

TABLE 3.1 Policing Arrangements for the Provinces and Territories of Canada

Province/Territory	Municipal	Provincial	Federal
Ontario	OPP (13) Independent (108) Regional (10)	OPP	RCMP
Quebec	Independent (160) Regional (1)	QPP	RCMP
Prince Edward Island	RCMP (4) Independent (5)	RCMP	RCMP
New Brunswick	RCMP (12) Independent (23) Regional (2)	RCMP	RCMP
Nova Scotia	RCMP (10) Independent (26)	RCMP	RCMP
Newfoundland and Labrador*	RCMP and RNC	RCMP	RCMP
Manitoba	RCMP (27) Independent (10)	RCMP	RCMP
Saskatchewan	RCMP (37) Independent (19)	RCMP	RCMP
Alberta	RCMP (61) Independent (10)	RCMP	RCMP
British Columbia	RCMP (43) Independent (12)	RCMP	RCMP
Yukon	RCMP	RCMP	RCMP
Northwest Territories	RCMP	RCMP	RCMP

SOURCE: Statistics Canada, 1990. Figures in parentheses denote the number of independent municipal departments and RCMP contract municipal detachments.

*Data for Newfoundland not available.

RANK STRUCTURE

Similarities exist among the rank structures of police departments in Canada. Figure 3.3 illustrates the typical seven-rank structure of a police department. There may be variations to this structure depending on the size of the force; for example, in Ontario there are nine ranks, the additional two being staff superintendent and staff inspector. Alternatively, smaller police agencies may have a smaller number of ranks, excluding the ranks of inspector, staff sergeant and superintendent as they deem appropriate.

FIGURE 3.3 Typical Rank Structure of a Police Department

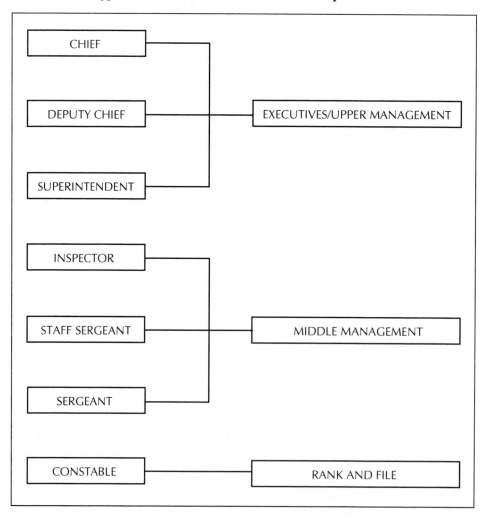

The RCMP has ten ranks. Table 3.2 illustrates these ranks and the number of officers assigned to each rank as of 31 March 1993 (RCMP, 1995).

TABLE 3.2 Rank Structure and Position Establishment for the RCMP

Rank	Establishment
Commissioner	1
Deputy Commissioner	5
Assistant Commissioner	21
Chief Superintendent	34
Superintendent	127
Inspector	355
Staff Sergeant	879
Sergeant	1,879
Corporal	2,993
Constable	9,903

A recent development has been a decline in the proportion of officers above the rank of constable. Edmonton Police Service has removed the rank of inspector in an attempt to flatten the hierarchy and the RCMP is currently reviewing policies along similar lines in order to remove the number of officers in middle management positions. Although the number of police officers in Canada declined by 2% between 1993 and 1994, this decrease was not uniform across all ranks; it is those positions above the rank of constable that have been most affected (Statistics Canada, 1996).

ACCOUNTABILITY AND GOVERNANCE

Police organizations can be called to account and asked to justify their actions with regard to legal and fiscal concerns, in addition to policy goals and policing objectives. This accountability can be either to an element within their own organizational structure, to a government department or, more broadly, to the community they serve.

The jurisdiction and structure of policing in Canada among national, provincial and local administrations is diverse (Stenning, 1981; Taylor, 1981). The Solicitor General in Ottawa is the minister responsible for federal policing while the provincial Attorneys and Solicitors General and Ministers of Justice are legally responsible for provincial and municipal policing, including where this has been contracted to the RCMP, the OPP or the QPP. All but two of the provinces and territories contract with the RCMP to provide provincial policing.

In addition, a number request that the RCMP undertake municipal policing under contract; therefore, the RCMP has responsibility for both provincial and municipal policing in most parts of the country.

Although many municipalities receive police services under contract with the RCMP, there is no formal local accountability of the detachment to the municipality. Instead, RCMP municipal services are legally accountable to the federal Solicitor General, the commanding officer of the division and the commissioner of the force. The relationship they have with the provincial ministry responsible for policing is primarily administrative. The relationship the RCMP has to local municipal governments does not involve any legal accountability. The situation is, therefore, complex when policing is contracted to the RCMP, as the RCMP commander is accountable through the RCMP organizational structure to the federal minister, despite the fact that the provincial minister has overall responsibility for policing.

The lines of demarcation, accountability and control are not always clear to the public, but the RCMP appears to see itself as legally, fiscally and operationally accountable to the federal, not provincial, government. One can question whether it is appropriate to have a provincial and municipal police force which owes its primary allegiance not to the province, but to its headquarters in Ottawa. This point has been made by Hann et al. (1985) who show how detachment commanders see their accountability to be owed to superiors within the force rather than to local government municipalities. It is reiterated by the RCMP itself, which confirms that in terms of the 'internal management' of the provincial and municipal police services, including administration and application of professional police procedures, control remains with the government of Canada (RCMP, 1995). This form of accountability, which recognizes a commitment removed from local jurisdiction, is therefore at odds with many of Peel's principles of policing and the current movement towards community policing (see Chapters 10 and 11) and periodically leads provinces to question their contractual arrangements with the RCMP. In examining the issue, a British Columbian Provincial Commission Report recently argued the RCMP needed to make fundamental changes and become more accountable to local needs (Oppal, 1994).

OTHER POLICE AGENCIES

In addition to the federal, provincial and municipal police forces, other agencies provide policing services in Canada. These include:

- Ports Canada Police
- Railway Police
- Aboriginal police agencies
- Private security and investigation agencies
- Government agencies

Ports Canada Police

The Ports Canada Police Service, sometimes known as the Harbour Board Police, is operated by the Federal Transport Ministry and has detachments in Sept Îles, St. John's, Halifax, Quebec, Montreal and Vancouver, with headquarters in Ottawa. In 1990, there were 136 fully sworn police officers (all male) employed across the country with the responsibility of coordinating port and interport security operations, including investigations, criminal intelligence, crime prevention, security and emergency planning (Statistics Canada, 1990). Ports Canada Police has recently been subject to review and its long-term future is yet to be determined.

Railway Police

In 1918, the Railway Act was introduced to enable railway companies to seek the appointment of people to act as police constables on and along their property. Although constables are recruited by the railway company, they are sworn police officers who have authority from the Railway Act and the Criminal Code. Their primary responsibility when conducting an investigation is to the Canadian justice system and as such, they act independently of the railway company. While they have powers to enforce both criminal and provincial laws, their efforts concentrate on thefts of goods in transit, theft of company property, fraud and mischief (Statistics Canada, 1990).

Aboriginal police

Recently, several autonomous Aboriginal police forces have been introduced in Canada. While most Aboriginal policing services began with limited powers and responsibilities, these have grown over time. However support, especially in the area of technical expertise, is frequently provided by the provincial police.

In December 1995, there were 34 self-administered First Nations police services in Canada. In addition, the RCMP had a total of 38 contracts to provide policing services to one or more Aboriginal communities. The Ontario Provincial Police provides law enforcement under one province-wide contract for 178 First Nations communities, and three municipal police forces have contracts with three Aboriginal communities (Aboriginal Policing Directorate, Ottawa, personal communication). As contracts are constantly being negotiated, these statistics are perpetually being reviewed.

The two largest Aboriginal-controlled police services operate in Ontario and Quebec. The Ontario First Nations Policing Program has been in operation since 1975 with approximately 125 members. Constables are hired by the bands and accountable to the band council and to the commissioner of the OPP. The OPP, in consultation with the bands, selects, trains and posts constables and provides supervision in the field. The Amerindian Police Program in Quebec operates in

23 communities (Statistics Canada, 1990). Both these forces are involved in policing reserves in the two provinces. Officers have full powers to enforce the Criminal Code and federal and provincial statutes as well as band by-laws. Smaller Aboriginal forces also exist in other areas of the country. Their enforcement powers vary, with some having full powers under provincial police acts and others limited to enforcing only band by-laws and certain provincial statutes. Aboriginal policing is discussed in Chapter 12.

Private security and intelligence agencies

It is argued that private and security police now outnumber the 'public' police (Cooper, 1981; Griffiths and Verdun Jones, 1994). Their numbers have grown considerably in the post-war years as private and public companies have felt the need to hire security firms. It is estimated there are about 125,000 full- and part-time private security officers in Canada of which about 75,000 are employed by private companies providing services on a contract basis. A further 50,000 work as in-house security personnel (Normandeau and Leighton, 1990). Their powers vary depending on the authority given to them under provincial statutes. Often they employ former and existing 'public' police officers (Stenning, 1989) and frequently share information with public police bodies. The issue of private policing has been addressed in a number of texts (Shearing and Stenning, 1987; Stenning, 1989; Stenning and Cornish, 1975) and will continue to be of interest in Canada as the number of private police officers grows.

Government agencies

Various federal government departments employ special constables with authority to enforce specific statutes such as income tax, custom and excise, immigration, and fisheries and wildlife. Provincial governments also delegate authority to individuals to enforce provincial statutes relating to issues such as public health, building codes and licensing. These officers of the federal and provincial government have only limited enforcement powers and areas of jurisdiction.

POLICE STRENGTH

In 1994, there were 74,902 people employed in providing police services in Canada. Of these, 55,865 were fully sworn police officers and 19,037 were civilian police personnel including 'special constables' who are not sworn police officers (Statistics Canada, 1996). These police officers were distributed among independent municipal police forces, the RCMP, the OPP, the QPP and the RNC. Ninety-one percent were male.

Municipal policing (including the RCMP and the OPP) accounted for 34,884 (62%) of police officers in Canada in 1994. The RCMP provides municipal police services under contract to 32% of municipalities, but RCMP officers make up only 9% of all municipal police officers. This is because the RCMP tends to police smaller municipalities; it is only in the province of British Columbia that the RCMP has municipal detachments numbering over 70 members. There are 14,327 police officers employed by the OPP, QPP, RCMP and RNC to provide provincial police services, and they account for 26% of all police officers. RCMP federal police officers number 5,180, 9% of all officers, while a further 1,474 (3%) of RCMP members undertake administrative tasks. RCMP officers comprise roughly a quarter of all police officers in Canada; 17% of RCMP officers work for provincial forces while approximately 57% are members of municipal forces (Statistics Canada, 1996).

In 1994, there was one police officer for every 523.5 Canadians; however, there is considerable variation in this 'population per police officer' figure, ranging from one police officer per 697 people in Prince Edward Island to one police officer per 266 people in the Yukon (Statistics Canada, 1996). Of all the provinces, Quebec has the lowest ratio (1:495). In cities with over 100,000 people, the ratio of police officers to population was lowest in Montreal (1:410), Toronto (1:434), Halifax (1:431) and Vancouver (1:463). Cities with the highest ratio include Surrey, BC (1:900), Richmond, BC (1:937), Halton Region (1:845) and Nepean, Ontario (1:855).

The five largest police forces account for 60% of all police officers (Statistics Canada, 1996):

RCMP	28%
Metropolitan Toronto	10%
Montreal Urban Community Police	8%
Ontario Provincial Police	8%
Quebec Provincial Police	8%

POLICE EXPENDITURE AND COSTS

Policing services costs increased by 206% between 1961 and 1981 (Woods, 1984). In 1985-86, the cost of policing Canada was $3.54 billion; two years later it amounted to $4.39 billion (Normandeau and Leighton, 1990) and in 1994-5, it totaled $5.78 billion, costing each Canadian $200 and representing a real increase in expenditure since 1985-86 of 20% (Statistics Canada, 1995). Provincially, policing costs are highest in Ontario and Quebec and lowest in the Atlantic provinces. The five largest police services accounted for nearly 70% of the total cost of Canadian policing. Municipal policing (including the RCMP and OPP) represents the greatest cost at 53% of the total, with provincial policing assuming 30%, federal policing, 9% and other RCMP expenditure, 8% (Normandeau and Leighton, 1990).

By far the greatest expenditure is on police officer salaries. In 1993, 82% of expenditure went to pay salaries, wages and benefits, 15% to operating costs and 3% to motor vehicle purchases and leases (Statistics Canada, 1995). Normandeau and Leighton (1990), quoting a Statistics Canada survey, illustrate that between 1966 and 1987, the average cost of a first class constable increased sixfold from $6,000 to $37,000. Taking the cost of living into consideration, this represents a real increase of 55%. Much of this increase occurred between 1965 and 1977 and can be attributed to employee demands and more vocal police unions (Forcese, 1992). The larger police agencies offer higher salaries for police officers, with the Atlantic police tending to have salaries 10-15% lower than their colleagues in central and western Canada (Forcese, 1992). Police salaries vary even within a geographical area: in 1995, the salary of an RCMP police recruit was $31,172, whereas the salary of a Vancouver Police Department recruit was $41,094. In the same year, constables with three years' service in the RCMP received $47,385, whereas those in the Vancouver Police received $54,074 (*Vancouver Sun*, 15 December 1995).

After years of perpetual growth, police expenditure—which increased on average seven percent between 1985 and 1993—has remained relatively unchanged since 1993. This trend reflects fiscal concerns as governments have been forced to make budget cuts to the public sector. Budget cuts have been evidenced by a two percent decrease in the number of police officers from 1993 to 1994 (Statistics Canada, 1996).

POLICE WORK

Between 1962 and 1993, the number of police officers more than doubled while the number of Criminal Code incidents (excluding traffic) increased fivefold (Statistics Canada, 1995). In 1994, there were 47.1 Criminal Code incidents per officer; in 1962, there were 19.7. Despite this increase, the clearance rate (the proportion of incidents reported to the police that are cleared by charge or by other means) has remained relatively stable: 37% in 1962; 35% in 1993 (Statistics Canada, 1995).

FEMINIZATION AND CIVILIANIZATION

As illustrated above, nine percent of police officers in Canada are women whereas in 1975 only one percent were. Over the recent past, the composition of Canadian police forces has altered to include more female officers each year. While there are still barriers women face in becoming police officers, their numbers in Canadian police forces are growing and, if the current trend continues, they will undoubtedly have an effect on the nature of police services. The issue of women in policing is discussed in Chapter 5.

Another recent personnel development is the increased use of civilians to provide services that in the past were performed by police officers. The civilianization of police agencies started during the 1970s in the United States, with the belief that it reduces police costs by freeing up expensively trained police officers to use their abilities where they are most needed. In Canada, civilian personnel are employed in areas such as communications units, where they take complaints, operate switchboards, dispatch officers and handle front-desk inquiries. Non-police personnel are also employed in the areas of crime prevention, court liaison and victim assistance, as well as in such administrative roles as accounting, computing and research. It is estimated that 23% of positions in BC police agencies were occupied by civilians in 1987 (Oppal, 1994). The gender breakdown of civilian personnel in 1994 illustrated that 68% of non-police personnel were women; in 1970, 50% were (Statistics Canada, 1996). The feminization of police agencies is therefore occurring in both police and non-police personnel.

SUMMARY

The structure of policing in Canada is characterized by three distinct levels—federal, provincial and municipal. As the population of the country continues to grow, so the cost of policing increases. This chapter has discussed policing as it exists in Canada today, it has not detailed the role of the police. This is the task of the following chapter.

QUESTIONS FOR DISCUSSION

1. In what provinces does the RCMP have no provincial jurisdiction?
2. What ministries are responsible for federal, provincial and municipal policing in your province?
3. What do you think are the advantages and disadvantages in municipalities contracting with the RCMP for police services?
4. What are the advantages and disadvantages of regionalization?
5. Should regionalization occur in your area?
6. What legal powers are granted only to the RCMP?
7. Explain why municipal policing costs are higher than federal and provincial policing costs.
8. Name the provincial police forces that exist in Canada.
9. Why do you think the image of the Mountie is so closely tied to the Canadian identity?
10. Give reasons why you think the proportion of police officers to population is so much higher in the Yukon than in Prince Edward Island.

FURTHER READING

Normandeau, A. and Leighton, B. (1990). *A Vision of the Future of Policing in Canada: Police Challenge 2000—Background Document.* Ottawa: Police and Security Branch, Ministry Secretariat, Solicitor General. This document is the result of a consultation process among the Solicitor General, police agencies and academics. It outlines issues which will influence policing in Canada in the next millennium, and advocates the adoption of community policing policies to address social and economic developments.

Statistics Canada *Juristat.* Ottawa: Centre for Justice Statistics Canada. These publications contain details on the size, composition and administration of police agencies. They are released annually.

Sewell, John (1985). *Police: Urban Policing in Canada.* Toronto: James Lorimer. This small book gives a general summary of urban policing in Canada. The author argues that policing urban areas shows a remarkable inconsistency. The discussion includes an historical analysis and addresses the issue of police-public interaction.

REFERENCES

Cooper, H.S. (1981). "The evolution of Canadian policing." In W.T. McGrath and M.P. Mitchell (Eds.) *Police Function in Canada.* Toronto: Methuen.

Forcese, Dennis P. (1992). *Policing Canadian Society.* Scarborough: Prentice Hall.

Griffiths, Curt T. and Verdun Jones, Simon N. (1994). *Canadian Criminal Justice.* Toronto: Harcourt Brace.

Hann, Robert G., McGinnis, James H., Stenning, Philip C. and Farson, Stuart A. (1985). "Municipal police governance and accountability in Canada: An empirical study." *Canadian Police College Journal, 9*(1).

Murphy, Christopher (1991). "The future of non-urban policing in Canada: Modernization, regionalization and provincialization." *Canadian Journal of Criminology, 33*(3-4).

Normandeau, A. and Leighton, B. (1990). *A Vision of the Future of Policing in Canada: Police Challenge 2000—Background Document.* Ottawa: Police and Security Branch, Ministry Secretariat, Solicitor General.

Oppal, The Honourable Mr. Justice Wallace T. (1994). *Closing the Gap: Policing and the Community.* Commission of Inquiry Policing in British Columbia. Victoria, B.C.: Attorney General.

Royal Canadian Mounted Police (1995). *Fact Sheets.* Ottawa: Ministry of Supply and Services.

Shearing, Clifford D. and Stenning, Philip C. (1987). *Private Policing.* Newbury Park, California: Sage.

Statistics Canada (1990). *Policing in Canada.* Ottawa: Canadian Centre for Justice Statistics.

Statistics Canada (1995). "Police personnel and expenditure in Canada 1993." *Juristat, 15*(8). Ottawa: Statistics Canada.

Statistics Canada (1996). "Police personnel and expenditure in Canada 1994." *Juristat, 16*(1). Ottawa: Statistics Canada.

Stenning, Philip C. (1989). "Private police and public police: Towards a redefinition of the police role." In Donald J. Loree (Ed.) *Future Issues in Policing: Symposium Proceedings.* Ottawa: Canadian Police College.

Stenning, Philip C. (1981). *Police Commissions and Boards in Canada.* Toronto: Centre for Criminology, University of Toronto.

Stenning, Philip C. and Cornish, M. (1975). *The Legal Regulation and Control of Private Police in Canada.* Toronto: Centre for Criminology, University of Toronto.

Taylor, I. (1981). "The law and order issue in the British general election and the Canadian federal election of 1979." *Canadian Journal of Sociology, 5*(3).

Vancouver Sun (15 December 1995). "Extra pay for Mounties opposed."

Woods, Gerald (1984). "Costs of municipal police services." *Impact, 2* 13-22.

THE POLICE ROLE

INTRODUCTION

To be able to understand what duties the police undertake and why, a discussion of their role is required. This chapter provides an analysis of the role of police in contemporary society. The first part reviews those agencies which influence the role of the police. This is followed by an account of what are widely regarded to be the three main roles of the police: law enforcement, order maintenance and service. Next, there is an historical discussion of police role development from the mid-nineteenth century to date, including an outline of the ongoing debates about the concept. The chapter concludes with a review of how politics affects the police role.

THE ROLE OF POLICING

Before attempting to examine the role of the police, the term 'role' must be defined. From a sociological stance, role refers to the position held by an individual in a communal setting (how others see him/her); from a psychological stance, role refers to the beliefs, attitudes and values attributed to the position, often by the individual in that role. In understanding the police role, both a sociological and psychological interpretation is required. One must consider both the behaviors and attitudes society expects of its police and the expectations police officers have for themselves (Dantzker, 1995). We need to define what we want our police to do so they can ensure their organization is set up to respond to these demands. Defining their role is important for the police as this role must be reflected in internal organizational policies and strategies. For example, educational and training initiatives need to reflect this role as do operational priorities.

The role of the police is shaped by a variety of social, legal, political and administrative factors (Alpert and Dunham, 1992; Broderick, 1987) and has been the topic of debate for many decades, although Roberg (1976) describes much of this literature as woefully inadequate with regard to promoting a true understanding of the issue. Questions concerning the role of the police began to be posed in the academic literature during the 1960s and continue to this day.

It is not only criminologists who have problems dealing with the police role; a survey of police officers illustrated that 85% agreed with the statement: "It is difficult to define the role of policemen in today's society" (Roberg, 1976). Defining the role of the police is therefore problematic both for society and the police agencies themselves.

The role of the police in western societies is widely regarded as being the maintenance of order. This concept is as old as policing and appeared in Peel's 1829 principles. It is contained in most documents setting out the duties of today's police officers, such as the RCMP Act (see Appendix A). To be able to determine the extent of this function, Shearing and Leon (1992) have argued that an understanding of what the police can do that others cannot is required. In addressing this issue, they state that access to the law as a means of maintaining order and the legitimate use of force are the two distinguishing characteristics of the police role.

POLICE USE OF FORCE

As discussed in Chapter 1, both Bittner (1970) and Klockars (1985) define the police by examining what makes them distinctive from other government agencies and suggest the use of coercive force to be their defining characteristic. With the exception of members of the Royal Newfoundland Constabulary who, like the British police, serve unarmed, all other police officers in Canada are armed. The issue of carrying guns leads to concern for their regulation. If a police force is given the authority to carry and use lethal weapons, then the appropriate checks and balances need to be established to ensure this activity is not abused. A number of guidelines exist for this purpose.

The legal basis for the use of force is found in Section 25 of the Criminal Code, which states that individuals exercising force must be undertaking a duty they are required or authorized to do; they must act on reasonable grounds; they must use only as much force as necessary and; they are responsible for any excess use of force. In addition, the provincial Police Acts add further guidance as do the discipline codes (see Appendix B for an example). Canadian society expects its police officers to maintain order and prevent crime, not as a separate governing force, but as an integral agent of society. In this respect, the police are given regulations and restrictions over the use of force. It is a delicate balance, for on the one hand, society demands guidelines to prevent the excessive use of force, while on the other, these guidelines cannot be so restrictive as to prevent officers from defending themselves (Oppal, 1994).

Police agencies can be defined as a non-military organizations which are given the general right by government to use coercive force to enforce the law. This unique function given only to the police therefore shapes what they do. Nevertheless, there are a number of other influences which also affect this role.

AGENCIES INFLUENCING ROLE DEFINITIONS

In addition to the police agency itself, there are a number of other influences which affect the police role. These include private citizens, legislative bodies, the media, courts and other police departments.

Private citizens

As clients of police services, private citizens may have a vested interest in defining the police role as they are often victims and sometimes offenders. Members of the population influence the police role through either individual action or pressure group efforts. This influence can be aimed directly at police departments, at federal, provincial and municipal governments, or at institutions and regulative bodies which oversee police agencies, such as police commissions and police boards (see Chapter 9).

Legislative bodies

The creation of laws by the federal, provincial and municipal governments influences the role of the police. For example, the introduction of the Canadian Charter of Rights and Freedoms in 1982 greatly affected what the police could and could not do during an investigation. In addition, these legislative bodies control funding to police departments and so may award money for specific initiatives and deny funding for others, thus dictating what the police do. (For example, municipal councils have recently allocated resources specifically for community policing initiatives such as storefront mini-stations and bike cops).

The media

By portraying the police either in fictional entertainment or via the reporting of news, the media shape the public's view of the police and frequently support a stereotypical police image. This image portrays the crime-fighting role of the police, often in a highly sensational way. For most people, the media are the only source of information about law enforcement; consequently, the media influence public opinion about the police role.

Courts

Courts influence the role of the police in two ways; firstly, by defining acceptable and non-acceptable police procedures in the collection and presentation of evidence and secondly, by the manner in which they respond to cases put before them. For example, if a court refuses to prosecute women for soliciting, or only awards a small fine for the offense, the police department may decide not to pursue these offenders, instead dedicating resources to other areas of work.

Other police departments

Canadian policing has undoubtedly been strongly influenced by policing initiatives that were pioneered and tested in the United States. The role of the police can be influenced by developments in other departments as new initiatives which are deemed to be successful elsewhere are adopted here.

THE POLICE ROLE: ORDER MAINTENANCE, LAW ENFORCEMENT OR SERVICE?

Kelly and Kelly (1976) contend that there has been a lack of written material on the role of the police and other law enforcement agencies in Canada. While this may be the case, there are a number of writers in both the US and UK who have provided in-depth discussions relevant to Canadian policing. These dialogues have tended to focus on the contradictory goals that result from the law enforcement and order maintenance role.

> A perennial chestnut of debate about the police role has been whether the police are best considered as a *force* with the primary function of enforcing the criminal law, or as a *service* providing balm for a sea of social troubles (Reiner, 1985, p. 111).

While Reiner (1985) recognizes the dichotomy to be between force and service, others have divided policing in other ways. For example, Whisenand and Ferguson (1973) simply cite law enforcement and order maintenance; likewise, Banton (1964) cites law enforcement and peacekeeping. Griffiths and Verdun Jones (1994) and McDowell (1993) have focused on what they regard as the three primary roles of the police:

- order maintenance
- law enforcement/crime control
- service.

Order maintenance

Order maintenance refers to preventing and controlling behavior which disturbs the public peace. In this role, the police regulate conduct and correct behavior seen to promote disorder, such as neighbors' disputes, loud parties, and conflict between citizens. As most forms of disorder are minor, the corresponding action taken by police officers is usually mild and only slightly coercive. Nonetheless, problems of order maintenance do have the potential to develop and become issues of law enforcement.

In many cases of order maintenance, there is little knowing who is right or wrong, but the police are asked to make judgments and ultimately resolve such incidents. If the issue involves a breach of the law, they have the option of invoking the criminal justice system, if not, they must negotiate, 'criminalize' or abandon the problem (McDowell, 1993). A key piece of research illustrating the order maintenance function of the police was conducted by Bittner (1967). In analyzing policing on skid row, he argues that peacekeeping, as he refers to it, is an integral part of the police role and requires a great deal of skill. Bittner was one of the first to identify the varied skills involved in patrol work and the peace-keeping role of the police.

Law enforcement

Law enforcement or crime control involves responding to and investigating crimes, apprehending offenders and undertaking preventative patrols. Law enforcement is aggressive and punitive; its objective is primarily the identification of law violators and their initial processing within the criminal justice system. This role is less ambiguous than that of order maintenance; the police are required simply to carry out the law and there are few 'gray areas.' This is a role which is solely assigned to the police and the one depicted most frequently in the media.

Service

The service role of the police recognizes their many other roles. The services they provide to the public, often as a consequence of their 24-hour availability, include giving advice and directions, assisting stranded motorists, looking for missing persons, escorting processions and informing relatives of sudden deaths.

> To whom does one turn when a family member is missing? Who answers the questions of strangers, citizens, businessmen in need of information? Who responds to accidents and emergencies? Often the police. Such roles of assistance are as much a police function as are coercive roles of authority (Reiss, 1971, p. 61).

Those who endorse the service role of the police state that it generates good will towards the police, is important for gaining information which may be used to combat more traditional crimes and fills a need in society. Critics state the service role raises problems such as the inflation of police budgets and a distortion of the apparent cost of crime control. It also prevents the professionalization of the police and diverts police attention away from their primary (law enforcement) role (Roberg, 1976).

The three roles of law enforcement, order maintenance and service are interrelated and result in contradictory and conflicting expectations. Should the police be primarily crime fighters or social workers? Where does order mainte-nance stop and law enforcement begin? These conflicting roles may acquire varying degrees of importance depending upon the geographical location of the police department (rural or urban), the size of the police department and the priorities of the individual police officers, resulting in operational-level questions about what the most important role is.

RESEARCH ON POLICE ROLE, TASKS AND ACTIVITIES

Research has illustrated that the police do in fact perform a multitude of tasks. Studies analyzing citizens' requests to police agencies have consistently shown the majority of requests do not relate to crime but rather to order maintenance, information and service-related activities (Ericson, 1982). These studies suggest the actual percentage of time a police officer devotes to law enforcement is between 10% and 30% with the remainder given to service or order maintenance. For example, Reiss (1971) found that only 17% of incidents reported to the police were of a criminal nature; the other 83% were classified as uncriminal (e.g. traffic, disturbances and lost people). Shearing (1984, pp. 20-22), in his study of a large police force in eastern Canada, found that calls to the police broke down as follows:

> internal police business: 23.6%
> accidents, collapses, illness: 16.3%
> suspicious circumstances: 8.9%
> traffic problems: 8.7%
> public nuisance: 7.4%
> other types of calls: 7.3%
> services: 7.2%
> reports of thefts: 6.7%
> disputes: 5.5%
> response of fire/ambulance service: 3.4%
> report of injury or damage to person or property: 2.5%
> return calls: 2.2%
> robbery or hold up: 0.3%

As can be seen, only a small number of calls relate to law enforcement. There now exists a consensus among criminologists that crime fighting is only a small part of the police role (Cordner, 1989). As previously mentioned, the role division was analyzed by Banton (1964) in what is regarded as one of the first empirical analyses of the police role. He discussed the difference between law enforcement and peace officers in the British and American police and found that uniformed police officers tended to be peace officers, whereas specialists such as detectives or traffic officers tended to be law enforcers.

> A division is becoming apparent between specialist departments within police forces (detectives, traffic officers, vice and fraud squads, etc.) and the ordinary patrolman. The former are 'law officers' ... whereas the patrolmen are principally 'peace officers' operating within the moral consensus of the community (Banton, 1964, pp. 6-7).

Most police departments embrace a mixture of order maintenance/service and law enforcement, with a patrol division responding to routine calls (order maintenance and service) and specialized units (e.g. detective teams) working on law enforcement matters, often after they have been identified as such by patrol officers (see Chapter 7).

THE IMAGE OF POLICING

Despite the recognition that the police spend the majority of their time on issues other than law enforcement, the public has generally accepted the image of policing as one synonymous with crime fighting. This image can be attributed to the media which perpetuate it through entertainment and news, depicting police officers as 'soldiers' fighting a 'war' on crime. This image is also promoted by the publishing and film industries and accepted by members of the community, who form expectations about police behavior based on their observations of popular television programs, books and films. The actual, everyday and frequently mundane life of the police officer is rarely portrayed by the media, which instead focus on the rarer 'sexier' issues that sell. It is not just the media that have been instrumental in the promotion of this image, the police have also supported it.

From a purely financial standpoint, the crime-fighting image is important to policing. The public fear of crime receives more financial attention than other (service) problems the police are asked to deal with. There are considerable dollar incentives for the police to promote an unrealistic image of their work as it is this image that will be financially compensated by governments. However, at the end of the day when questions are asked about what the police actually do, law enforcement is only one of their many roles.

The demands placed on the police have created what Manning (1971) has termed 'the impossible mandate.' Police officers cannot possibly develop a role or mandate, as satisfying the often conflicting demands of the groups that influence their task (politicians, public, victims, criminals, courts) is impossible. Manning argues that in trying to respond to these many demands, the police play up the heroic aspects of their work. The public wants crime controlled and criminals caught and so the police encourage the public to see them as addressing this role, a role that is glorified by media portrayals of the police. The actual proportion of time spent by the police on crime-related activities is small compared to their other tasks, but in emphasizing this role, both the police and the public come to see their raison d'être as law enforcement. The police see themselves as crime fighters and the public expects them to apprehend criminals, although the reality of policing involves much more than just addressing these concerns.

THE EVOLUTION OF POLICING

A better understanding of the role of policing can be achieved through an examination of police development through a time-role continuum (Dantzker, 1995). Explanations of role development have been advanced based on the historical development of policing. For example, Roberg and Kuykendall (1993) have reflected on the development of policing in the United States and argued the period from 1830 to date can be characterized by three distinct 'models' of police ideology: the political model (mid 1800s–1920s), the legalistic model (1920s–1960s), and the service/contingency model (late 1960s to date). In a similar analysis, Kelling and Moore (1989) have identified what they see as distinct phases of policing: the political phase (1840s–early 1900s), the reform phase (1930s–late 1970s) and the community phase (1980 to date). A more precise interpretation is provided by McDowell (1993) in his description of the political era (1884–1914), reform era (1914–1968) and post-reform era (1968–date). Dantzker (1995) divides his historical account into six categories: colonial (1700–1820s), pre-industrial (1820s–1850s), industrial (1850s–1920s), modernization (1920s–1960s), crisis (1960s–1980s) and today (1990s). Dantzker's industrial and modernization categories therefore match the eras and models devised by others.

All these authors base their analyses on the historical development of policing in the US. Their models are useful, but have reduced relevance to the police system in Canada. As will be illustrated, this is particularly the case for the 'political' or 'industrial' era of policing; however, the second two interpretations (legalistic/reform/modernization and service/contingency/post reform/crisis/community) do provide a useful basis for understanding the evolution of the police in Canada and give the necessary structure in which to ground a discussion of the role of policing in Canada.

THE POLITICAL/INDUSTRIAL ERA

This first era characterizes policing in the US at a time when it was politically dominated. Politics influenced every aspect of law enforcement, from who was employed, who was promoted and who was chief, to what services were provided. Individual police officers had a great deal of discretion; consequently, standards of enforcement varied widely between cities. Early police officers had only a vague idea of what they were supposed to do, with order maintenance being the primary task (McDowell, 1993). There was no official training; a police officer was given a badge and a gun and told to police. Job stability and security depended upon the political regime and police officers were often replaced to reflect the political complexion of the day (Dantzker, 1995). Consequently, role development was hampered as the police were constantly changing.

Political and economic corruption became a wide-scale problem within police departments. By the end of the nineteenth century, many were criticized for being difficult to manage, corrupt and politically dominated (Roberg and Kuykendall, 1993). Reforms took place at the beginning of the twentieth century, when religious leaders and civic-minded business and professional people argued for a more honest and efficient system, resulting in a movement away from a political orientation to a more bureaucratic and legalistic one.

In Canada, the development of policing from the mid-nineteenth century to the 1920s was characterized by three things: the introduction of provincial policing systems in Ontario and Quebec, the growth and development of municipal policing, and the expansion and introduction of policing to the prairies and western Canada by the NWMP. Unlike the US, historical accounts of policing in Canada during this period do not illustrate political domination nor widespread corruption but rather focus upon the many functions additional to law enforcement and order maintenance that were carried out by police officers. This is particularly the case for the NWMP, which was involved in rural policing, but is also true for municipal and provincial police agencies (Talbot et al., 1986). The era from the mid-nineteenth century to the 1920s in Canadian policing history must be seen as an introduction, expansion and development period in which the system of law enforcement was formalized by the creation of police bodies that had a number of diverse roles in the early years. In contrast to the political era of the US where the role of the police was primarily related to order maintenance, the role of the police in Canada in the expansion and development era incorporated law enforcement, order maintenance and service functions.

THE LEGALISTIC/REFORM/MODERNIZATION ERA

The second era of policing identified, from the 1920s to 1960s, is one dominated by a legalistic model. Roberg and Kuykendall (1993) contend this was the most significant period in the development of policing as it established the foundations for the professionalization of law enforcement. It is certainly an era of great change during which recognized standards were established, with crime control being the primary mission of the police. A number of factors characterized this period, including the application of science, key individuals who were successful in conveying their theories of reform to others and technological change.

The scientific approach

In both Europe and North America, attempts were made to apply science to police work; this became the cornerstone to what was regarded as the professional approach. One of the earliest applications of science was a system created by French anthropologist Alphonse Bertillion for identifying suspects. It involved four components: precise physical measurements, a description of distinguishing features, a photograph and fingerprints, thus becoming the first systematic process of record keeping for suspects, which still exists today. The scientific, rational, detached approach also provided a body of knowledge that could be and was conveyed in police training initiatives.

The architects of reform

In addition to scientific developments, a number of other reforms took place from the 1930s onwards. The field of public administration was in its infancy at the turn of the century but grew as police and other public administrators adopted principles from the private sector, such as scientific management as a way to reform their organizations and achieve efficiency at a reduced cost. Initiatives involving the standardization of behavior, training, professionalization and the development of organizational policies and procedures were adopted by public sector bodies including the police. Many of the reforms to professionalize the police have been attributed to two key North American innovators: August Vollmer and O.W. Wilson. Vollmer, chief of the Berkeley California Police Department was one of the key proponents of a professionalized police service. He developed police education programs, bicycle and automobile patrols and scientific crime detection aids, as well as founding the first school of criminology at the University of Chicago in 1916 (Roberg, 1976). His was the first police department to use forensic science (Uchida, 1993). O.W. Wilson, one of Vollmer's students, wrote what is regarded as one of the classical textbooks on police management, *Police Administration* (1977), which discusses police deployment, disciplinary measures and organizational structures. Wilson offered a variety of innovative concepts, many of which were controversial or radical, but some of which still exist today (Dantzker, 1995). During this period, the quality of police officers also improved, although the recruitment of college graduates did not occur.

Technological change

Technological changes facilitated the development of a more professional police. The automobile, two-way radio and the telephone all had a dramatic effect on the way the police operated and the manner in which the public utilized their services. The car ensured that calls could be responded to more quickly; it also lessened the contact between police officers and citizens, thereby reducing the opportunities for corruption. The car was regarded as a better way to allocate staff, as it allowed a greater area to be covered.

The two-way radio increased contact between sergeant and patrol officer allowing for more direct supervision, while the telephone enabled the public to have easier access to the police. The reactive capacity of the police was improved by use of the telephone. McDowell (1993) argues the telephone facilitated the development of the police as an order maintenance agency as well as one dealing with law enforcement because by using this method of contact citizens could report incidents without revealing their identity, thus increasing the number of calls to the police.

These developments transformed policing, allowing the foot officer whose response and duties were previously limited to provide a quicker service and to cover a wider area. The period from the 1920s to the 1960s was therefore one of significant change for police departments. However, during the 1960s, some of these reforms were questioned. It was argued that the police were becoming detached and separated from the communities they served and had developed an impersonal attitude towards the public. Prior to the advances in technology, there had been more interaction between the police and the public on an everyday basis. Technology removed the police from the people, resulting in less police-community contact. In addition, academic studies illustrated the police emphasis on crime fighting was inappropriate as the police actually spent only a small proportion of their time on this task. In the United States, urban riots and the growth of the civil rights movement led to challenges to the legalistic model, as a new generation refused to accept a police role portrayed as being the reactive agent of government.

While the political era characterized policing in the United States but not in Canada, the legalistic or reform era certainly existed in both countries. Although Canadian policing did not have the same architects of reform, the philosophies of Vollmer and Wilson were readily adopted. The technological and organizational changes which occurred in the US were clearly copied in Canada. The RCMP and other large metropolitan and provincial police departments became increasingly bureaucratic and professionalized and, like those south of the border, embraced new technology and scientific approaches. Unlike the US, violent confrontations and vocal criticisms of the Canadian police were not heard in the 1960s.

The legalistic era combined advances in technology with more stringent control over personnel to achieve a professionalization of policing. This led to an operational strategy focused on law enforcement and reflecting distinctive organizational values. These organizational values have been listed and summarize how the police role was interpreted during the legalistic era (McDowell, 1993):

- Police authority is based entirely on law. Professional police departments have the enforcement of law as their primary objective.

- Communities assist the police to enforce the law by providing information.

- Responding to citizens' calls is the highest police priority. All calls should be responded to in the fastest possible way.

- Social problems and other neighborhood issues are only of concern to the police if they threaten public order.

- The police are the experts in crime control and as such should be the ones entrusted with developing priorities and strategies.

THE SERVICE/CONTINGENCY/CRISIS/POST REFORM/COMMUNITY ERA

The legalistic era produced a number of reforms which tended to isolate the police from the community. This led to a series of recommendations which aimed to address this isolation and facilitate a closer relationship between the public and the police. Roberg and Kuykendall (1993) refer to this period as being characterized by a service or contingency model of policing; Dantzker (1995) calls it crisis, McDowell (1993), post reform. Kelling and Moore (1988) recognize a slightly later development and label it as community.

The service/contingency/crisis/post reform era has seen changes in three areas of police development: policy development, selection and training, and management and administration. Policies in the areas of police officer account-ability and the use of discretion have been developed. Selection criteria were introduced enabling the recruitment of more women and ethnic minority offi-cers and more highly-educated recruits. Training in human relations was also initiated. In the area of management and administration, community relations and crime prevention programs have been developed.

In the period 1940 to 1965, only six articles concerned with the police were published in the two leading American sociological journals (Niederhoffer, 1967). From the mid-1960s, research on the police grew tremendously in both the US and Britain. In 1968, in response to a number of reports, the United States Congress enacted the Law Enforcement Assistance Administration (LEAA). One of the most important undertakings of this new body was police research. Early influential studies included the Kansas City Patrol Experiment (Kelling et al., 1974), which examined the effectiveness of patrol and found that patrol officers devoted only 32% of their time to criminal matters, the Rand Corporate Criminal Investigation Process (Greenwood and Petersilia, 1975), which studied ways investigation techniques and processes could be improved and Team Policing (Sherman et al., 1973), which involved the deployment of police officers to specific areas (see Chapter 7). Knowledge was therefore gained about the efficiency and effectiveness of the police and led to questions about existing police procedures and roles.

The information that had existed in the legalistic era was based largely on the experience of police practitioners such as Wilson and Vollmer. During the late 1960s and 1970s, this knowledge was challenged not only by government-sponsored research such as that undertaken by LEAA, but also by social scien-tists studying police departments and conducting systematic research studies (e.g. Bittner, 1967; Reiss, 1971; Skolnick, 1966; Wilson, 1968). Many of their findings challenged the principles of the legalistic model.

While changes in the American policing system were occurring at the end of the 1960s, prompted by civil unrest, change in Canada lagged behind. Although many of the problems associated with the legalistic era were identified here, the nature and culture of Canadian society meant they were not as acute as in the US. Therefore, Canadian policing entered the service/contingency/crisis/post reform era later, during the 1970s, in what may be regarded as not so much a crisis but a recognition that the roles suggested elsewhere were more attractive.

COMMUNITY POLICING ERA

The community policing era, identified by Kelling and Moore (1988), has evolved from the third era. Because of this, it shares some of the same characteristics, but is also a distinctive period in policing. The community policing philosophy advocates that police organizations should not operate in isolation but should be sympathetic to the views of the community and should initiate policies which accord with community desires. It stresses the wider role of policing, advocating that police officers be involved in order maintenance and service functions as well as law enforcement. The community policing movement is characterized by a further shift away from the legalistic one and frequently advocates a partnership between the police and the community in recognizing and addressing issues. Community policing is discussed at length in Chapters 10 and 11.

This review of the three eras of policing illustrates the evolution of the police mandate and role in Canada. During the first era, the police role was not only to undertake law enforcement duties, but to assist in all aspects of the orderly occupation of newly-developing lands. The second era saw the role of policing as legalistic; many of the additional activities undertaken by the police during the previous period were eroded and the primary function was believed to be fighting crime. However, when studies were conducted on what the police actually do, their primary involvement in this role was questioned. This period was also characterized by a professionalization of the police. With the development of a third era, the role of policing again began to take a broader interpretation with an ideology that policing encompasses activities that are not solely crime related. Consequently, the role of the police has evolved and expanded, and with this expansion, role conflicts or debates occur.

ROLE DEBATES

Debates about the police role, while not mutually exclusive, can be positioned in the following categories (Roberg and Kuykendall, 1993). To some extent, these reflect the philosophies underpinning the different eras of policing:

- Bureaucratic or political
- Community norms or law enforcement
- Profession or craft

- Crime fighter or social worker
- Prevention or apprehension
- Proactive or reactive

Bureaucratic or political

This debate concerns the integration of the police into a democratic society. The bureaucratic approach sees the role of policing to be strictly controlled by a set of precise rules, policies and organizational procedures which give defined guidance to police officers. This rational, rule-oriented role ensures there is consistency between police departments, as theoretically every officer deals with an issue in the same way, a way prescribed by organizational guidelines. Consequently, there is little room for an individualized approach. This was the approach advocated by Vollmer and Wilson.

In contrast, the political approach argues the police need to be responsive to the demands of individual neighborhoods and communities. The bureaucratic role does not consider the unique character of communities and fails to recognize the diverse nature of society. The political role advocates the police should be flexible in order to respond to the needs of individual neighborhoods.

The movement from the legalistic era to community era has seen a change in police role from bureaucratic to political, with the acknowledgment that police agencies should tailor their service to the demands of the community and not adopt a 'one size fits all' approach. Despite this contention, there is a belief that larger police agencies—and especially the RCMP—have a preponderance of rules, policies and procedures and are bureaucratic to the extent that they face extreme difficulties in moving towards the political approach.

Community norms or law enforcement

This debate centres on the choices police officers and the community need to make as a result of the bureaucratic/political role debate. Should the police decide what are the most important issues in relation to crime and social disorder and introduce policies they deem most appropriate, or should the community make the decisions? For example, one community may not find the issue of drug dealing to be a problem, but may be concerned with noise from a rock club that closes in the early hours of the morning. The police, believing drugs to be more serious, could introduce an initiative to address the drug issue but ignore the rock club which is, in the views of the residents, effectively creating more trouble for the community.

Should the police enforce all laws in a bureaucratic, legalistic manner or be responsive to the demands of the community or citizen? There are often differences between the perceptions of the police and those of the public over certain crimes. For example, crimes such as recreational drug use, gambling and prostitution (so-called victimless crimes) may be viewed by some to be private matters which should not be regulated by the law. Those who engage in these behaviors are not likely to see themselves as criminals and resent law enforcement tactics which interfere with what they regard as a private habit.

Should the police ignore certain offenses if they are not deemed problematic by the community? Traffic law enforcement is an area where the police and the public are often at odds, with the public frequently arguing the police should not be concerned with this activity, as it does not constitute a problem, and instead go out and catch 'real' criminals.

Should the police 'over-police' an issue if there is pressure from one community, or a vocal pressure group within that community, to do so? By adopting this tactic, resources are concentrated in one area and other police functions may not be addressed, perhaps leading to a decline in the overall police service offered. These are all conflicts that arise in the debate of the police officer as law enforcer or preserver of community norms, and they acknowledge the fact that not all people are supportive of all legislation.

Profession or craft

The third role debate concerns whether policing is a professional activity or a craft, alternatively debated as profession or occupation (Alpert and Dunham, 1988). Policing in this analysis is either a rational, systematic undertaking which requires extensive formal preparation (profession) or alternatively, is common-sensical, with experience and intuition being the most important characteristics (craft). For an occupation to be considered a profession, it must have formal skill training for new members, a process to certify that new members are competent and methods to ensure that all members behave in a responsible way (Roberg and Kuykendall, 1993), as well as professional pride and high prestige (Niederhoffer, 1967). In contrast, a craft implies less training, intellectual exploration and discussion; the job is learned by experience over the course of time.

As illustrated above, during recent history police work has moved from being essentially a craft towards becoming a profession. Police officers in Canada are now rarely hired without university or college degrees, they go through an extensive period of recruit training, supplemented throughout their career with specialized professional development courses, and have managed to secure much higher incomes than their predecessors—indeed, higher than individuals in other well-established professions (e.g. university lecturers and architects). Policing is regarded as a status profession by most Canadians and has changed from being a task that could be undertaken with little formal training and few qualifications to one that demands a certain calibre of individual.

In listing the factors that distinguish a profession from an occupation, Alpert and Dunham (1988) have included prolonged membership, requirements for higher education, specialized training, controls over training, controls over licensing, a developed rhetoric, a shared perspective and a belief that work is worthy of a high esteem. Policing in Canada today includes many if not all of these attributes and therefore can be seen as a profession. However, there are considerable differences among individual Canadian police forces, for example, no uniform standards for admission, recruitment and training exist, and policies and operational procedures differ. Variations in size, in demands for service and in the availability of resources influence their ability to professionalize. The concept of professionalization may consequently be stronger in some police agencies than in others, a situation recognized in the United States (Lumb, 1994).

Despite the contention the police have been professionalized, analysis of how their time is spent suggests there are still significant craft elements. Bittner (1967), in his study of policing on skid row, eloquently argued the peacekeeping role is essentially a craft which must be learned and which requires practical skills. Policing order maintenance may require more craft than professional skill. Many police tasks remain menial in nature, which has been the greatest single roadblock in police professionalization (Roberg, 1976). In addressing this role debate from a Canadian perspective, Martin (1995) contends policing remains a craft, while others (Jackson, 1979) argue the police are in the process of professionalization, but are currently failing to meet standards warranting professional status. Lumb (1994) believes they fall into the category of semi-professional and will only achieve professional status following substantial change.

Crime fighters or social workers

Is the role of the police essentially to fight crime or should they be concerned with the broader issues and often related events which lead to crime? For a long time, early interpretations of policing argued that police work must be decisively determined by the duty to uphold the law; every action was interpreted in relation to this objective (Bittner, 1970). This analysis is in contrast to that which has arisen since the 1970s. By employing research techniques such as participant observation and ethnomethodology, criminologists in the US, UK and Canada have shown the proportion of a police officer's time spent on crime is relatively small compared to the multitude of tasks they undertake during the course of a day (Banton, 1964; Ericson, 1982; McConnville and Shepherd, 1992). This indicates that, despite the popular conception, the police work load contains only a minority of crime-related activities. Recognition of the police as *de facto* social workers occurred in the 1970s, leading one commentator to label them 'the secret social service' (Punch, 1979).

Again, the role debate of crime fighter or social service worker reflects the historical movement from the legalistic to community era. In the legalistic period, crime fighting was stressed; over the recent past, this has given way to a recognition of the social service aspect of the police. However, many police officers still do not accept the social service role. A 1983 study of police roles surveyed over 1,200 police officers in the United States and asked them to choose whether they perceived their role to be crime fighter or 'armed social worker';

72% chose crime fighter (Hunt et al., 1983). More recently, research undertaken in British Columbia found many police officers to be unsupportive of the social service role (Seagrave, 1995). The police may be preoccupied with crime fighting, but it is the social service role which occupies their time.

Prevention or apprehension

This role debate essentially concerns the management of police agencies. Should police officers and the organizational management of a police department focus on prevention or apprehension? Police departments that are prevention oriented allocate resources to policies such as school liaison, neighborhood watch, crime prevention and educational and counseling strategies in an effort to prevent crime. Departments that pay only minimal attention to such initiatives are by default more apprehension oriented. Prevention implies police-community interaction, with the belief that increasing contacts between the police and the public facilitates closer ties and establishes a partnership in addressing issues of crime and disorder. In contrast, an emphasis on apprehension results in more adversarial relationships, whereby the only contact the community has with a police officer is when the officer is apprehending an offender. The apprehension role is therefore evident in the legalistic era, with the prevention one a characteristic of the community era.

Proactive or reactive

Proactive policing relates to police-initiated activities undertaken by either the individual police officer or the organization; for example, giving a traffic ticket or initiating a crime prevention program. Reactive policing is when the police respond to a specific request by a citizen who has, for example, telephoned the police to report a crime. Traditionally, during the legalistic era, police departments were reactive in nature; with the development of community policing, they have been encouraged to adopt a more proactive role. There are problems with this, however, as proactive policing requires the police to initiate programs which the community may not want and may regard as an invasion of privacy. Proactive policing therefore may risk, and potentially could destroy, police-community relations.

This review of the role debates has not only illustrated the ongoing conflicts which exist within policing but also illustrates the way in which the functions, organization and priorities of policing have evolved. Table 4.1 positions these role debates under the three eras of Canadian policing, and illustrates that, in all but the craft/profession debate, police agencies in Canada are returning to many of the roles they undertook during the development era. Indeed, proponents of community policing see it as a return to the original priorities of policing (Leighton, 1994). On a note of caution it should be stressed that, while in ideal circumstances the community era of policing incorporates all these roles, in actual fact this may not be the case.

TABLE 4.1 Positioning of Role Debates Under the Recognized Canadian Policing Eras

Role debate	Development era	Legalistic era	Community era
Bureaucratic/ Political	Political	Bureaucratic	Political
Community/ Law enforcement	Community	Law enforcement	Community
Profession/ Craft	Craft	Craft	Profession
Crime fighter/ Social worker	Social worker	Crime fighter	Social worker
Prevention/ Apprehension	Prevention	Apprehension	Prevention
Proactive/ Reactive	Proactive	Reactive	Proactive

THE POLITICS OF THE POLICE ROLE

In addition to the debates identified above, the role of the police can also be discussed in relation to political ideologies. To a certain extent, policing reflects the political complexion of the day (this is distinct from political party affiliations which, while reflecting political ideologies, are not synonymous with them). Any analysis of the role of the police must be informed by these broader political ideologies. Reiner (1978) argues there are three political interpretations of the police role: conservative, liberal and radical.

Conservative

The conservative interpretation sees the police as a highly-disciplined, militaristic, bureaucratic force able to impose order on society with a strict chain of command capable of 'fighting' crime. Advocates of this approach were evident in the 1950s and 1960s (e.g., O. W. Wilson, cited above). This conservative interpretation depends on a conservative political ideology, which argues that criminal law and its enforcement provide a boundary over which individuals should not trespass. People are responsible for their own actions and should control them for the common good. Conservatives believe in the theory of general and specific deterrence, meaning that individuals are deterred from committing deviant acts by seeing others punished (general deterrence) or by being punished or recognizing the threat of punishment (specific deterrence). The police therefore exist to enforce the boundaries of acceptable and non-acceptable behavior. The legalistic era of policing appeared to be governed by conservative ideology because it emphasized patrol and investigation as the principal response to crime and argued that criminals could be deterred by arrest and prosecution.

Liberal

The liberal ideology believes that crime results from social influences (e.g., dysfunctional family, peer pressure, lack of economic opportunity). A liberal response to crime is to change society and to rehabilitate and reform the individual.

The development of the service/contingency/crisis/post reform era was in part a response to liberal assumptions about the causes of crime and how these should be addressed. The liberal approach believes that police efficiency in the enforcement of the law should be tempered by the right of the individual and of the accused to fair treatment. The ideal liberal ideology is a democratic police service practising authority by consent rather than by force.

Radical

The third interpretation of the police role advanced by Reiner is the radical approach. Here, the police are seen as an institution of the state, actively undertaking the role as an agent of social control, potentially having substantial influence on human behavior by enforcing the law and keeping the peace, and operating for the interests of one elite group in society.

The role debate discussed above can also be tentatively positioned under political headings. Table 4.2 illustrates how many of the role debates surrounding the police are grounded in political interpretations. The political environment in which the police operate may, of course, vary over time and from community to community. Political ideologies are important, as they dictate what are held to be the causes of crime and how the police should respond. The police are required to operate to produce order based upon the laws and rules which exist in society. As noted by Ericson (1982):

> The mandate of police patrol officers is to employ a system of rules and authoritative commands, to transform troublesome, fragile situations back into normal or efficient states whereby the ranks of society are preserved (p. 7).

Ericson goes on to note that the police do not produce a new order, but rather are charged with reproducing the existing order, thereby confirming the status quo. The police can never be totally removed from conservative ideologies about the causes of crime because they were created as the only agency to arrest offenders (Roberg and Kuykendall, 1993). As individuals, they are also more likely to hold conservative views.

TABLE 4.2 Positioning of Role Debates Under Political Ideologies

Role debate	*Conservative*	*Liberal*	*Radical*
Bureaucratic/ Political	Bureaucratic	Political	Bureaucratic
Community/ Law enforcement	Law enforcement	Community	Law enforcement
Profession/ Craft	Profession	Profession	Profession
Crime fighter/ Social worker	Crime fighter	Social worker	Crime fighter
Prevention/ Apprehension	Apprehension	Prevention	Apprehension
Proactive/ Reactive	Reactive	Proactive	Proactive

SUMMARY

This chapter has provided an analysis of the role of the police. Although much of the literature is from the United States, it can be applied to the context of Canadian policing. The primary debate centres on the law enforcement/service dichotomy. The popular image of the police is that of crime fighters, but the actual amount of time spent on this task is small compared to their other mandates. In giving an historical account of role development, this chapter has shown how it progressed over time. However, debates still exist over what the role and function of the police actually entails; many of these debates can be grounded in political ideologies. As will be illustrated in the following chapters, the debates surrounding the police role influence to a greater or lesser extent all other aspects of policing.

QUESTIONS FOR DISCUSSION

1. Who influences the role of the police and how?
2. What does Manning mean by the term 'impossible mandate'?
3. Identify the major changes that affected policing during the legalistic era.
4. Is policing a profession? Explain your answer.
5. Why do you think research on the police only started in the 1960s in the United States and later in Canada?

6. Should the police be involved in service type activities?

7. In what ways does the media's portrayal of the police conflict with the actual day-to-day role of the police?

8. What, if any, are the disadvantages of proactive policing?

9. How does political ideology influence the police role?

10. Should there be a clearly-articulated role for all police agencies in Canada, or should each individual department be free to develop its own role within defined legal boundaries?

FURTHER READING

Banton, Michael (1964). *The Police in the Community*. New York: Basic Books. Although somewhat old, this book contains many useful insights into the nature of policing. It is a comparative study of policing in the United States and Britain in which the police role is examined in relation to the demands of the public. It is regarded as one of the seminal works in policing.

Reiss, Albert J. (1971). *The Police and the Public*. New Haven: London Yale University Press. An empirical study of the police role in four cities. The text analyzes proactive and reactive police-citizen encounters.

Skolnick, Jerome H. (1966). *Justice Without Trial: Law Enforcement in a Democratic Society*. New York: John Wiley and Sons. This widely-quoted text is a classic within the policing literature. It examines the social foundations of the rule of law and accounts for police behavior by examining the police use of discretion and their interactions with the public.

REFERENCES

Alpert, Geoffrey A. and Dunham, Roger G. (1988). *Policing In Urban America.* Prospect Heights, Ill.: Waveland Press.

Banton, M. (1964). *The Police in the Community.* London: Tavistock.

Bittner, E. (1967). "The police on skid row: A study in peacekeeping." *American Sociological Review, 32.*

Bittner, E. (1970). *The Functions of Police in Modern Society.* Cevy Chase, Md.: National Institute of Mental Health.

Broderick, John J. (1987). *Police in a Time of Change.* Prospect Heights, Ill.: Waveland Press.

Cordner, Gary W. (1989). "The police on patrol." In D.J. Kenny (Ed.) *Police and Policing.* New York: Praeger Publishers.

Dantzker, Mark L. (1995). *Understanding Today's Police.* New Jersey: Prentice Hall.

Ericson, R. (1982). *Reproducing Order: A Study of Police Patrol Work.* Toronto: University of Toronto Press.

Greenwood, P. and Petersilia, J. (1975). *The Criminal Investigative Process.* Santa Monica: Rand.

Griffiths, Curt T. and Verdun Jones, Simon N. (1994). *Canadian Criminal Justice.* Toronto: Harcourt Brace.

Hunt, R.G., McCadden, K.S. and Mordaunt, T.J. (1983). "Police roles: Context and conflict." *Journal of Police Science and Administration, 11.*

Jackson, R. (1979). "Police labour relations in Canada: A current perspective." *Canadian Police College Journal, 3*(1).

Kelling, G.L. and Moore, M.H. (1988). "From political to reform to community: The evolving strategy of police." In J.R. Green and S.D. Mastrofski (Eds.) *Community Policing; Rhetoric or Reality.* New York: Praeger.

Kelling, G.L., Pate, T., Dieckman, D., and Brown, C.E. (1974). *The Kansas City Preventive Patrol Experiment: A Summary Report.* Washington D.C.: Police Foundation.

Kelly, W. and Kelly, N. (1976). *Policing in Canada.* Toronto: MacMillan.

Klockars, C.B. (1985). *The Idea of Police.* Toronto: MacMillan.

Leighton, B.N. (1994). "Community policing in Canada: An overview of experience and evaluations." In Dennis P. Rosenbaum (Ed.) *The Challenge of Community Policing: Testing the Promises.* California: Sage.

Lumb, Richard C. (1994). "Standards of professionalization: Do the American police measure up?" *Police Studies, XVII*(3).

Manning, P.K. (1971). "The police mandate, strategies and appearances." In J.D. Douglas (Ed.) *Crime and Justice in American Society.* Indianapolis: Bobbs-Merrill.

Martin, Maurice A. (1995). *Urban Policing in Canada: Anatomy of an Aging Craft.* Montreal: McGill-Queen's University Press.

McConnville, Mike and Shepherd, Dan. (1992). *Watching Police Watching Communities.* London: Routledge.

McDowell, Charles P. (1993). *Criminal Justice in the Community.* Cinncinnati, Ohio: Anderson Publishing.

Niederhoffer, A. (1967). *Behind the Shield.* New York: Doubleday.

Oppal, The Honourable Mr. Justice Wallace T. (1994). *Closing the Gap: Policing and the Community.* Commission of Inquiry Policing in British Columbia, Victoria, B.C.: Attorney General.

Punch, Maurice. (1979). "The secret social service." In S. Holdaway (Ed.) *The British Police.* London: Edward Arnold.

Reiner, R. (1978). *The Blue Coated Worker.* Cambridge: Cambridge University Press.

Reiner, R. (1985). *The Politics of the Police.* Brighton: Wheatshef Books.

Reiss, A.J. (1971). *The Police and the Public.* New Haven: Yale University Press.

Roberg, Roy R. (1976). *The Changing Police Role.* San Jose: Justice Systems Development Inc.

Roberg, Roy R. and Kuykendall, Jack (1993). *Police and Society.* Belmont California: Wadsworth Publishing Company.

Seagrave, J. (1995). *Changing the organizational culture: community policing in British Columbia.* Unpublished doctoral dissertation. Burnaby, British Columbia: Simon Fraser University.

Shearing, C.D. (1984). *Dial-A-Cop: A Study of Police Mobilization.* Toronto: Centre of Criminology, University of Toronto.

Shearing, Clifford D. and Leon, Jeffrey S. (1992). "Reconsidering the police role: A Challenge to a challenge of a popular misconception." In Kevin R.E. McCormick and Livy A. Visano (Eds.) *Understanding Policing.* Toronto: Canadian Scholars Press.

Sherman, L.W., Milton, C.H. and Kelley, T.V. (1973). *Team Policing: Seven Case Studies.* Washington D.C.: The Police Foundation.

Skolnick, J. (1966). *Justice Without Trial.* New York: Wiley.

Talbot, C.K., Jayewardene, C.H.S. and Juliani, T.J. (1986). *Canada's Constables: The Historical Development of Policing in Canada.* Ottawa: Crimcare Inc.

Uchida, Craig D. (1993). "The development of the American Police: An historical overview." In Roger G. Dunham and Geoffrey P. Alpert (Eds.) *Critical Issues in Policing.* Illinois: Prospect Heights.

Whisenand, Paul M. and Ferguson, Frederick R. (1973). *The Managing of Police Organizations.* Englewood Cliffs, N.J.: Prentice Hall.

Wilson, James Q. (1968). *Varieties of Police Behaviour: The Management of Law and Order in Eight Communities.* Cambridge Mass.: Harvard University Press.

Wilson, O.W. (1977). *Police Administration.* New York: McGraw Hill.

POLICE PERSONNEL: SELECTION, TRAINING, PROMOTION AND THE REPRESENTATION OF MINORITY GROUPS

INTRODUCTION

Many organizations believe their most important resource is the personnel they employ. This is also true of law enforcement because policing a democratic society requires competent individuals with a broad range of skills. Consequently, the recruitment, selection, retention and training of personnel is one of the most important functions of a police agency. This chapter looks at these issues as well as the role minority groups have recently assumed in police agencies.

HISTORY

Historically, the traditional recruit preference for North American and British police forces has been less educated, working-class males. Recruits who had a military background were also welcomed. Policing has always enjoyed the status of a respectable career; although salaries up until the mid-1960s were not high, the job was attractive because it offered security and respect. It was often chosen by working-class and rural Canadians and immigrants as a way to increase their social and economic standing.

Canadian police forces expanded at a rate that far exceeded the growth in population or the growth in crime during the three decades after the second world war (Forcese, 1992). In the 1970s, they experienced difficulties in attracting and recruiting suitable candidates, but by the following decade, these problems had been overcome. The early 1980s saw a decline in the recruitment rate. This can be illustrated by the figures from the RCMP training academy in Regina which trained classes of 1,000 or more in the 1970s, but from which only 23 graduated in 1983–4 (Forcese, 1992). Recruitment picked up again at the end of the 1980s when there was increasing pressure to recruit members of ethnic minorities and women.

For many years, Canadian police officers came from the working class strata of society. Policing offered these people a career path superior to that of their parents. For others, policing existed as a family tradition. Police recruits of the 1990s do not follow this pattern and, as will be shown below, are drawn from a far more diverse pool of applicants.

WHO WANTS TO BE A POLICE OFFICER?

As illustrated in the previous chapter, the sensationalized image of policing displayed in films and television does not accord with the reality of police work. Even today, this stereotype depicting the 'macho' image of danger, excitement and physical power still exists in the minds of many who want to be employed in law enforcement. Therefore, it is not unusual to find those who seek a career which they believe will provide these characteristics applying to the police.

While this image may be enticing to one group of people, factors such as the threat of physical danger, public hostility or apathy towards law enforcement, rotating shifts and emotional stress deter others from the occupation (Bonifacio, 1991). In the past, it has been minority groups in society, such as women and ethnic groups, that have not considered policing an option open to them. Furthermore, the fact that up until the 1970s few women and ethnic minority police officers were seen meant members of minority groups had few role models and were uncomfortable applying for police positions. In the same way that white males could identify with the personnel employed throughout police forces, minorities could not.

There has been considerable debate over why certain individuals are attracted to policing as a career. Early theories suggested that people with authoritarian personalities tended to seek police employment (Roberg and Kuykendall, 1993). These people, it was believed, had a predispositional personality and displayed traits such as cynicism, racism, secretiveness, loyalty and authoritarianism (Bonifacio, 1991) which drew them to policing. Theories of police personality are open to question (Burbeck and Furnham, 1985; Van Maanen, 1973) and it is now believed that, while many of these traits do exist in police officers, they are the product of socialization and experience gained while working in the police environment, not inherent personality traits. This issue will be discussed in the next chapter.

The literature suggests that police work attracts working-class, family-oriented white males interested in the security and salary working in law enforcement can bring. Individuals choosing this career do not do so casually, but rather enter policing believing it to be an elite organization, often already knowing something about police work, or personally knowing a police officer. They are also able to identify with the values and goals of the occupation (Van Maanen, 1973). Dantzker (1995) has shown the two primary reasons given by police officers for choosing their careers are 'to help society' and 'the nature of the job.'

To help society is a philosophical response, whereby the police officer indicates a desire to fight crime and address societal problems. Police officers in this category are somewhat unrealistic in their opinions about policing and take on the task for idealistic reasons. The second reason recognizes the intrinsic values of policing and the fact that few occupations offer such a diverse work environment without a strict routine. This, coupled with the fact that the job and its benefits will always exist, makes it a desirable career option. These individuals are more realistic in their perception of policing.

One further reason why people choose a policing career is because of some family connection. Arcuri (1976) found that having a police member in the family was a major reason why individuals became police officers.

RECRUITMENT

Recruitment strategies depend on how many and what kind of new recruits a police department wants to attract. If a number of positions are available, an agency may decide to place an advertisement in a newspaper; if only a couple of vacancies are created each year, the department may choose to target recruitment strategies towards those groups which are currently underrepresented in the organization. The way in which police agencies attract potential candidates varies among police departments and can incorporate any of the following strategies:

- **A team of recruiters.** The RCMP has a national recruitment team whose task is to encourage suitable, well-qualified applicants to consider working for the force.

- **An individual recruitment officer.** While larger police departments can afford recruitment teams, smaller departments assign the responsibility to an individual officer. It should be noted that the RCMP, in addition to the national recruitment team, also has an individual at each detachment responsible for recruitment (Walker, 1993).

- **Media advertising.** Advertisements placed in the media attract potential candidates. By targeting advertisements to specific, special-interest newspapers and magazines, police agencies have recently tried to attract minority candidates.

- **Unsolicited applications.** Many people who desire to become police officers contact the police force in which they seek employment directly to receive recruiting information. It is estimated that 85% of police departments receive unsolicited applications (Walker, 1993). Police departments often keep these applications on file and review them when a suitable vacancy arises.

- **Police volunteers.** Often people who have worked as volunteers for police agencies or have been employed by the police in a civilian capacity apply to become police officers.

- **Police presentations.** Police presentations at career fairs, high schools and colleges, ethnic festivals and cultural centres also attract potential candidates.

- **Direct mail.** In order to encourage applications from groups underrepresented in police departments, direct mail is sent to target groups. For example, in October 1995, the Vancouver police sent recruitment information to gay and lesbian organizations in BC in an attempt to entice more homosexual candidates (*Vancouver Sun*, 24 October 1995).

Once a prospective applicant has completed the required application form and submitted it to the police department for consideration, the next step is for that department to either accept or reject the application. If the application is accepted, the candidate must undergo a rigorous selection process.

SELECTION

One of the most critical first steps to policing is the selection of the most qualified and capable people to serve as police officers. Therefore, one of the most important functions a police agency must undertake is to establish effective recruit screening methods which are able to choose people at the outset who have attributes desirable to the police department and screen out those who do not. The appointment of inappropriate individuals results in considerable expense for police departments, as hiring and training recruits who leave during the probationary or training period naturally incurs costs. Also, the training of individuals who are not suited to police work may lead to citizen complaints that could damage the credibility of the department (Walker, 1993). A rigorously effective screening process is required to limit these potential problems.

On paper, it may appear that the basic qualifications for entering the police service are not that demanding. However, as the number of police jobs is held constant, increases only incrementally or declines, and the pool of individuals who aspire to enter the profession increases, police departments can become increasingly demanding in their selection process.

HIRING CRITERIA AND METHODS

Police departments, in association with police boards and commissions, develop their own selection criteria; therefore, the requirements for acceptance into recruit training vary among different police bodies. There are, however, a number of criteria that are commonly used by police for screening applicants. Walker (1993) notes that these criteria include written exams, oral interviews, special skills assessment, personality tests, cognitive ability tests, education and physical fitness tests. Although these criteria are common, what varies considerably among departments is the way the tests and initiatives are administered and structured.

Education

With the exception of forces in Quebec, where graduation from a community college is becoming a minimum entry standard, most forces require grade 12 education or its equivalent (Couttes, 1990). As the pool of applicants increases, the recruitment of a probationer constable with this level of education is now becoming increasingly rare. Although not formally stated, most new recruits have some university and college education.

Age

The minimum age requirement is usually between 18 and 21 with the maximum being from 35 to 65.

Height and weight

In the past, minimum height and weight requirements were demanded in most police departments; nowadays, very few forces have such criteria, which discriminated against women and minority groups. Most departments currently state they require a candidate's weight to be in proportion to height.

Physical performance

There is a wide degree of disparity in the requirements of the physical performance tests, with no provincial or national standards. The Police Officer's Physical Abilities Test (POPAT) was developed at the Justice Institute of British Columbia to provide standardized measures of fitness, health and physical ability for undertaking police duties (Couttes, 1990). The POPAT test includes a 2 km mobility/agility run, a pull and push activity, a modified squat thrust and stand station, a rail vault activity and a weight carry of 45.5 kg. The Ontario Police College has developed its own test, which requires a 2.4 km run, a sit and reach flexibility test, a 100 m sprint, a maximum number of sit-ups within one minute and a maximum number of push-ups within one minute. The RCMP has developed its own Physical Abilities Requirements Evaluation (PARE) for all candidates. The PARE simulates a scenario of three components, including a six-lap obstacle course, a pushing and pulling task and the carrying of a 36 kg torso bag over a 15 m distance within a set time (Walker, 1993).

Many of these physical strength and agility requirements were aimed at the macho-excitement image of the police and are unrelated to the actual job of policing (Roberg and Kuykendall, 1993). With the growing recognition that the police officer who can run a mile but does not possess any interpersonal skills may not be the most suitable for police work, questions have been raised about whether these physical tasks are truly job related or merely discriminatory against women and smaller males. Many police officers who passed these tests five years ago could not complete them today. There is now agreement that, while women should meet certain physical standards, these should be based on what the average woman can physically do, not the average man (Dantzker, 1995).

Psychological testing

In a study of recruitment policies and procedures in Canada, Walker (1993) found that 61% of respondents used psychological screening as a way to select applicants. The value of psychological testing rests on the assumption that, to be a police officer, one needs a number of stable, innate characteristics which are best measured by tests. These tests have been in vogue for a number of years (Cordingley, 1979), but have received criticism for identifying only the poor prospective candidates likely to cause trouble, and not the good prospects. This is, in part, attributable to the tests used (Couttes, 1990).

The most common psychological tests used in Canada are the Minnesota Multiphasic Personality Inventory and the California Psychological Inventory. After these tests have been taken, they are usually scored by a psychologist who is looking for serious emotional problems or for individuals who would not make good police officers. Applicants are screened out if their profile deviates from the established norm.

Considerable debate surrounds the use of psychological testing. Commentators have suggested there are significant methodological problems in the administration of these tests, and consequently, they should only be used in conjunction with other selection criteria (Burbeck and Furnham, 1985). Also there is much room for subjective interpretation by the psychologist (Inwald, 1985), leading to the recommendation that police agencies give more weight to background investigation and rely less on clinical judgments (Roberg and Kuykendall, 1993).

Background investigation

Background investigations are conducted on applicants by almost all police departments in Canada. The only exception seems to be small rural departments that retain personal familiarity with a large number of applicants (Nelson, 1992). The background investigation varies considerably, but basically attempts to assess candidates' general suitability for police work based on their past experience and lifestyle. Candidates have already provided the police department with an extensive personal history, which forms the basis for the background study. The investigator checks family ties, employment and credit history, employment and personal referees, educational record and criminal record in order to determine if each person is honest and would make a contribution to the department. Some departments carry out these investigations prior to testing, while others complete them just before the final interview (Couttes, 1990).

While little information is available on the background investigation in Canada, in the US, it is regarded as one of the most important aspects of the selection process (Bouza, 1990). A study by Cohen and Chaiken (1972) of the New York police found applicants rated as excellent in background checks later had the lowest incidence of misconduct, whereas applicants termed poor had the highest.

Interviews

Oral interviews measure attributes such as communication skills, confidence, interpersonal skills, and decision-making ability that are generally not measured elsewhere. The interview seeks to determine whether the candidate would make a good police officer and be an asset to the department. Typical questions might include: 'Why do you want to be a police officer?' 'What unique skills, strengths and abilities will you bring to the department?' 'How have you prepared yourself for this career?' 'What kind of magazines do you read?'.

Initial applicant interviews are usually carried out at the earlier stage of the application process by a sergeant in the personnel section (Couttes, 1990). If the candidate survives this process, a panel interview is then conducted with higher-ranking officers taking part. This interview is often chaired by the chief or deputy chief. Walker's (1993) study, cited above, showed that 94% of Canadian forces surveyed required candidates to pass an oral interview, but again the oral interview varies considerably among departments. It is at the interview phase of the selection process that opportunity for the greatest discrimination and subjective judgments occurs, leading some to suggest interviews are subject to interviewers' personal biases and may result in unfair evaluations (Nelson, 1992).

Written tests

Some police forces require candidates to undertake written tests on subjects such as 'Why I want to become a police officer' (Couttes, 1990), while others require an IQ test. Recently, these tests have been challenged as being culturally biased, discriminatory and not job related; consequently, there is a movement away from such testing.

Cognitive tests

Cognitive tests such as the Otis Quick Scoring Intelligence Test or the General Aptitude Test Battery (GATB) are widely used in North American policing. While a few Canadian forces have established their own in-house cognitive ability tests by using local professional psychologists, most use these two standardized tests (Couttes, 1990). Applicants usually have to pass this test in order to be considered for recruitment.

Polygraph tests

A polygraph, or lie detector, is a device that measures the physiological response to questions. It measures three variables: breathing, blood pressure and perspiration. Polygraphs are used to uncover aspects of an individual's character which are deemed undesirable to a police career. Nelson (1992) contends the use of the polygraph in western Canadian municipal police services is almost routine; however, Couttes (1990) argues only some Canadian departments use a polygraph to check the accuracy of the background information and to determine if there has been any inappropriate behavior in the applicant's past (e.g., criminal acts, drug use).

Medical exam

One final stage of the selection process is a medical examination conducted to determine the general health status of the candidate and to identify specific conditions, such as knee, back and heart problems. Any weaknesses that may be aggravated by police work will deny the candidate a police career (Roberg and Kuykendall, 1993).

The selection of a suitable recruit is an arduous task, but not a uniform process across all police agencies in Canada. Each department has developed its own selection criteria; some include all the categories listed above, others a reduced list. Two selection approaches (Couttes, 1990) are generally used: the multiple hurdle approach and the compensatory approach.

Multiple hurdle approach

The multiple hurdle approach is a method of assessment that requires the candidate to pass each of the selection criteria before passing on to the next one. Selection criteria are ranked, and failure to pass any hurdle means being rejected for the position. The premise of this approach is that the ability or skill being assessed at each stage is vital to the recruitment process and failure implies the candidate will not be able to do the job.

Compensatory approach

The compensatory approach is a system whereby candidates can compensate for deficiencies in certain areas by having ability in others. For example, a candidate who scores poorly during the cognitive test may be compensated by a good judgment score during the interview. This approach requires that the candidate undertake all the selection criteria, and it will not be until the end that an assessment is made.

While the selection criteria used in Canadian police forces vary, there are many problems inherent in the process. Couttes (1990) has argued police personnel selection practices do not incorporate state-of-the-art methods and techniques or include advances in personnel selection technology developed in other organizations. Some selection criteria, such as psychological and cognitive testing, are also open to serious methodological questions (Cordingley, 1979; Forcese, 1992) while other criteria, such as the oral interview and background investigation, are prone to subjective biases. As will be discussed below, the selection process has been amended during the last twenty years. One notable innovation, the assessment centre, has existed in British Columbia for a number of years, while in Ontario, change to a Police Learning System has been endorsed.

Assessment centres

An assessment centre can be used for recruit selection, personnel development and promotion. It utilizes occupational simulations to allow individuals to illustrate job-related skills, abilities and behavior. This information is then assessed with other relevant data to rate the quality of candidates. Assessment centres can also be used to introduce relevant training within a police academy. For example, assessment of an individual's oral, written and interpersonal skills can be used to focus academy training in this area if it is felt that these skills require improvement (Oppal, 1994). The Justice Institute of British Columbia is currently Canada's only assessment centre although the concept exists in a number of American states.

Police Learning System

In 1992, the Ontario Ministry of the Solicitor General published a report entitled *A Police Learning System For Ontario: Final Report and Recommendations*. This report advocates the introduction of a more holistic approach to police recruitment and training and recommends the introduction of a 'Police Learning System' which it defines as including:

> ...all aspects of police training, education and development including all formal and informal learning that takes place in the workplace, in the community, and in educational and other institutions. It includes trainers, co-workers, supervisors and managers as key learners and trainers (Ontario Solicitor General, 1992).

The report makes a large number of recommendations including:

- educational opportunities be delivered in a more open environment;
- a greater level of community imput be sought and;
- the needs of the learner be recognized.

In addition, the report stresses that new recruits must complete a two-semester 'Police Foundation' program at a community college to be eligible for hiring. The recommendations in this report are currently being implemented and will undoubtedly have a profound impact on police recruitment and training in Ontario.

TRAINING

The requirement to provide adequate training to individuals recruited to be police officers is a vital component of police agencies. Supervisors need to be confident the members of their staff have some fundamental skills and a knowledge of both the technical operations and human relations side of police work. In addition, in order to change the culture of the organization and to introduce new policies and philosophies such as those endorsed by community policing, training courses need to be developed to reinforce these philosophies. Policing skills are learned through the formal mechanisms of training and by operational experience. The nature and administration of police training varies across the country as, unlike some other countries such as Britain, Canada does not have a uniform training curriculum. There are two basic components to police training: basic training and ongoing training.

Basic training

Basic police training aims to provide cadets with the necessary skills to become constables. Basic training gives recruits instruction on a number of topics deemed relevant to their duties as generalists. Table 5.1 provides details of the RCMP Basic Recruit Training Program.

Normandeau and Leighton (1990) cite four models of basic training used by police forces in Canada, illustrating the diversity of training that currently exists.

1. The first model is based on the separation of police education and training from mainstream adult education. It provides training to recruits and police officers who have at least a grade 12 education in institutions that are separate and independent, for example, the RCMP Academy in Regina and the Ontario Police College.

2. The second model has many components similar to the first, but training takes place on a university campus. In such institutions, police staff provide classes on police administration and procedures, academic staff give classes on criminal justice and social services and lawyers and judges teach classes on criminal law, evidence and procedure. Examples of this model are the Saskatchewan Police College on the University of Regina campus and the Atlantic Police Academy at Holland College in Prince Edward Island.

3. The third model is premised on the assumption that police recruits should be exposed to the entire criminal justice system rather than being isolated. The Justice Institute of British Columbia provides training for police officers, probation officers, institutional personnel and court staff. Although basic training is designed for police recruits, courses dealing with issues pertinent to police officers, individuals working in social services and employees of other criminal justice agencies are also offered (for example, child sexual abuse and effective presentational skills).

TABLE 5.1 RCMP Basic Recruit Training Program

Operational training

Practical training
Report writing
First Aid
Handling of prisoners
Telecommunications
CPIC (Canadian Police Information Centre)
Typing
Police service dogs
Contingency planning
Officer survival

Identification services

Bombs and infernal devices
Crime scene protection
Crime detection laboratories
Plan drawing
Fingerprinting
Photography
Personal descriptions
Identification services
Fire scene investigations

Self-defense

Foot drill

History of police and RCMP

Police idea
Tradition

Law

Criminal code
Contacts and informants
Federal statutes
Official directives

Driver training

Driving
Traffic lectures
Point duty
Collision investigations

Firearms

Firearms practice
Care and handling of weapons
Shooting decisions
Safety lectures
Gas training

Physical training

Physical training
Personal performance test
Fitness field day test
Challenge circuits
PT lectures
Organized sports
Fitness and nutrition
Lifestyle development

Swimming

Swimming and lifesaving techniques
Cardio-pulmonary resuscitation (CPR)

Human relations

Police function
Effective presentations

Cross cultural

Cultural awareness
Cultures in conflict
Development and discrimination
Multiculturalism
Policing of minority groups

Human behavior and police intervention

Human interactions/relations
Problem solving
Intervention and defusion
The interview situation
Theory of stress

(RCMP, 1990)

4. The final model, found only in Quebec, attempts to integrate police education with adult education. Candidates first enroll in provincially-organized two-and-a-half-year college programs that include classes on criminology, law, and policing in addition to more general academic topics. Selected candidates then complete a ten-week course at the Quebec Police Institute in Nicolet. This model ensures recruits have some higher education (Normandeau and Leighton, 1990). As mentioned above, a similar model ensuring that all police recruits have some college education is currently under review in Ontario.

Basic recruit training represents a significant financial investment. The RCMP estimates the average cost of basic recruit training was about $40,000 in 1991-92; however, the extent and nature of this training varies considerably among police agencies and provinces.

In British Columbia, recruits are hired by the police department first. Basic training is then completed at the Justice Institute of BC and comprises:

• Block I: 14 weeks in the classroom.

• Block II: 8 weeks of field training.

• Block III: 10 weeks of classroom work then general duties (year one).

• Block IV: 3 weeks in the classroom (year two).

• Block V: one week in the classroom and three years' service establishes eligibility for promotion to the rank of first class constable.

In Ontario, recruits are also hired by the agency first. Basic training is completed at the Ontario Police College in Aylmer and consists of:

• Level I: 1-2 weeks' field training, which is undertaken at the individual agency.

• Level II: 60 days' classroom teaching.

• Level III: 3 months' field training.

• Level IV: 14 days' classroom training.

• Level V: general duties.

• Level VI: optional specialized training at the college and three years' service establishes eligibility for promotion to the rank of first class constable.

The RCMP hires individuals first, then requires they complete the 26-week basic training course at the RCMP Training Academy in Regina, followed by six months' field training. Recruits are then eligible for promotion to peace officer.

The academy gives formal and informal education about the police organization and is a vital component in the socialization process of a new recruit. Van Maanen (1973) has shown how the training academy provides a unique environment for a group of individuals to learn the traditions and culture of policing and how to become a front-line police officer. While some of this is through the formal classroom teaching, much is also learned by listening to the 'war stories' of experienced officers and by collectively learning the informal norms and values of policing. It is important to note that basic recruit training not only includes the instruction of predetermined topics but also incorporates an introduction to the broader issue of what being a police officer means.

Learning to be a police officer, therefore, involves two distinct socialization processes. Formal socialization is undertaken within the selection and training programs, where the organizational policies and procedures are learned from supervisors. Informal socialization occurs when recruits interact with older, more experienced, officers and their peers. The views learned from the process of informal socialization often contradict those of the formal process.

Field training

In field training, well-qualified, experienced police officers are trained to act as mentors for new recruits. Many provinces have a field training component interwoven into the basic recruit training; this period can last from six to twelve months. Field training prepares the recruit for the 'real world' of policing, often by assigning the recruit to a field training officer who provides on-the-job apprentice training.

There is a large volume of literature which has shown how in-service training seeks to modify and amend the academy instruction (Fielding and Fielding, 1987; Van Maanen, 1973). The rookie police officer, placed with an officer who 'knows the ropes,' is frequently informed to forget all that has been learned at the police academy as it is irrelevant to the actual world of policing. In addition, any enthusiasm and zeal displayed by the recruit is soon quashed with the instruction that low commitment and little activity are less likely to result in trouble (Forcese, 1992). Police agencies, therefore, experience difficulties instructing recruits on how they perceive policing should be done if these recruits are subsequently placed with field training officers who do not share the same philosophies of policing as those preached at the training academy. Even if the field training officer does share many of these philosophies, as the recruit starts to mix and socialize with experienced officers—many of whom display views that contradict those taught at the academy—the junior constable's outlook may change.

Ongoing training

In contrast to basic recruit training, ongoing training provides supplementary training on topics such as fraud, cultural relations, domestic disputes, child abuse and drug investigation, with the belief that social, legal and cultural changes continually occur and police officers need to keep abreast of such changes.

Ongoing training is also necessary when an individual wants to upgrade skills for promotion. Table 5.2 lists the ongoing training courses offered in the Saskatchewan Police College Course Calendar for 1996.

There are five categories of ongoing training:

1. **In-service training.** Here, the primary purpose is to regularly update members of a department with information necessary for them to function successfully. For example, training on new laws or newly-developed techniques may be provided. In-service training can also be used to address deficiencies identified in officer evaluations. For example, if an officer is recognized by his/her supervisor to use poor judgment or to be cynical about community policing philosophy, in-service training can be used to address these concerns (Alpert and Dunham, 1988). It has been suggested that, to keep qualified police officers informed of new developments, in-service training should account for between one and two percent of annual police budgets (Normandeau and Leighton, 1990).

2. **Multicultural training** teaches police officers to be sensitive to the ethnic and cultural diversities that exist in Canadian society. The RCMP was one of the earliest police forces to introduce multicultural training to police officers (Forcese, 1992); it is now a feature of both recruit and ongoing training. Other police forces have also recognized the need for such training in identifying a link between cultural sensitivity and police-community relations.

3. **Supervisory training** is geared to officers in first-line supervisory positions (sergeant and staff sergeant) and includes topics on leadership behavior, policies and procedures.

4. **Specialized training** prepares officers for specific tasks such as homicide investigation, fingerprinting, commercial crime. These courses are aimed at officers who take on specialized duties, work in separate units and do not undertake general patrol.

TABLE 5.2 Saskatchewan Police College Course Outline

Media communications course	Firearms instructors transition course
Fraud investigation course	Fire investigation course
Effective presentation skills course	Introduction to management
Operational investigators course	Police managers course
Cultural relations course	Child abuse investigators course
Senior identification technicians seminar	Drug investigation course
Statement analysis course	Gambling course
Senior constables development course	

5. **Management training** is provided for officers who have moved beyond the first-line supervisory position and require leadership skills. Training is provided on issues such as long-range planning, policy development and resource allocation.

While in-service, multicultural and supervisory training take place in the various provincial and regional training academies that provide recruit training, managerial and specialized training can take place at several locations. The largest and best known is the Canadian Police College in Ottawa. It was established in 1937 to provide special administrative and operations training for selected personnel from Canadian police forces (Kelly and Kelly, 1976) and is federally funded. It is managed by the RCMP and offers conferences, seminars and workshops in specialized areas, such as crime analysis, in addition to providing training for middle- and upper-level management, such as executive development courses and new officer training courses.

QUESTIONS SURROUNDING POLICE TRAINING

A number of commentators have recognized that some issues are controversial regarding the training of police officers. These include the following.

- The brevity of the training period. Policing is one of the most demanding jobs society asks an individual to undertake, and yet recruit training can be as brief as six weeks followed by a short period of supervision (Forcese, 1992). One can question whether this period is sufficient to train individuals to become police officers.
- Related to brevity is the content of training courses. Often, subjects are not dealt with in sufficient depth. In many cases, the new police officer has only a surface knowledge of issues and is not given sufficient instruction, for example, in the use of weapons or on how to handle domestic disputes.
- Critics have questioned whether the paramilitary focus of police training is dysfunctional for the police organization. Policing and soldiering are not alike, and yet police training has emphasized discipline and obedience, even though a great deal of police work involves individual discretion.
- Police training is seen to be biased towards the law and technological side of policing and not the social services and human relations role. The curriculum of police colleges is set by police personnel and has developed in an insular fashion. Questions can also be asked about the relevance of the curriculum, which has only recently begun to include classes on the social service role of the police, despite the fact this has been recognized as a major function of the police for over twenty years. Recently, courses on issues such as how to deal with the mentally ill and family crisis intervention have begun to address this shortcoming.

- Police training academies often exist as isolated institutions divorced from the rest of society. These training academies immerse new recruits in an environment that requires total commitment, conformity and loyalty (Forcese, 1992), isolating them from the rest of society.

- The quality of the instructors has been questioned. Instructors need both the ability to communicate effectively and practical recent experience with the issues they are asked to teach. A study of policing in BC (Oppal, 1994) found teaching methods dry, stale and inappropriate and advocated the application of more innovative techniques.

- The community policing philosophy, which is increasingly being advocated by police organizations in Canada, endorses a broader role for police officers, affecting training requirements. Training academies appear reluctant to respond to this need and have been slow to offer training in community policing. This has led to an ignorance of the concept among rank and file officers (Seagrave, 1996).

Attempts have been made to reform the training process by moving away from the traditional, classroom-instruction model. The use of role-playing has been advocated, in which professional actors simulate work experiences new police officers may face. Increasingly, films and multimedia techniques are also used as learning tools. Multicultural awareness training is now becoming more common and there is an attempt by police colleges to move away from the emphasis on physical competence and investigation procedures towards more community service and social work tasks. While these are worthwhile developments, the extent to which they are appreciated by police officers is debatable as many police officers, especially those who have many years' experience, regard them with suspicion or even hostility. The broader service role of the police has been described by police officers as 'bullshit' (Reiss, 1971), 'codswobble' (Reiner, 1978) and 'Mickey Mouse bullshit' (Reuss-Ianni, 1983) as it detracts from what they perceive as their primary crime fighting role. Some police officers do not recognize the value of these courses and are cynical and unsupportive of them.

PROMOTION

There are several factors that make policing a unique occupation in comparison to others. For example, virtually all officers begin as young constables and must work their way up the organizational hierarchy if they hold career aspirations. Other organizations tend to recruit individuals at a multitude of different levels (lateral entry). Other organizations also have specialist positions requiring externally-provided education and training; in contrast, police officers train and educate their own. Police agencies have been reluctant to endorse a system of lateral entry whereby a police officer could transfer from one police department to another, usually without losing seniority. It tends to be only chiefs and deputy chiefs who are recruited from outside the organization and even they have worked their way up through another Canadian police force. Police managers and unions have resisted change to this system, believing that management personnel would not function effectively without working their way up and obtaining street experience (Forcese, 1992). Police agencies also experience little attrition; once recruited, police officers do not tend to seek career change.

Promotion is, of course, a major motivator in police agencies and most have established formal promotional policies and procedures within their organizations. McGinnis (1989) identified several organizational factors which determine promotional prospects:

- **The rank structure and the availability of positions in each rank.** For example, McGinnis (1989) notes that in the RCMP there are 1.3 constables for each position above that rank, but in the Quebec Provincial Police the figure is 4.5, illustrating that promotion is easier in the RCMP.

- **Promotional policy and whether it favors youth or seniority.** Seniority means that virtually everyone will be promoted as each becomes the one with the most experience. If younger members are promoted they will occupy positions for longer periods of time, making the positions unavailable to others below them.

- **Retirement policy.** If generous pension plans allow police officers to retire after 25 years of service, this obviously clears the way for younger members. Alternatively, if such plans are only available after 30 to 35 years, then promotion is not so readily available as older officers remain in the organization longer.

- **Growth.** A growing organization generally creates new positions at most levels.

- **Force demographics.** If a department has a relatively young staff, there will be little opportunity for promotion for new recruits. At the same time, if the force recruits a number of individuals during the same period, competition for any promotions will be intense.

- **Attrition.** The number of individuals who leave the force.

- **Personnel policy changes.** Adding or removing a rank will, of course, create or remove a promotional opportunity. Also, changes in the promotional criteria (for example, stipulating a university degree) will remove certain individuals from the pool of potential candidates.

- **Size of the organization.** There is increased opportunity for constables to receive promotion in larger organizations where more opportunities exist than in smaller ones.

Promotion: constable to sergeant/staff sergeant

Most police officers aspire to become at least sergeants or staff sergeants within the organization (McGinnis, 1989), a process which involves two assessment hurdles: acquiring sufficient years of service and passing a promotional exam. Promotion to sergeant requires length of service as a first class constable to be between two and five years. In reality, most police officers who are promoted to this rank have between 11 and 15 years. Promotion to staff sergeant usually requires at least one year at the sergeant level.

Promotional examinations contain questions on law (federal and provincial statutes, the Criminal Code and municipal by-laws), departmental orders, policies and procedures and general principles of management. Police officers have to meet the length of service criteria and pass the promotional exam in order to be *considered* for promotion.

Once candidates are qualified to compete for sergeant or staff sergeant positions, they are evaluated on a number of issues:

- **Performance appraisals.** These are conducted by immediate supervisors and unit/divisional commanders and vary across forces, but most focus on factors such as initiative, judgment, acceptance of responsibility, interpersonal skills, written and oral communication, quality of work and leadership (Couttes, 1990).

- **Promotional potential rating.** These are incorporated within performance appraisals and rate the candidate's suitability for promotion based on the criteria in the performance appraisal.

- **Seniority.** Some forces do not credit seniority, while others believe it to be an important consideration when differentiating between applicants.

- **Promotional board interview.** These range in duration from twenty minutes to over one hour in length (Couttes, 1990) and can take the form of a series of structured questions, or questions relating to a number of 'what if' scenarios. They are usually conducted by three to five senior officers.

While these four criteria are the most common, there are at least two other factors which some forces also take into consideration:

- Self-improvement activities, such as the completion of in-service or university and college courses.

- Additional information, such as commendations, the amount of sick leave taken, the number of complaints (if any) received against the candidate.

Promotion: sergeant/staff sergeant to inspector

Promotions to the rank of inspector involve an evaluation process similar to that of sergeant/staff sergeant, in which a minimum length of time at the staff sergeant level (usually one to two years) is required, as is a promotional exam.

In some forces, sergeants are eligible for promotion to inspector rank and in the RCMP, corporals are. Once a candidate is eligible, similar criteria as applied to the sergeant level are used for promotions to the inspector rank, although less emphasis is placed on seniority.

Promotion to senior management

Promotions to the senior management levels of superintendent and staff superintendent do not involve formal assessment criteria. As noted by Couttes (1990):

> At these levels promotion decisions are usually made directly by the chief in consultation with the deputy chief. Their decisions often reflect a number of informal criteria such as the candidate's track record, breadth of experience...and his or her ability to 'fit in' with the existing management team (p. 103).

RETIREMENT

Police officers usually retire with 25 to 30 years of service. Over the course of the last twenty years, police unions have been successful in negotiating decent pensions for their members, so financially, retiring police officers are quite well off. However, retirees may find their problems are not financial, but rather lie with the idleness and social isolation that retirement brings. With few marketable skills, a police officer who was recruited at the age of 20 with no academic qualifications and retires at the age of 50 has little opportunity for a second career.

RETENTION

As illustrated above, the selection and training of police officers is a lengthy and expensive procedure. Police organizations aim to recruit those whom they believe will commit to a long-term career as a police officer. Research suggests that certain individuals are more likely to leave this career than others. A study undertaken by Linden (1985) showed that rates of attrition in the RCMP were substantially higher for women than for men. He found that 25% of females employed in the force after 1975 had left by September 1982 compared to 14% of males. The reasons given by these women for making this decision were not related to poor performance or low levels of job satisfaction, but rather were attributed to marriage-related factors, such as the strains caused by being located away from a spouse, conflicting shift schedules if the woman was married to a police officer and the difficulties of raising children in a dual-career household.

The issue of retention has been identified not only for women but also for ethnic minority police officers who leave after experiencing prejudice and alienation from the traditional white male culture of policing. In addition, those who enter policing with higher educational qualifications than has traditionally been the norm have also tended to leave at a greater rate. High turnover means the loss of experienced officers and the waste of considerable investment by the police organization. With these issues in mind, attempts have been made not only to recruit a broad cross section of the population but also to ensure that, once recruited and trained, they are retained. Unfortunately, there is little Canadian data on those who leave a police career and their reasons for making that decision.

HIGHER EDUCATION

Police work was once thought to require physical—not mental—ability. This opinion is now untenable as there has been a growing recognition the police need to be better educated. Many believe that police officers, especially those in senior ranks, would benefit from post-secondary education (Grant, 1984). The number of new recruits who hold degrees has increased recently, although, as mentioned previously, the formal entry requirement for most police agencies remains the completion of grade 12.

As one of the key issues for policing is the recruitment and retention of well-qualified individuals, concern has been voiced over the educational requirements of police officers and whether higher education will benefit policing (Normandeau and Leighton, 1990). The need for police officers to hold a degree has been tied to the concept of professionalism. Police departments are trying to become more professionalized, although the specific role of education in this process has not been clearly defined (Buckley, 1991). Higher education is seen to both improve the status of policing and provide police officers with a better understanding of society and their role in it.

The advantages that police officers with college and university education bring to the job have been described by a number of authors (Normandeau and Leighton, 1990; Roberg and Kuykendall, 1993) and can be listed as follows:

- Better communication with the public. Officers are more articulate and have better social and interpersonal skills.
- Improved written skills, resulting in better-quality of reports.
- Better performance, as evidenced by performance ratings from their superiors (Roberg, 1978).
- Fewer citizen complaints are received about them, presenting fewer problems for their departments.
- They show more initiative and are more adaptive to changes and new approaches to policing. Better-educated police managers are thought to be more creative.
- They are more professional. Research from the United States has shown that police officers with some college education are less authoritarian (Guller, 1972) and have stronger attitudes towards professional status (Miller and Fry, 1978).

- They are more likely to be promoted and to treat policing as a career rather than a job.
- They show more sensitivity, flexibility and discretion in dealing with different racial and ethnic groups.
- They are better decision makers.
- They appreciate the complexities of the criminal justice system and have a better understanding of the police position within the process.
- They have more job satisfaction. They tend to see their work from a broader perspective, believing they have some impact on society, whereas non-university educated officers are oriented to law enforcement (Weiner, 1974).

The disadvantages of recruiting police officers with higher education are:

- They are more likely to leave policing due to disillusionment.
- They are more likely to request reassignments.
- They tend to question orders and organizational policies more.
- Higher educational requirements disadvantage minority groups who tend to have lower educational qualifications. (This can be addressed with employment equity programs.)
- It has been suggested that better-educated police officers are less sympathetic to the problems faced by individuals in the lower socio-economic classes, as they are less likely to identify with them (Sherman, 1978).
- They have less job satisfaction because they are not challenged enough and have a harder time fitting in with the para-military structure of the organization (Fielding and Fielding, 1987).

In a study of Canadian police officers' attitudes towards higher education, Buckley (1991) found those who did not have a university education perceived it as having little value, whereas those who did held more positive views. Lesser-educated officers, especially the older ones, perceived university education as a threat to their careers. Further Canadian research (Seagrave, 1994) found a university degree is now considered vital for those who have aspirations of achieving senior management rank. The RCMP encourages and supports members who want to undertake a degree by providing periods of absence for officers to attend university. In the past, it has sponsored members to complete degrees.

As the pool of candidates wishing to pursue a police career increases in size, departments will have more scope to select applicants they feel are the most suited to policing. Many of these will have degrees and more formal education than those already employed in the organization. The injection of this group may change the quality and nature of policing and influence the culture of the police organization. This, coupled with the recruitment of groups that previously were not included within the ranks of the police, is an ongoing evolutionary process, which has only recently been actively encouraged.

MINORITY RECRUITMENT, EMPLOYMENT EQUITY AND AFFIRMATIVE ACTION

The recruitment of qualified personnel is a key area for police agencies. Over the last twenty years, there has been an increasing emphasis on employment equity. In 1984, The Report of the Royal Commission on Equality in Employment stated that employment equity seeks to identify any significant differences between participation and availability of four targeted (designated) minority groups—visible minorities, Aboriginal peoples, disabled peoples and women—within an employer's personnel figures. It asked employers to identify employment policies and practices that disadvantaged these groups. The 1977, the Canadian Human Rights Act (Section 16.1) gave further teeth to this report by asserting that it is not a discriminatory practice to adopt a special program or arrangement that is designed to eliminate disadvantages suffered by individuals in these minority groups. Employment equity does not mean hiring less capable individuals or discriminating against well-qualified white males, but rather developing new strategies and expending effort to actively recruit the targeted groups and increase the size of the target pool (Walker, 1993).

In discussing employment equity, Jackson (1992) suggested that police forces need to develop employment equity plans that embrace four elements:

1. Numerical goals for increasing the numbers of women, ethnic minorities, Aboriginal peoples and the disabled.

2. Elimination of barriers to the attraction, retention and promotion of designated groups.

3. Positive measures to enhance police agencies' attraction, retention and promotion of designated groups.

4. Accountability mechanisms to ensure the employment equity plans are being implemented.

Employment equity is often confused with affirmative action. While employment equity seeks to identify any significant differences between participation and availability of the four targeted minority groups, affirmative action goes one step further by stating the only way to ensure minority groups are represented in modern organizations, many of which formerly existed as male-dominated environments, is to move a significant number of previously excluded individuals into these organizations, thus changing their make-up and culture. Affirmative action policies, therefore, promote the recruitment of minority groups but are seen as discriminatory by many, especially white males. The issue has been a controversial one in Canada and the United States (Jackson, 1992). However, it is generally recognized that no alternative policy will work within an acceptable period of time (and may not work at all); consequently, affirmative action policies have been accepted.

Policing has long been regarded as a white male profession. Attempts have been made since the 1970s to recruit more minority groups so police agencies would reflect the communities they served. Today, police departments are becoming increasingly sensitive to pluralist, heterogeneous, multicultural and multiracial communities. Because of this, they have begun trying to recruit members of targeted minority groups into their organizations.

WOMEN IN POLICING

In 1970, the Royal Commission on the Status of Women in Canada published its report. One of the recommendations was that women take a more active role in policing. Despite this call, the number of Canadian women who choose policing as a career remains small, and our knowledge and understanding of these women is slight.

Research on policewomen

The fact that there have been comparatively few studies on women in law enforcement has been well recognized in the United States (Roberg and Kuykendall, 1993) and in Britain (Young, 1991). In the past, this has been attributed to the relatively small number of policewomen. Currently, in certain police departments in the United States, women comprise 20% of sworn personnel. As women appear in greater numbers and take a more active role, the number of studies should increase.

A text by Heidensohn (1992) provides one of the most comprehensive reviews of the literature. She argues that policing research has taken one of three approaches in assessing the role of women. The first approach is to completely ignore women. This has been the situation in the Canadian literature, where research on policewomen is practically nonexistent. The seminal work on the history of policing in Canada by Kelly and Kelly (1976) makes no reference whatsoever to women, and much of the broader police literature fosters the same silence (e.g., Sewell, 1985; Talbot et al., 1985). A notable exception to this is a series of studies by Linden (1983, 1984, 1985), commissioned by the Solicitor General, which examined the experiences of female officers. More recently, Walker (1993) completed a report on the status of women in Canadian policing.

The second categorization Heidensohn notes consists of studies undertaken in the 1970s, concerned with the effects of legal and policy changes made in these years, while the third approach she describes as a curious hybrid of studies that focus on males' attitudes to females.

To date, there has not been a Canadian feminist interpretation of women in policing. While female criminologists have been actively researching the experience of women as victims of crime and as offenders within the criminal justice system, they have not shown the same enthusiasm for women in law enforcement. Consequently, our information is limited.

Policewomen in Canada

The first Canadian policewoman was hired by the Vancouver police in 1912; during the next seven years, Toronto, Winnipeg and Edmonton also recruited women (Owings, 1969).

Little is known of the historical development of female police officers. Reviewing the history of policewomen in the Vancouver police, Halliday (1975) shows that the early policewomen were neither trained nor provided uniforms and were confined to certain duties, including clerical functions and the handling of women and youth. In 1952, Vancouver policewomen started to receive the same training as their male counterparts, but their duties remained restricted. During a period in the 1960s, they were removed from street policing tasks and awarded jobs only within the police station. In 1973, the first women were assigned to general patrol duties, after which the department changed its hiring policies so that, by 1977, women comprised five percent of the department's strength (Linden, 1983).

While the experience of Vancouver and other independent police departments illustrated an early commitment to female officers, the RCMP only gave serious consideration to the employment of women in the 1970s, following the Royal Commission on the Status of Women Report, which strongly recommended that this policy be adopted. Women had worked in the RCMP as civilian members and, as such, were subject to the same regulations, but did not wear uniforms or have police powers (Linden, 1984). The initial response of the RCMP to the Royal Commission was to study the issue for a number of years. However, in September 1974, a troop of women began training, graduating in 1975.

In 1977, the Canadian Human Rights Act was passed by Parliament, prohibiting employers from discriminating on the grounds of sex, unless there was justifiable occupational requirement for such discrimination. This legislation, along with the recommendations of the Royal Commission, no doubt influenced the recruitment of female officers.

In 1960, women comprised 1.2% of operational police officers in cities and districts with populations of more than 50,000. In 1977, this figure had increased to 1.8% (Linden, 1983). Table 5.3 illustrates how the number of female police officers has continued to increase.

It is important to note that this increase is not uniform across the country, as certain forces have a larger proportion of women, others a smaller proportion and some none at all. Although the number of women in Canadian policing is increasing, they are concentrated in the lower ranks. Among females, 93% hold the rank of constable compared to 68% of males, 0.75% are officers compared to 5% of males. In 1993, women made up 1% of officer ranks, 2% of non-commissioned ranks and 11% of constables (Statistics Canada, 1995).

TABLE 5.3 Numbers of Police Personnel in Canada 1965–1994

Year	Male	Female	Percent Female
1965	29,965	181	0.6%
1970	37,759	190	0.5%
1975	47,188	525	1.1%
1980	48,794	1,047	2.2%
1985	48,538	1,813	3.6%
1990	52,461	3,573	6.4%
1992	52,705	4,286	7.5%
1993	52,367	4,556	7.6%
1994	50,809	5,056	9.0%

(Statistics Canada, 1996; Walker, 1993).

Barriers to policewomen

It is not difficult to recognize how employment in a field that has traditionally shunned the inclusion of women and promoted a male-dominated image throughout its existence creates problems for those women who have chosen it. As noted by Martin (1993):

> Women threaten to disrupt the division of labor, the work norms, the work group solidarity, their already insecure occupational status and public image and the sexist ideology that undergirds the men's definition of the work as 'men's work' and their identity as masculine men (p. 334).

In a detailed study for the Solicitor General, Walker (1993) listed five barriers currently existing for women who pursue a career in policing:

1. **The barrier of tradition.** The traditional 'macho' image of the job acts as a significant barrier to women, who also face barriers in the form of sexual harassment, sexual jokes and sex-role stereotyping (Martin, 1990, 1993; Walker, 1993). Women are felt to be incapable of dealing with violent incidents and are blamed for absenteeism due to pregnancy, stress leave and family responsibilities.

2. **The barrier of credibility.** Women are not taken seriously in police organizations and have a difficult time establishing their careers. The selection and training process, with its emphasis on physical fitness and the use of force and the downplaying of the social service role of the police, means many of the attributes women bring to policing are not valued.

3. **The barrier of assumptions.** Policewomen are seen to be less committed to policing as a career. Having a female partner is presumed to put an officer at increased risk, as there is the belief that women are not supported by the

public and attract complaints. Balkin (1988) found police officers' wives object to their husbands having female partners because they feel that their spouses are both less safe and vulnerable to sexual liaisons.

4. **Self-made barriers.** Women can limit their opportunities by underrating their ability, for example, by remaining silent at meetings or by not competing in the promotional process. Many women lack the confidence displayed by their male counterparts.

5. **The barrier of isolation.** As there are still comparatively few women in police agencies, the chances of formal and informal networking and mentoring are slight, leading to a feeling of isolation. The structure and organizational culture of police departments is alienating to women; this may be particularly true of smaller police departments that employ only one or two women.

Effectiveness of policewomen

The meager amount of research that exists on women in policing, mostly from the United States, suggests they are better at diffusing violent situations (Bloch and Anderson, 1974), are less likely to be charged with improper conduct (Sherman, 1975) and have better interpersonal skills than their male counterparts, leading to the suggestion that, in many respects, women are better suited to police work (Van Wormer, 1981). In a detailed study, Sherman (1973) reported the benefits of women police officers.

• There was a reduction of incidents of violence between police officers and citizens.

• There was an increase in police service quality because women accentuate the service role of police more than men.

• There was improved police-community relations as women are more visible than men and make more citizen contacts.

• Policemen can learn from policewomen that force is not always necessary.

• Policewomen are more effective in settling problems reported by women and by those of the lower socio-economic classes.

• Police departments become more democratic and responsive to the community by employing women.

One of the most comprehensive studies of female police officers in Canada was undertaken by Linden (1983, 1984, 1985) in the early 1980s. He found no significant difference in their ability to undertake policing duties. He also noted that members of the public were positive and respectful to women officers.

The barriers identified by Walker (1993) and others, coupled with family and marriage commitments, means attrition among female officers is higher than for their male counterparts. In the RCMP, this is a particular problem, because its transfer policy, requiring a member to move every three years, has been cited by many women as a reason why they leave the force (Linden, 1985). In comparison to male colleagues, female police officers leave policing at a rate of 3:1 (Seagram and Stark Adamac, 1992).

There is resistance to the recruitment of women from men who believe a police officer requires certain physical attributes. Prejudice may be more evident amongst older officers, who were recruited into an all-male organization, than with the newer recruits, many of whom trained with women.

The opposition to women in policing lies with traditional views of gender roles held by male officers. With employment equity programs and organizational change, many of the barriers hindering the selection, recruitment, retention and promotion of women will be slowly addressed. As the number of female police officers continues to increase, the problems of integrating women into policing will likely diminish over time. In 1994, the first female chief of police was appointed in Guelph, Ontario (Statistics Canada, 1996). The following year, Calgary police, with over 1,100 officers, appointed a woman as chief constable. The movement of women into key management and leadership positions will undoubtedly assist in the increased acceptability of women in Canadian forces and, like the recruitment of more highly-educated officers, perhaps begin to alter the organizational culture of policing.

ETHNIC MINORITY POLICE OFFICERS

When Peel first laid down his principles of policing, he argued the police should be reflective of the community they serve. Policing is still a white male profession, and although increased recruitment of women has made some inroads into the male bastion, the recruitment of ethnic minorities has not been as successful. American research (Maghan, 1993) suggests the recruitment and hiring of ethnic minority police officers has been approached by police administrators with less than genuine enthusiasm, being frequently viewed as a political necessity rather than a professional opportunity.

Recruiting ethnic minority police officers is important for a number of reasons.

- For reducing existing tensions between the police and racial minority communities. Many municipal forces, for example in Montreal and Toronto, have been involved in conflicts with ethnic minority groups. The recruitment of members of these groups is seen as a way to ease potential conflicts.
- For reducing the homogeneous 'white' culture of traditional policing.
- For dispelling stereotyped images police officers have of minorities.
- For facilitating a diversity of attitudes and increased tolerance.

In a survey of Canadian police forces, Jain (1994) found visible minority representation ranged from zero to 4.7%, with almost all visible minorities being male. Of the larger police forces in 1990, the RCMP had 0.8% visible minority officers, Toronto 4.7%, Halifax 4.5%, Edmonton 2%, Montreal 0.5% and Vancouver

3.8%. Seven percent of the country's labor force is classified as visible minority and in areas such as Toronto and Vancouver, the figure is 16%. In comparison to the armed forces, visible minorities are poorly represented, yet they are better represented than in firefighting departments (Suriya, 1993).

During the last twenty years, police departments have been attempting to recruit minorities. In 1989, the RCMP created a national recruiting team aimed at recruiting visible minorities, indigenous people, francophones and women. A year later, the RCMP introduced the Aboriginal Constable Development Program, which aimed to facilitate an increase in the number of Aboriginal people eligible to become RCMP members. It is a two-year work-study program in which recruits receive educational upgrading and on-the-job training and, if successful, enter recruit training (see Chapter 12). The Ontario Provincial Police and other large municipal forces also have programs to encourage ethnic minorities to consider a career in policing. Some police departments have developed outreach recruitment programs for specific groups and have summer internship programs and pre-employment counseling and training to assist ethnic minority applicants.

Considerable publicity has surrounded the issue of ethnic minority recruitment. When visible minorities are recruited, they are placed in a 'fishbowl' conspicuous to the media, the public, management and their peers (Forcese, 1992). Minority recruits have found the traditional police environment uncomfortable and even hostile as they form a distinct group within the almost all-white organization, and receive a good deal of attention. They experience the challenges and stresses not only of wearing the uniform, but also of being a visible minority in a predominantly white organization. They are a subgroup within a subculture (Maghan, 1993).

As with the recruitment of women, the commitment to minority recruitment causes tensions with existing personnel who may regard any positive discrimination incentive as a system of unfair preferential treatment. This can be illustrated by the furor that accompanied the RCMP's 1989 decision to allow a Sikh recruit to wear a turban as part of the official police uniform. This decision prompted considerable debate both within the RCMP and by the public, and was seen by some police officers as the desecration of a tradition.

Resistance to the inclusion of ethnic minorities has come not only from within the organization. Some cultures do not regard policing as a status profession. Niederhoffer (1967) noted that Jewish communities do not see the job of police officer as a desirable one and research cited by Maghan (1993) on Asian communities indicates they have similar views. This trait has also been identified in Canada, where some ethnic minorities do not consider policing to be a respectable profession (Jayewardene and Talbot, 1990). Descendants of these cultures have been reluctant to join what they believe to be an organization with little credibility. To overcome cultural and social misconceptions, police agencies now place recruitment advertisements in ethnic language and cultural newspapers to encourage applicants. They have also addressed biases recognized in the selection and recruitment criteria (for example, height requirements and psychological testing). Despite these initiatives, the number of non-white police officers remains marginal.

Visible minority women are doubly disadvantaged (Suriya, 1993). In addition to being members of a visible minority, they experience gender-based discrimination, and so encounter additional obstacles to those of their male counterparts.

GAY POLICE OFFICERS

Although in the past Canadian police agencies have been reluctant to discuss homosexuality, more recently they have come to recognize the need to address the issue. In some instances (e.g., Vancouver police), they have actively directed recruiting material at the gay and lesbian community (*Vancouver Sun*, 24 October 1995). Previously, police forces have been loath to accept homosexuality, viewing it as a compromising perversion (Forcese, 1992). Heterosexual police officers working in the traditional masculine environment of policing tend to be hostile towards homosexuals, arguing that gay police officers lower society's respect for the police, cannot be counted upon to assist fellow officers and might force sexual attentions on other officers. Proponents argue that homosexuality does not affect the way a job is undertaken and the composition of policing should reflect the composition of the community; as a significant proportion of the population is gay, then this should be mirrored in police departments.

Toronto has the only Canadian support group for gay police officers. The Law Enforcement Gay Alliance was formed in 1989 by officers who felt harassed and discriminated against. In 1995, about 40 officers from all over Canada had sought support from the group (*Vancouver Sun*, 24 October 1995).

As more individuals 'come out' and declare their sexual preferences, it is likely that officers who are already employed in police departments but have concealed their sexual orientation will also do the same, but only if they feel they will not be discriminated against within the organization. This, coupled with targeted recruitment initiatives, may increase the number of overtly gay police officers in Canada, but, like other minority groups, they have a significant barrier to overcome.

SUMMARY

This chapter has discussed issues related to the recruitment, selection, training and promotion of police personnel in Canada. The importance of selecting high-quality personnel cannot be stressed too much, and recently, police agencies have been striving to attract more educated applicants. The recruitment of women and minority groups has increased over the last few decades, due primarily to equal employment opportunity policies and practices. Despite such initiatives, the proportion of women, ethnic minorities and homosexuals in police agencies remains small.

QUESTIONS FOR DISCUSSION

1. Outline some of the reasons why individuals choose to pursue a career in policing.
2. Do you think the polygraph test should be used as one of the selection criteria?
3. What do you think are the best components of basic recruit training and what are the worst?
4. What model of police training academy do you feel is most appropriate for the training of police officers and why?
5. Should the police use a system of lateral entry?
6. What are the barriers faced by female police officers in Canada? How easily do you think these will be overcome?
7. Do you think initiatives that encourage police forces to recruit minority candidates discriminate against white males?
8. Should all police officers hold a university degree?
9. Why should police departments encourage ethnic minorities to consider a career in policing?
10. In what way, if any, will the recruitment of minorities change policing?

FURTHER READING

Jayewardene, C.H.S. and Talbot, C.K. (1990). *Police Recruitment of Ethnic Minorities.* Ottawa: Canadian Police College. This text examines the recruitment of ethnic minorities into police agencies as a result of the increasing heterogeneity of Canadian society.

Walker, S. Gail (1993). *The Status of Women in Canadian Policing: 1993.* Ottawa: Solicitor General of Canada. This report gives a relatively recent analysis of the position of women in Canadian policing and provides a useful addition to the only previous Canadian literature on the subject by Linden.

Fielding, Nigel G. (1988). *Joining Forces: Police Training, Socialization and Occupational Competence.* London: Routledge. Although focusing on the British police, this text provides an in-depth account of the training and socialization process of recruits based on research conducted over a five-year period. The author relates his findings to policing in North America.

REFERENCES

Alpert, Geoffrey A. and Dunham, Roger G. (1988). *Policing In Urban America.* Prospect Heights, Ill.: Waveland Press.

Arcuri, A.F. (1976). "Police pride and self esteem: Indications of future occupational changes." *Journal of Police Science and Administration, 4*(2).

Balkin, J. (1988). "Why policemen don't like policewomen." *Journal of Police Science and Administration 16*(3).

Bonifacio, P. (1991). *The Psychological Effects of Policework.* New York: Plenum Press.

Bloch, P. and Anderson, D. (1974). *Policewomen on Patrol: Final Report.* Washington D.C.: Police Foundation.

Bouza, A.V. (1990). *The Police Mystique.* New York: Plenum Press.

Buckley, Leslie Brian (1991). "Attitudes toward higher education among mid-career police officers." *Canadian Police College Journal, 15*(4).

Burbeck, Elizabeth and Furnham, Adrian (1985). "Police officer selection: A critical review of the literature." *Journal of Police Science and Administration 13*(1).

Cohen, B. and Chaiken, J.H. (1972). *Police Background Characteristics and Performance.* Lexington Mass.: Lexington.

Cordingley, P. (1979). "Psychological testing in Canadian police forces." *Canadian Police College Journal, 3*(2).

Couttes, Larry M. (1990). "Police hiring and promotion: Methods and outcomes." *Canadian Police College Journal, 14*(2).

Dantzker, Mark L. (1995). *Understanding Today's Police.* New Jersey: Prentice Hall.

Fielding, N.G. and Fielding, J.L. (1987). "A study of resignation during British police recruit training." *Journal of Police Science and Administration, 15*(1).

Forcese, Dennis P. (1992). *Policing Canadian Society.* Scarborough: Prentice Hall.

Grant, Alan (1984). *The Police: A Policy Paper.* Ottawa: Ministry of Supplies and Services.

Griffiths, Curt T. and Verdun Jones, Simon N. (1994). *Canadian Criminal Justice.* Toronto: Harcourt Brace.

Guller, I.B. (1972). "Higher education and policemen: Attitudinal differences between freshmen and senior police college students." *Journal of Criminal Law, Criminology and Police Science, 3.*

Halliday, Carol-Ann (1975). *Many Minnies Later: Development of Women Police in British Columbia.* Vancouver: Vancouver Police Department.

Heidensohn, Frances (1992). *Women in Control? The Role of Women in Law Enforcement.* Oxford: Clarendon Press.

Inwald, R. (1985). "Administrative, legal and ethical practices in the psychological testing of law enforcement officers." *Journal of Criminal Justice, 13*(1).

Jackson, R.L. (1992). *Employment Equity and Ontario Police: Problems and Perspectives.* Kingston, Ontario: Industrial Relations Centre, Queen's University.

Jain, H.C. (1994). "An assessment of strategies of recruiting visible minority police officers in Canada 1985–1990." In R.C. Macleod and David Schneiderman (Eds.) *Police Powers in Canada: The Evolution and Practice of Authority.* Toronto: University of Toronto Press.

Jayewardene, C.H.S. and Talbot, C.K. (1990). *Police Recruitment of Ethnic Minorities.* Ottawa: Canadian Police College.

Kelly, W. and Kelly, N. (1976). *Policing in Canada.* Toronto: MacMillan.

Linden, R. (1983). "Women in Policing: A Study of Lower Mainland RCMP Detachments." *Canadian Police College Journal, 7*(1).

Linden, R. (1984). *Women in Policing: A Review.* Ottawa: Solicitor General.

Linden, R. (1985). "Attrition among male and female members of the RCMP." *Canadian Police College Journal, 9*(2).

Maghan, Jess (1993). "The changing face of the police officer: Occupational socialization of minority police recruits." In Roger G. Dunham and Geoffrey P. Alpert (Eds.) *Critical Issues in Policing: Contemporary Readings.* Prospect Heights, Illinois: Waveland Press.

Martin, S.E. (1990). *On the Move: The Status of Women in Policing.* Washington D.C.: Police Foundation.

Martin, S.E. (1993). "Female officers on the move? A status report on women in policing." In Roger G. Dunham and Geoffrey P. Alpert (Eds.) *Critical Issues in Policing: Contemporary Readings.* Prospect Heights, Illinois: Waveland Press.

McGinnis, James H. (1989). "Predicting Police Force Attrition, Promotion and Demographic Change: A Computerized Simulation Model." *Canadian Police College Journal, 13*(2).

Miller, J. and Fry, L.J. (1978). "Some evidence on the impact of higher education for law enforcement personnel." *Police Chief 45.*

Nelson, E.D. (1992). "'Employment equity' and the Red Queen's hypothesis: Recruitment and hiring in Western Canadian municipal police departments." *Canadian Police College Journal, 16*(3).

Niederhoffer, A. (1967). *Behind the Shield.* New York: Doubleday.

Normandeau, A. and Leighton, B. (1990). *A Vision of the Future of Policing in Canada: Police Challenge 2000.* Ottawa: Solicitor General of Canada.

Ontario Solicitor General (1992). *A Police Learning System For Ontario: Final Report and Recommendations.* Toronto: Ministry of the Solicitor General.

Oppal, The Honourable Mr. Justice Wallace T. (1994). *Closing the Gap: Policing and the Community.* Commission of Inquiry Policing in British Columbia. Victoria, B.C.: Attorney General.

Owings, Chloe (1969). *Women Police.* Montclair, N.J.: Patterson Smith.

Reuss-Ianni, Elizabeth (1983). *Two Cultures of Policing.* New Brunswick (USA): Transaction Books.

Reiss, A.J. (1971). *The Police and the Public.* New Haven: Yale University Press.

Reiner, R. (1978). *The Blue Coated Worker.* Cambridge: Cambridge University Press.

Roberg, Roy R. (1978). "An analysis of the relationship among higher education, belief systems and job performance of patrol officers." *Journal of Police Science and Administration,* 6(2).

Roberg, Roy R. and Kuykendall, Jack (1993). *Police and Society.* Belmont California: Wadsworth Publishing.

Royal Canadian Mounted Police (1990). *Fact Sheets.* Ottawa: Ministry of Supply and Services.

Seagram, Belinda Crawford and Stark-Adamec, Cannie (1992). "Women in Canadian urban policing: Why are they leaving?" *The Police Chief.*

Seagrave, J. (1994). "Advice for those who want to be boss." *RCMP Gazette,* 56(2).

Seagrave, J. (1996). "Defining community policing: Interpretations from the literature, police leaders and police officers." *American Journal of Police* 15(2).

Sewell, John (1985). *The Police Function in Canada.* Toronto: James Lorimer Company.

Sherman, L.J. (1973). "A psychological view of women in policing." *Journal of Police Science and Administration, 1.*

Sherman, L.J. (1975). "Evaluation of policewomen on patrol in a suburban police department." *Journal of Police Science and Administration, 3.*

Sherman, L.W. (1978). *The Quality of Police Education: A Critical Review with Recommendations for Improving Programs in Higher Education.* San Francisco: Jossey-Bass.

Statistics Canada (1996). "Police personnel and expenditure in Canada 1994." *Juristat,* 16(1). Ottawa: Statistics Canada.

Suriya, Senaka K. (1993). "The representation of visible minorities in Canadian police: Employment equity beyond rhetoric." *Police Studies,* 16(2).

Talbot, C.K., Jayewardene, C.H.S. and Juliani, T.J. (1985). *Canada's Constables: The Historical Development of Policing in Canada.* Ottawa: Crimcare.

Van Maanen, J. (1973). "Observations on the making of policemen." *Human Organization, 32.*

Van Wormer, K. (1981). "Are males suited to police patrol work?" *Police Studies,* 3(2).

Vancouver Sun "Police seeking recruits among gays, lesbians," 24 Oct. 1995.

Walker, S. Gail (1993). *The Status of Women in Canadian Policing: 1993.* Ottawa: Solicitor General of Canada.

Weiner, Norman (1974). "The effect of education on police attitudes." *Journal of Criminal Justice, 2.*

Young, Malcolm (1991). *An Inside Job: Policing and Police Culture in Britain.* Oxford: Clarendon Press.

THEORIES OF POLICE ORGANIZATIONS, SUBCULTURES, LEADERSHIP AND CHANGE

INTRODUCTION

This chapter reviews how police organizations have been viewed by management theorists and social scientists. As illustrated in chapter 4, the role of the police in Canadian society is highly complex, therefore, the management of such organizations is a complicated matter. The purpose of this chapter is to provide an overview of the management material and to offer an introduction to the issues most pertinent to police organizations. The first part of the chapter gives a history of police management theory, followed by an analysis of police subculture, leadership and organizational change. This chapter provides the theoretical grounding in which to contextualize much of the discussion in the following chapters.

DEFINING THE POLICE ORGANIZATION

An organization can be defined as a properly constructed social entity focused on a single goal or a set of specific goals. Police agencies are regarded not only as organizations but as bureaucratic organizations. As such, they possess the following defining characteristics (Alpert and Dunham, 1988; Dantzker, 1995).

- **Goals.** Goals are general statements of purpose identifying priorities the police agency has for itself and the public has for the police. Police departments have both specifically defined goals, such as law enforcement and crime prevention, and a number of other goals created by the population they serve and the government they are responsible to. Sometimes these goals conflict with one another; for example, the goal of repressing criminal activity can conflict with the goal of fostering good police-community relations. Organizational goals help to identify expectations the police and the public have concerning what the police are doing and how effective it is. These may be changed and modified over time as the nature of society alters.

- **Rational division of responsibilities.** Police agencies have developed a rational, hierarchical division of responsibility. In this respect, divisions of labor, power, authority and communication are well defined within their structures. For example, the patrol division is separated from specialist departments such as traffic, while the rank structure dictates who is responsible to whom.

- **Rules and norms.** Police departments are guided by two sets of rules: those stated by the government they serve, and those created internally to govern policies and procedures.

- **Authority centre.** Police departments create positions at the top of the pyramid to oversee the organization.

- **Reliance on written communication.** Written documentation is the customary form of communication in police organizations. This documentation acts as a way to supervise those who are on patrol by requiring them to keep a detailed log of their activities and provides a permanent record of events should they be required to reconstruct their activities. It has been estimated that between 40% and 80% of a police officer's time is spent filing reports and logs (Alpert and Dunham, 1988).

- **Hierarchical structure.** The rank structure in police organizations illustrates a visible chain of command, with each rank reporting to the one above. This pyramid structure has four basic elements:
  1. The chief, who provides overall leadership.
  2. Communications, which receives calls from the public and relays them to police officers.
  3. Patrol division, which responds to calls for service and initiates proactive patrols.
  4. Internal review, which controls police officers, ensures quality and monitors adherence to policies (Alpert and Dunham, 1988).

While these are the basic elements, most police departments have moved beyond this to create a more complex and diverse organizational structure.

APPROACHES TO THE STUDY OF POLICE ORGANIZATIONS

Academic interest in police organizations can be seen to have followed two distinct—although by no means exclusive—theoretical approaches: the normative approach and the empirical approach. Normative theories tend to prescribe the way in which police work should be done; they address management and administration issues and draw on a number of organizational theories to inform their analysis. In contrast, empirical theories look at the individuals who work in police organizations and what they do in order to offer an interpretation of police work. Normative theories, therefore, make recommendations on the 'best way' in which to operate a police organization, whereas empirical theories are explanatory, involve research and are concerned with describing why policing exists as it does.

Grimshaw and Jefferson (1987) suggest that the structure of police organizations is best studied from these two dimensions. They refer to the first as 'organizational,' depicting the vertical, hierarchical dimensions of rules, policies and procedures, command and control (the normative approach), and to the second as 'occupational,' relating to the norms, customs and practices of police officers themselves (the empirical approach). Normative theories have focused on the vertical structure of police organizations and addressed the rules, policies, management and administration of police organizations, whereas empirical theories have, for the most part, addressed the horizontal strata, primarily looking at the rank and file members.

Normative theories have been described by Grimshaw and Jefferson (1987) as studies conceptualizing the organization as a machine, focusing on how organizations ought to function by stressing standards and needs, rather than detailing how they actually work. As such, these theories are criticized for being idealistic. In contrast, empirical theories provide a rich interpretation of what actually occurs in police organizations by giving detailed accounts of day-to-day activities and by interviewing police officers themselves.

To give an analysis of what is known about the management and administration of police organizations and the individuals they employ, the next part of this chapter will review the literature on the police that has been conducted using both normative and empirical approaches. Much of this literature is from the United States and Britain.

NORMATIVE STUDIES OF POLICE ORGANIZATIONS

> The organizational element of police work is woefully neglected in much of our thinking about the police. Most studies treat police officers as the unit of analysis and do not take the total organization seriously (Guyot, 1977, p. 105).

Langworthy (1986) has illustrated how most theories of police organization are normative theories which give advice regarding "structures and behaviors associated with efficiency and effectiveness" (p. 7). These theories are frequently divided into three categories: classical/bureaucratic theories, democratic theories and system/contingency theories and have been used by academics working in the field of business administration to analyze the structure of many organizations. The terms are therefore borrowed from organizational theories developed by organizational scientists over the past century. To show how these theories relate to the police, it is necessary to briefly describe them, then outline their application.

Classical/bureaucratic theories

Classical organizational theory suggests that organizations can be regarded as machines and, as such, should develop rational systems and operate in the most efficient manner possible in order to obtain their goals. Classical organizational theorists sought an ideal form of organizational structure and a set of management principles upon which management practice could rest (Bradley et al., 1986). Henry Fayol, a French manager who attempted to design rules for managers, is regarded as the founding father of classical organizational theory.

Related to classical organizational theory is scientific management theory, which involves a similar type of rationality. Frederick Taylor developed this approach, which attempts to increase management control by separating the conception of tasks from their execution. While it is the manager's role to conceive plans and lay down rules, the worker merely conforms; thus a highly predictable (scientific), minute division of labor is created (Bradley et al., 1986).

Morgan (1986) argues that bureaucratic approaches to organizations have been popular for two reasons: firstly, because they are efficient, and secondly, because they reinforce and maintain existing patterns of power and control (the separation of workers from management).

Bureaucratic theories of police organizations

The literature on the police has tended to assume the police are organized according to traditional organizational theory and refers to the police organization as quasi-military (Bittner, 1970) para-military (Sandler and Mintz, 1974) and conventional (Angell, 1978). Early police management writers emphasized this bureaucratic approach, which included a need for rigid hierarchical structure, strong centralized control and authoritarian leadership. Police agencies, they said, should be organized along bureaucratic, military lines. Early theorists, in adopting this approach, were trying to create a more professional police organization. They stressed crime control and law enforcement with the belief that efficiency could be improved by applying classical principles.

Classical organizational theory has had more impact on police organizations than any other organizational theory. It has spawned works advocating the approach, both by Smith (1960), who saw the primary function of police as crime control and argued that not enough attention had been paid to administration, and the much-quoted work by O.W. Wilson (1950). These authors focus upon the ideal way organizations ought to work rather than how they actually operate (Grimshaw and Jefferson, 1987).

O.W. Wilson's work dominated the field of police management throughout the 1950s and 1960s, becoming the 'bible' of police administration (Roberg and Kuykendall, 1993). Wilson believed that police organizations need to be centrally organized and bureaucratic. He argued that procedures should be implemented and aimed at well-defined objectives that are highly operational (Thibault et al., 1990). Although spanning half a century, the issues raised by the bureaucratic theorists are similar and concur with each other. They emphasize the police role as law enforcement and advocate how police organizations ought to be organized. They advance the view that police departments should be administered according to size, with larger ones having bigger hierarchies to control the more specialized tasks. They all contend that the organization should be centralized, whatever its size (Langworthy, 1986).

The classical theories conformed well to the legalistic era discussed in Chapter 4. Reformers at that time wanted to make policing more objective and bureaucratic. With this approach came an emphasis on law enforcement, which led to the police being judged primarily for their crime control capabilities, such as their ability to make arrests (Roberg and Kuykendall, 1993).

Bureaucratic theories were criticized in the 1960s. Advocates of the bureaucratic model were uninterested in evaluation; consequently, their works were prolific on the criteria for organizational structure, but silent on how to evaluate the organization (Langworthy, 1986). An approach was therefore advanced, but no attempt was made to measure its success. Classical organizational theorists also failed to examine the relationship between the individual police officer and the police organization (Grimshaw and Jefferson, 1987) and ignored the complex nature of the police role within society by judging it to encompass only crime control.

Neoclassical/democratic theories

The neoclassical school of organizational theory developed during the 1940s and 1950s and challenged the traditional classical theories by introducing research from the behavioral sciences and by offering what was seen as a humanistic approach. They therefore started to consider the human dimension, incorporating the role of the individual within the organization and the influences of those external to the organization. The neoclassical theorists argued that organizations do not exist in isolation. They are influenced by many other agencies in their day-to-day activities, so should become more open. By applying the behavioral sciences to the study of organizations, the neoclassical school introduced an empirical impetus to the existing knowledge (Shafritz and Ott, 1987).

Neoclassical/democratic theories of police organizations

During the late 1960s, a considerable amount of research showed that police work involved significantly more than just law enforcement. Behavioral research illustrated that allegiance to a strict legal mandate would be ineffective in addressing the order maintenance and service functions of the police. Instead, the police needed qualified personnel who could use discretion on the wide array of issues they were asked to address. The legalistic model—and the classical organizational theories on which it was based—was therefore attacked.

Democratic theories of police organizations are based on different assumptions than bureaucratic theories, arguing that the role of the police officer is too broad and varied to make simple centralized bureaucracy work. Instead, they advocate a more flexible, decentralized structure.

The organization the democratic theorists prescribe is more open to allow informed, neighborhood-level problem identification. A hierarchical structure curtails participative staff interaction, so a new organizational structure is developed which has little or no structural specialization (neither by occupation nor by function). Police officers are granted a more comprehensive role to encourage professional responsibility (Langworthy, 1986).

Academics proposing this approach include Angell (1976), who suggests the conventional police organizational design has been responsible for the decline of police-community relations. He proposes the 'democratic' model, which involves the police adopting a more service and prevention-oriented role and a participatory, community-based police organization. Bittner (1970) has also advocated that the quasi-military structure of the police is and will always be at odds with the core of the police mandate, which he sees as not solely law enforcement, while Goldstein (1977) has argued that the police need to move from what he terms as an 'authoritative climate' towards a more democratic form of organization.

As illustrated earlier in the text, by the 1960s, the 'authoritative climate' was a common feature in police organizations. Police were criticized for their inability to respond to crime and for increasingly inappropriate management practices. The behavioral science research gradually began to influence police administration; however, the democratic model was frequently dismissed because it was seen to be too radical in advocating the abolition of middle management and an overhaul of the bureaucratic police structure.

Systems/contingency theories

The third normative approach to police organizations is system and contingency theories. Systems theory builds on the principle that organizations are 'open' to their environment and that they must achieve an appropriate relationship with that environment in order to survive (Morgan, 1986). Systems theory implies all parts of an organization are interrelated and dependent upon one another, so that change in one area will affect others. For example, if a police agency decides to put more resources into one area (e.g., tackling break and entry crimes) this will affect resources in other areas of the organization. In systems theory, organizations are not seen as autonomous entities divorced from the environment, but as dynamic structures which must change and adapt to the environment in order to survive.

Closely related to systems theory is contingency theory (Ott, 1989; Shafritz and Ott, 1987), which stresses the need to apply different managerial techniques to different tasks. The approach recognizes how both internal factors, controlled by the police agency (e.g., police personnel, technology, policies), and external factors, over which the police have no control (e.g., laws, funding, community priorities), influence organizational behavior. As these vary considerably, there is no one best way to organize and manage, therefore, a variety of different management practices and organizational structures may be necessary. It is the police leader's task to determine which practice is most relevant to the organizational environment in which he/she exists.

Systems/contingency theories of police organizations

Another interpretation of the police organization can therefore be found in the work of contingency theorists who compare different types of police organizations. They suggest that only through examining the environments in which police organizations function can one decide how they can best be organized.

The main advocate of contingency theory is Roberg who in 1979 wrote *Police Management and Organizational Behavior: A Contingency Approach*. Roberg claims there is a need to link management structure to practice and organizational design to characteristics of the environment. Roberg shows the police role is very complex. This factor, coupled with increasingly better-educated recruits and the ever-changing nature of the environment in which police forces act (new laws, heterogeneous population), must be considered when attempting to determine the most effective management practice (Roberg and Kuykendall, 1993).

The contingency approach therefore recognizes that a variety of management and organizational structures may be necessary, and that police agencies must adapt to situational circumstances. Elements of contingency theory have been applied to studies of community policing, where it has been shown that a police organization that has invested heavily in a traditional bureaucratic structure will have more difficulty in creating an environment conducive to community policing than a police organization that is less bureaucratic (Wilkinson and Rosenbaum, 1994).

Proponents of community policing (e.g., Goldstein, 1990; Skolnick and Bayley, 1988) may be regarded as offering a normative model of police work, in that they advocate and prescribe ways police organizations can improve the quality of their service by implementing community policing philosophies. As such, community policing is the latest development in the line of normative theories, although it clearly has similarities to both the democratic and contingency approaches.

POLICE ORGANIZATIONS TODAY

There would appear to be some disagreement over the type of organizational structure that exists in Canadian police organizations today. Indeed, it may be impossible to state that one organizational structure is prevalent in all police organizations for, as shown in Chapter 3, the size, location and composition of police agencies varies considerably among jurisdictions. Despite alternatives to the bureaucratic model, some have argued that most police departments operate on the traditional principles as they were first stated by O.W. Wilson (Swanson et al., 1988; Thilbault et al., 1990), and adhere to the traditional bureaucratic structure (Gaine, 1975). Lynch (1986), however, believes that since the 1950s, there has been a shift towards more democratic and participatory management structures as the behavioral sciences have had more influence on police managers, a development that has occurred in many large organizations. Others caution that models of change, such as community policing, may only survive for limited periods of time and that the bureaucracy will be a structure almost impenetrable to change (Swanson et al., 1988).

In general, police departments have not been able to break away from the classical bureaucratic structures advocated earlier this century. Consequently, they continue to display traits of the classical, hierarchical, pyramid model, which includes the following characteristics.

- Almost all contacts between personnel take the form of orders, which go down the organizational hierarchy, and results, which go up.
- Each subordinate receives instructions from one superior.
- All important decisions are made at the top of the pyramid.
- Superiors have a limited 'span of control' by supervising a limited number of individuals.
- With the exception of the top and bottom of the pyramid, individuals at any level only have contact with their boss and their subordinates.

(Roberg and Kuykendall, 1993).

PARA-MILITARY STRUCTURE

The organizational structure of policing is frequently referred to as para-military. The various hierarchical ranks are given military titles (sergeant, corporal) and uniform insignia (bars and strips), and the chain of command is adhered to strenuously. The military model requires obedience to the orders of superior officers and an implied loyalty (Forcese, 1992). Canadian police forces have been slow to move away from this model, although attempts have been made to do so recently, with the advent of community policing. For example, some police departments have changed their names from police *force* to police *service*. In addition, modification in the design of uniforms and less discipline over length of hair and beards has revealed a softening of the para-military approach. Saluting a senior officer is now almost a thing of the past. The extent to which these changes are superficial and not representative of large-scale organizational change is a point of conjecture.

As previously detailed, policing in Canada is characterized by a number of different police organizations. Its formal origins developed from those outlined by Peel in 1829 so, despite a strong commitment to the military model, police officers in Canada are regarded as 'citizens in uniform' (Forcese, 1992). Police forces vary in their adherence to the military structure and rigid chain of command. Some police agencies are more traditional and display more para-military characteristics, while others strive to move away from this. For example, it has been suggested that the RCMP, because of its size and organizational structure, is more hierarchical, bureaucratic and para-military than other smaller, independent departments (Seagrave, 1995). Despite these differences, all police forces retain some military characteristics, as can be seen by the hierarchical rank structure.

EMPIRICAL STUDIES OF POLICE ORGANIZATIONS

In addition to normative theories of police organizations, which prescribe how police departments should function, empirical theories have developed. These are sociological studies, which can be divided into two groups: structurally-grounded studies that look at the structure of police departments and portray them as bureaucratic, rule-dominated, deterministic environments; and action studies that focus on the dynamics of the organization and recognize the diversity of settings that influence behavior (Murphy, 1987). Alternatively, they have been described as environmental or subcultural models of police organizations (Grimshaw and Jefferson, 1987).

To a certain extent, this division reflects the research methodologies employed by those criminologists interested in policing. Structurally grounded/environmental studies adopt a formal empirical analysis, through the use of survey research such as questionnaires, in order to gain an understanding of police work. Action-oriented/subcultural studies try to conceptualize the wider context in which policing takes place by adopting an ethnographic approach and looking at the insiders' view through the use of interviews and participant and non-participant observation (Punch, 1983). In many respects, empirical studies test normative theories using a range of assumptions about how the police should function.

Structurally grounded/environmental studies

James Q. Wilson's book *Varieties of Police Behavior* (1968) is cited as one of the first empirical analyses of police organization. Wilson developed a typology of departmental styles by looking at eight US police departments. He demonstrated that the role of the police officer is different in each different style of department, which he termed the 'watchman', 'legalistic' and 'service oriented'. While these categories may be open to question, he was able to illustrate that the sum

of the police officers' actions produced different working styles in the departments and that these were related to the communities the police officers
patrolled. Thus, the watchman style was hierarchically flat and decentralized,
with an emphasis on order maintenance. Bureaucratization had barely developed. In these departments, police officers were awarded a large degree of
autonomy over the issues they were asked to address. The legalistic was specialized, hierarchically tall and centralized, operating a law enforcement approach
whereby universal standards were imposed upon all communities in a city. In
these departments, police officers tried to enforce the law and make arrests.
Finally, the service oriented style was administratively centralized, operationally
decentralized, specialized and hierarchically tall, with a stress on community
involvement. In these departments, order maintenance problems deemed
important to the community and the police received attention, in addition to
standard policing concerns. Wilson's categories are clearly linked to the discussion of police roles undertaken in Chapter 4.

Wilson's work promoted a number of studies that examined the relationship
between police organization, community and behavior. Rossi et al. (1974)
undertook an empirical study in the 1960s of police practices, public opinion and
police and political leaders' attitudes. Their findings illustrated that certain cities
were more law-and-order oriented and others were more civil rights oriented,
and that policing styles seemed to be closely associated with the views of the
local politicians and the police chief. The study concluded that operational styles
and practices seemed to be a feature of the whole organizational culture.

More recently, research in Canada (Seagrave, 1995) revealed differences
between RCMP and municipal police officers in British Columbia, not only in the
constraints their respective organizations placed on them (with the RCMP being
more bureaucratic and hierarchical) but also in their opinions about policing. The
RCMP officers showed more commitment and allegiance to policing and to their
own organization than did their colleagues in other municipal departments.

These structurally grounded/environmental studies suggest that there are
significant distinctions in the organizational culture of policing in different areas
and illustrate important differences between police organizations. However, the
extent to which these variations are the result of conscious efforts made by
police departments is unspecified.

Action-oriented/subcultural studies

In contrast to these structural interpretations of police organization, "action-oriented studies of the police...challenge the ideal bureaucratic models proposed by
police administrators and undermine the overly deterministic conceptions
offered by most formal structural analysis of police organizations" (Murphy,
1987, p. 29). Theories of this type attempt to offer alternative interpretations of
police structures by providing information on the informal processors and
behaviors that occur in police organizations. They focus on the activities of the

police officers themselves—usually the lower-ranking officers—as a way to understand police organizations. Much of the work of these action-oriented academics draws attention to the subculture of the police as a mechanism for understanding how the police organization operates. Grimshaw and Jefferson (1987), in fact, label what Murphy (1987) sees as action-oriented studies, 'subcultural'. They argue that, in relation to organizational theory, subcultural analysis borrows from the notion of 'informal organization' and the behavioral science approach that was a reaction to the classical management school. This subcultural approach focuses on the less rational elements of human behavior and examines the characteristics of specific occupational groups. In most cases, this is the group of lower-ranking operational police officers.

SUBCULTURE

A subculture can be viewed as any social group that demonstrates particular patterns of behavior, distinguishing it from other groups in society. Subcultures represent alternative forms of cultural plurality that exist within the wider culture (Brake, 1980). For example, within Canadian society, it is possible to have a youth subculture, gay subculture, Chinese subculture, all existing within the broader Canadian culture. Downes (1966) argues that subcultures emerge in response to collectively-experienced problems, where a number of individuals have similar problems of adjustment to a shared common dilemma. This view is similar to that of Cohen (1955), who, like Downes, states the emergence of a subculture must involve "...effective interaction with one another, of a number of actors with similar problems of adjustment" (p. 59). While Cohen's work is essentially related to the development of deviant subcultures, he does discuss the general theory of subcultures, which is directly applicable to an analysis of policing. He states a complete subcultural theory would detail the conditions under which a subculture emerges and state ways to predict the content of subcultural solutions. Cohen's criteria for the analysis of subcultures can therefore be applied to the policing subculture.

THE POLICE SUBCULTURE

Despite a contention that our knowledge of the police occupational subculture remains slight (Holdaway, 1989), police subculture has been of interest to police researchers since Westley (1970) Niederhoffer (1967) and Skolnick (1966) wrote the initial texts on policing in the United States. These early works have been supported by a wealth of sociological literature illustrating that this subculture has a profound effect on policing policy and initiatives in a variety of contexts (e.g. Bittner, 1967, 1970; Chatterton, 1976, 1983; Ericson, 1982; Fielding, 1988; Graef, 1989; Grimshaw and Jefferson, 1987; Holdaway, 1979, 1983; Manning, 1977, 1979; Punch, 1983; Rubinstein, 1973).

Subcultures are learned through a process of socialization. All social groups have some way to teach new members the norms, values and attitudes that are highly valued by all members of that group. In turn, the new recruits internalize these. This is the process of socialization, which incorporates a complex process of social learning (Alpert and Dunham, 1988). For police officers, some of this socialization is formal and occurs within the training academy, but most of it is an intergenerational process whereby new recruits are indoctrinated and acquire a set of beliefs, values and attitudes by working alongside more experienced officers. As illustrated in Chapter 5, police officers experience a period of intense training together; this training, and the subsequent work they undertake, leads to the development of a strong occupational subculture.

It has been argued that police management in North America, which is promoted out of the rank and file, operates within the context of one of the strongest vocational subcultures (Thibault et al., 1990), and that policing is dominated by a culture that is most evident within the rank and file (McConnville and Shepherd, 1992). This subculture of the lower echelons is depicted as so uniform and sustained that any attempts by senior management to alter policy or practice are frequently subverted by the police officers' actions (Fielding, 1988).

A considerable volume of policing literature has attempted to detail and explain the subculture of policing. There is general agreement that police agencies encourage a broadly coherent set of outlooks, beliefs, customs and norms among police officers, and that this is reinforced, resulting in a distinct police 'subculture' (Holdaway, 1984; Jermier et al., 1991), or 'cop culture' (Grimshaw and Jefferson, 1987; Jefferson, 1990; Reiner, 1985) or 'occupational culture' (Ericson, 1982; Fielding, 1988; Hunt and Magenau, 1993; Manning, 1979; McConnville and Shepherd, 1992; Reiss, 1971). Certain commonalities of police outlook are discernible among British and American police officers (Manning, 1979) and from the reports and studies of policing across many countries (Bayley, 1985; Das, 1993; Mawby, 1990).

The literature states that, in conjunction with the formal, hierarchical, bureaucratic, militaristic structure of the police organization, the police subculture acts as a distinct system of internal control (Goldsmith, 1990) in which the lower ranks of the profession control their own work situation (Holdaway, 1979). As such, the "occupational culture of the police has found reference points in virtually every publication about policing" (Holdaway, 1989, p. 55).

Skolnick (1966), like many other commentators (e.g., Chatterton, 1976; Ericson, 1982; Fielding, 1988; Holdaway, 1984; Hunt and Magenau, 1993; McConnville and Shepherd, 1992), argues that the subculture of the police is attributable to the police function itself, and that this subculture manifests itself at the rank and file level. Skolnick suggests there are unique facets to a police officer's role which attribute to what he terms a 'working personality'. These facets are: danger, authority and the constant pressure to appear efficient.

- **Danger.** Policing is a unique job, as it requires police officers to regularly enter situations where there is an element of risk and to cope with unpredictable and potentially dangerous situations. Although policing is actually less hazardous than occupations such as construction, transportation, mining and logging (Griffiths and Verdun Jones, 1994; Reiner, 1985), officers become preoccupied with danger because of the unpredictable nature of the work. This affects the way they do their work and influences the development of a 'working personality'.
- **Authority.** Danger is linked to authority. Police officers represent authority, backed up by the use of legitimate force. In every encounter, police officers present a symbol of authority (the law) and are the only public servants with this role. New recruits soon learn it is this authority that allows them to carry out their work.
- **Pressure for results.** Police officers experience pressure to produce results, often because of a particularly bad crime or spate of crimes, or when there is a need to address spiraling crime statistics. Sometimes this creates unrealistic expectations for the police. Public expectations of the police, in addition to their own perceptions, stress the crime fighting role and further add to this pressure.

According to Skolnick (1966), it is the police officer's unique role that leads to the development of this working personality, or as others term it, the police subculture.

Characteristics of the police subculture

In reviewing much of the literature on the topic, Reiner (1985) provides a list of what he sees as the seven core characteristics of 'cop culture':

1. 'Mission - action - cynicism - pessimism'. He sees these traits as intermingling and reinforcing each other. *Mission* refers to the way that policing is seen not as a job, but as a way of life, a trait identified by those who have looked at the RCMP (Seagrave, 1995). *Action* relates to the hedonistic, action-centred guise of the cop culture, a trait recognized by McConnville and Shepherd (1992) and termed the 'blue light syndrome', while *cynicism* and *pessimism* are evidenced in the way police officers become hardened to the work they are asked to do.

2. Suspicion is a characteristic, actively encouraged in police training, that leads to the stereotyping of certain individuals as well as a requirement to keep a look out for signs of trouble, dangers and clues. Related to this characteristic is that of 'secrecy,' which Brogden et al. (1988) highlight when arguing that the occupational subculture values secrecy and colleague loyalty. The issue of secrecy has also been recognized by others (Punch, 1983; Ericson, 1982) including Westley (1970) who described it as a 'code of silence'.

3. The effects of shift work, erratic hours and the overall stress of the job are seen to result in internal solidarity, coupled with social isolation. This 'us and them' division is recognized by others to be the foremost characteristic of the police subculture (Goldsmith, 1990). It was initially identified by Westley (1970), who used the term 'pariah' to describe the social estrangement officers felt. It continues to be noted today (Bouza, 1990), with the belief that police officers alone share and understand the full extent of the job; therefore they can identify and comfortably socialize only with other police officers.

4. Research in the United States (Skolnick, 1966), Britain (Reiner, 1978) and Canada (Lee, 1981) has shown that the police hold political and moral views that are conservative.

5. Reiner argues the police exhibit 'old fashioned machismo' characteristics that manifest themselves in alcoholic and sexual indulgences. Analysis of the problems faced by ethnic minority and female police officers has also illustrated this machismo trait; female and ethnic minority officers have commented on the male dominance pervading police organizations (Young, 1991).

6. Racial prejudice. Again, research in North America and Britain has found that the police frequently display prejudiced views. While some authors have attributed this to psychological characteristics (Colman and Gorman, 1982), Reiner concludes it is both necessary and sufficient to explain police views of ethnic minorities by the police function and circumstances of police work.

7. The final characteristic Reiner defines as pragmatism; a preoccupation with practical, down-to-earth, concrete events and a reluctance for innovation, experimentation and research. Police officers want to get on with the job and are reluctant to spend time reading or exploring new or alternative ways of policing.

Reiner's review of the core characteristics of the police subculture has been developed from his own research and from studies by other academics in both the United States and Canada. Others have provided a narrower characterization, for example, Punch argues that solidarity and secrecy are the distinguishing characteristics of police occupational culture (Punch, 1983). The 1970s saw a burgeoning of research on the police subculture, often employing participant observation techniques (Holdaway, 1979; Chatterton, 1976; Manning, 1977; Van Maanen, 1973). More recently, the police subculture has been recognized as a barrier to new developments in policing (McConnville and Shepherd, 1992).

Subcultural analyses of police organizations have been done in the United States (Jermier et al., 1991; Skolnick, 1966; Neiderhoffer, 1967; Van Maanen, 1973), England (Banton, 1964; Cain, 1973; Chatterton, 1976; Holdaway, 1979) and, to a lesser extent, in Canada (Ericson, 1982; Shearing, 1981) as a way to conceptualize and understand the activities of the police. Sociological studies of police work in Canada indicate similar patterns to those found in Britain and the US (Mawby, 1990). The pioneering work of Becker (1963) provided the theoretical underpinnings for studies of this nature. As Becker illustrated the process by which an individual becomes a marijuana user through acquiring the norms, values and the 'know how' of smoking, so academics interested in police subculture have found that the actions of police officers become defined by their occupational culture. The training academy and probationary period provides the initial introduction into this subculture (Fielding, 1988; Van Maanen, 1973), and an intensive socialization process occurs on the streets (Chatterton, 1979; Punch, 1979), resulting in core subcultural characteristics. Characteristics of police adaptation to their role and status have been developed to such an extent that, although the subculture may vary among police departments and police officers, the overall recognition that there is a distinct police subculture is an accepted fact. The characteristics of the police subculture, as detailed by Reiner and others, offer plausible explanations of how police officers see their world and their role in it.

Issues relating to police subculture

Overall, a considerable amount of commentary presents the occupational subculture of policing as solid and cohesive, although, more recently, this interpretation has been under review (Fielding, 1988). Commentators have noted that policing can be differentiated into variants or subcultures based on rank, with the management subculture being different from the rank and file subculture (Reuss-Ianni, 1983), function, with detective and other specialized units displaying distinguishing characteristics (Van Maanen, 1986), and local environment (Wilson, 1968). While each subcultural variant will be distinctive in some ways, at the same time, they are all seen as 'variations on a theme' (Hunt and Magenau, 1993; Reiner, 1992). As noted by Fielding (1988): "...being a cop is not an either/or but a more or less thing" (p. 204).

The extent to which these subcultures are indeed all 'variations on a theme' is debatable. The structurally grounded/environmental studies that have identified variations among police organizations would suggest that the emphasis on the autonomy of the rank and file subculture requires qualification. There is a need to analyze police subcultures *within* and *among* police organizations and to build upon the few works that have been able to identify a variety of police subcultures within policing. Research of this nature would help support or refute the few studies that have recognized different police subcultures and lead to a more comprehensive understanding of police subculture.

Despite the contention that a police subculture exists, an emerging body of research in Britain, Canada and the United States has called the subculture concept into question and suggested that there may be considerable diversity in the extent to which officers exhibit certain characteristics. Some of the theories of police subculture were constructed over twenty years ago. Policing has evolved since then, therefore, the extent to which this police subculture exists today may be questioned. These questions include:

- Will the recruitment of female and ethnic minority police officers change the police subculture? For many years, policing was a white male occupation; as the police population diversifies, so will the social values of the officers, diluting the macho image. The recruitment of ethnic minority officers may also break down racial prejudices that exist in police organizations.

- Will the increased educational qualifications of police officers influence their propensity to be socialized into the police subculture? The professionalization of policing may make police officers more open to new approaches to policing and less pragmatic.

- To what extent do recent recruits socially isolate themselves? Canadian research conducted by Vincent (1990) found that younger police officers who were more educated had a wide circle of friends, many of whom were not police officers, while older police officers tended to socialize only with other officers.

- To what extent do police officers actually feel that there is a strong division between themselves and the rest of the population (the 'us and them' syndrome)? Shearing (1981) found that, rather than the police distinguishing between themselves and the rest of the population, they distinguished between people who were supportive of them (or at least neutral), and whom they did things *for* and people they referred to as 'dregs' or 'scum,' whom they did things *to*.

- Questions have been asked concerning the 'task environment' in which police officers work. Policing in Canada means policing in a wide variety of environments, from small rural communities to large urban metropolises. It is unlikely that police officers, employed by the same police organization, deployed in small rural communities display attitudes and behaviors similar to their colleagues deployed in urban centres simply because the nature of the environment is so different. Core subcultural characteristics as identified by Reiner (1985), Skolnick (1966) and others may be less evident in certain environments.

- It is possible to question the degree to which the police subculture is evident in all police departments. Canadian policing is characterized by a wide variety of police agencies (RCMP, provincial, municipal). The proposition that all police officers in all these organizations share the same characteristics is clearly open to question.

Variations in police subculture

In further explorations of the police officer subculture, various academics have developed typologies of different police orientations and styles. While some of these police officers share the same core characteristics, it has been suggested the police rank and file does not constitute one uniform group, but can be broken down. Broderick (1987), for example, recognized four types of working personalities for police officers:

- The **Idealist**, who places value on individual rights and due process and sees policing as a profession.

- The **Enforcer**, who is more concerned with social order and keeping society safe than with individual rights and due process. He/she believes the police are an isolated minority surrounded by a hostile public.

- The **Realist**, who accepts society at face value and places little worth on either individual rights or due process, seeing both society and the police in a cynical light.

- The **Optimist**, who values individual rights highly and sees the job as being people-oriented because it provides a variety of opportunities to help people.

In a similar analysis undertaken in England, Reiner (1978) distinguishes among:

- The **Bobby**, a police officer who both applies the law by using common sense and is committed to the peacekeeping role.

- The **Uniform Carrier**, who is a cynical and disillusioned police officer shirking responsibility whenever possible.

- The **New Centurion**, who is dedicated to fighting crime and disorder, and who regards detective work as the *raison d'être* of the police.

- The **Professional Policeman**, who is ambitious and career conscious and has an appreciation of all aspects of policing.

Broderick undertook his research in the US, Reiner in England. Research of a similar nature has been undertaken in Canada by Shearing (1981), whose four-part typology identified:

- **Wise Officers**, who were committed to the police work.

- **Real Officers**, who were hard-nosed officers working to become 'heroes' of the cop culture by controlling 'scum'.

- **Good Officers**, who saw policing as a profession and who were dedicated to liberal democratic values.

- **Cautious Officers**, who had essentially dropped out and were alienated from the purpose and principles of policing.

Although these studies were conducted in different countries at different times, they do categorize police officers in similar ways. These overall categories can be grouped as follows:

1. The traditional 'ideal' police officer who undertakes all police duties (service, order maintenance and law enforcement) as they are assigned, but who has few career aspirations. Bobby (Reiner), Optimist (Broderick), Wise Officer (Shearing).

2. The police officer who stresses law enforcement over every other role and wants to 'fight' crime. New Centurion (Reiner), Enforcer (Broderick), Real Officer (Shearing).

3. The disillusioned and cynical police officer who does his/her time but little else. Uniform Carrier (Reiner), Realist (Broderick), Cautious Officer (Shearing).

4. The career police officer who sees policing as a profession. Professional (Reiner), Idealist (Broderick), Good Officer (Shearing).

These typologies exist as 'ideal types' and refer to police officers at the bottom end of the hierarchy. Obviously, factors such as the location of the police department, its size and organizational structure all influence policing. What is interesting is the degree of similarity among the typologies, despite their geographical differences. The fact that different types of police officers have been identified by these authors has implications for police management. For example, the police officers who see themselves as crime fighters will be reluctant to undertake a broader service role, while those who are cynical may also demonstrate the same reservations. Management has to cope with and address this reluctance. Police managers are only able to promote a certain number of individuals within their organizations, and may find they have a number of career-oriented individuals they are not able to promote. This is another management issue, as indeed is police deviance and misconduct, which is discussed in Chapter 9, and which is more prone to occur in officers who are disillusioned with policing.

As illustrated at the outset, subcultural theory emphasizes collective adaptation to shared problems. Policing is a unique function with many stresses and contradictions. In order to deal with these, police officers develop a subculture which has characteristics that can be understood as coping mechanisms police officers use to undertake their job. The review of the literature demonstrates that the characteristics of the police subculture can be seen as a means of addressing shared problems inherent in the policing role itself.

Two policing subcultures

Most of the studies of police subculture have focused on the rank and file members. A study undertaken in the 1970s (Reuss-Ianni, 1983) showed, for the first time, the organization of policing is best understood in terms of the interaction between *two* distinct subcultures: a street cop culture (the rank and file) and a management cop culture. The existence of two distinct subcultures has implications for how academics view the police organization, and again, calls into question the notion of one subculture.

Hunt and Magenau (1993) state the two cultures idea can be understood as an institutional collision between an established occupational culture of policing—the police subculture detailed above—in which the police officer is the protagonist, and the contemporary social and political forces advocated by management that aim to change this subculture. The acknowledgment of two cultures has also been made in the Canadian literature, where Loree (1988) has shown there to be perceptual separation between those who manage the organization and those who work on the street. This reiterates the division, identified by Holdaway (1977), of what he termed the 'practical professionalism' of the rank and file subculture and the 'managerial professionalism' of the higher echelons, a distinction also acknowledged by Punch (1983).

While previous research has illustrated that the style of policing may vary among different police agencies (Cain, 1973; Wilson, 1968), the existence of various subcultures across levels of the same organization has been recognized, but rarely explored systematically.

POLICE LEADERSHIP

While action-oriented/subcultural theories on rank and file police subculture provide a rich insight into the daily activities of police work, they ignore the wider aspects of the organization and the policies and practices of senior management. As Grimshaw and Jefferson (1987) observe "...the 'realistic' examination of rank and file beliefs and activities is, ironically accompanied by a hopelessly idealistic conception of the beliefs and activities of police managers" (p. 9).

Several authors have pointed out the dearth of research on police leadership (Crank, 1986; Cohen, 1980; Hunt and Magenau, 1993; O'Reilly and Dostaler, 1983; Reiner, 1991; Potts, 1982; Seagrave, 1995), although the importance of leadership style in affecting policy and exploring police officer perceptions has been acknowledged (Cohen, 1980; Talarico and Swanson, 1982; Wilson, 1968) and recently has been argued to be the single most important factor in determining whether or not community policing innovations will succeed (Loree, 1988).

The lack of research on police leadership may be attributed to the commitment to participant observation research techniques, which precludes an understanding of the upper echelons of the organization (Cain, 1979), in addition to the politics of access, whereby access to this elite group is denied so researchers are only able to gain information from the rank and file. It has also been suggested that those granting access are reluctant to have their own environments placed under scrutiny (Punch, 1981), as the knowledge gained is less useful to this group and can even be dangerous to them (Reiner, 1991).

The concept of police leadership has been treated as a panacea in the policing literature. While management theorists working in the field of business studies have devoted considerable attention to the distinction between management and leadership functions, chief executives in policing have recognized little difference between the two (Roberg, 1979). Although this may not be a concern in a small organization, it is critically important in a large bureaucracy. Management includes planning, controlling and directing the organization to ensure the job gets done. In contrast, leadership requires innovators, change agents, risk takers, who are open to criticism and have an orientation to the future. Any understanding of police leadership must account for the organizational structure in which the leaders are working, as this may influence their ability to direct and change the organization. It must also identify whether the police leader's role is that of leader initiating change, or manager pursuing the status quo.

The few studies of police leadership that have been conducted have been undertaken from different theoretical positions, using both quantitative and qualitative research techniques. Hoover and Madner (1990) examined the attitudes of police chiefs towards private sector management principles, such as letting employees have input into the decisions of the organization, and recognizing what the client wants and delivering that service. They constructed a questionnaire and mailed it to 100 police chiefs in the state of Texas. They found the chiefs accepted and supported the principles but believed that police personnel of the lower ranks would not accept the implementation of these principles.

In 1992, the RCMP External Review Committee, an independent body that reports directly to Parliament, surveyed the membership of the Canadian Association of Chiefs of Police, the Canadian Police Association and the Directors of Human Resources in 143 private-sector companies. The research found that Canadian police managers were more authoritarian than private-sector managers and sought to control the activities of their subordinates. The report went on to state that this need to control is detrimental to the introduction of community policing (Koenig, 1992).

The few studies that have been conducted suggest that police executives display managerial—rather than leadership—qualities more than their colleagues in other organizations and are more conservative and cautious about change.

ORGANIZATIONAL CHANGE

Police agencies do not exist in static environments. Community leaders, government officials, citizens and employees all influence law enforcement. The dynamic nature of society, coupled with changes in the law and the criminal justice system, influences the police environment as do internal pressures. Police organizations are therefore subject to external and internal influences advocating change.

There are two ways in which change can be implemented: reactive or planned. Reactive change happens when problems occur first and the police agency responds (after the fact) to the problem. For example, in 1994, a riot occurred in Vancouver following the Stanley Cup hockey game. The Vancouver police were criticized by certain members of the community for the way they responded to the incident; this criticism resulted in them reviewing their policies on the policing of large crowds; change in this instance was reactive. In contrast, planned change involves attempts by police departments to change the status quo. As previously shown, police agencies in Canada are currently in the process of adopting community policing philosophies and practices that encompass a wider police role than allowed for in traditional bureaucratic theories. Many police agencies are also trying to introduce planned organizational change in the form of community policing (see Chapters 10 and 11).

Alpert and Dunham (1988) have recognized three dimensions of organizational change: structure, technology and personnel.

- Structural change is the most difficult, as it involves comprehensive revisions to the organization incorporating policies and procedures. For example, allowing lower-ranking police officers more input into the decision-making process would be a structural change. Community policing is also a structural change.
- Technological change involves new working methods, new tools and new equipment which results in new information being obtained. DNA testing is an example of a change in technology.
- Personnel changes involve demands made on personnel for new skills, a modification of attitude or motivation. The recruitment of more highly-educated individuals and more women into police organizations is an example of a personnel change.

In discussing change, it is important to define what sort of change is being proposed and by whom. In police organizations, change can either be promoted from within the organization itself or be the result of external pressures from governments or interest groups, or the community. Compared to other organizations, the rate of change in police organizations has to date been shown to be slow and incremental in nature. The reason for this could lie with the police leader or with the police subculture, or could be a combination of both.

Police leadership and change

In reviewing organizational change, Campbell and Wright (1993), Goldstein (1990), Hunt and Magenau (1993) and others have stressed the importance of leadership in articulating a sense of purpose for an organization and for shaping direction. Leaders must be able to accept why organizational change is desirable, understand how to effect the appropriate restructuring and deal with the resistance against it (Angell, 1976). The police leader has been recognized to be instrumental in changing the culture of the organization (Wilkinson and Rosenbaum, 1994). In Canada, the role of top management in this regard has been ignored (Clairmont, 1991), although it was recently acknowledged as crucial to the success of community policing in one Canadian province (Oppal, 1994) and in Canada as a whole (Campbell and Wright, 1993).

The leadership style of the police executive is important in promoting policy making and in defusing opposition to it (Angell, 1976). Hunt and Magenau (1993) adopted what they term an "institutional and organizational analysis" of North American police chiefs. Their work draws heavily on the biographies of police chiefs of large departments to illustrate the changing role of the chief. The final chapters of their book provide a discussion of the importance of police leadership in initiating change, and the barriers that exist to inhibit this change. They conclude:

> Of course management is important to operating any organization but the essential function of the principal executive is leadership: the will and the ability to articulate a mission, an agenda and a set of legitimizing values for an enterprise to develop operational means and for their expression (pp. 145-6).

Research conducted by Descza (1988) attempted to show, by drawing on the corporate culture and leadership literature, how Canadian police managers communicate purpose to operational police officers when trying to bring about organizational change. The methodology he employed involved 44 in-depth, semi-structured interviews with chiefs, deputy chiefs, superintendents and inspectors, lasting 45 minutes, in three municipal police departments. The study concluded chiefs were in a unique position to transform their organizations by providing a new direction and sense of purpose and that communication processes lay at the centre of this change. It would, therefore, appear chiefs in some jurisdictions are in a position to change the nature of their organizations, if they have the desire to do so. Another Canadian study conducted in BC (Seagrave, 1995) examined the different perspectives chief constables and RCMP Officers in Charge of municipal police detachments had towards community policing and organizational change. The research concluded the independent chief constables had more autonomy and fewer constraints than did the RCMP Officers in Charge, as they were in less bureaucratic, smaller organizations. This study showed the ability of the chief to introduce change was dependent, not only upon personal characteristics, but also upon the organizational structure in which he/she was working, the size of the department and the police subculture.

The desire of police leaders to initiate change is an important consideration within the organizational change process. Police leaders need to articulate an abiding commitment to the values they espouse and must have the support of the rank and file. Police leaders may achieve change by a number of ways:

- By concentrating on informing younger members of the department that change is required, with the belief that these individuals will be more open to new ideas.
- By urging the retirement of the old guard who are resistant to change and by hiring new officers.
- By flattening the hierarchy to enable communication to flow more easily between the ranks.

- By determining who, specifically, is resistant to change (and if all else fails, sanctioning them).
- By sending trained middle management out as team leaders to convey and 'sell' new ideas (Skolnick and Bayley, 1986).

In the United States, a new generation of police chiefs, trained in public administration, sociology and criminal justice, is now attempting to implement progressive ideas (Manning, 1977) and, over time, may succeed in promoting change.

Organizations may resist change if they are deemed to be currently successful. Police organizations in Canada have enjoyed a steady increase in funding over the past few decades and opinion polls routinely report high overall public support for the police (Griffiths and Verdun-Jones, 1994). With these facts in mind, police leaders may find any arguments endorsing change untenable.

Police subculture and change

It is not only police executives who need to alter their philosophies in order to accommodate change, the police rank and file subculture must also adapt; yet it is this level of the organization that has been shown to be the most resistant to change. The same features of the police organization that provide cohesiveness and integration make it resistant to change and innovation (Manning, 1977), prompting one commentator to state that promoting change in the rank and file subculture is as easy as 'bending granite' (Guyot, 1979). Descza (1988), in summarizing the literature on the Canadian police subculture, has detailed three costs to policing that this subculture promotes:

1. police alienation from the public and its institutions (and vice versa).
2. police officer alienation from management.
3. resistance to changes that could assist in addressing personal and organizational problems.

One of the most recent additions to the subcultural area of research details the police subculture as unsympathetic towards the service model of policing, with little time for community policing (McConnville and Shepherd, 1992). This disregard is not attributed to characteristics of individual officers, but rather is the result of the police subculture. While this study illustrates the discrepancy between the views advanced by police managers and the views of the rank and file, it draws primarily on the opinions of police officers at the lower levels of the organization and not those of the more senior ranks. In England and Wales, a study (*Operational Policing Review*, 1990) to compare the opinions of operational police officers with those of the Association of Chief Police Officers (ACPO) was undertaken. The study found that the rank and file favored a 'strong' approach to policing and dismissed community policing as 'soft'. In contrast, the ACPO ranks implied strong support for many aspects of the community policing approach. They placed greatest value on community-related activities, such as liaison with schools and ethnic minorities, and placed less importance on law and order approaches. Reiner's (1990) British study of police chiefs illustrated that many had a broad view of the police role, only identifying crime as one aspect of it, unlike operational police officers who focused on law enforcement. These studies suggest that there is more resistance to change within the lower ranks of policing.

Despite the volume of findings that suggest significant organizational change in policing is extremely difficult, there is evidence that it can take place. Large-scale changes have occurred, evidenced by the creation of provincial police forces in Ontario and Quebec, regionalization, the increased use of technology during the legalistic era and the amalgamation of a number of police forces. While all these examples illustrate structural change, there are fewer examples of cultural change away from the military model. One recent exception is found in a study by Foster (1987), who conducted research in London, England, and illustrated how alterations occurred in police management, community initiatives and training in order to improve police-community relations in one subdivision. Change was achieved because it was backed by the entire management hierarchy. Similar findings are also presented by Skolnick and Bayley (1986) in their review of six innovative police chiefs in the US. However, the extent to which these changes were sustained over time is unclear.

In discussing change in police organizations, it is important to consider the rate and extent of change. Foster's (1987) research illustrated that change was possible, but her sample was small. Skolnick and Bayley (1986) argued change was possible but did not show whether change was retained over time. The extent to which the police subculture influences the movement towards community policing and other initiatives management wants to introduce will vary among different police organizations. The size, location and structure of these organizations will influence their desire and ability to adopt new strategies. Another factor in this equation of change is police unions and associations.

An understanding of police culture as it exists at every level of the organization is important, not only in understanding organizational change and the barriers that may exist to it, but also in understanding what being a police officer means. This issue will be explored in the following chapter.

POLICE UNIONS AND ASSOCIATIONS

Police unions have existed in Canada since the turn of the century, although their presence in the past was sporadic. In Canada today, almost all large police forces have some form of employee group, known as either a union or an association, that bargains with civic officials over wages and benefits. The exception to this is the RCMP, which since 1972, has had a system of divisional representatives to present issues of employee concern to management. Although there

were moves in the 1970s to introduce unions into the RCMP, the system of divisional representatives, coupled with a force policy to match RCMP compensation
and benefits levels to those of other major municipal forces, diluted calls for
unionization in the organization (Forcese, 1992).

In commenting on the composition of police unions and associations in
Canada, Forcese (1980) lists a number of defining characteristics:

- All major municipal forces and most forces in smaller communities are union-
  ized, ensuring collective bargaining to be a well-established practice.
- Most unions have little interest in strikes.
- Associations and management are well prepared for the bargaining process.
- Many of the senior officers who now comprise management were themselves members of police associations, consequently, they are well informed
  of the frustrations unions have in bargaining with management. As noted by
  Jackson (1986): "Unlike industry and business, members of police management are drawn from the same social classes, have similar backgrounds and
  a common 'ideology' or view of themselves and their role to those of the
  association" (p. 95).
- Despite this empathy, there is a recognizable division in the rhetoric of management and the rank and file, with management believing itself restricted by
  employee organizations.
- Police unions have been able to bargain for issues other than wages.
- Unions have aided the professionalization of policing by making gains in the
  areas of benefits, working conditions, disputes and promotional procedures.
- There has been an increased aggressiveness on the part of both unions and
  management. This can be evidenced by unions seeking to influence law
  enforcement policy "...and in so doing challenging the public's conception of
  the neutrality of the police" (Forcese, 1980, p. 88).
- Unions have been instrumental in gaining improved equipment and, to a lesser extent, personnel.

Jackson (1986) adds one further characteristic: the brotherhood syndrome.
Police officers share similar outlooks and attitudes; the conditions of the job also
isolate them socially and professionally.

Police associations have become increasingly vocal over the last few decades.
In this respect they have mirrored other white-collar and government employee
groups, which have moved from a position of little organization to one of solidarity and militancy (Jackson, 1979). As with other employee bodies, they assign high
priority to job security and benefits, but they also address broader issues. While
the views of police chiefs are expected to be politically neutral, police unions often
enter debates on a variety of issues, such as police weapons, parole, sentencing
policy and capital punishment, frequently seeing management's reluctance to

enter such debates as 'soft'. Jackson (1986) sees this as a recent development and terms it 'going public'. He argues that police associations have found themselves in the unique position of being able to speak for the institution of policing and law enforcement itself, a luxury management cannot afford. This privilege is fragile and must be used with caution, as insensitive or thoughtless comments by associations may jeopardize public support (Forcese, 1980).

During the 1960s, unions were successful in achieving a number of goals, both in terms of wage increases and by influencing and overturning management decisions they found disagreeable. For example, in some areas, they successfully fought for the retention of two-officer patrol cars when management wanted to introduce one-officer cars (Martin, 1995). They have also been instrumental in debating issues such as hats, scheduling, promotion and tenure, and dress and grooming standards (Jackson, 1979). Police militancy can take the form of work slowdowns, violation of dress codes and, in the most extreme cases, strikes. In Nova Scotia, New Brunswick and Saskatchewan, the police have the right to strike, in other areas, such as Ontario, Quebec and Alberta, the police are prohibited from striking, while in some places, this option is dependent upon collective agreements (Forcese, 1992). Where strikes have occurred, the RCMP has often been brought in to maintain order.

Unions influence departmental policies and philosophies. As they are largely comprised of the rank and file police officers, they reflect the views of this subculture. In this respect, unions have been recognized as a barrier to organizational change. They tend to endorse the traditional law enforcement ideology and remain "...conservative, even rigid, seemingly unprogressive" (Martin, 1995, p. 139).

Because they contain characteristics derived from the rank and file subculture, police associations are often reluctant to sanction organizational changes that do not accord with their world views. They have been accused of hindering the professionalization of policing and of presenting an obstacle to reform. This, however, may be a management view, reflecting the dynamic relationship between structure and subculture. At the very least, it alerts us to the role unions have in influencing organizational change.

SUMMARY

The organization of police departments is bureaucratic in nature and still retains many components of the military model. Studies of police organizations have been conducted using two approaches, normative and empirical. The first approach utilizes organizational theory to describe and prescribe how police departments are and should be managed. In contrast, empirical approaches draw attention to the human dimension of police work and focus on police subculture. Most of the work on the police subculture concentrates on the activities of the rank and file who carry out everyday police work. Although the theoretical understanding of this subculture has come a long way in the last twenty years, only a few of these studies have addressed middle management and police leadership. At best, the police literature informs us about the bottom end of the hierarchy, but not the top or middle. An understanding of all levels of the police organization and the environment in which that agency operates is important for an analysis of organizational change.

An understanding of police culture is important in understanding organizational change and to inform our analysis of what being a police officer means. The following chapter will explore the police rank and file subculture in action.

QUESTIONS FOR DISCUSSION

1. Why do you think the bureaucratic theories of policing are still evident today?

2. Describe what you think the goals of a police department should be.

3. What para-military characteristics do police agencies contain?

4. Describe J.Q. Wilson's three departmental styles. How appropriate do you think these categories are for Canadian policing?

5. What is the difference between street cop cultures and management cop cultures?

6. Why have so few studies been done on police middle management?

7. How relevant do you think Reiner's list of police subcultural characteristics is to an understanding of police resistance to organizational change?

8. Describe the difference between reactive and planned change.

9. What is the difference between management and leadership? Are chief constables leaders or managers?

10. Why would the research suggest police executives are more open to community policing philosophies than the rank and file?

FURTHER READING

Niederhoffer, A. (1967). *Behind the Shield*. New York: Doubleday. This book is written by a former New York City police officer and provides insight into policing by discussing numerous concerns, including organization, relationships with the public, bureaucracy, professionalism and cynicism, from a sociological stance.

Wilson, James Q. (1968). *Varieties of Police Behavior: The Management of Law and Order in Eight Communities*. Cambridge Mass.: Harvard University Press. This classic text explores police discretion, develops three distinctively different policing styles and attributes them to the structural characteristics of the organization in which the officer is working.

Reuss-Ianni, Elizabeth (1983). *Two Cultures of Policing: Street Cops and Management Cops.* New Brunswick: Transaction Books. Based on two years' fieldwork, this book examines two competing—and often conflicting—cultures within one police organization: the culture of the rank and file and management. It also explores the tensions inherent in bureaucracies.

Westley, W. (1970). *Violence and the Police: A Sociological Study of Law, Custom and Morality.* Cambridge Mass.: MIT Press. An in-depth analysis of the nature of policing and issues surrounding role definitions. The text provides a critical review of why reform in police departments is difficult to achieve.

REFERENCES

Alpert, Geoffrey A. and Dunham, Roger G. (1988). *Policing In Urban America.* Prospect Heights, Ill.: Waveland Press.

Angell, John E. (1976). "Organizing police for the future: An update of the democratic model." *Criminal Justice Review, 1*(2).

Banton, M. (1964). *The Police in the Community.* London: Tavistock.

Bayley, D.H. (1985). *Patterns of Policing: A Comparative International Analysis.* New Jersey: Rutgers University Press.

Becker, H. (1963). *Outsiders.* New York: Free Press.

Bittner, E. (1967). "The police on skid row: A study in peacekeeping." *American Sociological Review, 32.*

Bittner, E. (1970). *The Functions of Police in Modern Society.* Cevy Chase, Md.: National Institute of Mental Health.

Bouza, A.V. (1990). *The Police Mystique.* New York: Plenum Press.

Bradley, David, Walker, Neil and Wilkie, Roy (1986). *Managing the Police: Low Organization and Democracy.* Sussex: Wheetshef Books.

Brake, M. (1980). *The Sociology of Youth Culture and Youth Subculture.* London: Routledge and Kegan Paul.

Broderick, John J. (1987). *Police in a Time of Change.* Prospect Heights, Ill.: Waveland Press.

Brodgen, M., Jefferson, T. and Walklate, S. (1988). *Introducing Policework.* London: Unwin Hyman.

Cain, M. (1973). *Society and the Policeman's Role.* London: Routledge and Kegan Paul.

Cain, M. (1979). "Trends in the sociology of policework." *International Journal of the Sociology of Law, 7*(2).

Campbell, Peter and Wright, Susan (1993). "Leadership in turbulent times." In The Ministry of the Solicitor General of Canada *Canadian Community Policing Series.* Ottawa: Minister of Supplies and Services.

Chatterton, M. (1976). "Police in social control." In J. King (Ed.) *Control Without Custody.* Cropwood Papers No.7. Cambridge: Institute of Criminology.

Chatterton, M.R. (1979). "The supervision of patrol work under the fixed points system." In S. Holdaway (Ed.) *The British Police.* London: Edward Arnold.

Chatterton, M.R. (1983). "Police and Work Assault Charges." In M. Punch (ed.) *Control in the Police Organization.* Cambridge: MIT Press.

Clairmont, D.H. (1991). "Community-based policing: Implementation and impact." *Canadian Journal of Criminology, 33*(3-4).

Cohen, A.K. (1955). *Delinquent Boys: The Culture of the Gang.* Chicago: Free Press.

Cohen, B. (1980). "Leadership styles of commanders in the New York City Police Department." *Journal of Police Science and Administration, 8.*

Coleman, A. and Gorman, L. (1982). "Conservatism, dogmatism and authoritarianism in British police officers." *Sociology, 16*(1).

Crank, J.P. (1986). "Cynicism among police chiefs." *Justice Quarterly, 3*(3).

Dantzker, Mark L. (1995). *Understanding Today's Police.* New Jersey: Prentice Hall.

Das, Dilip K. (1993). *Policing in Six Countries Around the World.* St. Louis: The C.V. Mosby Company.

Deszca, G. (1988). "The communication of ideology in police forces." *Canadian Police College Journal, 12*(4).

Downes, D. (1966). *The Delinquent Solution: A Study of Subcultural Theory.* London: Clarendon Press.

Ericson, R. (1982). *Reproducing Order: A Study of Police Patrol Work.* Toronto: University of Toronto Press.

Fielding, N. (1988). *Joining Forces: Police Training, Socialization and Occupational Competence.* London: Routledge.

Forcese, Dennis (1980). "Police unionism: Employee management relations in Canadian police forces." *Canadian Police College Journal, 4*(2).

Forcese, Dennis P. (1992). *Policing Canadian Society.* Scarborough: Prentice Hall.

Foster, J. (1989). "Two stations: An ethnographic study of policing in the inner city." In D. Downes (Ed.) *Crime and the City.* Macmillian: London.

Gaine, Larry Keith. (1975). *An Examination of Organizational Model in Traditional and Innovative Police Departments.* Unpublished doctoral dissertation. Sam Houston State University.

Goldstein, H. (1977). *Policing a Free Society.* Cambridge Mass.: Ballinger.

Goldstein, H. (1990). *Problem Oriented Policing.* New York: McGraw Hill.

Grant, A. (1980). *The Police: A Policy Paper.* Montreal: Law Reform Commission of Canada.

Goldsmith, A. (1990). "Taking police culture seriously." *Policing and Society* 1(2).

Graef, R. (1989). *Talking Blues.* London: Collins Harvill.

Griffiths, Curt T. and Verdun Jones, Simon N. (1994). *Canadian Criminal Justice.* Toronto: Harcourt Brace.

Grimshaw, Roger and Jefferson, Tony (1987). *Interpreting Policework: Policy and Practice in Forms of Beat Policing.* London: Allen Unwin.

Guyot, D. (1977). "Police departments under social science scrutiny." *Journal of Criminal Justice, 5.*

Holdaway, Simon (1979). *The British Police.* London: Edward Arnold.

Holdaway, Simon (1984). *Inside the British Police: A Force at Work.* Oxford: Basil Blackwell.

Holdaway, S. (1989). "Discovering structure. Studies of the British police occupational structure." In M. Weatheritt (Ed.) *Police Research: Some Future Prospects.* Aldershot: Gower Publishing Company Ltd.

Hoover, Larry T. and Madner, Edward T. (1990). "Attitudes of police chiefs towards private sector management principles." *American Journal of the Police, 9*(4).

Hunt, Raymond G. and Magenau, John M. (1993). *Power and the Police Chief: An Institutional and Organizational Analysis.* Newbury Park: Sage.

Jackson, R. (1979). "Police labor relations in Canada: A current perspective." *Canadian Police College Journal, 3*(1).

Jackson, R. (1986). "Canadian police labor relations in the 1980s: New environmental concerns." *Canadian Police College Journal, 10*(2).

Jefferson, T. (1990). *The Case Against Para-Military Policing.* Milton Keynes: Open University Press.

Jermier, John M., Slocum, John W., Fry, Louis W. and Gaines, Jeannie (1991). "Organizational cultures in a soft bureaucracy: Resistance behind the myth and facade of an official culture." *Organizational Science, 2*(2).

Jones, S. and Levi, M. (1983). "The police and the majority: the neglect of the obvious." *Police Journal, LVI:4.*

Koenig, Daniel J. (1992). *Secondary Employment: A Discussion Paper.* Unpublished paper for the RCMP External Review Committee. Ottawa.

Langworthy, Robert H. (1986). *The Structure of Police Organizations.* New York: Praeger.

Lee, J.A. (1981). "Some structural aspects of police deviance in relations with minority groups." In C. Shearing (Ed.) *Organizational Police Deviance.* Toronto: Butterworth.

Loree, D. (1988). "Innovation and change in a regional police force." *Canadian Police College Journal, 12*(4).

Lynch, Ronald G. (1986). *The Police Manager: Professional Leadership Skills.* New York: Random House.

Manning, P. (1977). *Police Work.* Cambridge Mass.: MIT Press.

Manning, P. (1979). "The social control of police work." In S. Holdaway (Ed.) *The British Police*. London: Edward Arnold.

Martin, Maurice A. (1995). *Urban Policing in Canada: Anatomy of an Aging Craft.* Montreal: McGill-Queen's University Press.

Mawby, R.I. (1990). *Comparative Policing Issues: The British and American System in International Perspective.* London: Unwin Hyman.

McConnville, Mike and Shepherd, Dan (1992). *Watching Police Watching Communities.* London: Routledge.

Morgan, G. (1986). *Images of Organization.* Newbury Park: Sage.

Morgan, R. (1987). "Police accountability: developing the local infrastructure." *British Journal of Criminology, 27*(1).

Murphy, C. (1987). *The Social and Formal Organization of Small Town Policing. A Comparative Analysis of RCMP and Municipal Policing.* Unpublished doctoral dissertation, University of Toronto.

Niederhoffer, A. (1967). *Behind the Shield.* New York: Doubleday.

O'Reilly, Robert R. and Dostaler, Ann (1983). "Police managers development study." *Canadian Police College Journal, 7*(1).

Operational Policing Review (1990). Joint Consultative Committee of the Police Staff Associations, Surbiton, Surrey: The Police Foundation.

Oppal, The Honourable Mr. Justice Wallace T. (1994). *Closing the Gap: Policing and the Community.* Commission of Inquiry Policing in British Columbia. Victoria, B.C.: Attorney General.

Ott, Steven J. (1989). *The Organizational Culture Perspective.* Chicago: The Dorsey Press.

Potts, Lee W. (1982). "Police leadership: Challenge for the eighties." *Journal of Police Science and Administration, 10*(2).

Punch, Maurice (1979). *Policing the Inner City: A Study of Amsterdam's Warmoesstraat.* London: Macmillian.

Punch, Maurice (1983). *Control in the Police Organization.* Cambridge, Mass.: MIT Press.

Reiner, R. (1978). *The Blue Coated Worker.* Cambridge: Cambridge University Press.

Reiner, R. (1985). *The Politics of the Police.* Brighton: Wheatshef Books.

Reiner, R. (1991). *Chief Constables: Bobbies, Bosses or Bureaucrats.* Oxford: Clarendon Press.

Reiner, R. (1992). *The Politics of the Police* (second edition). Hemel Hempstead: Harvester Wheatsheaf.

Reiss, A.J. (1971). *The Police and the Public.* New Haven: Yale University Press.

Reuss-Ianni, Elizabeth (1983). *Two Cultures of Policing.* New Brunswick (USA): Transaction Books.

Roberg, Roy R. (1979). *Police Management and Organizational Behavior: A Contingency Approach.* St. Paul, Minnesota: West Publishing Co.

Roberg, Roy R. and Kuykendall, Jack (1993). *Police and Society.* Belmont California: Wadsworth Publishing Company.

Rossi, P., Berk, R. and Eidson, B. (1974). *The Roots of Urban Discontent.* New York: Wiley.

Rubinstein, J. (1973). *City Police.* New York: Ballatine.

Sandler, G. B. and Mintz, E. (1974). "Police organizations: Their changing internal and external relationships." *Police Science and Administration, 2.*

Seagrave, J. (1995). *Changing the organizational culture: Community policing in British Columbia.* Unpublished doctoral dissertation, Simon Fraser University.

Shaftritz, J.M. and Ott, J.S. (1987) *Classics of Organizational Theory.* Chicago: The Dorsey Press.

Shearing, C. (1981). *Organizational Police Deviance: Its Structure and Control.* Toronto: Butterworths.

Skolnick, J. (1966). *Justice Without Trial.* New York: Wiley.

Skolnick, J.H. and Bayley, D.H. (1986). *The New Blue Line.* New York: The Free Press.

Skolnick, J.H. and Bayley, D.H. (1988). *Community Policing: Issues and Practices Around the World.* United States: National Institute of Justice.

Smith, B. (1960). *Police Systems in the United States.* 2nd rev. ed. New York: Harper & Row.

Swanson, Charles R., Territo, Leonard and Taylor, Robert W. (1988). *Police Administration.* New York: Macmillian.

Talarico, Sussette M. and Swanson, Charles R. (1982). "An analysis of police perceptions of supervisory and administrative support." *Police Studies, 5*(1).

Taylor, Frederick, W. (1947). "The principles of scientific management." *Scientific Management.*

Thibault, E.A., Lynch, L.M. and McBride, R.B. (1990). *Proactive Police Management.* Engelwood Cliffs, N.J.: Prentice Hall.

Van Maanen, J. (1973). "Observations on the making of policemen." *Human Organization, 32.*

Van Maanen, J. (1986). "Power in the bottle: Informal interaction and formal authority." In S. Srivasta (Ed.) *Executive Power.* San Francisco: Jossey-Bass.

Vincent, C. (1990). *Police Officer.* Ottawa: Carleton University Press.

Westley, W. (1970). *Violence and the Police: A Sociological Study of Law, Custom and Morality.* Cambridge Mass.: MIT Press.

Wilkinson, Deanna L. and Rosenbaum, Dennis P. (1994). "The effects of organizational structure on community policing: A comparison of two cities." In Dennis P. Rosenbaum (Ed.) *The Challenge of Community Policing: Testing the Promises.* California: Sage.

Wilson, James Q. (1968). *Varieties of Police Behavior: The Management of Law and Order in Eight Communities.* Cambridge Mass.: Harvard University Press.

Wilson, O.W. (1977). *Police Administration.* New York: McGraw Hill.

Young, Malcolm. (1991). *An Inside Job: Policing and Police Culture in Britain.* Oxford: Oxford University Press.

POLICE DECISION-MAKING, BEHAVIOR AND PATROL

INTRODUCTION

This chapter discusses police behavior, decision-making and patrol. It initially reviews theories of police behavior and then proceeds to analyze the factors that affect police decision-making. The final part examines police patrol.

As illustrated in Chapter 4, the police role is influenced by a variety of social, legal, organizational and political factors and has been the subject of considerable, ongoing debate. The preceding dialogue is directly relevant to an analysis of police behavior, for any debate over the definition of police role clearly affects the discussion of the skills required to undertake that (albeit poorly-defined) role, the decision-making process and police behavior.

THEORIES OF POLICE BEHAVIOR

Theories of police behavior can be grouped into two categories. The first, predispositional theory, argues that individuals who seek careers as police officers have certain characteristics, values and attitudes, such as cynicism and authoritarianism, that these traits are evident before an individual embarks on a policing career and that they affect decision-making. Predispositional theory was challenged during the 1960s, when criminologists began to argue that police behavior was not determined by personal characteristics but by a process of socialization. This is the second category of police behavior theory. As shown in the preceding chapters, police officers learn the values and norms of policing by a process of formal socialization, conducted through the selection and training process, and informal socialization, as they begin to work within the police agency and learn from their peers what it means to be a police officer. It is now widely held that this process of formal and informal socialization into the police subculture has the greatest effect on police behavior and decision-making.

SKILLS OF POLICING

In discussing how police officers learn the skills of policing, Bayley and Bittner (1993) illustrate that experience gained on the job contributes to learning about three important factors: goals, tactics and presence.

Goals

Through experience, officers learn goals. These refer to individual objectives and include:

- Meeting departmental norms, such as issuing a required number of parking tickets, or filling out the necessary forms for dealing with a specific incident.
- Preventing crime. Bayley and Bittner (1993) argue that an essential part of the officer's task is to take charge and restore order in the hope the incident will not be repeated. Often this work is superficial and does not address the causes of the problem, but does succeed in responding to the officer's concern to restore order.
- Avoiding physical injury by being future oriented and by deciding when it is appropriate to use critical sanctions and when it is not.
- Avoiding provocation, which could result in an angry reaction by the public and challenge their careers. Police officers worry a lot about the repercussions of their actions; there are many things the organization instructs officers to do to avoid the glare of public scrutiny.

Tactics

The second area which Bayley and Bittner (1993) claim is essential to learn is tactics. These are the various approaches to, and solutions for, problems encountered. There are three stages of police-citizen interaction—contact, processing and exit—and at each of these stages, police officers have a great deal of discretion. Police learn by their own experience and from colleagues what works and what doesn't, "...choice is an operational necessity and they see trial and error as the only way to learn about it" (Bayley and Bittner, 1993, p. 120).

Presence

The third factor that experience teaches is presence. Policing does not involve simply doing something, it means *being* something. Police officers must display external calm and be non-provocative, adopting a demeanor which pacifies and mollifies, while at the same time being watchful and alert for signs of danger. This demeanor is again learned as an officer gains experience and is part of the ongoing socialization process.

Learning the role of a police officer involves both formal and informal social-ization. Acquiring information on goals and tactics is gained from the formal channels of training, departmental policies, organizational procedures and from mixing with other police officers. Presence is something learned only from working with others. Knowledge about goals, tactics and presence ensures police officers obtain the "skills of policing" (Bayley and Bittner, 1993). These skills have been the subject of a number of research studies.

RESEARCH ON POLICE BEHAVIOR

Social scientists have long been interested in police decision-making and behav-ior, especially the behavior of the rank and file police officer employed in rou-tine patrol work. The first, and most notable, study was conducted by Westley (1970) in the 1950s in the United States. He showed how older, more experi-enced officers indoctrinate the rookies and inform them that to be good officers they need to gain control over a situation. Westley's research also showed how police officers saw the public as unsupportive. This trait, together with the need to control, influenced behavior.

Research by Banton (1964) showed how police officers behaved differently if they were assigned different tasks. Banton recognized a division between 'peacekeepers', who undertake routine patrol duties, and 'law enforcers', who work in specialized positions. He showed that police behavior was dependent on the work assigned.

In 1966, Skolnick wrote *Justice Without Trial*, which analyzed two US police departments. Skolnick found police behavior was influenced by the goals and objectives of the organization; so, for example, if a department was preoccu-pied with crime control, an officer would be aggressive in making arrests and issuing tickets.

Niederhoffer (1967) developed a socialization theory of police behavior by showing there to be four stages to a police officer's career development:

- commitment, the early phase when an officer is dedicated to helping people and tackling crime.
- frustration, when the officer begins to realize that little can be done to address crime.
- disenchantment, when the original ideals of the job are rejected.
- cynicism, when the officer is disillusioned and pessimistic about the job.

Similarly, Van Maanen (1973) advanced a four-stage socialization theory of police behavior, illustrating how individuals develop and learn about policing in four processes:

1. by deciding to pursue a career as a police officer.
2. by being admitted and trained at the academy.

3. by working with other police officers and gaining experience.

4. by adjusting to the realities of police work.

The work of both Niederhoffer (1967) and Van Maanen (1973) has parallels with previously quoted research on police subculture, which discussed different police officer orientations and styles (Broderick, 1987; Reiner, 1978; Shearing 1984). These different styles—which affect decision-making and behavior—have also been discussed by others (Brown, 1981; Muir, 1977).

The most notable Canadian study on police behavior was conducted by Ericson (1982), who looked at police patrol in an eastern city. Ericson showed how the police construct 'recipes for action', a sort of organizational shorthand, which enables them to classify and order events and to reclassify them based on whether there is potential for police involvement. These 'recipes for action' are developed from a collection of 'recipe' rules, or rules of thumb, learned on the job which combine actual events, police department rules and legal codes. The community, the law and the organization give the police officer 'recipe rules', which in turn provide the officer with a sense of order, influence his/her conduct and lead to 'recipes for action'. 'Recipes for action' influence police decision-making and are, in turn, influenced by the area policed and its population. Ericson's work also illustrated how a number of socio-economic, cultural and personal factors affect decision-making.

This selective review of the literature illustrates that research on police behavior and decision-making has had a long history in criminology. The findings from these studies and others have informed what is known about police discretion. They also provide insights into the three skills of policing as detected by Bayley and Bittner (1993).

POLICE DISCRETION

Discretion is an unavoidable feature in policing (Stansfield, 1996) and is a characteristic of all agencies within the criminal justice system. While it is frequently conveyed as being a problem, it should more realistically be treated as a necessary component of a police officer's role. Discretion grants an individual the power to choose among various alternatives and is an inevitable function of policing. Once this factor is accepted, the real issue becomes not whether discretion should be exercised, but the criteria that are applied in order to make an informed decision.

There exists a considerable amount of research on police discretion and the way in which discretionary decisions are made at every level of the organization. Goldstein (1977) has identified various levels of discretion exercised by police organizations. His first two may be defined as police goals, the later three as police tactics:

- Prioritizing how resources will be allocated by accounting for the competing demands placed on the department. Even before a police officer is dispatched to an incident, police telephone operators and dispatch officers receive citizen requests for service by telephone and assess whether police intervention is needed. With limited organizational resources, police must prioritize the requests they receive.

- Senior managers exercise discretion in setting and enforcing departmental priorities and policies. For example, a police department could decide to have a crackdown on speeding, thus giving priority to dangerous driving over other concerns.
- Police officers display discretion in responding to calls for service and in the way the call is treated. The fewer the rules that apply to the situation, the more discretion the police officer has. Police officers therefore have considerable scope in deciding how to act.
- Goldstein's (1977) fourth level relates to the third and concerns the decisions police officers make regarding how to dispose of a case; for example, whether to arrest, mediate, warn or make a referral.
- The final level of discretion is the decisions made by police investigators in gathering evidence.

Discretionary decision-making takes place a long time before a police officer arrives at the scene. Research by Shearing (1984) on the Metropolitan Toronto Police Department found that officers receiving telephone calls from the public had a system of prioritizing these calls, with those relating to bodily injury and serious property damage being given a higher priority than others. Shearing noted that the decisions of the complaint officer were influenced by the demeanor of the caller and the officer's perception of the amount of trouble represented by the call. When the complaint officer decided the dispatch of a patrol car was justified, the request went to the dispatch officer, who engaged in further discretionary behavior in deciding what resources, if any, to send. This decision was based on the demand for service and the resources available.

Police discretion exists both at the individual and at the administrative level. Patrol officers make choices on a regular basis, such as how quickly to respond to calls for service, how long to spend at each call, how to spend uncommitted time, where and how to patrol and whom to arrest and stop. At the administrative level, decisions are made concerning staffing, the allocation of personnel and resources, policies, procedures, training and enforcement priorities. Brooks (1993) shows that when organizational rules are strict, less discretion is awarded to the police officer; conversely, when rules are vague, the police officer exercises more discretion. The purpose of departmental policy is to reduce officer discretion (Alpert and Fridell, 1992), but this aim can never be fully achieved due to the varied and unpredictable nature of police work.

The extent and degree of discretion exercised by a police officer is dependent on the nature of the call for service. If a serious law has been broken, the officer may only need to establish guilt in order to proceed with a predetermined process. Discretion does, however, play a larger role in cases of order maintenance, where laws can be interpreted in various ways and where there are many different alternatives open to the police officer. Research by Wilson

(1968), discussed in Chapter 5, showed how police officers in different departments demonstrated different styles of policing, with the 'watchman style' being concerned with maintaining order, the 'legalistic style' being more law-enforcement oriented and the 'service style' stressing community service. His study supports the view that the management style of a police department will affect police officer judgment and decision-making by affecting both the development and the implementation of policies and procedures within the department.

It is somewhat of an anomaly that the patrol officers, who occupy the lowest rung on the organizational ladder, exercise the greatest discretion. It is at this level that most of the academic interest in police decision-making has been focused. In a classical study of police discretion, Davis (1975) argued that, while police discretion could not be eliminated, it should be structured, confined and controlled and parameters should exist within the police organization to restrict discretionary powers. Although this may be the aim of police managers, and is indeed articulated in the numerous organizational rules that exist in police departments, in the end, street policing is a process performed by trained individuals but subject to personal interpretations.

Essentially, patrol officer discretion involves three decision processes (Roberg and Kuykendall, 1993):

- Whether or not to get involved in the incident. (The police officer may have little choice in this if sent by the organization).
- How to behave and act with citizens.
- Selecting alternatives to solve the problem.

Police officers can observe a violation of the law and decide to prosecute or, alternatively, do nothing. These are discretionary acts, most of which are made with the knowledge of only a few individuals (suspect, victim, colleague). Police decision-making is a low-visibility activity often known only to one other individual in the organization.

FACTORS AFFECTING POLICE BEHAVIOR

Brooks (1993) has analyzed research concerning the variables that influence police behavior and decision-making and has categorized them as: organizational, neighborhood, situational and officer.

Organizational variables

The organizational variables that influence police discretionary behavior place constraints on the amount of discretion police officers exercise and socialize officers into making certain decisions. Organizational variables include: the degree of bureaucracy, the extent of professionalization, the size of the organization, the stability of the assignment and the span of control.

Bureaucracy. Highly bureaucratic, militaristic, impersonal departments have tall hierarchical structures and are characterized by rigid rules governing police officer behavior. Organizations like this tend to emphasize crime fighting more than service activities; for police officers to be viewed as effective, they must make arrests. Impersonal relationships within the organization may be transferred to impersonal relationships with the community. Bureaucratic departments exert punitive disciplinary measures in an attempt to control police officer behavior, which may result in officers doing very little to avoid getting into trouble.

Professionalization. The degree of professionalization is another factor in police officers' decision-making. A professional police department is one in which education, service and citizen respect and support are essential (Goldstein, 1977). If professional departments do not become too bureaucratic they offer a different type of police environment and style of policing to that of the bureaucratic model.

Size. The size of a police department affects police behavior. Officers from larger police departments tend to be less sympathetic, and have a detached relationship with the citizens they serve. Officers from smaller agencies are less aggressive and not primarily oriented towards law enforcement.

Stability of assignment. Departments that frequently rotate their personnel into different beats, shifts or units inhibit the development of close community ties. If a police officer remains in one area, his/her understanding of and empathy with the people in the area grows, resulting in fewer aggressive police actions. In contrast, 'stranger policing' (Murphy and Pate, 1977) results in areas that frequently rotate officers and is characterized by a more law-enforcement style. Related to the stability of the assignment is the size of the geographical area the officer is required to patrol. The smaller the area, the more likely that the service, rather than law enforcement, orientation will exist.

Supervisor's span of control. Larger bureaucratic police departments have the strictest and most impersonal supervision, due to the masses of people who must be supervised. The degree of supervision affects police officers' behavior, with larger organizations exerting more supervision and control.

In Canada, organizational characteristics vary considerably, from the large bureaucratic RCMP structure, which regularly relocates members, to small independent departments with less than 20 members who remain in one location. To date, there has not been any Canadian research exploring how these organizational variables affect police discretionary behavior.

Neighborhood variables

Neighborhood or environmental variables associated with police discretion include racial composition, socio-economic status, heterogeneity, crime rate and attitudes towards the police.

Racial composition. There is a considerable amount of research in both Britain (Policy Studies Institute, 1983) and the United States (Bayley and Mendelsohn, 1969; Rossi and Eidson 1974) and, to a more limited extent, Canada (see Jayewardene and Talbot, 1990) that the police write more reports, make more arrests, receive more requests for intervention and, as a result, get to know people better in minority areas than in non-minority areas. Police view minority areas as places where crimes are more likely to occur and where their authority is more readily challenged.

Socio-economic status. The social class of an area affects both the crime rate (with lower-class areas reporting more crime) and police behavior (Wilson, 1968). Research by Westley (1970) showed that the police believed they had to be tougher in lower-class areas, where force was often required to achieve and maintain respect. In contrast, middle-class people in more affluent areas were treated differently. People in nice areas are considered nice people, whereas people in not-so-nice areas are thought not so nice. Research in Canada also confirms this view (Ericson, 1982).

Heterogeneity. The greater the diversity of an area in terms of both race and social class, the greater the likelihood the police will feel insecure, become aggressive and make arrests (Roberg and Kuykendall, 1993). Heterogeneous neighborhoods are less amenable to routine procedures and imply the use of more discretion and autonomy.

Crime rate. Areas with high crime rates affect officer perceptions, increasing the likelihood the officer will resort to legalistic and aggressive tactics. At the same time, due to the sheer volume of work in such locations, officers must be selective and may be forced to ignore trivial offenses.

> When confronted with high rates of crime officers develop higher thresholds of crime tolerance. They may be less accommodating or more aggressive in the police-citizen encounters in high crime neighborhoods...Police may be more hostile to citizens and treat all residents as potential criminals (Brooks, 1993; p. 153).

In contrast, when policing low-crime areas, officers have more time for service activities and are prepared to become involved in trivial incidents.

Citizen attitudes. Most police-citizen encounters are the result of citizens calling the police. The decision on whether or not to involve an officer is, to some extent, dependent on an individual's view of the police and involves discretionary behavior by the citizen (Reiss, 1971). The views and opinions individuals have of the police influence their decision to contact and, in turn, affect police behavior.

All these demographic and attitudinal variables are, in some respects, interrelated; all play a role in accounting for the discretionary behavior of the police.

Situational variables

Situational variables thought to influence police discretionary behavior include the characteristics of the suspect and complainants, the type of offense/nature of the call, the visibility of the encounter, the type of mobilization and the presence of others.

Characteristics of suspects and complainants. Brooks (1993) lists a number of personal characteristics that have been recognized to influence police behavior. These include the following.

- **Demeanor.** A considerable amount of research, including Ericson's (1982) study of a Canadian police department, has shown that disrespectful and uncooperative suspects are more likely to be arrested than those who are deferential and display a civil manner. Likewise, uncooperative complainants are likely to receive less assistance.

- **Socio-economic status.** Suspects from lower socio-economic classes receive harsher treatment than those who are more affluent. Ericson (1982) found that, with minor complaint situations, the police were more likely to provide advice and assistance to lower-status individuals; in more serious cases, the police were more likely to write a report if the complainant was of higher social status.

- **Race.** It is generally suggested by literature from the United States (Rossi, 1974) and Britain (Policy Studies Institute, 1983) that race influences police decision-making. However, in Canada, Griffiths and Verdun-Jones (1994) argue that there is no conclusive evidence that the police discriminate in their arrest practices on the basis of the ethnicity of the suspect, a view contested by others (Forcese, 1992; Harding, 1991). A number of official inquiries have identified conflict between the police and racial minorities. For example, the 1992 Ontario Race Relations and Policing Task Force Report (Lewis, 1992) identified this problem, as have a number of provincial justice inquiries (Hickman, 1989; Hamilton and Sinclair, 1991). In examining testimony to the Quebec Human Rights Commission Report (Bellemare, 1988) on police relations with ethnic minorities, Normandeau (1990) notes that some citizens view the police as unwelcoming to certain ethnic minority groups, that low numbers of ethnic minority police officers creates a climate of harassment and prejudice against minorities within the organization and that low representation means role models are not created for young ethnic minorities. The risk of racial tension increases as the proportion of visible minority groups increases in an area (Normandeau and Leighton, 1990). The high arrest rates for Aboriginal peoples and the ongoing conflicts between ethnic minorities and police in many urban areas (e.g., Montreal and Toronto) suggest the issue of race in Canadian police officers' decision-making, involving both suspects and complainants, justifies further analysis.

- **Age.** This is a further variable that seems to influence police behavior. Research suggests that people under 25 and over 65 are more likely to be sanctioned than individuals in between these two ages, perhaps because young people are more likely to challenge authority, and older citizens have a 'know it all' attitude (Roberg and Kuykendall, 1993).

- **Gender.** Although early research suggested that gender did play an important role in the way police officers treat suspects and complainants, Brooks (1993) argues this is less prominent than was first thought and may be linked with demeanor.

- **Relational difference.** If the relationship between the suspect and the complainant is close, it would appear the police are more reluctant to make an arrest, believing it would create further problems between the parties in the future. The complaint is less likely to be considered a police matter.

- **Preference of the complainant.** While police officers do not always follow the wishes of the complainant, Ericson (1982) found that in one third of cases, they complied totally, in one third, partially, and in the remaining, not at all. Brooks (1993) cites other research showing that police officers do consider the demands of the complainant when deciding what action to take.

The personal characteristics identified by Brooks (1993) are interrelated. For example, demeanor can be a product of gender while socio-economic status and race are often linked. Determining whether one characteristic by itself influences police behavior is a difficult, and perhaps impossible, task to undertake.

In his study of policing in a Canadian city, Ericson (1982) concluded that demeanor, socioeconomic status, race, age, gender and the preference of the complainant all influenced police officer decision-making. Although this research was conducted over 15 years ago in only one area of the country, it does suggest that the characteristics of the suspects and complainants can influence the behavior of Canadian police officers.

Type of call/nature of call. Generally speaking, the more serious the crime, the greater the possibility of a formal, harsher disposition. In addition, property-related crimes, even if minor, have a high rate of official response by the police, primarily because of insurance requirements (Ericson, 1982; Roberg and Kuykendall, 1993).

Visibility of the encounter. It has been suggested that police officers are more likely to respond harshly in a public setting than in a private one. This would appear to be attributable to a number of factors, including the type of crime (which is often more serious), the need to appear in control of the situation and the fact that the encounter is more likely to be police initiated.

Type of police mobilization. Police-initiated activity, or proactive policing, results in arrest, detection and official report writing more often than does citizen-involved or reactive policing. Brooks (1993) attributes this to two factors. Firstly, proactive policing means police officers enter a situation on their own initiative and have to be more forceful and aggressive to gain legitimacy and control. Secondly, if police officers enter a situation on their own, they have obviously made a prior decision that it warrants attention.

Presence of others. The presence of other officers and bystanders influences police behavior. If colleagues are part of the scene, a police officer may behave in a way he/she believes is expected. Roberg and Kuykendall (1993) argue this behavior is important to being accepted into the police brotherhood. There is also evidence to suggest officers working alone make more arrests than those working in pairs, as a single officer feels more need to exert control over a situation.

While situational and neighborhood variables clearly influence police officers' decision-making, they are also subject to organizational pressures that require the officer to handle cases efficiently and effectively. Lundman (1980) shows how officers use their experience to classify police work into two categories: 'real' police work and 'bullshit'. Most police calls for service fall within the second category and include minor traffic accidents, neighbors' disputes, drunken people, barking dogs and are felt by police officers to have little to do with the real purpose of policing. Lundman argues that police officers establish standard ways to deal with these situations. This point is reiterated by Ericson (1982).

Officer variables

Officer variables that influence police behavior include age, experience, education, gender and race. The effect of education and gender on behavior was discussed in Chapter 5.

It is difficult to separate age and experience, as most individuals start police careers in their twenties, and as they grow older, gain more experience. It is contended that less experienced officers work harder, are more aggressive and more punitive than older officers, but older officers produce higher-quality work when this work is measured by the number of convictions (Brooks, 1993).

Due to the small numbers, there is no Canadian research on how the race of a police officer influences behavior. Research on this issue has been conducted in the United States (Banton, 1964; Rossi, 1974), but as the ethnic and cultural diversity there is significantly different to that of Canada, the findings of the research cannot be applied here.

One further variable affecting police officer decision-making relates to the attitudes officers hold. For example, police officers who believe they have citizen support and respect are likely to behave differently than ones who do not have this view. The role police attitude plays in determining behavior towards domestic assault has been shown to affect decision-making. Attitudes towards family violence and women as victims has historically resulted in low arrest rates for such crimes. Although this situation is being addressed, the example illustrates how attitude influences decision-making. To date there has been little research examining police officers' attitudes (Brooks, 1993).

Many different factors, including organizational structures, the nature of the environment, the situation and the characteristics of the police officer, affect police officer discretion and behavior. Much of the information on police discretion is from the United States; there is clearly a need for more Canadian studies.

As illustrated in Chapter 3, policing in Canada is characterized by a variety of different environments, from sparsely-populated rural prairie settlements, to large urban areas, to remote Inuit communities. In addition, municipal and provincial police departments are frequently responsible for a number of ethnically, culturally and economically diverse neighborhoods within their overall jurisdictions. A critical issue is whether police departments should take into consideration the diversity of populations and tailor decision-making to the needs and requirements of each different group or try to develop one policy for all. At present, we are unaware of the extent to which decision-making and discretionary behavior in Canadian police agencies is subject to organizational, situational and environmental variables.

THE CANADIAN CHARTER OF RIGHTS AND FREEDOMS AND POLICE POWERS

Before leaving the topic of police discretion, it is important to briefly discuss the influence that the Canadian Charter of Rights and Freedoms has had on police powers since its enactment in 1982.

Prior to its introduction, the police in Canada enjoyed considerable freedoms and were less constrained than police in many other countries. For example, all evidence, even that which had been obtained illegally, was admissible in court and cases were not dismissed if a police officer had violated an individual's rights. There was also no clear requirement that police officers inform suspects of their legal options and rights. This changed after the Charter. Forcese (1992) shows how three clauses in particular affect police conduct:

- *Section 8*. Everyone has the right to be secure against unreasonable search and seizure.

- *Section 9*. Everyone has the right not to be arbitrarily detained or imprisoned.

- Everyone has the right on arrest and detention to (a) be informed promptly of the reasons therefore, (b) to retain and instruct counsel without delay and to be informed of that right, and (c) to have the validity of the detention determined by way of *habeas corpus* and to be released if the detention is not lawful.

Upon introduction, the Charter was vigorously opposed by many police officers, including the Canadian Association of Police (Marquis, 1991) who actively lobbied against it, believing it would 'Americanize' Canadian law enforcement and unfairly constrain police officers (Forcese, 1992), leaving them to fight crime at a considerable disadvantage (Griffiths and Verdun Jones, 1994). In contrast, commentators such as Ericson (1982) have shown the Charter to have little direct impact on the rights of individual citizens; it exists to ensure a framework of official discretion for the police, enabling them to proceed with their routine social control tasks. Despite this contention, it has been noted (Griffiths and Verdun Jones, 1994) that, after the initial decade, there has been a shift in balance between police powers and those of individual citizens and that this shift has favored the citizen.

This debate demonstrates an ever-present and ongoing tension between police powers and the need to ensure democratic and civil rights, a tension that is continually being addressed and readdressed. The police walk a difficult tightrope in trying to enforce law and order while, at the same time, not violating the rights of the individual. The Charter has undoubtedly influenced their decision-making and powers and can be counted as another factor that affects what they do.

Police behavior is influenced by a number of factors. These factors converge and produce different patterns of discretion in different police departments and police officers, and can be observed in the many facets of police work, the most common and visible being police patrol.

POLICE PATROL

Patrol is considered to be the 'backbone of policing' (Chamelin et al., 1979; Dantzker, 1995; Roberg and Kuykendall, 1993) and can be defined as the deployment of police officers in a given area with the responsibility to prevent and deter crime and provide day-to-day police services. It is the most visible element of the police agency, identifiable by police vehicles and uniformed officers who are the front line and the first point of contact between the community and the organization.

Chamelin et al. (1979) state that police patrol is important, complicated, conspicuous and delicate. Important, because it provides a 24-hour, seven-day-a-week protection and service to the community. Complicated, because it has a vast array of tasks to perform. Conspicuous, because many of these tasks are undertaken in public, and delicate, because officers need to ensure a balance is maintained between the rights of the citizen and the need for law and order.

Although estimates vary on the proportion of police officers who are assigned to patrol, it is proposed that, in the United States, between 50% and 75% undertake this function (Thibault et al., 1990). In Canada, approximately two thirds of police personnel do so (Forcese, 1992), although the proportion can vary significantly among police departments.

The patrol division is important not only for its visibility and contact with the public, but also because it is the starting point for most rookie police officers. It accounts for the greatest number of police personnel and is the most expensive part of the police service, yet patrol officers are the lowest-paid and the least-consulted personnel in the organization (Dantzker, 1995), receiving the lowest status (Alpert and Dunham, 1992). As noted by Forcese (1992):

> They are usually the first on the scene of accidents, crimes and calls for help. Yet their tasks are viewed as the least prestigious, the bottom of the policing order, the assignment for rookies and dead-end older constables (p. 107).

The work is often boring and routine, but regarded as an important way to gain street experience. Many police officers remain in patrol throughout their careers.

In addition to the generalist 'routine' patrol officer who performs a variety of patrol functions, there are specialists who investigate crimes and provide a more focused service by directing efforts at identified problems. Often, a patrol officer is dispatched to the scene of a crime, undertakes a preliminary investigation and then refers the incident to detectives, or others who have more specialized knowledge, for further follow up.

THE GOALS OF PATROL

Historically, the goals of patrol, as outlined by the London Metropolitan Police, were to prevent and deter crime and provide a sense of security to the community. Theoretically, it was believed, patrol eliminated the opportunity for crime by creating a proactive police presence. The police are seen to be doing their job by patrolling and making citizens feel safe. Although deterrence and security were the mainstays of policing in the past (Dantzker, 1995), today, these roles have been expanded. Roberg and Kuykendall (1993) list the goals of patrol as:

- Crime prevention and deterrence.
- Apprehension of offenders.
- Creating a sense of community security and satisfaction.
- Provision of non-crime-related services.
- Traffic control.

The first two goals relate to the law enforcement role of the police, the third and fourth to the order maintenance/service role, while traffic can incorporate any of these roles.

Patrol is undertaken to achieve three related outcomes (Alpert and Dunham, 1988):

- To achieve visibility. The presence of an officer may eliminate the opportunity for someone to commit a crime, also allowing the officer to investigate leads and observe infractions of the law.

- Patrolling allows the police officer to be proactive by determining the opportunities for criminal behavior and initiating preventive strategies to address these potentials. This proactive behavior facilitates contact with the community and encourages cooperation and trust between officer and citizen.

- Patrolling provides the officer with an opportunity to respond or react quickly to calls for service.

THE TASKS OF 'ROUTINE' PATROL

As noted by Wrobleski and Hess (1979) and Dantzker (1995) there is nothing routine about routine patrol, as it includes the vast array of demands and challenges placed on police by the public. What is routine is not the incident itself (be it a traffic stop or a neighbors' dispute), but the procedure used. Training and departmental policies theoretically ensure all officers respond to an incident in an established 'routine' way, but, as discussed above, a number of situational, organizational, environmental and personal factors influence responses. While the procedure used to handle or perform an activity may be routine, each event will itself be different.

Patrol functions can be divided into five categories: preventive patrol, calls for service, administration, self-initiated tasks and directed patrol.

Preventive patrol. In the US, it is estimated that preventive patrol takes about 40% of a police officer's time (Thibault et al., 1990; Wrobleski and Hess, 1979). It involves detecting crime, apprehending criminals, recovering stolen property, maintaining a sense of public security and confidence in the police and satisfying public demands for non-criminal services (Thibault et al., 1990). The theory behind preventive patrol is that highly-visible, mobile patrol units will help prevent crime. This is achieved by uniformed officers moving at random through an assigned area during what is referred to as 'uncommitted time'. Sometimes, priorities are set for preventive patrol; for example, if there has been a series of break and entry offenses in a particular area, officers will be directed to concentrate their uncommitted time in that area.

Preventive patrol is good public relations, as it shows citizens the police are 'out there' doing their job. It also provides a number of non-criminal services to the community.

Calls for service. Calls for service is the single most important element of patrol and requires the police officer to be dispatched to the citizen requesting assistance.

While certain smaller Canadian police departments pride themselves on being able to personally answer every call, the 'no call too small' philosophy, larger urban police departments do not have this luxury and instead, in certain instances, take details over the telephone and do not dispatch a police officer to the scene. It is estimated that 40% of calls could be handled this way (Thibault et al., 1990). Most police departments have a system of prioritizing calls so that, for example, a report of a rape or attempted suicide would justify an immediate response, but one of a burglary or theft of a motor vehicle would be dealt with when time allowed.

Calls for service depend upon the nature of the environment. In rural settlements or small towns with low crime rates, police officers can spend more time with victims or complainants. In contrast, in busier urban areas, police officers may have no time to conduct preventive patrol, as their shifts are stacked with calls for service.

Administrative tasks. Over the recent past, attempts have been made to cut down the amount of time uniformed officers spend on administration. Nonetheless, an issue that constantly plagues police officers is their administrative functions—particularly the paperwork—as numerous forms have to be completed and reports written in the course of their work. It is estimated that police officers in the United States spend one quarter of their time on administrative duties (Wrobleski and Hess, 1979) and, within the RCMP, the preponderance of paperwork and administration has been identified as a particular organizational problem (Seagrave, 1995).

Self-initiated tasks. Officer-initiated activities usually result from observations made while on patrol and involve community relations and crime prevention activities, such as questioning suspicious people, citizen contacts, operating radar and car and vehicle checks. Self-initiated tasks are a form of proactive policing and depend on the individual police officer's initiative and willingness to be involved in such activities.

Directed patrol. Directed patrol can be defined as the allocation of patrol services in a planned and rational manner (Thibault et al., 1990). It is proactive and uses uncommitted time to undertake a specified activity based on problem or crime analysis. By collecting information from field reports, arrest sheets and dispatch logs, supervisors can analyze data and make rational decisions on where to deploy patrols. Instead of police officers randomly patrolling an area, crime analysis is performed to determine if there are any patterns of criminal activity in certain areas, and if so, resources are deployed to these identified locations. For example, in the early 1990s, Edmonton Police Service found through crime analysis that certain areas of its jurisdiction provided very few calls for service, whereas, in other areas, demand was heavy. The Edmonton Police therefore developed a policy of directing patrol to the areas it was most needed. Directed patrol produces more information, heightens citizen awareness of the police and requires the police to be more alert and active (Roberg and Kuykendall, 1993).

Crime analysis can also be used to redesign patrol shifts. Criminal activity increases between 4 p.m. and 2 a.m. and over the weekend. Workload distribution is not equal across time periods, and yet traditionally, police resources have been allocated equally over a 24-hour period. Through crime analysis, police departments are attempting to construct models that respond to these differences. More officers are allocated to work in time periods and areas that historically have initiated more calls for service and fewer officers in periods and areas that are known to be relatively quiet.

SPECIALIZED PATROL

Operations includes not only routine patrol, but also specialized services such as detectives, drug units, fraud investigation units, sexual abuse squads, motor vehicle theft and crime prevention. Both routine patrol and specialized patrol fall under the banner of field operations, where the bulk of police personnel are allocated. Specialized patrol is geared to handling problems that require a coordinated, concentrated effort. The assignment of a specialized unit to a problem is based on an analysis of crime data. These units are seen to have a number of advantages (Thibault et al., 1990).

- Accountability to management over the responsibility for a particular crime problem.
- High morale and teamwork are frequently features of specialized units.
- Improved skills, acquired over a period of time, mean specialized expertise can be called upon by all members of the department.

The relationship that exists between the routine patrol unit and the specialized units is one of potential conflict. Effective communication between the two is vital, but frequently tensions arise over communication (or the lack thereof). The specialized unit has more status within the organization, with officers being allowed to wear civilian clothes and to work on higher profile cases, while the patrol officer is assigned to deal with, to use Lundman's (1980) phrase, 'bullshit' calls. There exists the belief by patrol officers that anything 'interesting' is taken away, leaving them to answer just the routine calls for service. While a patrol officer may identify a problem and carry out the initial or preliminary investigation, if the issue is deemed serious enough, it is the specialists who follow up and develop a case, providing conflict between the plain-clothes and uniform branches (Ericson, 1982). As illustrated by Banton (1964), the behavior of police officers working in specialized areas is characterized as being 'law enforcement', whereas officers doing routine patrol display a 'peacekeeping' role. The division of patrol between routine and specialized functions creates a hierarchical split within the organization, with detectives seen as the elite, and general duty officers as lesser beings (Bryatt, 1989).

METHODS OF PATROL

There are a number of different patrolling methods, the most common being car, foot and bicycle.

Automobile patrol

This is the dominant form of police patrol, providing the police with the greatest flexibility and mobility, allowing for wide coverage of an area and a rapid response. The police car also provides communication with headquarters and CPIC (Canadian Police Information Centre) through the radio and computer and is a means to transport equipment, prisoners, suspects and victims. The car is believed to be the most cost-effective patrol method, but it does distance the police from the community and limits police-community contacts.

When police cars were first introduced, two officers were assigned to each car; however, many police departments now assign only one officer. While officers themselves prefer to work in pairs, American research (Boydstun et al., 1977; Kessler, 1985) suggests that one-person cars are more effective in terms of making arrests, filing crime reports and receiving fewer citizen complaints. They are also more economical.

Foot patrol

Foot patrol is the oldest form of patrol and has the advantage of engendering close citizen contact. The introduction of the two-way portable radio, and now the cellular telephone, has improved the communication capacity of the foot patrol officer. Foot patrols are limited in their mobility and ability to respond rapidly, but are highly visible and are generally deployed in areas of high public concentration (shopping malls, commercial streets). Foot patrols have increased with the development of community policing, drawing strong support from citizens. They have been found to decrease fear of crime and change the nature of police-community contacts, making them more positive and less adversarial. In studying the effects of foot patrol, Kelling (1987) found:

- Fear of crime decreases when foot patrol is added to an area and increases if it is withdrawn.
- Citizen satisfaction with police services is increased when foot patrols are added.
- Police who patrol on foot have a greater appreciation of the community and its residents than those who patrol by car.
- Police who patrol on foot have greater job satisfaction, less fear and higher morale than those who patrol in cars.

Bicycle patrol

Bicycle patrols have become increasingly popular with the introduction of community policing, as they are seen to offer good mobility and interaction with the public. The Canadian climate means that, in most jurisdictions, they exist only in the summertime, but in places such as Vancouver, Victoria and the lower mainland of British Columbia, they are used every day of the year.

Other forms of patrol

Motorcycles are often used for traffic patrol and in highly-congested areas. Well-trained dogs may be used for tracking and apprehending suspects and for searches of buildings; some forces also use horses for patrol in certain areas. Some departments, most notably the RCMP, operate boat and air patrols. These latter forms of patrol are extremely expensive, but ensure a widespread area can be covered and are a necessity for many of the policing tasks undertaken in the remote and rural areas of Canada.

RESEARCH ON PATROL

One of the most widely-quoted and influential studies designed to measure the effectiveness of the police function was the Kansas City Preventive Patrol Experiment (Kelling et al., 1974). The aim of the study was to determine the effect random patrol had on crime rates and the public's perception of safety. Fifteen beats in the south patrol division of Kansas were selected and matched based on crime data, calls for service and population characteristics. These were then divided into five groups, each containing three similar beats. The beats in each group were then assigned three different levels of police patrol:

1. Reactive. No preventive patrol. Police cars entered these areas only when responding to calls for service.
2. Proactive. These beats were assigned two to three times the normal number of patrol units.
3. Control. These beats were assigned the normal number of patrol vehicles (one per beat).

The results of the study showed the three experimental conditions had no effect on crime rates (e.g., burglary, theft of cars, robberies, vandalism), citizens' fear of crime, citizens' attitudes towards the police or rates of reported crime. The research findings fundamentally challenged the dominant philosophy that routine preventive patrol deters crime and fear of crime. The Kansas City experiment found that traditional preventive patrol was not effective and that adding more officers to routine patrol would not reduce crime. The results undermined the very philosophy on which patrol was based. The experiment has been criticized for faulty methodology and flawed design, but succeeded in promoting considerable discussion on the benefits of preventive patrol.

One further piece of research added still more questions to the traditional interpretation of patrol. Until the 1970s, it had always been presumed the police needed to respond rapidly to calls for service in order to apprehend suspects and foster public satisfaction. Considerable research has subsequently shown that it is the citizens' reporting time, not the police response time, that increases the likelihood of arrest. Spelman and Brown (1983) found that in only 2.9% of serious arrest cases could the arrest be attributed to rapid response, while Pate et al. (1976) showed that citizens wait an average of six minutes before reporting a crime. They found citizen satisfaction was based, not on rapid response, but on knowing approximately when an officer would arrive.

Studies questioning the premise of preventive patrol led to a questioning of traditional methods and the development of alternative patrol strategies.

TEAM POLICING

One of the forerunners of community policing, which developed following criticism of traditional patrol methods, was "team" or "zone" policing, introduced into Canada during the early 1970s. The aim of team policing was to restructure the delivery of policing services by moving away from the traditional response-to-call and enforcement model, to one that concentrated on crime prevention and service to the community. It advocated the deployment of officers in well-defined neighborhood areas so their knowledge of one area, and their efforts, increased. Team policing in both Canada and the United States received a great deal of attention when it was initially introduced; however, it met with a number of problems, most notably:

- A staunch resistance by midline managers. Team policing endorsed a decentralization of authority, whereby more autonomy was awarded to the operational officer. Many midline police officers saw this as a loss of power and consequently resisted the change.

- Patrol officers also resisted change, as they felt traditional crime control strategies were being compromised with the introduction of team policing methods.

Despite these criticisms, the concept of team policing illustrated that alternatives to traditional patrol strategies were available. It was also an important precursor to the development and introduction of community policing.

SUMMARY

This chapter has reviewed police behavior, decision-making and patrol. It has shown policing as discretionary behavior, the nature of which is inherently linked to the police role. While a number of organizational and legal constraints are placed upon police officers, they have a considerable amount of discretion in undertaking the task of policing. Ironically, members of the police department with the greatest discretion are those at the bottom of the organizational hierarchy who do routine patrol. In examining the patrol function, it was shown that the greatest number of police officers and the largest proportion of expenditure is dedicated to routine patrol.

Police behavior is subject to a number of interrelated organizational, situational, environmental and personal variables. Police patrol—and the discretion it requires—places a number of demands on the officer and can lead to considerable stress. The issue of police stress is the subject of the following chapter.

QUESTIONS FOR DISCUSSION

1. According to Bayley and Bittner (1993), what are the 'skills of policing' and how are they gained?

2. To what extent can the race of a suspect be said to influence police officer decision-making in Canada?

3. To what extent is it possible to say that the race of a police officer influences police decision-making in Canada?

4. List the various levels of discretion that exist in police organizations.

5. What organizational variables influence police officer behavior?

6. What does Ericson (1982) mean by 'recipe rules' and 'recipes for action'?

7. How has the Charter affected police behavior?

8. What are the tasks of routine patrol?

9. Why does conflict occur between routine and specialized patrol units? Discuss ways in which it could be addressed.

10. What patrol methods are there and which are most effective?

FURTHER READING

Ericson, Richard (1981). *Making Crime: A Study of Detective Work*. Toronto: Butterworths. Richard Ericson is one of the most renowned scholars of Canadian policing. This text details an observational study of detective work in Peel Regional Police Force. He finds it is reactive, rather than proactive, and influenced by organized legitimized structures which help shape definitions and awareness of crime.

Ericson, Richard (1982). *Reproducing Order: A Study of Police Patrol Work*. Toronto: University of Toronto Press. This book interprets police work from an interactionist perspective. Encounters with victims, suspects and colleagues are detailed in order to provide an account of police decision-making, discretion and interpretation of crime.

Rubinstein, Johnathon (1973). *City Police*. New York: Farras, Strauss and Giroux. This book gives a description of the day-to-day work of patrol officers in the Philadelphia Police Department.

REFERENCES

Alpert, Geoffrey A. and Dunham, Roger G. (1988). *Policing In Urban America.* Prospect Heights, Ill.: Waveland Press.

Alpert, Geoffrey A. and Friddell, L. (1992). *Police Vehicles and Firearms: Instruments of Deadly Force*. Prospect Heights, Illinois: Waveland Press.

Banton, M. (1964). *The Police in the Community.* London: Tavistock.

Bayley, David T. and Bittner, Egon (1993). "Learning the skills of policing." In Roger D. Dunham and Geoffrey P. Alpert (Eds.) *Critical Issues in Policing: Contemporary Readings*. Prospect Heights, Illinois: Waveland Press.

Bayley, David H. and Mendelsohn, H. (1969). *Minorities and the Police*. New York: Basic Books.

Bellemare, J. (1988). *Investigation into Relations between Police Forces, Visible and Other Ethnic Minorities*. Montreal: Quebec Human Rights Commission.

Boydstun, J.E., Sherry, M.E. and Moelter, N.P. (1977). *Patrol Staffing in San Diego.* Washington D.C.: Police Foundation.

Broderick, John J. (1987). *Police in a Time of Change*. Prospect Heights, Ill.: Waveland Press.

Brooks, Laure Weber (1993). "Police discretionary behavior." In Roger D. Dunham and Geoffrey P. Alpert (Eds.) *Critical Issues in Policing: Contemporary Readings*. Prospect Heights, Illinois: Waveland Press.

Brown, M.K. (1981). *Working the Street: Police Discretion*. New York: Russell Sage Foundation.

Bryett, Keith (1989). "Police socialization: A reassessment." *Canadian Police College Journal, 13*(4).

Chamelin, Neil C., Fox, Vernon B. and Whisenand, Paul M. (1979). *Introduction to Criminal Justice*. Englewood Cliffs, N.J.: Prentice Hall.

Dantzker, Mark L. (1995). *Understanding Today's Police*. New Jersey: Prentice Hall.

Davis, K.C. (1975). *Police Discretion*. Minneapolis: West Publishing Co.

Ericson, R. (1982). *Reproducing Order: A Study of Police Patrol Work*. Toronto: University of Toronto Press.

Forcese, Dennis P. (1992). *Policing Canadian Society*. Scarborough: Prentice Hall.

Goldstein, H. (1977). *Policing a Free Society*. Cambridge, Mass.: Ballinger.

Griffiths, Curt T. and Verdun Jones, Simon N. (1994). *Canadian Criminal Justice*. Toronto: Harcourt Brace.

Harding, Jim (1991). "Policing and Aboriginal justice." *Canadian Journal of Criminology,* *33*(3-4).

Hamilton, Associate Chief Justice A.C. and Sinclair, Associate Chief Judge C.M. (1991). *Report of the Aboriginal Justice Inquiry of Manitoba. The Justice System and Aboriginal People.* Vol. 1. Winnipeg: Queen's Printer.

Hickman, T.A. (1989). *Royal Commission on the Donald Marshall Jr. Prosecution.* Nova Scotia: Queen's Printer.

Jayewardene, C.H.S. and Talbot, C.K. (1990). *Police Recruitment of Ethnic Minorities.* Ottawa: Canadian Police College.

Kelling, G.L. (1987). *Foot Patrol.* Washington D.C.: National Institute of Justice.

Kelling, G.L., Pate T., Dieckman, D. and Brown, C.E. (1974). *The Kansas City Preventive Patrol Experiment: A Summary Report.* Washington D.C.: Police Foundation.

Kessler, D.A. (1985). "One or two officer cars? A perspective from Kansas City." *Journal of Criminal Justice, 13.*

Lewis, C. (1992). *The Report of the Race Relations and Policing Task Force.* Toronto: Solicitor General.

Lundman, R.J. (1980). *Police and Policing - An Introduction.* New York: Holt, Rinehart and Winston.

Marquis, Greg (1991). Canadian Police Chiefs and Law Reform: The Historical Perspective. *Canadian Journal of Criminology 33* (3-4).

Muir, W.K. (1977). *Police: Streetcorner Politicians.* Chicago: University of Chicago Press.

Murphy, P.V. and Pate, T. (1977). *Commissioner.* New York: Simon and Schuster.

Niederhoffer, A. (1967). *Behind the Shield.* New York: Doubleday.

Normandeau, A. (1990). "The police and ethnic minorities." *Canadian Police College Journal, 14*(3).

Normandeau, A. and Leighton, B. (1990). *A Vision of the Future of Policing in Canada: Police Challenge 2000 - Background Document.* Ottawa: Police and Security Branch, Ministry Secretariat, Solicitor General.

Pate, T., Bowers, R.A., Ferrara, A. and Lorence, J. (1976). *Police Response Time: Its Determinants and Effects.* Washington D.C.: Police Foundation.

Policy Studies Institute (1983). *Police and the People in London.* London: Policy Studies Institute.

Reiner, R. (1978). *The Blue Coated Worker.* Cambridge: Cambridge University Press.

Reiss, A.J. (1971). *The Police and the Public.* New Haven: Yale University Press.

Roberg, Roy R. and Kuykendall, Jack (1993). *Police and Society.* Belmont California: Wadsworth Publishing Company.

Rossi, P., Berk, R. and Eidson, B. (1974). *The Roots of Urban Discontent.* New York: Wiley.

Seagrave, J. (1995). *Changing the organizational culture: community policing in British Columbia.* Unpublished doctoral dissertation. Burnaby, British Columbia: Simon Fraser University.

Shearing, C.D. (1984). *Dial-a-Cop: A Study of Police Mobilization.* Toronto: Centre of Criminology, University of Toronto.

Skolnick, J. (1966). *Justice Without Trial.* New York: Wiley.

Spelman, W. and Brown, D.K. (1982). *Calling the Police.* Washington D.C.: Police Executive Research Forum.

Stansfield, Ronald T. (1996). *Issues in Policing: A Canadian Perspective.* Toronto: Thompson Educational Publishing.

Thibault, E.A., Lynch, L.M. and McBride, R.B. (1990). *Proactive Police Management.* Engelwood Cliffs, N.J.: Prentice Hall.

Van Maanen, J. (1973). "Observations on the making of policemen." *Human Organization, 32.*

Westley, W. (1970). *Violence and the Police: A Sociological Study of Law, Custom and Morality.* Cambridge, Mass.: MIT Press.

Wilson, James Q. (1968). *Varieties of Police Behavior: The Management of Law and Order in Eight Communities.* Cambridge, Mass.: Harvard University Press.

Wilson, O.W. (1977). *Police Administration.* New York: McGraw Hill.

Wrobleski, Henry M. and Hess, Karen M. (1979). *Introduction to Law Enforcement and Criminal Justice.* New York: West Publishing Company.

STRESS AND THE HAZARDS
OF POLICE WORK

INTRODUCTION

The fact that police officers form a unique occupational group in Canadian society has been documented throughout this text. They are called upon to perform a variety of functions, from providing advice and information, to enforcing the criminal law and maintaining order. They are distinctive because of the authority society has vested in them; they can request that citizens follow a certain course of action, arrest them and, in some circumstances, they have the authority to take a life. Policing is a unique job and as such has frequently been acknowledged a stressful occupation.

This chapter examines stress in relation to police officers. After defining the concept, the text reviews the sources of stress experienced and the physiological, psychological and social effects that stress induces. Finally, the various mechanisms that have been introduced to deal with stress are discussed.

An understanding of the concept is important for the management of human resources within the organization and because this understanding may, in part, inform our comprehension of police subculture, discussed in Chapter 6, and police deviance, the subject of Chapter 9. It should be noted that literature on stress and Canadian police officers is rare; consequently, most of the research discussed in this chapter comes from academics from the United States and Britain. Much of the stress experienced by Canadian police officers relates to the nature of the work they undertake, work that is comparable to that performed by their colleagues in other western democracies.

DEFINITIONS OF STRESS

Stress is a term frequently used but rarely defined. It has been described as "...mental, emotional and physical tension" (McDowell, 1993, p. 254), "...the body's non-specific response to any demand placed on it" (Selye, 1974, p. 60) and as "...any event or situation which causes a person to react, either negative-ly or positively...(the) reaction can consist of psychological and physiological adaptations" (Gaines, 1993, p. 539). Physiological stress deals with the biological reactions that occur, such as ulcers, migraines, headaches, heart disease and high blood pressure, while psychological stress is less precise, and refers to anxiety and emotional experiences which can result in clinical depression, drug and alcohol abuse, aggression and suicide.

Stress can be both negative and positive. Selye (1974) identifies positive stress as 'eustress'. This is pleasurable and takes place when, for example, an officer receives an award or promotion. Negative stress, known as 'distress', refers to negative situations, for example, when an officer is reprimanded or has to inform someone about the death of a close relative. The most common and frequent use of the term is in regard to negative situations. This type of stress (distress) can, in turn, be broken down into two groups, referred to as either acute vs. chronic stress (Farmer, 1990), or crippling vs. routine stress (McDowell, 1993). Acute/crippling stress relates to the one-time incidents that occur due to a single traumatic event, such as the death of a colleague, or a shooting. Chronic or routine stress is regarded as the long-term build-up of a number of different factors, resulting from the day-to-day routine nature of the job, which increase gradually over time and are not attributed to any one thing. It is the routine stresses experienced by most police officers that create the most significant problems (McDowell, 1993).

One term frequently employed in the literature on police stress is 'burnout'.

> Burnout occurs when officers have experienced debilitating stress for extended periods of time to the point that they are no longer able to cope. At this point they give up or withdraw (Gaines, 1993, p. 545).

Burnout is a form of physical, emotional and mental exhaustion, resulting from an accumulation of job stress over a period of time, which has had no avenue for release. Symptoms include a dip in energy level, lowered resistance to illness, increased pessimism, reduced sense of humor, social withdrawal and an increase in physical complaints (McDowell, 1993). Forcese (1992) argues the tensions that are endemic to police work are translated into cynicism, suspiciousness, an unwillingness to talk about policing to others and even self-dislike. He characterizes these symptoms as 'burnout'. Officers are also more prone to alcohol abuse. As these symptoms begin to manifest themselves, so can poor job performance.

THE STRESS PROCESS

Selye (1956) has described a three-stage process in adapting to stress, which he termed the General Adaptation Syndrome (GAS). The first stage is alarm, the second, resistance and the third, exhaustion.

- The alarm stage occurs when the individual is totally aroused and confronted with a stressful situation. All resources are focused on the 'stressors', which are the environmental agents or activities powerful enough in their impact to elicit a reaction from the body (Swanson et al., 1993). This is known as the 'fight or flight' response and takes place when a person is exposed to threatening or frightening stimuli (Brown and Campbell, 1994). It results in psychological reactions, such as fear and trepidation, and physiological responses, including adrenaline release. If the situation subsides or dissipates, the individual returns to a state of normality (Gaines, 1993).

- The stage of resistance occurs when the individual adapts to external stressors and the symptoms of stress either increase or are contained. At this stage, attempts are made to bring the effects of the stressors to tolerable levels. If this containment is successful, the stress is overcome, if unsuccessful, the individual will continue to be stressed.

- If the stressors are sufficiently severe or prolonged, the third, exhaustion stage results. Any defenses against stress are removed and the stress becomes dominant. The person can no longer adapt and physiological symptoms as severe as heart attacks and death may result. The exhaustion stage occurs when the individual has been overwhelmed and has no resources to fight the threat (Gaines, 1993).

In discussing these three stages in relation to Canadian police officers, Perrier and Toner (1984) liken Seyle's three stages to the erosion of shorelines, arguing that stress gradually wears down the physical and emotional health of police officers and affects their ability to cope with situations.

RESEARCH ON POLICE STRESS

The media, and to a certain extent police and academics, have argued policing is a stressful occupation. There has been a tendency to present an alarmist perspective with respect to the level of stress in policing (Roberg and Kuykendall, 1993), despite the fact empirical evidence does not support this conclusion (Malloy and Mays, 1984). Webb and Smith (1980) find the evidence is contradictory over whether policing is more stressful than other occupations; for example, Somodeville (1978) stated that policing is the most emotionally hazardous job, whereas French (1975) says the pressures of policing are not that much worse than for other occupations. Brown and Campbell (1994) argue that many of the assumptions about the nature of police stress are based on anecdotal evidence or unempirical statements from police organizations. Forcese (1992) notes that the issue should be not whether the police face more stress than workers in other occupations, but the acknowledgment that stress exists and influences the role police officers are asked to undertake.

In reviewing the literature, Brown and Campbell (1994) draw on the work of Malloy and Mays (1984) and document responses to what they see as the five dominant assumptions about the nature of police work.

1. Police work is inherently stressful. It would appear that policing is inherently stressful, but that a number of individual and organizational factors affect the propensity for stressful situations.

2. Police officers suffer stress to a significant degree. Being exposed to stressors results in a variety of physiological and psychological symptoms; identifying these is difficult. The research would suggest a proportion of police personnel suffers adverse symptoms, but again, this varies among individual officers, police departments and countries.

3. Policing is more stressful than other occupations. This assumption is incorrect. A number of other jobs, such as air traffic control and medicine, have been found to be more psychologically stressful, while mining, construction and agriculture are considered more physically stressful.

4. The police deserve special attention to reduce causes and consequences of stress. Anything that will eliminate or ameliorate stress should be attempted for the well-being of the organization and the individual.

5. Policing will become more stressful in the future. The ever-changing nature of the social, cultural and economic make-up of society, coupled with the technological developments that affect the police department, are likely to introduce new sources of stress.

Stress is, therefore, a serious concern for police agencies; it is important to acknowledge its existence and deal with it effectively. Failure to do so can result in severe consequences for the individual police officer who suffers social, psychological and physiological problems and the department that has to deal with the effects of stress. The effects of stress on the administration of a police department can be manifested in a number of ways. These can be human resource issues such as stress-related absenteeism, long-term sick leave and medical retirement, poor or substandard performance leading to citizen complaints and disciplinary measures, and the creation of an organizational environment that is unconducive to the delivery of good policing services.

SOURCES OF STRESS

A number of studies have been conducted, which examine the perceptions of police officers and nature of police work in order to account for stress. From these, sources of stress have been broken down into four categories (Alpert and Dunham, 1988; Gaines, 1993; Kroes, 1976; McDowell, 1993; Roberg and Kuykendall, 1993; Perrier and Toner, 1984):

1. Organizational and administrative practices, stressors internal to the police department.
2. External stressors evident from outside the police organization.
3. Stressors inherent in the nature of police work—task-related functions or operational stress.
4. Stressors for the individual police officer (personal stressors).

Organizational and administrative stressors

These stressors emanate from the police department itself and include: policies and procedures; poor training, supervision, equipment or pay; internal investigations that examine citizen complaints; excessive paperwork; inadequate career development programs; few rewards or reinforcement systems for good work and overall lack of administrative support. The staffing, organization and administration of police departments contribute to officer stress. Supervision is autocratic and authoritarian; police officers are told to act and behave in a prescribed way by those in management, who are often divorced from the situation itself (Golembiewski and Kim, 1990). The bureaucratic, hierarchical nature of the organization ensures police officers have little input into the development of departmental policies and procedures, even though many of these may lead to stress (McDowell, 1993). Crank and Caldero (1991) found that stressors created within the organization itself were the most frequently cited sources of stress by police officers.

External stressors

The nature of the interaction between the police officer and the environment is an important source of stress. Several stressors have been recognized to come from factors external to the police department. The most notable of these is frustration with the criminal justice system, namely courts and corrections.

Court-specific stressors include the problems of scheduling appearances, court decisions limiting police discretion, being cross-examined and giving testimony, the belief courts are too lenient with offenders, the lack of consideration shown to the police officer by courts, the perceived ineffectiveness of rehabilitation sanctions and the fact that court appearances interfere with work assignments, personal commitments and sleeping patterns (Golembiewski and Kim, 1990; Goolkasian et al., 1985). In studies of police stress, Kroes et al. (1974) found 56% of police officers in the United States reported stress in dealing with courts, while the stressors ranked highest by RCMP members was the frustration of working within the judicial system (Logan, 1995). Furthermore, when police officers see defendants not receiving their full sentence and obtaining probation and parole, they perceive they have little cooperation in fighting crime from the other two components in the criminal justice system.

Another stress-producing factor external to the police environment is the failure to receive cooperation and support from citizens. As illustrated by a number of victims' surveys, many people do not report crimes and are reluctant to involve the police in their lives (Perrier and Toner, 1984). Although most people are supportive of law enforcement, specific groups, such as ethnic minorities, have negative views which can result in poor police-community relations and be a source of stress to the officer.

One further external stressor is the controversial and distorted images of police frequently displayed in the media, forming another source of stress the police cannot control.

Inherent stressors

Also referred to as task-related stressors (Alpert and Dunham, 1988), or occupational stressors (Logan, 1995), this category relates to the duties and responsibilities of police officers. These include job fragmentation, workloads and role conflicts. As discussed in Chapter 4, police officers experience a number of problems defining their mandate and role in society, the most fundamental being the debate over whether they are crime fighters, whose *raison d'être* is to enforce the law, or social workers, involved primarily in service and order maintenance functions. Confusion over what role society expects its police officers to undertake, and how this role is performed, is an inherent form of stress.

Shift work disturbs eating and sleeping patterns and affects social and family life. In working irregular hours, police officers find it difficult to plan for social or family events, a pressure that can lead to conflict in relationships with spouses and family members. Shift work puts a strain on officers and has been recognized by numerous studies to be a major job stressor (Brown and Campbell, 1994), although it is a characteristic found in a number of other occupations.

The constant exposure to suffering and people with problems is another stress-producing factor inherent to policing. Clients of the police are frequently those who occupy the lower socio-economic classes, and who have a number of social problems, such as drug and alcohol abuse, poor financial resources and no family or support network. In perpetually working with the 'underbelly of society' in the course of their day-to-day lives, considerable stress is placed on those police officers assigned to the routine patrol activities that demand high levels of interaction with the public. As noted by Perrier and Toner (1984):

> No other representative of society is available 24 hours a day to provide services such as marriage counseling during disputive family arguments, settling neighborhood disputes, searching for lost children...the common element underlying these daily activities of the police officer is the constant exposure to the stress of others (p. 19).

Boredom and inactivity and the fact that police officers spend long periods of time in routine activity can lead to stress. Both work underload and work overload have been associated with stress. Having 'too much work to do' was identified in a British study, cited by Brown and Campbell (1994), of police upper management as the most likely source of stress.

One further source of stress is fear and danger. In 1994, one police officer was the victim of homicide while on duty in Canada, compared to two in 1993, one in 1992 and three in 1991. In contrast, 76 police officers were killed in the United States while on duty in 1994 (Statistics Canada, 1995). Police officers are taught in the training academy about the dangers inherent to policing and the fact they are constantly at risk (Gaines, 1993). This orientation affects police operations and management philosophy. Officers are trained to treat everyone with suspicion and caution, while at the same time, demonstrating authority and control. Certain situations will engender fear, which is often suppressed because of mistaken beliefs that police officers should not be afraid. The 'macho' image endorsed by the subculture is at odds with what an officer may feel during tense circumstances, but the subcultural pressure to hide emotions and deny fear may be considerable. Failure to acknowledge and address fear may result in stress.

At the most extreme level, police officers experience considerable stress if they have witnessed or used deadly force, as this is the most serious single act a police officer can perform, with far-reaching and irreversible consequences (Yarmey, 1988). Lethal force resulting in death produces a series of psychological reactions. Witnesses typically experience emotional reactions that may be understood in three separate stages (Yarmey, 1988).

1. **Impact stage.** Victims at this stage feel vulnerable and helpless. They experience reactions such as lack of breath, upset stomach, a feeling of weakness, sleep disturbance and loss of appetite.

2. **Recoil stage.** This stage is often described as post-traumatic stress disorder, in which victims feel a loss of equilibrium, have difficulty concentrating, experience guilt and trauma and have a fear of returning to the scene of the event.

3. **Reorganization stage.** This is the stage at which victims reestablish themselves and move beyond the fear and anger emotions. Although flashbacks may occur, they will not be as extreme or debilitating as in the previous stage.

Police officers who witness or undertake a shooting experience shock, but may also be reluctant to face this fact. It could be a considerable time after the event that the officer suffers psychosomatic illnesses such as fatigue, nightmares and flashbacks (Yarmey, 1988).

Inherent stressors were found to be the most prominent concern in a study of RCMP members (Logan, 1995). However, in contrast to studies predominantly from the United States, this Canadian research did not identify issues such as danger or encountering death as high on the list of concerns, probably because of the relative infrequency of these events in Canada.

Individual stressors

These include factors related to police work but outside its immediate scope (McDowell, 1993). It is difficult to provide an assessment of individual stressors, as these are prone to an individual's subjective interpretation; a situation that is profoundly stressful for one person may not be so for another because stress tolerance levels vary significantly from one individual to the next (Goolkasian et al., 1985; Roberg and Kuykendall, 1993). Individual characteristics that can contribute to stress include becoming preoccupied with fear of potential dangers and worrying about competency and performance at work.

If an officer lacks self-confidence or feels insecure, stress may result (Perrier and Toner, 1984). The home and family life of an officer acts as a stressor, as family routine is dictated by the demands of the job. Spouses often live in the shadow of their partner's work, but are not a part of it; problems encountered at work can lead to problems at home, and vice versa.

One final individual stressor is encountered by ethnic minority and female police officers. As discussed in Chapter 5, policing has traditionally been a white male occupation; the relatively recent addition of minority groups has meant they have additional stress to contend with. Non-white officers frequently face resistance and negative perceptions from peers, friends and family and may not be accepted into the 'police family', which is a mechanism of support, camaraderie and occupational identity for other officers. Female officers face similar stressors, which include the questioning of their competence by the police subculture. The policewoman frequently has to act in an environment in which colleagues question her ability to deal with the physical and emotional rigors of policing. Like her male colleague, she must overcome her doubts over performance ability and effectiveness, but unlike him, she has to do it alone (Perrier and Toner, 1984). Research examining sources of stress for policewomen also found sexual harassment among those cited most often (Wexler and Logan, 1983). The sexist culture evident in policing, and the sexism displayed by male colleagues, is an additional concern for female officers.

In discussing stressors and the police occupation, Roberg and Kuykendall (1993) and Brown and Campbell (1994) consider a distinction between stressors unique to policing and those which are shared by other occupations. Many of the stressors reviewed above can be found in other occupations. For example, health professionals, social workers and firefighters all have stressors such as role conflict, inactivity, inadequate or poor resources, work overload and job complexity. In looking at stressors found only in policing, Kroes and Hurrell (1975) identify four.

1. The courts and their treatment of police officers.
2. A negative public image manifested by unfavorable attitudes and a critical media.
3. Racial situations, whereby police officers are in conflict with ethnic groups.
4. Line of duty/crisis situations, incorporating circumstances that pose a threat to the officer's emotional and psychological well-being.

MANIFESTATIONS OF STRESS

As mentioned above, the effects of stress vary among individuals and may broadly be described as physiological, psychological and social in nature.

Physiological

One of the most recognizable areas in which symptoms of stress manifest themselves is in physiological problems. These include a wide range of disorders: backaches, muscle cramps, headaches, asthma, hyperventilation, mouth and gum disease, high blood pressure, ulcers and thyroid disorders. Stress plays an important role in causing these disorders, which frequently result in early medical retirement and absenteeism. This, in turn, presents personnel and financial problems for a police department. The most common ailments found among officers are digestive disorders, respiratory ailments and cardiovascular problems (Alpert and Dunham, 1988). Compared to other occupations, the incidence of physiological illness, such as ulcers, high blood pressure and intestinal viruses, is held to be extremely high among police officers (Goolkasian et al., 1985; Perrier and Toner, 1984), although this finding has been questioned by others (Golembiewski and Kim, 1990).

Psychological

Among the most devastating effects of stress are the psychological problems that can result (Dantzker, 1995). Psychological stress causes symptoms such as anxiety, depression, irritability and mental fatigue. Police officers who are restless, agitated, defensive or preoccupied may be experiencing psychiatric disorders. The most common psychiatric problems found are depression, anxiety and alcohol abuse (Brown and Campbell, 1994). Within the police literature, the psychological stress most frequently addressed relates to alcohol and drug misuse and suicide.

Alcohol and drug misuse. Alcohol and drugs may be used to lessen anxiety and reduce the effects of stress. Brown and Campbell (1994) argue that alcohol or drug use becomes abuse when:

- the individual cannot stop or cut down use.
- work, family and social life is negatively affected.
- the abuse problem has existed for at least one month.

The use of alcohol by police officers has been shown to be part of the police subculture (Van Maanen, 1986) and commonplace among police officers whose environment includes social drinking. In the United States, Kroes and Hurrell (1975) reported that as many as 25% of police officers had alcohol abuse problems, while Alpert and Dunham (1988) showed that some police chiefs indicated half of their officers drank heavily. While normal, or social, drinking does not cause concern, it becomes a problem when drinking affects decision-making and job performance. People who experience stress and who drink learn that alcohol temporarily allows them to escape from their problems. Social drinking may develop into utilitarian drinking when an individual begins to use drinking to alleviate stress (Alpert and Dunham, 1988). High levels of stress, coupled with utilitarian drinking, can lead to a psychological and physical dependence on alcohol known as alcoholism.

Police officers are believed to be at risk from alcoholism because drinking is a norm of the subculture. As illustrated in Chapter 6, police officers frequently socialize together by relaxing after work over drinks. This subcultural norm, coupled with the stressors inherent in the occupation itself, can contribute to alcohol-related problems.

There is little data on drug use and police officers, although, in the United States, police departments have started to use drug testing to screen out applicants with drug use problems. No Canadian data exist.

Suicide. Whether police officers have a higher suicide rate than members of the general population is currently a matter of debate. Forcese (1992) shows, by drawing on media accounts, that police suicide in Canada is six times that of the national average, with officers having a greater risk of death by suicide than in the line of duty. This finding is questioned by Stansfield (1996), who cites research by Stenning reporting that, between 1983 and 1987, the police suicide rate was half that of a comparable group in the general population. In Britain, male police officers have a lower suicide rate than men in other occupational groups (Office of Population Census and Surveys, 1988) and in Australia, the rate is also relatively low (Brown and Campbell, 1994). Research in the United States suggests a different scenario, with some police departments reporting low rates, others high. For example, Dash and Reiser (1978) showed that members of the Los Angeles Police Department had a low suicide rate. This they attributed to:

- the use of thorough physical and psychological screening methods to screen out individuals prone to stress.
- the development of training programs.
- the availability of counseling and mental health services.

In contrast, Wagner and Brzeczek (1983) showed the suicide rate for Chicago Police Department officers was greater than average, while another study found police officers had the second-highest rate when compared to 36 other occupations (Labovitz and Hagedorn, 1971). Reasons advanced for the high suicide rate include the following (Alpert and Dunham, 1988):

- Policing is a male-dominated profession and males have a higher rate of suicide than females.

- The availability of weapons.
- The psychological effects of being exposed to death and serious injury may influence the decision to commit suicide.

The conflicting evidence presented in the studies suggests that no generalization about police officer stress-induced suicides can be made.

Social

Social stress manifests itself in the development of family and personal relationship problems, the most notable of these being marital disorder, divorce and social isolation. The nature of policing causes instability for the families of police officers who have to organize their schedules to accommodate shift work and learn to live with job-related stress. Police officers are involved in a constant engaging and disengaging among the roles of mother, wife, cop or father, husband, cop; this demands cognitive and emotional adjustment (Logan, 1996). Police officers frequently work weekends, holidays and evenings/nights and forfeit taking part in family activities. The nature of the job prevents officers from establishing a 'normal' family life. Spouses often complain of being married to the job, with their lives revolving around the demands of the organization. They must learn to accept the anxiety of having a police officer for a partner and are often called upon to act as therapist and counselor (Alpert and Dunham, 1988), leading to more emotional stress. In addition, as noted by Gaines (1993), citizens have certain standards that they impose on police officers and their families. Consequently, spouses and children are expected to conform to these standards, promoting feelings they are constantly under scrutiny. The effects of police stress as it relates to the officer's family is an under-researched area (Logan, 1996).

Territo and Vetter (1981) list police stressors that contribute to marital and family discord as follows:

- **The over-protection of family members.** Officers are exposed to a variety of depressing and traumatic incidents in the course of their work. This results in them being overprotective of family members.
- **Problems with children.** Children can receive negative reactions from peers because of their law enforcement connection.
- **Hardening of emotions.** Police officers have to suppress their emotions in order to deal with the demands of the work; this characteristic is transferred to their own personal relationships.
- **Sexual problems.** The pressures of police work, coupled with diverse hours, lead to intimacy problems which, in turn, can develop into frustration and anxiety.

As with alcohol-abuse and suicide rates, the argument that divorce is higher for police officers has been advocated by some and contested by others. Terry (1981) reviewed the literature from the United States and concluded divorce rates were lower than the national average. Roberg and Kuykendall (1993) argue that the divorce rate itself is not the issue; instead, it is important to acknowledge that police stressors do lead to family problems which can have an impact on job performance.

One further social problem for police is isolation (Dantzker, 1995). As illustrated in the review of police subculture in Chapter 6, police officers tend to choose their friends from among colleagues and primarily socialize with other police officers. This attribute causes stress, as conversations with fellow police officers ultimately focus on job-related topics. Being a police officer inhibits non-police friendships and ultimately means the officer is never away from the police environment and its stressors.

Kroes et al. (1974) found that the police occupation influences the social aspects of an officer in three ways:

1. by affecting the quality of family and personal life, especially with respect to keeping non-police contacts.

2. by affecting the amount of time spent with children and family and socializing.

3. by generating a negative public image for the family.

DIFFERENTIAL EFFECTS OF STRESS

Stress resulting from performing the duties assigned and from undertaking a poorly-defined role does not affect all in the same way. Police work is not a single homogeneous entity across which stressors are evenly placed (Brown and Campbell, 1994). Many different factors influence who will suffer adverse consequences when exposed to stress and who will be able to mitigate these. Factors which have been examined include: age/experience, gender, occupational characteristics such as rank and specialization, and the availability of social and family support. In a detailed analysis of stress in the RCMP, Logan (1996) found that members reporting the most stress were uniformed constables with between nine and twelve years' experience. Issues of concern were raising children, workload, promotional opportunities, emotionally-draining work and the feeling of being always on duty. These encompass each of the above-named sources of stress (organizational, external, inherent and individual).

Research cited by Gaines (1993) showed that, as police officers pass through different stages of their career, they experience different levels of stress. He draws on the work of Niederhoffer (1967) to illustrate how the four career stages of policing influence the stress levels experienced by officers.

1. **Alarm stage** (0-5 years). During this stage, police officers are exposed to the realities of police work. They experience stress in a number of different ways: through the constraints placed on them by the criminal justice system, through organizational and departmental policies, through the anger and lack of cooperation they face from certain members of the public and through boredom and isolation.

2. **Disenchantment stage** (6-13 years). At this stage, the years of policing and the stress begin to take their toll. Officers may lose interest in their job and experience 'burnout'.

3. **Personalization stage** (14-20 years). This is when police officers learn to cope and accept the stress of the job by focusing on personal and family goals. They attempt to see work as nothing more than a job.

4. **Introspection stage** (20 years and over). Upon approaching retirement, police officers have little stress; they have seen everything and take policing in their stride.

This analysis of different stress patterns relates primarily to officers who remain within the lower levels of the organization. The different ranks engender different types of stress, with higher-ranking officers experiencing organizational and management stressors, and operational police officers experiencing stressors faced in their day-to-day dealings with the public and management. Different units of a department also experience different stressors; for example, detectives are less likely to experience the stress of shift work or dealing with the public than are patrol officers. As previously mentioned, women and other minority groups experience stress that is attributable to their culture and gender characteristics.

In one of the few Canadian studies on police stress and burnout, Burke and Kirchmeyer (1990) argue that individuals who enter policing with different orientations experience varying levels of stress and burnout during their working lives. They draw on a four-part career orientation model advanced by Cherniss (1980) to inform their work.

• **Social activist.** These individuals enter policing to change the status quo and are idealists and visionaries. As the actual experience, realities and demands of policing do not accord with these initial ideals, stress and burnout occur.

• **Self investors.** These individuals choose policing just because it is a job and a way to earn a living. Their primary interests are external to work. They illustrate symptoms of poor 'person-to-job' fit and, consequently, experience job dissatisfaction, alienation and poor physical and emotional well-being later in their careers.

• **Careerist.** These individuals seek work success through prestige, responsibility, financial security and recognition from superiors. They experience the least work/non-work conflict and, compared to the aforementioned categories, have less stress.

• **Artisan.** These individuals seek intrinsic rewards, such as personal development, challenges and obtaining new skills. They are the best suited for the demands of a policing career and are the least susceptible to burnout and its effects.

Burke and Kirchmeyer (1990), therefore, argue that stress is attributable to the orientations police officers have when they enter policing. Research by others has illustrated similar findings (Russo, Engel and Hatting, 1983) and suggests that effective recruit screening methods may reduce stress later on in careers.

STRATEGIES FOR MANAGING STRESS

Canadian police forces have been slow to respond to the problems of stress, tending to treat them as isolated incidents, and have, in the past, been unsympathetic towards officers with stress-related problems (Forcese, 1992). A study of RCMP members found that 57% had no training in stress management (Logan, 1995). Increased awareness of stress-related problems has led to stress reduction programs being introduced (Perrier and Toner, 1984).

There are three strategies police departments can adopt for dealing with an overstressed member (Brown and Campbell, 1994).

1. **Primary prevention.** This involves two approaches: an attempt to eliminate or reduce the sources of stress; and the selection of recruits whose personal characteristics make them relatively immune to the adverse effects of stress.

2. **Secondary intervention.** This involves intervention before psychological problems have a chance to develop and could include debriefings following exposure to a traumatic event and the recognition and treatment of the early symptoms of stress.

3. **Tertiary intervention.** This involves all arrangements for those who are suffering from psychological problems, including counseling services and medical discharge.

In discussing stress-related programs that have developed, Gaines (1993) distinguishes between those that are proactive—aimed to prevent stress—and those that are reactive—designed to deal with the problem once it is identified in the officer.

Proactive stress-reducing programs

Proper screening and refined selection processes have been advocated as a way for departments to select individuals less prone to stress. Applicants who are evaluated in terms of their potential for stress go through a series of psychological tests and background and character investigations. In-depth, thorough selection procedures can benefit the organization in the long run by identifying individuals who are less prone to anxiety.

Training programs that include information on the realities of policing and the stressors inherent to the job alert officers to the various problems associated with policing and better prepare them for the stressful situations they have to face.

Some departments, for example Montreal and Nepean, have experimented with spousal programs in an effort to reduce the stress experienced by police officers and their families. These initiatives inform the officer's partner about the realities of policing and encourage ride-alongs, in which spouses learn first hand about the nature of policing.

Reactive stress-reducing programs

One of the best known and earliest stress-reduction programs was introduced in the Boston Police Department in 1974 by one of its officers, Bill Donovan, who had experienced alcoholism, divorce and suicidal tendencies (Forcese, 1992). It is essentially a counseling program to assist officers suffering from stress and other related problems. Counseling programs that ensure confidentiality for the police officer have been recognized as a way to cope with stress and have been introduced in the form of employee assistance programs (EAPs). These entail establishing a counseling centre away from the police department to which officers can be referred by management, or attend independently, to seek help (Gaines, 1993).

An initiative by the RCMP incorporates both reactive and proactive strategies. In the 1980s, the force introduced psychological services for its employees (Loo, 1985; 1987). This initiative emphasized a preventive approach, advancing a number of strategies for promoting and maintaining the psychological well-being of members. These initiatives included:

- The use of psychological procedures for recruitment and selection.
- Education about mental health incorporated into recruit and officer training.
- Regular examinations and check-ups.
- Psychological assessments before and after particularly stressful duties.
- Introduction of an employee assistance program.

Other police forces, for example, in Calgary, also employ psychologists to attend to mental health problems related to policing (Forcese, 1992). Many forces, including the RCMP, have introduced stress leave and integrated stress management education into existing training courses, while the Canadian Police College has developed three training videos on police stress (Logan, 1995).

SUMMARY

This chapter has reviewed the issue of police stress and shown that there are a number of different factors that contribute to this condition. Much of the research about the extent, nature and effects of stress is inconclusive, but it would appear that police officers are susceptible to a number of different stressors throughout the course of their careers. Some of these stressors will be dealt with effectively by the officer, while others may result in social, physical or psychological problems and require treatment if they are not to lead to long-term harm for both the individual and the department.

QUESTIONS FOR DISCUSSION

1. What is the difference between positive and negative stress?
2. Describe Seyle's (1956) General Adaptation Syndrome.
3. How does burnout differ from stress?
4. Describe some of the physical symptoms that stress can create.
5. Is police work more stressful than other occupations?
6. What stressors external to the police agency promote stress for officers?
7. In what way does the family of a police officer experience stress?
8. At what stage in their career do police officers experience the most stress? The least?
9. Describe reactive stress-reduction programs.
10. What stressors are unique to policewomen?

FURTHER READING

Brown, Jennifer M. and Campbell, Elizabeth A. (1994). *Stress and Policing: Sources and Strategies*. Chichester, West Sussex: John Wiley and Sons Ltd. This recent book provides a comprehensive discussion of the sources and consequences of stress experienced by those who work in law enforcement and draws on studies from a number of western democracies to inform its analysis.

Kroes, W.H. (1976). *Society's Victim, the Policeman: An Analysis of Job Stress in Policing*. New York: Charles C. Thomas. This text discusses the major stressors police officers face and distinguishes between those unique to policing and those also experienced in other occupations. Stressors unique to police management are also reviewed.

REFERENCES

Alpert, Geoffrey A. and Dunham, Roger G. (1988). *Policing In Urban America*. Prospect Heights, Ill.: Waveland Press.

Brown, Jennifer M. and Campbell, Elizabeth A. (1994). *Stress and Policing: Sources and Strategies*. Chichester, West Sussex: John Wiley and Sons Ltd.

Burke, Ronald J. and Kirchmeyer, Catherine (1990). "Initial career orientations, stress and burnout in policeworkers." *Canadian Police College Journal*, 14(2).

Cherniss, C. (1980). *Professional Burnout in Human Service Organizations*. New York: Praeger.

Crank, J.P. and Caldero, M. (1991). "The production of occupational stress in medium sized police agencies: A survey of line officers in eight municipal departments." *Journal of Criminal Justice, 19*.

Dantzker, Mark L. (1995). *Understanding Today's Police.* New Jersey: Prentice Hall.

Dash, J. and Reiser, M. (1978). "Suicide among police in urban law enforcement agencies." *Journal of Police Science and Administration, 6.*

Farmer, R.E. 1990. Clinical and Managerial Implications of Stress Research on the Police. *Journal of Police Science and Administration 17.*

Forcese, Dennis P. (1992). *Policing Canadian Society.* Scarborough: Prentice Hall.

French, J.R.P. (1975). "A comparative look at stress and strain in policemen." In W.H. Kroes and J.J. Hurrell (Eds.) *Job Stress and the Police Officer: Identifying Stress Reduction Techniques.* Washington D.C.: Department of Health Education and Welfare.

Gaines, Larry K. (1993). "Coping with the job stress in police work." In Roger G. Dunham and Geoffrey P. Alpert (Eds.) *Critical Issues in Policing.* Prospect Heights, Illinois: Waveland Press.

Golembiewski, Robert T. and Kim, Byong-Seob (1990). "Burnout in police work: Stressors, strain and the phase model." *Police Studies: The International Review of Police Development, 13(2).*

Goolkasian, Gail A., Geddes, Ronald W. and DeJong, William (1985). *Coping with Police Stress.* Washington D.C.: National Institute of Justice.

Kroes, W.H. (1976). *Society's Victim, the Policeman: An Analysis of Job Stress in Policing.* New York: Charles C. Thomas.

Kroes, W.H. and Hurrell, J.J. (1975). *Job Stress and the Police Officer: Identifying Stress Reduction Techniques.* Washington D.C.: Department of Health Education and Welfare.

Kroes, W., Margolis, B. and Hurrell, J. (1974). "Job stress in policemen." *Journal of Police Science and Administration, 2.*

Labovitz, S. and Hagedorn, R. (1971). An analysis of suicide rates among occupational categories. *Sociological Inquiry 41.*

Logan, Matt (1995). "A systems application to stress management in the RCMP." *RCMP Gazette, 57(11-12).*

Loo, R. (1985). "Police development for psychological services in the Royal Canadian Mounted Police." *Journal of Police Science and Administration, 13.*

Loo, R. (1987). *Police Stress and Social Supports.* Paper presented at the 48th Annual Convention of the Canadian Psychological Association, Vancouver B.C.

Malloy, T.E. and Mays, G.L. (1984). "The police stress hypothesis: A critical evaluation." *Criminal Justice and Behaviour, 11.*

McDowell, Charles P. (1993). *Criminal Justice in the Community.* Cincinnati, Ohio: Anderson Publishing.

Niederhoffer, A. (1967). *Behind the Shield: The Police in Urban Society.* New York: Doubleday.

Office of Population Census and Surveys, (1988). *Occupational Mortality.* Series DS No 6. London: HMSO.

Perrier, David C. and Toner, Reginald (1984). "Police stress: The hidden foe." *Canadian Police College Journal, 8*(1).

Roberg, Roy R. and Kuykendall, Jack (1993). *Police and Society.* Belmont California: Wadsworth Publishing Company.

Russo, Philip A., Engel, Alan S. and Hatting, Steven H. (1983). "Police and occupational stress: An empirical investigation." In Richard E. Bennett (Ed.) *Police at Work: Policy Issues and Analysis.* Beverly Hills: Sage.

Selye, H. (1956). *The Stress of Life.* New York: McGraw Hill.

Selye, H. (1974). *Stress Without Distress.* Philadelphia: Lippincott.

Somodevilla, S.A. (1978). "The psychologists role in the police department." *Police Chief, 39.*

Stansfield, Ronald T. (1996). *Issues in Policing: A Canadian Perspective.* Toronto: Thompson Educational Publishing.

Statistics Canada (1995). "Homicide in Canada 1994." *Juristat 15*(11). Ottawa: Statistics Canada.

Swanson, Charles R., Territo, Leonard and Taylor, Robert W. (1993). *Police Administration: Administration, Processes and Behaviour.* New York: Macmillan Publishing.

Territo, L. and Vetter, H.J. (1981). *Stress and Police Personnel.* Boston MA: Allyn and Bacon.

Terry, W.C. (1981). "Police stress: The empirical evidence." *Journal of Police Science and Administration, 9.*

Van Maanen, J. (1986). "Power in the bottle. Informal interaction and formal authority." In S. Srivasta (Ed.) *Executive Power.* San Francisco: Jossey-Bell.

Wagner, M. and Brzeczek, R.J. (1983). "Alcohol and suicide: A fatal connection." *FBI Law Enforcement Bulletin.* August.

Webb, S.D. and Smith, D.L. (1980). "Police stress: A conceptual overview." *Journal of Criminal Justice, 8.*

Wexler, J.G. and Logan, D.D. (1983). "Sources of stress among women police officers." *Journal of Police Science and Administration, 11.*

Yarmey, A. Daniel (1988). "Victims and witnesses to deadly force." *Canadian Police College Journal, 12*(2).

POLICE DEVIANCE, ACCOUNTABILITY AND CONTROL

INTRODUCTION

Police organizations can be asked to justify their actions with regard to legal and fiscal concerns, policy goals and policing objectives. Police officers can be accountable to an element within their own organizational structure, to a government department or, more broadly, to the community they serve. This chapter examines the issue of accountability. It commences with a discussion of police deviance, what it is, why it exists, its extent and nature and how it is addressed. The text then considers police accountability and examines the internal and external mechanisms in place to monitor, restrict and control police services.

DEFINITIONS OF POLICE DEVIANCE

Police actions are controlled by a number of different rules and regulations. Some are formally written down in the Criminal Code and various Police Acts (see Appendix A and B), while others are undocumented and exist in the expectations society—and the police department itself—has for officers. The rules and regulations constraining police behavior exist in a variety of formats. For example, the Criminal Code contains rules for the police use of deadly force, detailing formal rules to which the police are subject. Police Acts also contain the same guidelines, but, in addition, include rules governing neglect of duty, insubordination, discreditable conduct and dress, thus incorporating controls relating to legally-relevant behavior, organizational expectations and personal conduct. Furthermore, although not formally articulated, rules relating to demeanor and police-citizen interaction are prescribed by society, which expects officers to maintain certain ethical standards. Police deviance refers to behavior that violates any of these norms (Ellis, 1987) and, therefore, covers a wide range of activities from minor infractions of departmental policies, to engaging in criminal activities.

Standards of police behavior can be derived from three perspectives: ethical, organizational and legal (Roberg and Kuykendall, 1993). Ethical standards are linked to morality and concern an individual's moral values, including integrity and responsible behavior. If a police officer does not hold moral and ethical standards, he/she may be more prone to deviant behavior. Organizational standards are established by individual police departments, police boards and commissions, while legal standards are outlined in substantive and procedural law. Police deviance may involve an infraction of any one of these.

Barker and Carter (1987) describe police deviance as: "...a generic description of police officer activities which are inconsistent with the officer's legal authority, organizational authority and standards of ethical conduct" (pp. 2-3). This provides a broad definition that can be dissected. Obviously, some forms of police deviance are of little consequence to either the police organization or the public (for example, an untidy or unshaven officer) yet still violate regulations of the organization. This behavior is clearly different from that classed as a serious violation of rules and regulations, such as corruption or excessive use of force. An important distinction exists between behavior that is tolerated, or receives only minor reprimands from the organization, and behavior that fundamentally breaches the trust society has placed in police. Therefore, in discussing police deviance, a wide range of activities can be included, some involving only minor infractions, and others representing serious forms of deviance.

THEORIES OF POLICE DEVIANCE

Sherman (1974) developed a useful typology to distinguish different levels of corruption that exist at different levels of the police organization: rotten apples and rotten pockets; pervasive unorganized; and pervasive organized.

Rotten apples and rotten pockets

This theory purports that police corruption is limited to a small number of police officers who were probably dishonest prior to their employment within law enforcement. The 'rotten apple' is the one officer engaged in deviant behavior; the 'rotten pocket' refers to a few officers who engage in corrupt activities as a group. This type of deviance has little or no organization, is not tied to organizational structure and receives no support from administrators or managers (Alpert and Dunham, 1988).

The 'rotten apple' theory is the one advanced most frequently by police leaders and by the police themselves, when indiscretions come to light (Alpert and Dunham, 1988; Ellis, 1987). Society, too, may be more willing to accept this interpretation, not wanting to believe corruption extends further than one or two officers.

Pervasive unorganized

The pervasive unorganized level of corruption takes the rotten apple level one step further by suggesting deviance and corruption are not limited to a few, but that a number of police officers are actively and passively involved in corrupt activities. Even though the number of police officers involved has increased, the corruption is characterized by its unorganized and independent nature. A greater number of police officers may be involved, but they are not acting in a coordinated way.

Pervasive organized

For corruption to become organized, every level of command and a large number of police officers must be involved. While pervasive unorganized deviance is learned through informal socialization processes, pervasive organized deviance is formally taught by the police organization; consequently, it is the most serious form of police misconduct. Organizational deviance occurs when police misconduct violates external expectations of what a department should be doing, but, simultaneously, is supported by peers, the police subculture and the internal operating norms of the organization itself (Lundman, 1980). Misconduct that is a characteristic of the police organization, environment and subculture has been referred to as 'organizational police deviance' (Shearing, 1981).

The rotten apple theory of police deviance was prevalent in the 1960s and 1970s. Following media reports of wide-scale corruption, there has been a reluctant acknowledgment that pervasive unorganized, and perhaps pervasive organized, police deviance has been a feature of certain Canadian police forces in the past. Indeed, Forcese (1992) provides numerous accounts of every level of police deviance occurring in Canada.

Theoretically, the rotten apple or psychological interpretation has been severely criticized by sociologists, who emphasize the social determinants of police deviance (Ellis, 1987). Instead of seeing it as attributable to the personality traits of one individual, they believe it results from a number of different factors, including subcultural pressures, organizational laws, department rules and the presence of groups in society who want the police to perform a variety of roles.

As illustrated before, the police subculture acts as a powerful force in the socialization of police officers, by teaching those new to policing the norms and expectations of the police department. A police officer's identity is developed through a process that includes social isolation from the community, coupled with support from the subculture. The officer is, therefore, subject to intense peer group influence and control, which can include the acceptance of deviant behavior.

REASONS FOR POLICE DEVIANCE

A number of reasons can be advanced explaining why police misconduct exists and why, in many respects, it is almost inevitable. The seminal work on this issue was conducted by Sherman (1974) in *Police Corruption: A Sociological Perspective*. He and others showed that a number of factors make corruption and deviance possible.

- The large number of police officers. This ensures the inevitability that a few will be deviant. Statistically, it is reasonable to expect a proportion will misbehave, as would be the case in any organization.

- As illustrated in Chapter 7, a lot of police work is undertaken without direct supervision. The low visibility of patrol officers' actions encourages the opportunity for misbehavior. Likewise, most incidents of police patrol are neither visible nor known to the public, facilitating the opportunity for deviance.

- The complex task of policing, which incorporates law enforcement, order maintenance and service functions, and yet places strict limits on the powers of the police, can lead to misconduct. Shearing (1981) argues that police misconduct in Canada is attributable in some part to the complexity and ambiguity of the modern police role and the strain that places on police.

- Both the discretionary power of the police and the nature of the work provide police officers with numerous opportunities to partake in deviant behavior. The nature of police work, especially the law enforcement component, is adversarial. The fact that complaints arise from such interactions is not surprising (Wagner and Decker, 1993). Any time an officer is called upon to exercise discretion, the possibility of deviance exists.

- Contacts formed during the course of their work with deviant and criminal subcultures can introduce the officer to deviance.

- The police subculture exists as a powerful mechanism of group solidarity which—while not overtly sanctioning—is reluctant to openly recognize and condemn deviance. Sherman (1974) refers to this as a 'code of secrecy' that contributes to the opportunity structure for police deviance. New recruits are socialized into a system that teaches the values and norms of policing and may include corruption and deviance.

- Police managers are part of the police subculture, having worked their way up the ranks. Consequently, they have the same code of secrecy, making it difficult for supervisors to objectively monitor police deviance.

- Although the status and economic reward of a police career have improved over the recent past, police officers continue to believe they are underpaid and undervalued by society. This creates a rationality for corruption and lawbreaking.

TYPES OF POLICE DEVIANCE

Police deviance can be broken down into three broad, overlapping categories: police misbehavior; police corruption; and police abuse of power.

Police misbehavior

Police misbehavior, or misconduct, refers to violation of organizational rules and regulations, standards, or policies and procedures and includes offenses such as improper dress or untidiness, sloppy work habits, damage to police property, neglect of duty, insubordination, discreditable conduct and abuse of authority. Police officer behavior is expected to accord with societal values and norms. Therefore, actions that contradict this, such as racism, sexism and discrimination, are deemed inappropriate.

Police misconduct may also be described as 'conduct unbecoming to a police officer' (Forcese, 1992); this behavior may not violate public norms, but is regarded as unsuitable. For example, drunkenness or engaging a prostitute may not be practices widely condemned by the public, but they are deemed unsuitable for a police officer and invoke disciplinary measures. Police officers must be exemplars in personal conduct, and therefore, are subject to more stringent controls than individuals in other occupations.

Police corruption

Corruption has been defined in a variety of ways by different commentators; for example, Sewell (1985) defines it as where the police act as a group for personal gain. Most others see it as an activity engaged in either by police officers acting alone or as a group. Shearing (1981) defines it as behavior that results in private gains at the public's expense, while Forcese (1992) describes it as the acceptance and extortion of benefits by the police, who use their position to engage in crime for profit. As with misbehavior, there are many levels of corruption. Dantzker (1985) has identified three: graft, criminal activity and administrative practices.

Graft is often referred to as gratuities, and is the acceptance of something of value by the police officer. Gratuities can be in the form of free coffee or meals, free admission to a movie or event, or a small gift. Many police departments have explicit policies that preclude accepting gratuities and the practice has been deemed unethical by the International Association of Chiefs of Police (Roberg and Kuykendall, 1993). It is unknown to what extent the practice exists in Canada today, although the formal policy is that police officers can accept nothing (Sewell, 1985).

Members of the public give police gratuities to show appreciation for the job they do and to ensure that police officers frequent their businesses, allowing the business to receive more protection. Some have applauded this practice, arguing these gifts are voluntary and the police should freely accept minor gratuities, as they are the building blocks of positive social relations between themselves and the public (Kania, 1988). Others illustrate that their acceptance leads to unfairness in police services, as one area receives more policing than another. This is unjust; as everyone pays taxes, police services should be equal. It is also held that this practice may lead to other, more serious, forms of corruption. The acceptance of gratuities is a low-level form of corruption and has occurred in the past. For example, in the 1970s, a number of Toronto fast-food restaurants reported giving free coffee and meals to police officers. Following reports in the media, the chief of police ordered the practice to stop (Forcese, 1992).

An important distinction needs to be made between accepting gratuities, which are gifts to the officer without any form of payback, and bribery, which is an arrangement between a police officer and a citizen whereby the officer does not enforce the law in return for some financial, sexual or other reward. While minor forms of gratuities are often accepted and do not involve a significant breach of organizational policies, the acceptance of bribes is a serious matter.

The second type of corruption identified by Dantzker (1995) is criminal activity. This may occur in one of two ways: by an officer appropriating goods or money during the course of an investigation, or by the actual commission of an offense. The appropriation of money or merchandise is the more common activity, and includes retaining drugs or money during a seizure or arrest, failing to turn in confiscated goods and the removal of goods from the scene of a crime (Dantzker, 1995). These crimes occur because of the opportunistic situation officers find themselves in. In addition, officers may engage in criminal activity because of privileged information at their disposal.

The third type of police corruption is the one that is most difficult to identify and relates to the administration of justice. Police officers may decide not to investigate certain events or individuals because of personal liaisons, or may overtly hinder investigations or make deals to stop them for a variety of political and personal reasons. They may also tell lies in court or to police commissions and inquiries to protect fellow officers (Ellis, 1987). Interfering with the course of an investigation is a form of administrative corruption, as is perjury.

It is important to note that the fallout caused by police deviance extends beyond the department itself. It facilitates criminality, decreases law enforcement and reduces public confidence in the police, inhibiting citizen cooperation with crime prevention measures (Murphy and Caplan, 1993).

POLICE MISUSE OF FORCE

Police misuse of force is an issue of paramount concern in policing democracies. There have been incidents of police misuse of force in many metropolitan areas (e.g., Vancouver, Toronto and Montreal) and they have become the subject of heated debate, with far-reaching consequences. For example, in 1992, a black man was fatally shot in Toronto by a police officer; this incident led to a street riot (Stansfield, 1996), and in 1994, during the Stanley Cup hockey celebrations which got out of hand in Vancouver, a man was shot and wounded by a police officer. Incidents such as these illustrate the delicate and emotive issues surrounding the use and misuse of force.

In attempting to enforce the law, police officers may resort to some form of coercion, which can be defined as the use of deception, threats or force to obtain information or compliance. Roberg and Kuykendall (1993) note that there are four types of coercion.

1. **Verbal coercion.** The use of deceit, threats, promises and derogatory language.

2. **Physical coercion.** The use of the officer's physical strength, for example, neck restraints.

3. **Non-lethal coercion.** The use of a weapon in addition to the officer's strength, for example, pepper spray, capsicum spray, baton, police dog.

4. **Lethal coercion.** The use of a deadly weapon in such a manner that a person is likely to be injured or killed—usually by a firearm.

These various levels of authority and coercion can be either appropriate or not depending on the encounter as determined by law, organizational policies and community expectations. Police officers are taught to assess a situation and select appropriate action, progressing as necessary to the last option, the use of firearms and deadly force. They are taught to use the least violent option initially and, if this is unsuccessful, proceed to the next level (Oppal, 1994). For the police officer, there are numerous anomalies for which few organizational policies and procedures exist. As each encounter is different, strict guidelines governing when each level of coercion is appropriate are difficult to legislate. As shown previously, policing is a discretionary activity, and often the guidance given with regard to non-lethal force is vague.

Police brutality is defined as excessive force, as determined by organizational policies and procedures, or perceived by citizens to be excessive. Physical abuse, or excessive force, occurs when an officer uses more force than is necessary, which may or may not result in physical injury. For example, in arresting a suspect, a police officer may put handcuffs on too tightly, causing discomfort but not injury. This is an instance of abuse of power. Forcese (1992) lists three reasons why the police engage in excessive use of force.

1. Police training policies have traditionally focused on working-class males who come from an environment that supports aggression and violence.

2. Police training is based on the military model and emphasizes the use of force.

3. The working environment of the police officer frequently promotes encounters with individuals who are prone to violence and who may become violent, requiring the use of physical coercion.

In addition, Forcese (1992) comments the increasing presence of police paraphernalia acts as a form of self-fulfilling prophecy, and illustrates how the use of full riot gear can lead to an escalation in the perceived seriousness of a matter and an abuse of power. The relatively recent development of tactical squads designed to deal with extremely unusual incidents is another example of this development which may lead to an increased propensity to use excessive force for incidents that previously would have been dealt with differently.

To ensure accountability, some police forces (e.g., Ontario, Edmonton, Calgary, Saskatoon) require officers to complete a use of force report form to assess the extent and nature of police use of force in their organizations. Criteria for the use of these forms varies. Some are required when, for example, an officer discharges a firearm, points a firearm, uses a weapon, injures a person through force, uses a vehicle to chase someone or uses a dog to arrest someone. While some police departments require officers complete these forms, others do not (Oppal, 1994).

POLICE DEVIANCE IN CANADA

Police agencies in the United States have a long history of corruption, dating back to the beginning of the century, and still evident today. Well-publicized cases, such as the video recording of the beating of a black man, Rodney King, by the Los Angeles Police Department and the subsequent inquiry, suggest deviance is a far greater problem in the US than it is in Canada. Canadian accounts of 'the dark side of policing' (Ellis, 1987) are not as numerous as those from the US, and range from those that dismiss it as a non-issue to those purporting that every police agency is harboring some form of deviance. Sewell (1985) accords with this first category. In writing about police deviance, he dismisses a vast amount of police officer wrongdoing by stating:

> When an officer acts for his own personal gain or satisfaction, such as pocketing money found during a search, it is referred to as misbehavior. This kind of individual deviance can occur in any bureaucracy and nothing further needs to be said about it here (p. 181).

Sewell presents the startling opinion that what occurs everywhere but is still a crime does not warrant attention when undertaken by a police officer. In contrast, Forcese (1992) provides numerous details from press reports during the 1970s and 1980s illustrating every level of police corruption (individual, pervasive unorganized and pervasive organized), while Ellis (1987) selects a few notable examples to illustrate that police deviance does occur. He argues that the Canadian evidence of police deviance illustrates four things:

- It is a recurring pattern of activity, not an isolated phenomenon.
- Supervisory officers condone illegal activity by not doing more to investigate it.
- Police officers often justify their actions by referring to their 'good intentions'.
- Illegal activity by police officers is widely distributed across Canada.

Canada's most famous incident of police misconduct occurred in the 1970s and resulted in two public inquiries: the Keable Commission and the McDonald Commission. In 1974, a corporal of the RCMP Security and Intelligence Branch injured himself while planting a bomb outside the Montreal home of a supermarket executive. Subsequent inquiries into the actions of the RCMP noted a number of illegalities, including many that were established RCMP departmental practices rather than isolated incidents, such as opening private mail, burglary, theft and arson (Forcese, 1992; Mawby, 1990). It was also shown that the RCMP had been assisted by the Quebec Provincial Police and the Montreal Urban Community Police. This form of police deviance became known as 'dirty tricks' and resulted in the removal of surveillance on Canadian citizens from the mandate of the RCMP. A civilian body, the Canadian Security and Intelligence Service (CSIS), was given this power.

Obtaining statistics and data about police deviance and corruption is difficult. Police misconduct that breaches organizational policies is treated in an informal way within the organization (Kean, 1992). The dominant police subculture and 'brotherhood' has aimed to keep issues of police misconduct, whatever the scale, as internal matters. Consequently, more serious issues only come to light through public pressure and media reports. These media reports can be the catalysts to public inquiries, as was the case in 1993, when the government of British Columbia established a commission of inquiry into policing (Oppal, 1994) following two particularly alarming use of force incidents by lower mainland police departments. One other mechanism, developed over the last twenty years, is the process of civilian review introduced to ensure that public complaints about the police are dealt with effectively.

CONTROLLING THE POLICE

Mechanisms for ensuring accountability and control can be divided into two categories, internal review processes and external review processes. Internal review processes refer to those policies and procedures that exist in individual police departments and are enforced through a chain of command; they include internal affairs, discipline boards and command and management supervision. External review procedures relate to agencies, such as police boards, police commissions and public inquiries, external to police organizations which monitor police agencies. In addition to these two categories, civilian review bodies exist and can be characterized as either internal or external review processes.

THE CIVILIAN REVIEW PROCESS

As a concept, civilian review involves the creation of a group of civilians to review instances of alleged police misconduct (Alpert and Dunham, 1988). While this form of accountability is popular with the public, the police have resisted the intrusion into what they deem their exclusive area of expertise. Reasons for this resistance include the need for secrecy; civilian oversight compromises police operations, which frequently have to be secret. In addition, there is the belief that only those who have been police officers can understand the intricate and diverse problems police officers have to deal with. Opponents of civilian oversight also argue the police are well versed in matters of law and procedure and are in the best position to render competent decisions on complaints, and state further that the use of civilians will mean the process will lack credibility with police officers (Wagner and Decker, 1993). Despite this resistance, civilian review boards have flourished as public demand for accountability from law enforcement agencies has grown.

The aim of the civilian review process is to ensure police accountability. Fyfe (1985) lists the objectives of the process as follows:

- To determine whether individual complaints against an officer are founded and, where appropriate, take disciplinary or corrective action.
- To identify patterns of wrongdoing by officers who are subject to a number of complaints.
- To provide feedback to the chief and the organization about police policies and procedures.
- To demonstrate police credibility and responsiveness to the public by showing them grievances are taken seriously.

A number of authors (Grant, 1992; Goldsmith, 1988; Oppal, 1994; Wagner and Decker, 1993) have discussed the various models that can be implemented for dealing with police-citizen complaints. Grant (1992) provides five alternatives for dealing with the issue.

1. The 'in-house' model. In this instance, the task of recording the complaint, investigating it and recommending a course of action is in the hands of the police with no civilian oversight.

2. The externally supervised 'in house' model. In this example, the investigation and adjudication of the complaint are undertaken by the police, but at the end of the process, the entire procedure is reviewed by an individual external to the police department to ensure the case received just and fair treatment.

3. The police investigation with independent adjudication model. Here, the investigation is conducted by the police but, once completed, the adjudication is in the hands of a body independent of the police.

4. The independent investigation with police adjudication model. This model advocates that the investigation of a complaint be undertaken by individuals employed specifically for the purpose under the control of an ombudsman, who reports back to the chief with recommendations. The final disposition is in the hands of the police.

5. The truly independent model. In this model, the entire procedure is carried out externally to the police. The chief would be informed of the outcome of the investigation, but would have no authority to disagree with it.

Model five, therefore, gives the greatest public involvement in the complaints procedure and model one, the least.

Metropolitan Toronto was the first city in Canada to create a Public Complaints Commission (PCC) following a series of misconduct scandals and official inquiries (Goldsmith, 1988). It represented the most striking concession to the perceived need for greater civilian involvement in policing (Goldsmith and Farson, 1987). The seeds of this form of civilian review were sown in 1972, when the Ontario provincial government introduced legislation to enable the establishment of civilian review boards anywhere in the province. The legislation was abandoned following unanimous opposition by the chiefs of police in Ontario (Forcese, 1992).

In December 1981, a three-year pilot project was initiated to improve methods of processing complaints by members of the public against police officers on the Metropolitan Toronto Police Force (Ellis, 1987). In 1984, the Metropolitan Police Force Complaints Act came into effect, ensuring a formal procedure whereby complaints against the police could be heard. Prior to the creation of this body, an individual had to complain directly to a Toronto police officer. The Public Complaints Commission consists of a staff of investigators, clerks and lawyers. The procedure by which a member of the public submits a complaint follows a predetermined path (Sewell, 1985).

- A complaint is filed with the police or with the PCC.
- The police begin an investigation, and must report, in writing, within thirty days to the PCC and to the complainant on the course of the investigation. If the investigation has not been completed, the report must detail its state; if it has been completed, the complainant is told of the disposition. Police investigators gather evidence and a senior police officer independent of the investigation decides on the basis of the evidence what action should be taken. After the first thirty days, the PCC is permitted to intervene in the investigation if it does not appear to be proceeding.
- If the complainant is unhappy with the outcome, he/she can ask the PCC to review the matter. The PCC can then undertake a further investigation to seek clarification.
- If the complainant remains dissatisfied, the PCC can be asked to order a hearing. Board members of the PCC then adjudicate after receiving accounts from all those involved.

The model of dealing with complaints in Toronto can be classified as 'police investigation with independent adjudication'. Toronto was the first area of Canada to actively involve civilian oversight. The civilianization of the police complaints procedure has now been expanded throughout Ontario and other police departments have drawn from the Toronto experience (Watt, 1991). For example, in Manitoba, a civilian commissioner of the Law Enforcement Review Agency (LERA) is concerned with the investigation of all complaints relating to independent municipal police officers, from the moment they are lodged to their disposition, removing the traditional belief that police officers themselves should take on the initial stage of investigation and disposition (Goldsmith, 1988). The Manitoba model, therefore, accords with Grant's (1992) 'truly independent model'.

Canada's largest police force, the RCMP, created the RCMP Public Complaints Commission in 1988 with the mandate to examine the disposition of complaints made about the conduct of members (see Appendix A). The Commission does not take an active role in the initial investigation; only when/if the complainant is dissatisfied with the RCMP's disposition of the complaint does the Commission become involved. At this stage, the Commission begins an investigation and, through this procedure, attempts to ensure the RCMP is fair and thorough. The Commission's chair produces a final report that is submitted to the RCMP Commissioner, who is not bound to fulfill any of the recommendations, nor act on any of the findings (Scorer, 1994). The RCMP, therefore, accords most closely with Grant's (1992) 'in house' model.

As can be seen with the examples of Toronto, Manitoba and the RCMP, there is considerable diversity in the way public complaints are treated by Canadian police forces.

The results of investigations into citizen complaints can fall into four categories:

- **Sustained complaint.** The complaint is justified.
- **Unsustained complaint.** The complaint, in the opinion of those making the decision, cannot be sustained as either true or false.
- **Unfounded complaint.** The complaint did not occur as alleged by the complainant.
- **Exoneration.** The allegation is found to be true, but the officer's behavior is considered justified, legal and within organizational policy (Grant, 1992; Roberg and Kuykendall, 1993).

The response of police supervisors and managers to sustained complaints can range from taking no action at all, to counseling or training for the officer concerned, to some form of disciplinary action, such as a verbal reprimand, written reprimand, suspension, demotion or termination. As would be expected, the more serious the behavior the more serious the punishment.

The decision to file a complaint is, of course, a subjective process dependent on a number of personal and situational characteristics. Research by Russell (1978) in England showed that individuals only initiated complaints after considerable thought, and normally did so for one of the following reasons:

- They were advised they had a good chance of having their complaint upheld.
- They were able and prepared to make the effort to complain, in the belief justice would be done.

- They believed their complaint would deter police officers from misbehaving, and would therefore be in the public interest.
- They did not believe there would be any revenge sought by the police officer concerned or his/her colleagues.

Those deciding not to report did so because of the following:

- They were advised by a significant other not to.
- They could not be bothered and were apathetic.
- They were concerned and apprehensive over reprisals that might occur as a result of their complaint.
- They had a fatalistic attitude that nothing would be achieved by complaining.
- They believed police work was difficult and problematic enough and did not want to add to these difficulties.
- They were ignorant of the complaints procedure.

RESEARCH ON CITIZEN COMPLAINTS

Research concerning the number, types and dispositions of complaints is limited (Roberg and Kuykendall, 1993), but a number of studies do provide an insight into citizen complaints. In analyzing the complaints received by the Metropolitan Toronto Police in 1985, Goldsmith and Farson (1987) stated that these numbered 750, but each complaint averaged two allegations of misconduct. The most common complaint was failing to act in accordance with police procedure (482), followed by threat or verbal abuse (450) and physical assault/excessive force (385). In all, a total of 1,253 police officers were cited in complaints, representing just under one-quarter of police officers employed in the force.

Statistics concerning the 12 municipal police departments in BC, which employ approximately 1,800 police officers, showed that from 1989 to 1993, a total of 817 complaints were received, often involving more than one allegation. Eighty-five percent involved complaints about the abuse of authority, 49% complained of a police officer's attitude, 41% complained about excessive use of force and 22% about quality of service (Oppal, 1994).

More complaints are filed against younger, less experienced officers than against older officers (Ellis, 1987), indicating that as police officers gain experience, they become more adept at handling the public. In addition, the type of police work influences the number of complaints received, with police officers involved in enforcing traffic by-laws and working in criminal investigations receiving more complaints as these officers experience more police-citizen contacts.

In an exploratory study of minor disciplinary matters (e.g., tardiness, sloppy work habits and the violation of department procedures) in three British

Columbian municipal police forces, Kean (1992) found that, in deciding what sanctions to invoke, supervisors have a choice of (a) proceeding under the Police Act, (b) administering an informal action or (c) taking no action. His study found that informal undocumented techniques were the prevalent form of action.

In 1983, complaints were made against 1,062 Toronto police officers. No action was taken against 1,008 (94%) (Ellis, 1987). The fact that approximately 5% of complaints result in some form of disciplinary action has been noted by others (Goldsmith and Farson, 1987). Most complaints are deemed to be unfounded or unsubstantiated and the ones that are sustained are largely dealt with by 'counseling', whereby the officer concerned receives advice or admonition from a superior (Grant, 1992). While police officers and their supporters hold that this level of disciplinary action reflects the true nature and reality of policing (the 'rotten apple' theory), other groups, such as civil liberties associations, question these findings and the process whereby police officers are asked to investigate and adjudicate themselves.

POLICE ACCOUNTABILITY

The extent to which the police are controlled by the public raises the question of accountability (Mawby, 1990). Accountability of the police is based on the premise that the state has a duty to provide a fair and equitable police service to the public. Accountability in relation to policing refers to the way in which both individual police officers and the police department are held accountable, responsible and capable of explaining actions, objectives, goals and productivity (Dantzker, 1995). It is also concerned with control, whereby standards are established to restrict and monitor behavior. As police officers are among the few public servants authorized to use force, accountability measures must be established so this authority is not abused. The use of force, and other powers granted to them, makes the issue of accountability more important for policing than for other professions.

Police services are accountable in at least four different ways (Normandeau and Leighton, 1990).

1. **Administratively.** They must be fiscally accountable, be able to justify the use of resources and personnel and prove they provide an effective and efficient service.

2. **Politically.** Police services must adhere to the RCMP Act and provincial Police Acts (see Appendix A and B) and must follow the guidelines stated by local police boards, police commissions and elected officials.

3. **Legally.** Police officers must uphold and enforce the criminal law while recognizing the existence of civil rights. The Charter of Rights and Freedoms ensures that individual rights are maintained and that the police do not abuse the powers vested in them.

4. **To the community.** The advent and development of community policing has strengthened the view that the police should not operate in isolation and should work with communities to set agendas and priorities for policing. As a vast proportion of the police budget comes from the local community, police officers have a responsibility to these jurisdictions.

The police are, therefore, accountable to a number of different groups: to elected and appointed officials in government, to the general public, to those individuals who receive police services (victims and suspects) and to other parts of the criminal justice system (lawyers, courts, judges). They are accountable for their behaviors and actions and for the services they provide. In this respect, an individual police officer can be held accountable for his/her actions or, alternatively, a police department can be held accountable for the actions of its members.

Assessing accountability

One of the issues surrounding police accountability is how it should be measured. An administrative way to evaluate a police agency is to establish measures of effectiveness and efficiency. Effectiveness takes into account such things as crime and arrest rates, the number of calls for service, reports taken and cases cleared, levels of fear of crime in the community and public perceptions of the police. Efficiency is concerned with how resources are used by the organization. Departmental accountability can, therefore, be assessed by looking at such measures as crime rates—when the crime rate is low, the public perceive the police to be doing a good job, when it increases, police performance is questioned. The crime rate provides quantifiable data on specific crimes; however, many services provided by the police are not so easily measured. For example, preventive patrol, and the many non-crime-related services patrol officers give in the course of their day-to-day activities, go unreported by police departments and are regarded as intangibles, even though they are highly valued by the public. These intangible services form an integral part of policing, but cannot be measured, further complicating the issue of assessing the accountability of the police.

INTERNAL REVIEW PROCESSES

There are a number of different levels of internal review designed to ensure police officer accountability. The most formal structure can be found in the internal affairs unit of police departments, which is designed to monitor internal accountability. This unit has three basic functions (Alpert and Dunham, 1988):

- Investigation of citizens' complaints.
- Review of incident reports filed by police officers, such as police pursuits and the drawing and discharge of weapons.
- Self-initiated investigations into possible misconduct.

Officers working in internal affairs are often viewed with suspicion and mistrust by colleagues, as their role incorporates policing the police. They walk a delicate tightrope in trying to convey an image to the public that the police can effectively police themselves, if required, while at the same time, demonstrating to peers that they are fair and equitable. Internal affairs officers are often unpopular with colleagues (Roberg and Kuykendall, 1993), as their investigations may result in disciplinary measures being recommended to discipline boards for officers who have violated policies and procedures. There is also the perception that an officer is wrong until proven right, and that, once an officer is reported to the internal affairs unit, his/her job is in jeopardy (Dantzker, 1995).

Other forms of internal accountability include the activities of midline managers and supervisors, who are held responsible for the effectiveness and actions of their subordinates. Officer evaluations, undertaken by managers, establish an additional level of internal accountability. Training policies ensure officers are able to meet acceptable standards of behavior and performance and form another mechanism of accountability, as do audits whereby officers maintain logs and worksheets of their activities. Police departments, therefore, contain a myriad of structures to ensure their own internal controls are enforced.

EXTERNAL REVIEW PROCESSES

In addition to the process of civilian review discussed above, three other forms of external review can be recognized: police boards, police commissions and public inquiries.

Police boards

Police boards oversee the administration of a number of municipal police agencies, and are broadly tasked with ensuring the police department is administered effectively and adheres to contracts and budgets. In undertaking a discussion of police boards, it is important to note that a wide array of boards exist in Canada, making generalizations about the nature of these boards dangerous. The history of police boards can be traced back over one hundred years, with the first ones being established in the 1850s in Ontario (Hann et al., 1985). In 1981, there were 130 police boards in Canada; more than half were in the province of Ontario. Police forces governed by police boards therefore represent less than one-third of municipal forces in the country (Stenning, 1992). Boards do not exist in Prince Edward Island, New Brunswick or Newfoundland (Martin, 1995).

There is debate over the functions of boards. Martin (1995) argues their practices are quite similar, while Stenning (1992) notes their range of functions is diverse and varies considerably among boards. Stenning lists their functions as follows.

- Preparation of the police force budget.
- Collective bargaining.

- The development of rules and regulations.
- Supervision of recruitment, hiring, promotions, suspensions and dismissals.
- General policy direction and approval.
- Public and community relations.
- Internal disciplinary matters and complaints.
- Miscellaneous functions, for example, reviewing reports, responding to requests for information, licensing persons to carry on various businesses.

Most police boards consist of between three and five members, although larger boards exist in Montreal and Nova Scotia. The composition of the board tends to be drawn from the ranks of 'professional' people (lawyers, businessmen, teachers, doctors). In British Columbia and Saskatchewan, the head of the municipal council is always a member of the board (Hann et al., 1985; Stenning, 1992).

Martin (1995) argues that police boards impose accountability on a department in the area of administration, but stay away from the specialized and functional areas, such as setting police priorities. In this respect, they ensure police departments are administered effectively, that there is adherence to contracts and budgets and that political intervention is avoided, but take a minimal role in establishing police policies, programs and priorities.

Police commissions

The first police commission was established in 1962 in Ontario to fill a perceived need for the standardization of law enforcement in the province. Prior to this time, a system had developed in which each municipal force governed itself. Ontario's lead was followed six years later by Quebec. In Canada today, police commissions exist in Ontario, Quebec, Nova Scotia, British Columbia, New Brunswick and Saskatchewan. Prince Edward Island, Newfoundland and Alberta do not have them. In Manitoba, the police commission was dissolved in 1992 and its functions absorbed by the Justice branch of government (Ainslie, 1994).

In a detailed analysis of police commissions, Stenning (1981) argues they were established to achieve a number of objectives.

- To bring about greater coordination and efficiency of police services in a province.
- To establish and impose minimum standards of recruitment, training and working conditions.
- To provide an independent authority to review local decision-making with respect to internal discipline matters and police complaints.
- To plan and implement overall police policy in a province.

Police commissions have the general mandate to promote efficient and effective police services through specific and varied powers of control and supervision of police forces (Stenning, 1981). They provide support services to police boards, create statistical information and conduct and disseminate research. They can also provide advice to government ministers on a number of issues, such as the amalgamation of police departments and the negotiation of contracts with the RCMP. Provincial police commissions are also involved in training programs for provincial and municipal police officers.

Commissions vary considerably in size of membership, staff and budgets. In some respects, this reflects the size of the policing problems they are asked to address. For example, in Ontario and Quebec, the commissions oversee provincial police forces and municipal police services operating in the province, whereas in British Columbia, the commission is only concerned with 12 municipal forces. It is important to note that, like police boards, commissions are not responsible for policing services delivered by the RCMP. As noted by Mawby (1990) "...local accountability does not appear to exist for the RCMP, even when under contract to the provincial or municipal government" (p. 86). A recent provincial inquiry into policing in BC recognized that the province had limited control over the RCMP, which has a total of 2,161 police officers on municipal contract and a further 1,505 on provincial contract working in the province (Oppal, 1994). Therefore, while police boards and commissions oversee municipal and provincial police forces, they have no jurisdiction over the RCMP.

Public inquiries

Public inquiries into police conduct can be federally or provincially initiated; they are frequently instigated following an issue of police-community conflict or concern. For example, in the 1980s, following national publicity concerning the guilt of a 17-year-old Micmac, the government of Nova Scotia ordered a Royal Commission to examine, not only the events surrounding the case, but the treatment of ethnic minorities by the Nova Scotia justice system (Sunahara, 1992). Other public inquiries, such as the Manitoba Justice Inquiry (Hamilton and Sinclair, 1991) and the Blood Tribe Inquiry (Alberta), have also been prompted by specific events that have strained police-community relations.

Public inquiries have been conducted without the catalyst of a well-publicized incident. The Alberta Aboriginal Justice Inquiry arose in 1990 in response to a general problem between the criminal justice system and Native people in Alberta. The Inquiry into Policing in British Columbia, which comprised "...virtually every aspect and issue related to policing" (Oppal, 1994, p. i), was also not instigated as the result of one specific incident, although, as mentioned above, there had been concern over police use of force in the province.

Public inquiries, like civilian review boards, are frequently disliked and resisted by police, who see them as demoralizing (Forcese, 1992). While a great deal of publicity frequently surrounds their initiation and the publication of their final report, their effectiveness depends on the recommendations they make and whether these are implemented. The BC inquiry resulted in a report over 700 pages in length, containing over 300 recommendations; a year after its publication, very few of these had been implemented. In contrast, the McDonald Commission, which investigated the activities of the RCMP, resulted in the creation of the Canadian Security and Intelligence Service.

External review procedures, therefore, incorporate police boards, police commissions, civilian review procedures and public inquiries. Police commissions and police boards have no jurisdiction over the RCMP, which sees itself as legally, fiscally and operationally accountable to the federal, not provincial or municipal, government. Provinces and municipalities that have their own police forces are able to exert more local accountability and control than those areas that have chosen to contract with the RCMP. With the introduction of community policing, questions arise regarding the appropriateness of a provincial or municipal force that owes its primary allegiance—not to the province—but to its headquarters in Ottawa. This point was made by Hann et al. (1985) who showed how RCMP detachment commanders see their accountability to be owed to superiors within the force, rather than to local government. It is reiterated by the RCMP itself, which confirms that, in terms of internal management of provincial and municipal services, including administration and application of professional police procedures, control remains with the government of Canada (RCMP, 1990).

SUMMARY

This chapter has examined police deviance and the civilian review process that attempts to ensure police agencies are responsive to citizens' concerns. It went on to discuss accountability and the mechanisms of internal and external control that have been developed to facilitate the governance of the police. In reviewing these procedures, it was noted that municipal and provincial forces have more procedures for external accountability than does the RCMP.

QUESTIONS FOR DISCUSSION

1. Outline Sherman's (1974) typology of police deviance.

2. To what extent can the police subculture be said to support police wrongdoing?

3. Provide examples of police misconduct and corruption.

4. Outline the arguments for and against the police acceptance of gratuities.

5. Why is it difficult to measure police effectiveness and efficiency?

6. How are complaints against police officers dealt with in the Toronto Metropolitan Police and the RCMP?

7. What are the four levels, described by Normandeau and Leighton (1990), to which police services are accountable?

8. What are the major limitations of police boards?

9. In what ways do police commissions differ from police boards?

10. Can the police police themselves?

FURTHER READING

Shearing, C. (1981). *Organizational Police Deviance: Its Structure and Control.* Toronto: Butterworths. This collection of work argues that police corruption in Canada can be attributed to the complexity of the police role and the problems this brings.

Sherman, Lawrence W. (1974). *Police Corruption: A Sociological Perspective.* Garden City New York: Anchor Books. This American text provides an in-depth sociological account of the theories and analysis surrounding the issue of police corruption.

Stenning, Philip C. (1981). *Police Commissions and Boards in Canada.* Toronto: Centre for Criminology, University of Toronto. Although now a little dated, this book provides the most comprehensive review of police boards and commissions in Canada.

REFERENCES

Ainslie, Mary T. (1994). *The Role, Organization and Operation of the British Columbia Police Commission.* Report submitted to the Commission of Inquiry Policing in British Columbia. Victoria, B.C.: Attorney General.

Alpert, Geoffrey A. and Dunham, Roger G. (1988). *Policing In Urban America.* Prospect Heights, Ill.: Waveland Press.

Barker, T. and Carter, D.L. (1986). *Police Deviance.* Cincinnati: Anderson.

Dantzker, Mark L. (1995). *Understanding Today's Police.* New Jersey: Prentice Hall.

Ellis, D. (1987). *The Wrong Stuff—An Introduction to the Sociological Study of Deviance.* Don Mills, Ontario: Collier Macmillan.

Forcese, Dennis P. (1992). *Policing Canadian Society.* Scarborough: Prentice Hall.

Fyfe, James J. (1985). *Police Management Today.* Washington D.C.: International City Management Association.

Goldsmith, Andrew J. (1988). "New directions in police complaints procedures; some conceptual and comparative departures." *Police Studies: The International Review of Police Development, 11*(2).

Goldsmith, Andrew and Farson, Stuart (1987). "Complaints against the police in Canada: A new approach." *Criminal Law Review, 11.*

Grant, Alan (1992). "The control of police behavior." In K.R.E. McCormick and L.A. Visano (Eds.) *Understanding Policing.* Toronto: Canadian Scholars Press.

Hamilton, Associate Chief Justice A.C. and Sinclair, Associate Chief Judge C.M. (1991). *Report of the Aboriginal Justice Inquiry of Manitoba. The Justice System and Aboriginal People.* Vol. 1. Winnipeg: Queen's Printer.

Hann, Robert G., MacGinnis, James H., Stenning, Philip C. and Farson, Stuart A. (1985). "Municipal police governance and accountability in Canada: An empirical study." *Canadian Police College Journal, 29*(1).

Kania, R.R.E. (1988). "Should we tell the police to say 'yes' to gratuities?" *Criminal Justice Ethics, 7.*

Kean, Darrell W. (1992). *Informal and formal control mechanism: An exploration of minor discipline within police organizations.* Unpublished masters dissertation, Simon Fraser University.

Lundman, R.J. (1980). *Police and Policing—An Introduction.* New York: Holt, Rinehart and Winston.

Martin, Maurice A. (1995). *Urban Policing in Canada: Anatomy of an Aging Craft.* Montreal: McGill Queen's University Press.

Mawby, R.I. (1990). *Comparative Policing Issues: The British and American System in International Perspective.* London: Unwin Hyman.

Murphy, Patrick V. and Caplan, Dean Gerald (1993). "Fostering integrity." In Roger G. Dunham and Geoffrey P. Alpert (Eds.) *Critical Issues in Policing: Contemporary Readings.* Prospect Heights, Illinois: Waveland Press.

Normandeau, A. and Leighton, B. (1990). *A Vision of the Future of Policing in Canada: Police Challenge 2000—Background Document.* Ottawa: Police and Security Branch, Ministry Secretariat, Solicitor General.

Oppal, The Honourable Mr. Justice Wallace T. (1994). *Closing the Gap: Policing and the Community.* Commission of Inquiry Policing in British Columbia. Victoria, B.C.: Attorney General.

Roberg, Roy R. and Kuykendall, Jack (1993). *Police and Society.* Belmont, California: Wadsworth Publishing Company.

Royal Canadian Mounted Police (1990). *Fact Sheets.* Ottawa: Ministry of Supply and Services.

Russell, Ken (1978). *Complaints Against the Police: A Sociological View.* Leicester: Milltak Limited.

Scorer, G. (1994). *The Royal Canadian Mounted Police Complaints and Discipline.* Report submitted to the Commission of Inquiry Policing in British Columbia. Victoria, B.C.: Attorney General.

Sewell, John (1985). *Police: Urban Policing in Canada.* Toronto: James Lorimer.

Shearing, C. (1981). *Organizational Police Deviance: Its Structure and Control.* Toronto: Butterworths.

Sherman, Lawrence W. (1974). *Police Corruption: A Sociological Perspective.* Garden City New York: Anchor Books.

Stansfield, Ronald T. (1996). *Issues in Policing: A Canadian Perspective.* Toronto: Thompson Educational Publishing.

Stenning, Philip C. (1981). *Police Commissions and Boards in Canada.* Toronto: Centre for Criminology, University of Toronto.

Stenning, Philip C. (1992). "The role of police boards and commissions as institutions of municipal police governance." In K.R.E. McCormick and L.A. Visano (Eds.) *Understanding Policing.* Toronto: Canadian Scholars Press.

Sunahara, David F. (1992). "Public inquiries into policing." *Canadian Police College Journal, 16*(2).

Wagner, Allen E. and Decker, Scott H. (1993). "Evaluating citizens complaints against the police." In Roger G. Dunham and Geoffrey P. Alpert (Eds.) *Critical Issues in Policing: Contemporary Readings.* Prospect Heights, Illinois: Waveland Press.

Watt, Susan (1991). "The future of civilian oversight of policing." *Canadian Journal of Criminology, 33* (3-4).

COMMUNITY POLICING: DEFINITIONS AND INTERPRETATIONS

INTRODUCTION

The aim of this chapter is to provide a discussion of the various definitions and interpretations of community policing that have been advanced and discussed in the academic literature and to describe the various policies and programs that have been introduced under the community policing banner. This information provides a framework in which to understand the development of community policing in Canada, which is the subject of Chapter 11.

Community policing is seen by some to represent a paradigmatic shift (Bayley, 1989; Chacko and Nancoo, 1993; Greene et al., 1994) and an entire philosophy of policing (Goldstein, 1987), rather than a specific program. This philosophy advocates an expanded police role in society, internal organizational change and a greater linkage between the police and the community (Clairmont, 1991). Most commentators agree that it involves, not only increased police involvement with the public, but a complete overhaul of police management and structure. In this respect, it is seen to propose the most fundamental change to policing this century (Bayley, 1989).

Although community policing has been a subject of academic interest for almost 20 years, confusion exists over what it actually is. Both academics and practitioners have failed to devise a common definition of it and, consequently, have been content to treat it as an intangible, fluid and nebulous concept.

There are advantages to leaving the term undefined. In so doing, any renamed or add-on program that a police agency wishes to adopt can be called community policing, even if, upon closer examination, it may not be community policing. However, there are also numerous advantages in trying to understand how academics, police officers and the community define the community policing concept in order to determine how community policing is being interpreted and enacted. After reviewing the various definitions of community policing, this chapter details the various programs and policies that have been introduced in the name of community policing.

COMMUNITY POLICING DEFINED

> What is possibly so fascinating about community policing is that it is not easily amenable to a particular definition...but it is clearly a highly appealing concept (Friedmann, 1992, p. 3).

Community policing, sometimes referred to as community-oriented policing or community-based policing, is most broadly regarded as a philosophy requiring significant organizational change. It is, therefore, distinct from both the professional, para-military, bureaucratic policing model (see Chapter 6) and from specific policing initiatives, such as community relations policies (discussed below). Both of these argued for a defined response, advocating a narrow, bureaucratic approach to a recognized problem and not a fundamental philosophical change in the overall structure of a police department (Trojanowicz, 1990). However, a review of the term community policing illustrates that confusion exists over how this concept is being interpreted, enacted and defined.

There are a wide array of options offering themselves as definitions, redefinitions, potential definitions, and interpretations of community policing. This is quite understandable when two such commonly accepted terms as community and police are linked (Friedmann, 1992). This has led one commentator (Murphy, 1994) to propose that the term be abandoned and another be introduced which: (a) does not become confused with community relations; (b) connotes the structural changes involved; (c) emphasizes the collaborative relationship between the police and community; and (d) distinguishes these developments from previous policing philosophies.

Although fluid, definitions or ways in which the community policing concept has been interpreted can be derived from the literature. This study of definitions is not critical or evaluative, but rather descriptive. Written definitions given by others comprise the information to be worked with by the social scientist. Definitions must be developed in order to have effective communication and to facilitate evaluations.

An understanding of the term community policing can be gained from reading and rereading the community policing literature. This analysis suggests five interpretations or ways of seeing community policing (Seagrave, 1996). These categories represent the primary meanings discussed by the referenced source and are mutually exclusive, representing the clearest articulation of that cited interpretation of community policing. Therefore, they represent content areas under which definitions or interpretations of community policing advanced by others can be placed.

These five categories see community policing as follows.

1. A meaningless **rhetorical** term, including every and any initiative.
2. A **philosophy** focusing on the police and community working together to influence the management and delivery of police services.
3. A particular crime prevention **program**.
4. A form of increased social **control**.
5. An **imprecise** notion, impossible to define.

Rhetorical

Some have suggested that community policing is no more than a consensus rallying cry, used to convey a sense of nostalgia, with the word community carrying considerable emotional appeal (Mawby, 1990). Community policing evokes powerful metaphors that play to contemporary cultural concerns (Manning, 1984) and does little more than summon up images of a world we have lost, providing inspiration for a better future (Weatheritt, 1987). Community policing is therefore seen to be a new legitimating mandate that evokes powerful metaphors of democracy, small town morality and local autonomy (Crank, 1994), but may lack substance and be little more than rhetorical. In commenting that the community policing concept is rhetorical, it should be noted that many other terms used in the social sciences (e.g., power, justice, economy) suffer from the same criticisms and yet are utilized extensively. The rhetorical interpretation sees community policing as having little depth, being merely a buzz-word designed to persuade or impress.

Philosophy

The philosophy definition of community policing is the one most frequently discussed in the academic literature. The community policing philosophy frequently advocates a 'partnership' between the police and the community to address numerous social issues. Often the key elements or ingredients or definitions of community policing are listed and have been condensed to three points by some commentators (Clairmont, 1991; Goldstein, 1987), four by others (Kelling and Moore, 1989; Manning, 1984; Skogan, 1990; Skolnick and Bayley, 1988; Wycoff, 1989), six by one other (Murphy, 1988), eight by yet another (Loree, 1988), and more recently extended to include twelve points (Normandeau and Leighton, 1990).

Skogan (1990) cites four broad principles of the community policing movement:

- A commitment to a broader problem-oriented policing philosophy and a move away from a focus on crime fighting.
- Decentralization, new patrol tactics and a two-way communication between police and citizens.
- Police respond to the citizens' definitions of their problems.
- Police help neighborhoods help themselves by serving as catalysts.

Broderick (1991) has noted that these last two principles are not that different from those proposed by Shaw and Mackay (1942) at the Chicago School and put into practice by Saul Alinsky and his colleagues, supporting the conclusion by some that community policing is really just old wine in new bottles.

In practice, the community policing philosophy advocates not only listening to (elusive) community input, but also creating the opportunities for the community to have its say in policing policy. It therefore promotes the need for structural change within police departments. This is a big step for most police agencies, which, throughout their existence, have seen themselves as professionals who know better than anyone else what needs to be done to maintain social order and enforce the law (Skolnick and Bayley, 1988).

The philosophy definition of community policing, therefore, advocates that the police and the community work together to identify issues of concern. This definition also implies the need for internal organizational change and is a radical departure from the traditional professional model of policing.

Program

From philosophical definitions, one can go to much more focused interpretations. These see community policing as requiring only three things: community policing councils, inter-agency cooperation, and community constables (Alderson, 1982). Some believe community policing exists as a program that can be added onto the existing organizational structure.

Although no clear definition of community policing may exist, a number of programs and policies that include community involvement or facilitate increased contacts between the police and the community are frequently cited as being compatible with it. These include neighborhood foot patrols, zone policing, mini-stations or storefronts, community consultative groups, neighbourhood watch and crime prevention initiatives. Community policing in operational terms is a program which, in its most facile interpretation, requires only a deployment decision.

To a certain extent, the program category corresponds to elements from the era of crime prevention and community relations initiatives—such as team policing—which preceded community policing and which sought to facilitate police and community contacts by add-on policies, not structural organizational change.

Control

A critical interpretation of community policing has been given by Klockars (1989), who claims that the movement from bureaucratic to community policing is best understood as the latest in a long tradition of 'circumlocutions', whose purpose is to conceal, mystify and legitimize police use of nonnegotiable coercive force. Other circumlocutions were legalization, militarization and professionalization of policing. He regards the progression towards community policing not as a radical shift, but as a cumulative process. Community policing is, therefore, a more covert way to penetrate communities to acquire information, or a confidence trick where a velvet glove hides the iron fist and is, in reality, a mechanism for state control (Kinsey, Lea and Young, 1986; Taylor, 1980). The control definition, in seeing community policing as a form of social control, exists as a critique of the concept.

Imprecise

While the rhetorical interpretation sees community policing as having little depth, being merely a buzz-word, the imprecise interpretation recognizes that there is substance to the concept, but that this substance has yet to be defined. Various authors have noted that, despite the term 'community policing' being readily adopted, the words 'community', 'policing' and 'community policing' are open to numerous definitions (Mawby, 1990). There is, consequently, confusion over the exact nature of community policing, so some have suggested that there are *no* standard definitions at this point in time (Hunt and Magenau, 1993) and that it is indistinguishable from traditional policing (Broderick, 1991). Existing definitions range from those that see it as a variety of forms of social control involving community effort (Alderson, 1982) to any initiative that includes the police and the community (again undefined) working together (Leighton, 1991; Murphy, 1989; Skolnick and Bayley, 1988). More cynically, it has been described as a term "used to describe virtually any policing activity which its proponents approve" (Weatheritt, 1987, p. 7), and as any form of policing so long as it gains the support of the community (Mawby, 1990). A recent survey of chief constables in England and Wales found that 45% believed it to be a meaningless expression (Reiner, 1991).

Table 10.1 provides a summary of the five categories of community policing definitions.

DEFINING COMMUNITY POLICING IN CANADA

In their publication for the Solicitor General, Normandeau and Leighton (1990) argue that community policing involves a police-community partnership to deal with crime and that this "new blue line" should incorporate twelve ingredients, most of which are mentioned by other commentators.

1. **The role of the police should be that of peace officers.** Police officers become involved with the reduction and prevention of crime and promote public order and individual safety, thus extending their role beyond law enforcement and crime control to offer a more comprehensive service. In many respects, this represents a return to the original principles of policing advocated by Peel (see Chapter 2). This aspect has been acknowledged by many police departments, which have changed their names from police 'department' to police 'service'.

2. **The police should adopt a strategy of community consultation.** The consultative process helps the police establish short- and long-term goals for addressing the crime and disorder problems that are seen as priorities for the citizens they serve. In addition, citizens learn of the problems associated with policing through this interactive process, and so comprehend the difficulties police officers face in addressing crime. This consultative process is a radical departure from the professional model of policing, which was premised on the view that the police knew best the needs of the community and could devise policies without community input.

TABLE 10.1 Summary of Definitions and Interpretations of Community Policing Derived from the Literature

Community Policing	Interpretation	Source
Rhetorical	"Meaningless." Metaphorical.	Weatheritt (1987) Manning (1984)
Philosophy	Community influences management and delivery of police services.	Murphy (1988) Goldstein (1987) Normandeau and Leighton (1990)
	Organizational change.	Skolnick and Bayley (1988)
Program*	Blockwatch, team policing, consultative groups, crime prevention. No organizational change.	This interpretation is often advanced by police officers themselves. (Seagrave, 1996)
Control	Covert way to penetrate communities to acquire information. Social control.	Klockars (1989) Bunyan (1981) Taylor (1981)
Imprecise	Numerous definitions. No definition. Indistinguishable from traditional policing. New definition needed.	Mawby (1990) Hunt and Magenau (1993) Broderick (1991) Murphy (1994)

*While there are few recent academic commentators that suggest community policing is a program, when the concept was first discussed, it was confused with crime prevention initiatives (see Trojanowicz, 1990 for a review of this confusion).

3. **The police should become proactive and identify local crime and disorder problems.** Instead of the police passively waiting for calls or randomly patrolling, police officers, in conjunction with the community, should proactively identify crime and disorder problems. By analyzing the calls for service and the nature of crimes in a given area, a greater understanding of crime-related issues is available; whereupon strategies for addressing specific problems can be proposed.

4. **A problem-oriented policing strategy should be adopted.** No single tactic is associated with community policing; rather, a wide array of strategies needs to be employed to help address specific issues of crime and disorder. In this respect, tactics associated with the professional model of policing remain necessary, such as rapid response teams and specialist units dealing with issues of, for example, domestic violence, but coexist with

other services that increase the level of contact between the police and the community, such as mini-stations and foot patrol officers. (The link between community policing and problem-oriented policing is discussed below).

5. **The police need to tackle the underlying causes of problems.** The police should identify opportunities to reduce crime through crime prevention techniques. Examples of these initiatives include Crime Prevention Through Environmental Design (CPTED) courses, in which police officers are taught to identify environments susceptible to crime so they can suggest how such areas may be altered.

6. **There should be more inter-agency cooperation between the police and other service delivery agencies.** While the police exist as the first response to crime and many other crises, other agencies are often better equipped to deal with the underlying causes of crime, such as poverty, unemployment, poor health and inadequate housing and to assist the victims. The police need to work in conjunction with other service agencies, such as local government housing departments and social services, to address the social issues that influence crime and disorder.

7. **Police personnel should act as information managers who engage in 'interactive policing'.** By increasing contacts with the community, police officers become more knowledgeable about the community they serve and the public becomes more willing to communicate with the police. This interaction means information is more readily available should crime problems arise in the area. Again, this premise departs from the professional model of policing, which advocated distancing the police from the community.

8. **Tactics should be developed to reduce fear of crime.** Certain groups in society, such as the elderly and women, are particularly fearful of crime. The police need to ensure that these groups take reasonable crime prevention measures, thereby reducing this fear.

9. **Police officers should be encouraged to become career generalists rather than specialists.** Under the professional model, police officers were not awarded the autonomy to be responsible for a broad range of policing activities. The community policing model stresses that police officers should adopt a more professional approach, work on their own initiative and move away from the 'blue collar' image by becoming responsible for a wide range of activities.

10. **There should be greater management decentralization.** More autonomy and independence is awarded to operational police officers, who are responsible for neighborhood policing; in addition, resources are allocated to accommodate the needs of individual neighborhoods.

11. **There should be a change in the organizational structure from the hierarchical para-military model.** Community policing advocates a flattening of the hierarchical structure, in which loyalties are placed not with the chain of command and the police department, as in the past, but with the Charter, the Criminal Code, the common law and the community.

12. **The police should become accountable to the community.** Through mechanisms such as public consultations, the police should review their policies and procedures. This form of informal accountability supplements the legal accountability that already exists through external review bodies (Normandeau and Leighton, 1990).

DIMENSIONS AND PERSPECTIVES OF COMMUNITY POLICING

Definitions and interpretations of community policing highlight different policies, components and principles and do not yield a single description. In discussing this issue, Cordner (1995) has cited three major dimensions of community policing: the philosophical dimension, the strategic dimension and the programmatic dimension.

Philosophical

The philosophical dimension is similar to the philosophy category outlined earlier, and suggests a broad interpretation of policing, incorporating citizen input and policing tailored to local needs. This dimension is the most comprehensive, consisting of a paradigm shift away from traditional bureaucratic policing practices and a movement towards a police function that includes more than crime fighting and law enforcement alone. It incorporates both citizen input into the policies and practices of police departments, and neighborhood variation, in which policing priorities are based on local norms and values.

Strategic

The strategic dimension incorporates the operational aspects and translates the philosophy to action. In this regard, the strategic dimension represents the link between the philosophical assumptions and the specific programs that are to be implemented. The strategic dimension frequently involves more geographically-focused policing, whereby officers are awarded 24-hour responsibility for a specific area rather than 10-hour responsibility for an entire area, an emphasis on preventive and proactive policing and a more focused attempt to address problems in the area.

Programmatic

The programmatic dimension translates philosophies and strategies into programs, tactics and behaviors, and involves problem-solving techniques and community involvement. Cordner (1995) shows that, despite the preponderance of studies on the issue, it is only within the programmatic dimension that we have empirical evidence illustrating beneficial effects for both police and community.

Cordner's (1995) dimensions are all interrelated and provide a comprehensive interpretation of community policing. Friedmann (1992) argues that, to understand the new philosophy, community policing should be examined from three perspectives: that of the police, that of the community, and that of the police and the community. As will be illustrated in the next chapter, there is scant Canadian empirical research on how these groups regard the introduction of community policing.

COMMUNITY POLICING AND PROBLEM-ORIENTED POLICING

The terms community policing and problem-oriented policing have been used interchangeably by some (e.g., Riechers and Roberg, 1990). Neither lends itself to precise definition. Trojanowicz and Bucqueroux (1990) argue that community policing refers to police activities focused on community-level issues (whatever these may be), in which the police cooperate with citizens to deal with problems, and citizens have input into the policing agenda. In contrast, problem-oriented policing develops to address specific problems, and does not require open-ended input from citizens. Problem-oriented policing attempts to improve policing by emphasizing a proactive and analytical police response to repetitive problems in the community (Murphy, 1992).

In 1990, Goldstein published *Problem Oriented Policing*. In this text, he undertakes to redefine the operational role of the police and the relationship the police have with the public, in order to develop a distinct perspective on policing. This work expands on an original article, published in 1979, which advocated the problem-oriented policing approach. This approach has been readily adopted in the United States and, to a lesser extent, in England (Weatheritt, 1986).

A problem-oriented approach implies that the police develop a systematic method for examining and handling the issues the public expects them to address (Goldstein, 1979). There are basically four stages to the process, which has become known as the SARA model.

1. **Scanning.** This involves looking for and identifying possible problems. Categories such as 'crime' and 'theft' are too broad; problems need to be defined more specifically so that characteristics of offenses can be recorded. By collecting detailed data, a full understanding of the extent and nature of the issue is possible.

2. **Analysis.** This requires an understanding of the problem's cause, scope and effects. Analysis implies researching the problem from perspectives other than those of the police, in order to establish a comprehensive understanding of the issue to be addressed.

3. **Response.** Acting to alleviate the problem. Response requires a broad search for solutions, which may extend beyond the police and the criminal justice system and may well include other government agencies, community resources and private sector agencies.

4. **Assessment.** This means determining whether or not the response worked. In order to assess whether the problem-oriented approach has been successful, a thorough evaluation of the entire process is required.

Community policing and problem-oriented policing have been regarded as a particular management ethos taken from the private sector and incorporated under the umbrella of 'total quality management' (Hunt and Magenau, 1993). This movement stresses the obligation to understand customer needs and analyze problems to improve the quality of service offered. Many of the clichés advanced in the total quality management arena find parallels in those articulated by proponents of community policing and reflect the movement to recognize the similarities between police agencies and private sector organizations.

In Canada, training in problem-oriented policing has recently been implemented within the RCMP, and courses also exist at the Justice Institute of British Columbia. The RCMP has developed its own version of SARA: CAPRA, standing for Clients, Analysis, Partnership, Response and Assessment; this basically follows the SARA model outlined above. Goldstein advocates problem-oriented policing, as he believes it is more feasible and has fewer 'downside risks' (Hunt and Magenau, 1993). Indeed, problem-oriented policing stresses the need for police officers to specifically define problems and emphasizes the role of research in the ongoing monitoring and evaluation process (Weatheritt, 1986). As illustrated above, one of the criticisms of community policing is that it is not adequately researched, an issue addressed by problem-oriented policing. However, overlaps are obvious: problem-oriented policing, like community policing, involves significant organizational change and is regarded by some to be the precursor to community policing in traditional police agencies (Leighton, 1994).

COMMUNITY POLICING AND CRIME PREVENTION/ COMMUNITY RELATIONS

Community policing is most broadly regarded as a philosophy requiring significant and fundamental organizational change. It is, therefore, quite distinct from earlier policing initiatives, such as crime prevention and community relations, which argued for a more limited approach, implying a narrow bureaucratic response to a particular problem and not a fundamental philosophical change in the overall mission and expectations of a police department. In undertaking a

TABLE 10.2 Comparison of community policing and police community relations

Community policing	Community relations
Goal: Solve problems—improve relations with citizens	Goal: Change attitudes— project positive image
Regular contact between officers and community	Irregular contact between officers and community
Citizens identify problems and cooperate with police to set agenda	Selected committees identify problems and instruct police
Police accountability is ensured by citizens receiving the service	Police accountability ensured by civilian review boards and formal police supervision
Meaningful organizational change; restructuring of recruitment, training and evaluation	Traditional organization remains and new programs are added. No organizational change
Department-wide philosophy and acceptance	Isolated acceptance often in one unit
Influence from the bottom up. Community sets the priorities which influence police policy	Influence from the top down. Police hierarchy makes decisions
Officer is accessible, has local contact through decentralized office	Intermittent contact with the community. Contact is made through central headquarters
Success is determined by the reduction in fear, neighborhood disorder and crime	Success is determined by traditional measures such as crime rates.

(Trojanowicz, 1990)

review of the differences between previous community relations approaches and current community policing strategies, Trojanowicz (1990) illustrated the distinctive nature of the community policing philosophy. His work is detailed in Table 10.2 and provides a neat summary of the distinctiveness of community policing.

OBJECTIVES OF COMMUNITY POLICING

The discussion so far has centred on defining and interpreting the community policing concept and recognizing how it is distinct from previous policing initiatives. Community policing has been identified as an exceptional policing process which, in theory, departs significantly from the professional policing model. It therefore inherently contains objectives and expectations that distinguish it from policing initiatives of the past. These objectives can be summarized as follows.

1. **Greater police legitimacy and public acceptance.** Community policing advocates a movement away from the traditional, hierarchical, bureaucratic style of policing towards a model that is more responsive, accountable and inclusive. By drawing on the support and cooperation of various community groups, including ones that, in the past, have been critical of the police (e.g., youth, ethnic minorities), police agencies hope to gain legitimacy and project a better image.

2. **Increased police accountability.** The value and importance of community input into policing policies and practices is recognized by the community policing model. Through more collaborative and consultative practices, the police become more accountable—formally and informally—to the citizens they serve.

3. **More efficient use of police services through changes in organization and management.** By utilizing community resources and by sharing responsibilities in a collaborative effort, police agencies become more efficient. In addition, new styles of management, focusing on problem solving, directed patrol, the monitoring of effectiveness and call prioritization, produce a more efficient service.

4. **Increased effectiveness through innovation.** By adopting proactive innovative policing strategies that address the underlying problems of crime, rather than simply reacting to them, the fundamental causes of crime and disorder may be addressed.

5. **Decreased fear of crime and public safety.** Increasing police visibility in a neighborhood by introducing foot patrols and mini-stations reduces public fear and enhances the relationship between the police and the community.

6. **Increased job satisfaction and officer productivity.** Community policing allows police officers more autonomy, limits bureaucratic and supervisory control and promotes positive non-confrontational contacts between the police and citizens. In theory, this leads to a more rewarding work environment for the officer (Hornick et al., 1991; Oppal, 1994).

While these may exist as the ideal objectives and goals of the community policing movement, the extent to which they have been attained is questionable. As will be illustrated in Chapter 11, research on community policing in Canada is scant; consequently, our understanding of whether the community policing movement is meeting its objectives is currently open to debate.

COMMUNITY POLICING PROGRAMS

There are a number of programs and initiatives that have been identified as oriented towards the community policing philosophy, including foot and bike patrols, community consultative committees, problem-oriented policing approaches, mini-stations, police-community relations programs, customer surveys and crime prevention initiatives. This section will describe the most common of these initiatives and provide examples of their existence. This review is not exhaustive. The very nature of community policing implies that any initiative receiving support from the police and the community may fall under the rubric of community policing; therefore, unique programs that exist in only one or two areas are not described. Instead, this review concentrates on the most frequently introduced programs that are deemed to be examples of community policing.

Foot patrols

Although foot patrols have been a characteristic of British policing throughout its existence, they became less prevalent in North America with the advent of the automobile. Recent questioning of the effectiveness of the mobile patrol led some police departments to experiment with reintroducing foot patrols in the belief that they improve police-community relations. Foot patrol officers are responsible for patrolling small, well-defined neighborhoods and are often given more autonomy than mobile patrols in the tasks they perform. They are expected to undertake proactive policing and often work out of smaller, decentralized police stations. As foot patrol officers are highly visible, citizens observe them undertaking their duties. This, theoretically, may lead to a reduction in fear of crime. In addition, it is suggested that foot patrol officers learn more about the community they serve

Research on the effectiveness of foot patrols has been conducted in the United States and, to a more limited extent, Canada. While studies have shown that foot patrols, like mobile patrols, do not have a significant impact on the crime rate, they do influence fear of crime by increasing citizens' feelings of personal safety. Research undertaken in the United States illustrates that there are advantages to both the community and police personnel. A study by the Police Foundation (1981) into foot patrols in Newark, New Jersey found that residents were more satisfied with services delivered by foot patrols, while in Flint, Michigan, foot patrol officers reported higher levels of community support and greater levels of familiarity with the neighborhoods they served, as well as feeling safer at work, than did officers in motorized patrol (Trojanowicz and Banas, 1985).

In Canada, foot patrols are used quite rarely. The most notable exception is the Edmonton Police Service, which began a neighborhood foot patrol project in 1987, assigning officers to 21 areas of the city recognized to have a high number of crime and disorder incidents as well as a number of repeat calls for service. An evaluation of the project found that use of foot patrols resulted in a reduction of repeat calls for service in high incident areas, increased levels of community satisfaction with the police and increased levels of job satisfaction for officers (Hornick et al., 1990).

Bike cops

Falling halfway between the motorized police response and the beat cop is the police officer deployed on mountain bicycle. This is a relatively new community policing initiative that has grown out of the current interest in mountain biking. While the bicycle has a long history of use in Britain, the application of the mountain bike to policing is truly a North American development that has grown significantly over the last ten years.

Surrey RCMP detachment in British Columbia was the first RCMP agency to put police officers on bikes, doing so in 1990. Since this time, the initiative has broadened, so bikes are used in a number of detachments. Similarly, bikes are a regular detail of many metropolitan police departments. In British Columbia, the police training academy now runs a one-week bike training program for officers assigned to bike patrol. While bike patrols are a year-round detail for police departments in the lower mainland of British Columbia, the climate in the rest of Canada prohibits this.

Bike patrols clearly provide a quick, quiet and effective way to deploy police officers. They are effective in cities, where traffic is frequently a problem, and do not place the police officer inside a machine, distancing him/her from the community. Unfortunately, there have, to date, been no evaluations of bike cops in Canada, so assessment of their influence on crime and disorder problems is not available. Police and community perceptions of this mode of deployment are also unknown.

Community consultative committees

One of the community policing programs most frequently discussed is the community consultative committee, or advisory committee, which has been in existence in other countries (e.g., England and Australia) for over ten years, but has only been introduced in Canada this decade. The objective of these committees is to facilitate the police-community partnership in dealing with issues of crime and disorder through a consultative process. In practice, this means that members of the community meet on a regular basis with their police agency and have input into policing by:

- identifying problems and areas of concern.
- setting police priorities.
- developing tactics to solve, reduce and prevent crime and disorder issues.
- allocating resources to problems (Leighton, 1994).

The community consultative process may address a number of different issues.

- Issues that are of concern to an identified group or subculture of people. For example, racial and ethnic issues such as racial attacks, sexuality issues such as gay bashing, or issues affecting women such as rape and domestic violence.

- All issues of crime and disorder occurring in one geographical location.
- Specific crime issues, such as gangs, prostitution, drug dealers, which are a concern in one geographical location.

The consultative group may be composed of all members of the community in a given location, or all individuals who belong to an identified subculture. Alternatively, the consultative committee may comprise only invited representatives of the community (e.g., local business representative, high school student, homemaker, clergy, etc.) or representatives of the identified subculture. Consultative committees are police initiated. In seeking input, the police agency decides whether to open up the consultative process to all members of the community or to select 'representatives' of the community. In choosing to invite selected representatives to meetings, the police are screening the process, as certain groups may not be invited to take part. While this may be the safest option for the police—criticisms and comments may be less severe—it does not fill the mandate of a true community consultative process.

Many police agencies in Canada have adopted community consultative groups as part of their commitment to community policing. The Ontario Police Services Act (see Appendix B) emphasizes community consultation, while the Ontario Provincial Police have made it a part of their mission statement (Leighton, 1994). In addition, the Vancouver Police introduced community consultative forums in 1991, in order to address one of the objectives of their corporate strategy, which was to: "mutually agree with the communities we serve the priorities for police service." Probably the largest commitment to this community policing program was made by the RCMP in 1989, when the directional statement of the commissioner instructed all RCMP detachments of a certain size to establish such committees. A year later, the Aboriginal and Community Policing Directorate was created to oversee the establishment of community consultative groups (Seagrave, 1993).

As with many other community policing initiatives, evaluations of these projects in Canada have yet to take place. Currently, the community consultative process, if truly open to all members of the community, offers a viable way for community members to have direct input into policing policies and initiatives.

Mini-stations

The community policing philosophy advocates the decentralization of police services and a greater local accountability. With this in mind, a number of police agencies have started to introduce mini-stations—sometimes called storefront offices or community police stations—in order to decentralize their service and provide a local police presence.

The scope of activities undertaken within these mini-stations varies and in ideal circumstances, is tailored to reflect the needs of the community served. Details on crime prevention and programs such as Neighborhood Watch and

Operation Identification are often available. The mini-station also offers a drop-in facility, where citizens can provide information on a number of different issues. Mini-stations are generally staffed by volunteers, with police officers assigned responsibility for the local area coming in to make phone calls, write and receive reports and provide advice.

The historical development of the mini-station concept can be traced back to 1974, when Detroit established small, locally-accountable police stations. Nine years later, the concept was introduced in Canada by the Toronto police, who opened the first mini-station on Danforth Avenue. In 1986, a second was opened in Parkdale. The goal of these two mini-stations was to create an enhanced understanding of police-community partnership (Lambert, 1988) and followed a recommendation by a working group of municipal council representatives who were addressing the issue of race relations. In 1987, probably the most widely known Canadian program of mini-stations was initiated in Victoria, BC. The Community Police Station Program (CoPS) was comprised of several mini-stations staffed by one uniformed officer, who was assisted by a number of volunteers (Walker and Walker, 1989).

While the historical development of the mini-stations in Canada shows them to have been police initiated, recently, community groups have been involved in pressuring for, organizing and establishing their own community police stations. This has often meant the solicitation of funds from provincial and municipal councils and private business in order to set up the resource. Police involvement in these community-initiated mini-stations is present in much the same way as it is in the police-sponsored projects; the difference is in the early identification of the need for this provision.

Police-community relations programs

As illustrated above, there are important differences between community policing and community relations; however, community relations designed to improve the relationship between the police and the public is a basic building block to community policing (Griffiths and Verdun Jones, 1994). Community relations programs aim to increase community understanding of policing, and vice versa. Many of these programs were started before the community policing revolution, but have now been incorporated under the banner of community policing. Often, these programs are directed at a specific group of individuals, such as victims of crime, youth, the elderly or women.

Programs directed at crime victims exist in most police departments in Canada. Victim assistance programs provide details to victims on the progress of their case, facilitate the return of property and act as a referral agency for other support groups in the community. They may also provide training for police officers in dealing with victims of crime. These initiatives often rely heavily on the support of volunteers, and sometimes incorporate a collaborative agreement between the police and a community agency. For example, in Ottawa, the

Salvation Army works with the Ottawa Police Department to supply a victim support service, while in Montreal, the Integrated Victim Assistance Program is operated by the University of Montreal in cooperation with the Montreal Urban Community Police (Griffiths and Verdun Jones, 1994).

In addition to these programs, some police departments have developed specific victim services for battered and sexually abused women and children, the elderly and for victims of specific offenses such as robbery.

Police school liaison programs provide another example of the community relations effort undertaken by police departments. While some of these involve the police officer visiting the school on a regular basis to make presentations and facilitate contact, others demand a greater commitment, whereby the police officer is resident in the school on a full-time basis during school hours. It is important to see these programs, not as ways to reduce crime, but as vehicles that promote and facilitate police-community relations by promoting positive contacts and communications. In this respect, they fall within the community policing philosophy.

Crime prevention programs

There exists a vast array of crime prevention programs, such as Neighborhood Watch, Operation Identification, citizen patrols, Crime Prevention Through Environmental Design (CPTED) and media initiatives. Some of these, like community relations, started before community policing became the dominant rhetoric. The objective of these programs is to reduce levels of crime and increase citizens' perceptions of safety by reducing fear of crime (Rosenbaum, 1986). Most crime prevention programs are designed to reduce the incidence of property crimes, by identifying opportunities for it to occur and altering these conditions.

Probably the best-known crime prevention program is Neighborhood Watch or Block Watch. Originating in the United States during the 1970s, this initiative involves mobilizing the community to be the 'eyes and ears' of the police. It is also designed to promote a sense of community in neighborhoods by encouraging citizens to look out for each other. The program is run by volunteers. Usually two individuals, who are not resident in the same house but who live in close proximity, become coordinators for the project. It is their task to mobilize the community. Variations on this theme are Block Parent schemes designed to watch out for children.

Research on the effectiveness of Neighborhood Watch is inconclusive. Bennett and Lavarakas (1989) found that it did reduce fear of crime, while research by Rosenbaum (1987) found evidence to the contrary.

Citizen patrols have also been initiated over the last few years. The most organized and well known is The Guardian Angels, which is active in the United States and also retains a presence in Canada. Citizen patrols can either be on foot or mobile, and work by reporting to police incidents they deem need attention. Evaluations of these initiatives in Canada are not available, but evidence from Europe and the United States suggests they may be effective in reducing property crime and fear of crime (Pennell et al., 1989; Van Andel, 1989).

Property identification schemes aimed at deterring theft have been introduced by Operation Identification (for private residences) and Operation Provident (for businesses). These programs involve citizens and businesses marking their property with identification numbers, thus making the disposal of stolen goods more difficult, and the recognition of items easier. An evaluation of Operation Identification and Operation Provident programs by the Solicitor General found them to be successful in deterring theft; however, research, cited by Griffiths and Verdun Jones (1994), in the United States and Wales did not produce such optimistic results.

The media have also been involved in promoting crime prevention initiatives by screening programs such as Crime Stoppers and America's Most Wanted. Research undertaken by Carrier (1987) in Canada and by Rosenbaum et al. (1989) in the United States found that these programs received widespread public support.

Crime Prevention Through Environmental Design (CPTED) involves altering the physical environment to discourage potential offenders. The program promotes the use of better lighting to allow for increased surveillance, controlling access to areas to reduce the potential for victimization and the use of architectural and landscape designs to prevent crime. Courses in CPTED are now taught in Canadian police colleges, although there remains little evidence that altering the physical environment has a significant impact on crime (Griffiths and Verdun Jones, 1994).

While the research evidence may not present an optimistic picture of crime prevention programs having a quantifiable influence on levels of crime or fear of crime, it is important to see such initiatives for their wider potential. They do promote police-community contacts and make the community more aware of crime prevention initiatives. However, the extent to which they are known and adopted by all communities, irrespective of their socioeconomic composition, is anything but uniform. As will be shown in the next chapter, the problem of community involvement in crime prevention and other community policing initiatives has been recognized as an issue for the development of community policing. Research from the United States (Skolnick and Bayley, 1986) suggests there are examples of police-community initiatives working well that have led to new policing strategies. Skolnick and Bayley argue this has led to a 'new blue line' in the form of community policing, which has been successful in providing new ways of dealing with traditional crime and order problems.

Community surveys

In order to gain an understanding of community priorities for policing, some police departments have undertaken community surveys or satisfaction surveys when developing policing policies and practices. These surveys usually take the form of an interview or questionnaire and may have a variety of objectives:

- to evaluate the success of alternative policing measures, such as foot patrols.
- to gauge the impact of crime prevention initiatives.
- to monitor public perceptions of the police.
- to identify public concern with crime.
- to discover which issues the community deems as priorities for police action.
- to develop a community profile detailing the characteristics of the community.
- to investigate the 'dark figure' of crime (crimes unreported to the police).
- to identify training and recruitment needs (Sacco, 1994).

In Canada, community surveys have been undertaken in a number of cities, including Toronto (Murphy and de Verteuil, 1986), Regina (Hylton, 1980), Winnipeg (Forde, 1992), New Brunswick (Baseline Market Research Ltd, 1991), and Vancouver (Seagrave, 1993). The methodologies employed in the collection of data vary, and the extent to which police departments act on the survey results is a point of conjecture; nevertheless, they do promote police-community contacts and have been introduced only recently.

Other community policing initiatives

Additional widely-known community policing programs include problem-oriented policing strategies, which have been attempted in a number of police departments, and zone policing, which is similar to team policing in that it divides policing jurisdictions into smaller zones. Halifax introduced zone policing in the mid-1980s. As mentioned above, any program designed to promote and facilitate police-community relations can be introduced onto the community policing bandwagon. This review has concentrated on those programs that are most commonly applied by police agencies.

The community policing philosophy advocates comprehensive organizational change. With the notable exception of the Edmonton Police Service, which is held to be at the forefront of community policing, evidence of police departments introducing large-scale change are rare. However, there are attempts to change the organizational culture in a number of police departments. Over the course of the next decade, it will be possible to assess the extent to which the community policing philosophy has (or has not) taken hold in Canadian policing.

SUMMARY

This chapter has illustrated the imprecision that surrounds the concept of community policing. It showed that interpretations of community policing fall into five categories, with the philosophical interpretation providing the broadest, most ideal definition. Community policing was then discussed in relation to problem-oriented policing and police-community relations to show its similarities and differences with these approaches. The overall objectives of the community policing movement were detailed and the various policies and programs that have been introduced under the community policing umbrella were outlined. The following chapter deals with how the community policing concept has been introduced in Canada.

QUESTIONS FOR DISCUSSION

1. Describe the difference between problem-oriented and community policing.
2. Provide three examples of community policing programs.
3. To what extent are the objectives of community policing 'pie in the sky' dreams?
4. Discuss the reasons why you think the term 'community' is frequently applied to policies of reform. For example, community art, community architecture, community radio, etc.
5. Outline Cordner's dimensions of community policing. To what extent can they be treated in isolation from one another?
6. Describe the 'control' interpretation of community policing. How applicable is it in an analysis of policing in Canada?
7. What, if any, similarities exist between community policing and community relations?
8. What is meant by the term 'interactive policing'? Why is this different from what has gone before?
9. Provide three examples of structural organizational change that may occur when a police department implements community policing.
10. To what extent do you think the 'philosophy' interpretation of community policing exists in police agencies in Canada? Give reasons for your response.

FURTHER READING

Goldstein, H. (1990). *Problem Oriented Policing.* New York: McGraw Hill. This work commences by reviewing the criticisms and problems faced by the traditional model of policing and then outlines the advantages of the problem-oriented approach. Examples of the successes and failures of the method are given.

The Ministry of the Solicitor General of Canada (1993-5). *Community Policing Series.* Ottawa: Minister of Supplies and Services. This is a series of reports, written primarily for police personnel, on various community policing strategies, for example, leadership development, the use of surveys, community consultation, problem-oriented policing and crime and incident analysis.

Walker, Christopher R. and Walker, Gail S. (1989). *The Victoria Community Police Stations: An Exercise in Innovation.* Ottawa: Canadian Police College. This document describes the program of introducing community police stations in Victoria, B.C.

REFERENCES

Alderson, J. (1982). "The future of policing." In T. Bennett (Ed.) *The Future of Policing.* Cambridge: Institute of Criminology.

Baseline Market Research Ltd. (1991). *Public Attitude Survey: Crime, Safety and Policing Services in New Brunswick.* New Brunswick: Department of the Solicitor General.

Bayley, D.H. (1989). "Community policing: A report from the devil's advocate." In J.R. Green and S.D. Mastrofski (Eds.) *Community Policing; Rhetoric or Reality.* New York: Praeger.

Bennett, S.F. and Lavarakas, P.J. (1989). "Community-based crime prevention: an assessment of the Eisenhower Foundations Neighborhood Program." *Crime and Delinquency, 25*(2).

Broderick, J. (1991). "Review essay: Community policing and problem oriented policing." *American Journal of Police, X*(4).

Bunyan, T. (1981). "The police against the people." *Race and Class, 23*(2-3).

Carriere, K.D. (1987). Crime stoppers critically considered. *Canadian Criminology Forum, 8.*

Chacko, James and Nancoo, Stephen E. (1993). *Community Policing in Canada.* Toronto: Canadian Scholars' Press Inc.

Clairmont, D.H. (1991). "Community-based policing: Implementation and impact." *Canadian Journal of Criminology, 33*(3-4).

Cordner, Gary W. (1995). "Community policing: Elements and effects." *Police Forum, 5*(3).

Crank, J.P. (1994). "Watchman and the community: Myth and institutionalization in policing." *Law and Society Review, 28*(2).

Forde, D.R. (1992). *Public Attitudes Towards Crime and Police Services: Survey Findings of Winnipeg in 1989 and 1992.* Winnipeg: Department of Sociology, The University of Manitoba.

Friedmann, Robert R. (1992). *Community Policing: Comparative Perspectives and Prospects.* Hemel Hempstead: Harvester Wheatsheaf.

Goldstein, H. (1987). "Towards community oriented policing: Potential basic requirements and threshold questions." *Crime and Delinquency, 33*(1).

Goldstein, H. (1990). *Problem Oriented Policing.* New York: McGraw Hill.

Green, Jack R., Bergman, William T. and McLaughlin, Edward J. (1994). "Implementing community policing: Cultural and structural change in police organizations." In Dennis P. Rosenbaum (Ed.) *The Challenge of Community Policing: Testing the Promises.* California: Sage.

Griffiths, Curt T. and Verdun Jones, Simon N. (1994). *Canadian Criminal Justice.* Toronto: Harcourt Brace.

Hornick, J.P., Burrows, T.A., Tjowvold, I. and Phillips, D.M. (1990). *An Evaluation of the Neighbourhood Foot Patrol Program of the Edmonton Police Service.* Ottawa: Solicitor General of Canada.

Hornick, J.P., Burrows, B.A., Phillips, D.M., and Leighton, B. (1991). "An impact evaluation of the Edmonton neighbourhood foot patrol program." *The Canadian Journal of Program Evaluation,* 6(1).

Hunt, Raymond G. and Magenau, John M. (1993). *Power and the Police Chief: An Institutional and Organizational Analysis.* Newbury Park: Sage.

Hylton, J.H. (1980). "Public attitudes towards crime and the police in a Prairie city." *Canadian Police College Journal,* 4(4).

Kelling, G.L. and Moore, M.H. (1989). "From political to reform to community: The evolving strategy of police." In J.R. Green and S.D. Mastrofski (Eds.) *Community Policing: Rhetoric or Reality.* New York: Praeger.

Kinsey, R., Lea, J. and Young, J. (1986). *Losing the Fight Against Crime.* London: Routledge.

Klockars, C.B. (1989). "The rhetoric of community policing." In J.R. Green and S.D. Mastrofski (Eds.) *Community Policing: Rhetoric or Reality.* New York: Praeger.

Lambert, Leah (1988). "Police ministations in Toronto: An experience in compromise." *RCMP Gazette,* 50(6).

Leighton, B.N. (1991). "Visions of community policing: Rhetoric or reality in Canada." *Canadian Journal of Criminology,* 33(3–4).

Leighton, B.N. (1994). "Community policing in Canada: An overview of experience and evaluations." In Dennis P. Rosenbaum (Ed.) *The Challenge of Community Policing: Testing the Promises.* California: Sage.

Loree, D. (1988). "Innovation and change in a regional police force." *Canadian Police College Journal,* 12(4).

Manning, P.K. (1984). Community policing. *American Journal of the Police,* 3(2).

Mawby, R.I. (1990). *Comparative Policing Issues: The British and American System in International Perspective.* London: Unwin Hyman.

Murphy, C. (1988). "Community problems, problem communities and community policing in Toronto." *Journal of Research in Crime and Delinquency,* 24(4),

Murphy, C. (1989). "The development, impact and implications of community policing in Canada." In J.R. Green and S.D. Mastrofski (Eds.) *Community Policing: Rhetoric or Reality.* New York: Praeger.

Murphy, C. (1992). "Problem oriented policing." In Ministry of the Solicitor General of Canada *Canadian Community Policing Series.* Ottawa: Minister of Supplies and Services.

Murphy, C. (1994). *Community-Based Policing—A Review of the Issues, Research and Development of a Provincial Policy.* Report prepared for the Commission of Inquiry Policing in British Columbia. Victoria, B.C.: Attorney General.

Murphy, C. and de Verteuil, J. (1986). *Metropolitan Toronto Community Policing Survey: Working Paper No. 1.* Ottawa: Solicitor General of Canada.

Normandeau, A. and Leighton, B. (1990). *A Vision of the Future of Policing in Canada: Police Challenge 2000—Background Document.* Ottawa: Police and Security Branch, Ministry Secretariat, Solicitor General.

Normandeau, A. and Leighton, B. (1991). "Police and Society in Canada." *Canadian Journal of Criminology, 33*(3-4).

Oppal, The Honourable Mr. Justice Wallace T. (1994). *Closing the Gap: Policing and the Community.* Commission of Inquiry Policing in British Columbia. Victoria, B.C.: Attorney General.

Pennell, S., Curtis, C., Henderson, J. and Tayman, J. (1989). "Guardian Angels: A unique approach to crime prevention." *Crime and Delinquency, 35*(2).

Police Foundation (1981). *The Newark Foot Patrol Experiment.* Washington, D.C. The Police Foundation.

Reiner, R. (1991). *Chief Constables: Bobbies, Bosses or Bureaucrats.* Oxford: Clarendon Press.

Riechers, Lisa M. and Roberg, Roy R. (1990). "Community policing: A critical review of underlying assumptions." *Journal of Police Science and Administration, 17*(2).

Rosenbaum, D.P. (1986). *Community Crime Prevention? Does it Work?* Beverly Hills, California: Sage Publications.

Rosenbaum, D.P. (1987). "The theory and research behind neighbourhood watch: Is it a sound fear and crime reduction strategy?" *Crime and Delinquency, 33.*

Rosenbaum, D.P., Lurigo, A.J. and Laurakos, P.J. (1989). Enhancing citizen participation and solving serious crime: A national evolution of the Crime Stoppers Progam. *Crime and Delinquency, 35.*

Sacco, Vincent F. (1994). *Community Surveys.* Ottawa: Ministry of the Solicitor General of Canada.

Seagrave, J. (1993). "Obtaining information for the corporate strategy: The Vancouver Police telephone survey." *Police Studies: The International Review of Police Development, 16*(4).

Seagrave, J. (1996). "Defining community policing: interpretations from the literature, police leaders and police officers." *American Journal of Police 15*(2).

Shaw, Clifford R. and Mackay, Henry D. (1942). *Juvenile Delinquency in Urban Areas.* Chicago: University of Chicago Press.

Skogan, W.G. (1990). *Disorder and Decline: Crime and the Spiral of Decay in American Neighborhoods.* New York: The Free Press.

Skolnick, J.H. and Bayley, D.H. (1986). *The New Blue Line: Police Innovation in Six American Cities.* New York: The Free Press.

Skolnick, J.H. and Bayley, D.H. (1988). *Community Policing: Issues and Practices Around the World.* United States: National Institute of Justice.

Taylor, I. (1980). "The law and order issue in the British general election and the Canadian federal election of 1979." *Canadian Journal of Sociology, 5*(3).

Taylor, I. (1981). *Law and Order: Arguments for Socialism.* London: MacMillan Press.

Trojanowicz, R.C. (1990). "Community policing is not police community relations." *FBI Law Enforcement Bulletin.*

Trojanowicz, R.C. and Banas, D.W. (1985). *Perceptions of Safety: A Comparison of foot patrol versus motor patrol officers.* Michigan: National Foot Patrol Centre, Michigan State University.

Trojanowicz, R.C. and Bucqueroux, D. (1990). *Community Policing: A Contemporary Perspective.* Michigan: Anderson Publishing.

Van Andel, H. (1989). "Crime prevention that works: The case of public transportation in the Netherlands." *British Journal of Criminology, 29*(3).

Walker, C. and Walker, Gail S. (1985). *The Victoria Community Police Stations: An Exercise in Innovation.* Ottawa: Canadian Police College.

Weatheritt, M. (1986). *Innovations in Policing.* London: Croom Hall.

Weatheritt, M. (1987). "Community policing now." In P. Willmott (Ed.) *Policing and the Community.* London: Policy Studies Institute. Discussion Paper 16.

Wycoff, M.A. (1989). "The benefits of community policing: evidence and conjecture." In J.R. Green and S.D. Mastrofski (Eds.) *Community Policing: Rhetoric or Reality.* New York: Praeger.

COMMUNITY POLICING: THE CANADIAN PERSPECTIVE

INTRODUCTION

This chapter outlines the historical development of community policing. The first part shows how community policing evolved in Canada as a reaction to traditional policing practices, which were recognized as costly and detrimental to police-community relations. The chapter then illustrates the extent to which community policing has been discussed and adopted by police agencies in Canada and concludes with a discussion of the problems and issues associated with the concept.

COMMUNITY POLICING HISTORY

Some writers on the subject of community policing believe that it started in Britain with the introduction of Robert Peel's force in 1829 (Jones, 1983; Normandeau and Leighton, 1990; Leighton, 1991). In America, it was initiated as early as 1914 by the then commissioner of the New York City Police, Arthur Woods (Skolnick and Bayley, 1988). Others contend that there has always been community policing, especially in rural areas (Wasson and Crawford, 1977) and that, as a concept, it offers no clear definition that allows us to distinguish it from conventional bureaucratic policing (Murphy and Muir, 1985).

Most commentators regard it as a development of the last twenty years, which has arisen in response to a number of social, political and economic factors (Anderson, 1982; Green and Taylor, 1989; Kelling, 1986; Kelling and Moore, 1989; Leighton, 1991; Wasson and Crawford, 1977). As such, community policing is a reaction to the heavily bureaucratic police organization and encourages community involvement so the police can deal with community problems in a proactive, innovative and creative way (Trojanowicz and Bucqueroux, 1990).

It is also possible to combine both of these perspectives and to view community policing as a re-emergence of the original style of policing, rather than as something that developed over the last twenty years.

PHASES OF POLICING

Some have argued that policing is currently in a period of transition. As mentioned in Chapter 4, Kelling and Moore (1989) have identified three distinct phases to policing in the United States:

1. The political phase, which characterized early development from 1840-1900.

2. The reform phase, which dominated policy from the 1920s until quite recently, and incorporated notions of advanced organizational and technical thinking and professionalism.

3. The transition phase from the reform to the community strategy of the moment.

While these phases may be regarded as simplistic, offering only limited applicability to other nations, policing in many western democracies, including Canada in the 1990s, can be identified as being in this transitional phase. As such, community policing should be regarded as an ongoing evolving process (Oettmeir and Brown, 1989).

For many years, the police in North America and Britain existed within a paradigm characterized by rapid response, militaristic style and a detachment (accentuated by technology) from the community they served. This paradigm has been referred to as 'modern state' (Clarke, 1987) 'professional' (Normandeau and Leighton, 1990) and 'bureaucratic' (Manning, 1989). This style of policing is significantly different from the concept of policing first envisaged by Robert Peel.

Early systems of policing were based on the premise that police officers provide a comprehensive service to the communities they serve through self-initiated strategies. In this regard, they were responsible for a number of broad functions in addition to law enforcement. During the twentieth century, with the advent of the automobile, telephone and more recently, computers, policing has become reactive in nature. Police cars replaced foot patrols, centralized dispatches replaced local police stations and police officers were assigned areas of expertise and specialization, but had little knowledge of local neighborhoods. As a result of these developments, policing became incident driven and a reactive style of policing developed. Oppal (1994) describes the characteristics of this style of policing as follows.

- **Incident oriented.** Operational focus is directed to responding to individual incidents, which are treated in isolation from each other. Little attempt is made to recognize patterns or similarities in the calls received.

- **Response oriented.** Incidents are responded to when they arise and priority is given to response capability and capacity. Little attention is paid to proactive, self-initiated policing or preventive measures.

- **Focused on limited analysis.** Analysis and information gathering are confined to specific situations. There is sparse analysis into the underlying causes of a wide variety of incidents.

- **Focused on narrow response.** The response of police personnel is to apply standard law enforcement strategies, not explore alternative ways to address issues.
- **Focused on means rather than ends.** Efficiency is valued over effectiveness. Scant attention is awarded to policing strategies that prevent, reduce or eliminate the problem.

Anomalies in this incident-oriented, reactive style of policing were discovered in the 1960s and early 1970s (e.g., expenditure and efficiency were questioned, as was the use of discretion and treatment of ethnic minorities). These anomalies reached crisis proportions in Britain, leading to the 1981 riots that took place in certain urban centres and resulted in the subsequent Scarman Report (1982), and (less precisely) in the United States, leading to the increasingly vocal disillusionment with policing (Crank, 1994). It is important to view any impetus for change in Canada in light of the political and economic climate of the day and in relation to the influences of other western democracies particularly the United States.

COMMUNITY POLICING IN THE US

Since the 1980s, there has been a slow and steady increase in the number of community policing texts in the US. While few references could be found on the subject in 1985, volumes of literature exist now. Although initial works illustrated some skepticism over the philosophy, more recently, authors have displayed an "unbiased enthusiasm for the changes, an enthusiasm uncommon in the social sciences" (Broderick, 1991, p. 130). Research that draws a distinction between community policing and traditional policing can be traced back to the 1960s. For example, Bittner (1967) provided an analysis of policing on skid row to illustrate the peacekeeping role of police officers; this would be seen by many as community policing today.

The development of community policing in Canada may be seen, in part, as a reaction to what has occurred in the United States (Normandeau and Leighton, 1990; Murphy, 1989). However, any analysis along these lines must be undertaken with caution as, for the most part, Canadian policing has not had to deal with the same concerns as American police, such as allegations of widespread corruption and political influence (Leighton, 1991). Community policing emerged in the US in response to a number of factors, including expensive and expansive police services, declining neighborhood safety in urban areas, class- and race-based conflict and an academic critique of police efficiency. Although some of these social, economic and political factors have been recognized as influencing the shift to community policing as long ago as 1969 (Germann, 1969), they have been reiterated and expanded over the last twenty years, when the position of the police has been undermined by social change, a better-educated, heterogeneous population, a more critical media and a greater devotion to individual rights (Marquis, 1991). The change in political complexion towards the conservative policies of Reagan and Mulroney aided this development.

There was clearly a crisis in policing in the US in the 1960s; the police were seen as distant from the populations they served (Crank, 1994). This issue was compounded by the increased use of technology (Kelling and Moore, 1989; Leighton, 1991; Mawby, 1990) and epitomized by the widespread introduction of the patrol car and improved communication, addressing the proposed need for rapid response. While police agencies in North America readily adopted these strategies, it soon became obvious that anomalies existed within the professional model of policing. The questionable effectiveness of the professional model, driven by technological advances, and the resulting detrimental influence on police-community relations can be summarized as follows.

- From the 1930s onwards, there was increased use of the patrol car, which took the police officer off the street. Most crimes are solved through the information provided by victims and witnesses, therefore, the police need to establish and maintain close contacts with the communities they serve in order to facilitate the communication process. The patrol car restricted this process.

- All calls for service, irrespective of their nature, were responded to in the same manner. During the 1960s, rapid response to calls for service was shown to be an ineffective way to address demands from the public, as most victims delay reporting incidents to the police. Prioritizing calls based on urgency and offering a differential response permits better use of police resources.

- There is no evidence that random motorized patrol deters criminals, reduces crime, increases the apprehension of offenders or reduces fear of crime. In contrast, foot patrols are believed to reduce fear of crime and increase public satisfaction with the police.

- Throughout the 1960s and early 1970s, there was a belief that crime could be addressed by dedicating more financial resources to its control. Ever-increasing police budgets were demanded, but the crime rate still grew. It became apparent that merely adding police personnel and dedicating more resources to police services does not increase effectiveness in solving crime. Instead, resources need to be targeted and directed at specific crime and disorder problems in order to show results.

In addition to these factors, fear of crime and the perceived incivilities illustrating signs of disorder led to a demand for the police to address order maintenance and quality of life problems. Considerable reaction against 'fire brigade' policing, articulated in the 1960s by the *President's Crime Commission*, stimulated a variety of initiatives, so that by the 1970s, team policing, problem-oriented policing and community policing approaches were being advocated (Mawby, 1990). Policies such as team policing (see Chapter 7), which attempted to democratize and decentralize policing, were the forerunners to community policing (Green and Taylor, 1989).

Recently, community policing has been described as the centrepiece of the Clinton administration's anti-crime policy (Rosenbaum and Lurigo, 1994), with the administration setting aside $150 million in the 1993 supplemental budget to hire 100,000 community police officers (Grinc, 1994). Despite this commitment, a recent Canadian study that reviewed American literature found that, for most US police forces, community policing remains largely theoretical (Oppal, 1994).

COMMUNITY POLICING IN CANADA

Leighton (1994) has argued that, in adopting community policing, police organizations in Canada are simply returning to their nineteenth-century origins after a few years of 'flirting' with the professional policing model. Others see the adoption of community policing policies and practices to be influenced by events in the US (Mawby, 1990) and, to a lesser extent, in Britain (Friedmann, 1992). Canada has traditionally looked south for new ideas because of the lack of indigenous research and innovative police leadership (Murphy, 1989). There are merits in both these positions. In addition, the development of community policing may be viewed as a response to other social and economic concerns.

Community policing sits well with programmatic policies. As concern has been expressed over the efficiency and effectiveness of policing, community policing, by involving the community, is beneficial in both fiscal and political terms. In shifting some responsibilities and costs for policing back to the community and reducing the finances for government-funded public policing, community policing is both a pragmatic and politically appealing reform (Murphy, 1988).

A number of developments in Canada were regarded as distancing the police from the community. For example, both the Canadian Police Information Centre and the Police Information Reference System have strained police-community relations because of the belief that these developments have increased the ability of the police to collect information on the public—the existence of which the public is not aware and to which it does not have access (Taylor, 1980). However, the actual amount of pressure—both internal and external—to reform Canadian policing has not been extensive (Leighton, 1991).

The extent to which police departments and detachments in Canada are paying lip service to a vague and untested idea developed in the United States is a point of conjecture. Although some believe that, in comparison to five years ago, Canadian policing has firmly embraced the community policing paradigm (Chacko and Nancoo, 1993; Leighton, 1994), a recent study of policing in British Columbia found that, despite recent developments, concern over other policing issues, such as investigation procedures, performance measurement, race relations and domestic violence, has diminished the importance of community policing (Oppal, 1994). There would appear to be a gap between the optimistic rhetoric and the implementation reality.

The inception of the community policing philosophy in Canada can be traced back several years to a publication sponsored by the Solicitor General, *Community Based Policing: A Review of the Critical Issues*, which argued there was a strong mandate for reassessing current police beliefs and practices. This document went on to stress that community policing offers a viable and creative management response to what was seen as a restrictive police environment (Murphy and Muir, 1985). Since that time, the community policing movement has gained momentum so that, more recently, it was described as the "official morality" of policing in Canada (Clairmont, 1991, p. 469) and that there is now "no turning back" (Kennedy, 1991, p. 286).

In 1990, the Solicitor General of Canada, Pierre Cadieux, stated community policing was "the most effective way to police the Canada of the future," and called upon line officers and police chiefs to "get on with the business of systematically implementing community policing" (Cadieux, 1990). It has subsequently been endorsed by the Canadian Police College and further supported in the document *A Vision of the Future of Policing in Canada: Police Challenge 2000* (Normandeau and Leighton, 1990), which was issued by the office of the Solicitor General. While this publication articulated neither defined policies to be adopted, nor implementation strategies, it did promote discussion and confirm that the Solicitor General supported community policing. The authors of the report claimed community policing is the object of a growing consensus and that no competing views of policing exist. More recently, the Ministry of the Solicitor General (1994) produced a series of reports on community policing. These reports aimed to assist police agencies with the implementation of community policing initiatives and were prepared as a joint project with the Ontario Ministry of the Solicitor General and Correctional Services. They were subsequently adopted by the OPP and the RCMP.

There is evidence that, as an idea, community policing has been awarded increasing attention and has been "lauded by community and police leaders alike" (Kennedy, 1991, p. 279). Canadian police leaders have adopted "as their conventional wisdom that community policing represents the most progressive approach to contemporary policing" (Leighton, 1991, p. 486) and have made sweeping promises to implement the philosophy (Leighton, 1994). Researchers and academics have voiced their opinions by arguing that fundamental changes must be made to the traditional, centralized organizational culture found in many police departments (Descza, 1988).

Firm evidence of formal commitment can be found in the 1990s mission statements of every major force in Canada, all of which use the term community policing (Bayley, 1991; Horne, 1992). In addition, federal, provincial and municipal police agencies and federal and provincial governments have enthusiastically endorsed and advocated the community policing philosophy.

COMMUNITY POLICING AND THE RCMP

As early as 1981, the RCMP started to discuss the possibility of community polic-ing (Oppal, 1994). However, it has been during the recent past that the RCMP has developed a number of different policy documents that include reference to community policing. In the 1989 directional statement, the Commissioner com-mitted the RCMP to adopting the community policing concept. This statement directed all detachments of more than 12 to establish advisory committees (Seagrave, 1994) and, while not grounded in a rational plan for community policing, still had an impact (Leighton, 1994). In 1990, the RCMP developed a strategic action plan for the implementation of community policing. It defined community policing as "an interactive process between the police and the com-munity to mutually identify and resolve community problems" and went on to characterize community policing in 14 points. The plan stated that the "Senior Executive Committee of the RCMP has decided that this community policing approach will be adopted to the delivery of police services." One of the recom-mendations of this plan was to rename the contract policing function communi-ty policing. The 22-page document proceeded to define the strategic goal which was to implement community policing throughout the RCMP by 1993. Twelve objectives were detailed and awarded a time frame in which they were to be undertaken. Costings were also discussed as were staffing requirements; howev-er, due to imprecise wording, the actual role of each rank in the change process was not specifically outlined.

In 1991, the RCMP mission statement provided a lengthy definition of com-munity policing, which now appears in both official languages on a poster in all reception areas of RCMP detachments. In addition to the consultative commit-tees, recruit training is increasingly being oriented towards community policing, while certain individual detachments are being given autonomy to experiment with the concept (e.g., Burnaby, BC).

COMMUNITY POLICING AND PROVINCIAL POLICE

The Ontario Provincial Police (OPP) and the Sûreté du Québec (SQ) are in the process of implementing community policing with the OPP promoting the phi-losophy through an action plan aimed at small towns in the province. The 1990 Ontario Police Services Act legislated community policing through a number of principles (see Appendix B), and in 1990, the OPP started appointing communi-ty police officers with responsibility for several small municipalities, who were given the freedom to structure their work according to the demands of the com-munity (Bayley, 1991). In addition, the SQ is promoting a change in organiza-tional culture and practice through training (Leighton, 1994). Both forces have been developing a number of policies and programs reflecting the community policing philosophy, an ongoing process.

COMMUNITY POLICING AND MUNICIPAL POLICE

A number of municipal police agencies have made significant moves towards the introduction of community policing. Community policing has been a primary objective of the Metropolitan Toronto Police since the early 1980s (Lambert, 1988). Throughout the decade, the force was involved with a number of different programs, including the opening up of mini-stations and community consultation. In 1992, it published *Beyond 2000...The Strategic Action Plan of the Metropolitan Toronto Police*, which advocated the comprehensive implementation of community policing. One of Toronto's neighboring forces, the Halton Regional Police Force, has also introduced mini-stations, in addition to other community policing initiatives.

Storefront offices have proven to be one of the most popular community policing programs, being introduced in a number of different locations, including Halifax, Fredericton, Ottawa, Edmonton, Vancouver and Victoria. They often exist in conjunction with a number of other community policing programs. As described in Chapter 10, while detailed evaluations of the success of these and other community policing initiatives is sketchy, some comprehensive studies do exist and illustrate positive results. However, the picture is not all rosy, as certain municipal forces have experienced problems in the introduction of community policing.

Since the mid-1980s, the Montreal Urban Community Police has established storefront offices and implemented zone policing in an effort to move towards the community policing model. Despite these attempts, a number of racial incidents occurring over the recent past has meant implementation in Montreal does not appear to have been as successful as in other jurisdictions. Winnipeg also seems to have suffered set-backs in its implementation of community policing following commissions of inquiry investigating racial bias towards Aboriginal people (Leighton, 1994).

Notwithstanding these regional problems, there exists firm evidence that community policing programs are being adopted by municipal police departments across the country.

COMMUNITY POLICING AND THE FEDERAL GOVERNMENT

In 1990, the Solicitor General issued a policy paper on policing in Canada entitled *A Vision of the Future of Policing in Canada: Police Challenge 2000*. Andre Normandeau, from the University of Montreal, and Barry Leighton, from the Ministry of the Solicitor General, were commissioned to write the report. The background research for this document involved reviewing the policing literature, talking to academics and police practitioners, interviewing 50 key individuals involved with policing, group discussions with approximately 500 interested individuals and a seminar on the future of policing in Canada.

After providing data and statistics on policing in Canada, the report discusses the environmental factors that will influence policing in the next decade, including demographics, technology, crime patterns and economic, cultural, political and social trends. The report then proceeds to discuss community policing, contrasting it with bureaucratic traditional policing and endorsing it as the way policing should develop. In predicting how policing will change during the 1990s, the report states:

> A fundamental shift will take place from the professional elitist style of policing to community policing. Problem solving, the human element and accountability to the public will supplant the reactive, militaristic and aloof organizations of the past (Normandeau and Leighton, 1990, p. xiii).

In arguing for change, the authors suggest police agencies need to look to the private sector, adopt approaches that have been successful there and apply them to their own organizations. Peters and Waterman's book *In Search of Excellence* is quoted as an example of how private sector principles and philosophies may be used for public sector agencies. Throughout the sections that advocate change, the authors cite processes that have occurred in the private sector as mechanisms for changing police agencies. Therefore, the importance of developing mission statements, adopting strategic planning and developing leadership skills is endorsed with the view that, "...police organizations in the future will pursue excellence much like private organizations" (p. 138). In such agencies, the public is seen as the consumer of police services to whom police departments are accountable.

The dominant themes presented in this federal policy document are community policing, management and administration and organizational change. As noted by Melchers (1993), *A Vision of the Future* was not intended for scholars, but rather for government officials and police practitioners. While the text advocates the importance of developing a vision and stresses leadership as the catalyst to change, it offers little in the way of pragmatic implementation suggestions. Although it includes a broad discussion of the management and administration of police agencies, the document prefers to address leadership and strategic planning issues and, as such, provides a rhetorical discussion with little practical applicability. In many respects, it should be read as a mission statement illustrating the direction of change, not a programmatic one showing how change can be achieved. This publication has been followed by the *Canadian Community Policing Series* (1994), produced by the Ministry of the Solicitor General. This series contains a number of pragmatic policy documents detailing how community policing initiatives, such as consultative committees, community profiles and problem-oriented policing, can be implemented by police departments.

A Vision of the Future (1990) provided the catalyst for many police agencies to seriously consider changing their operational policies and introduce community policing practices. It endorses community policing, argues for fundamental change and recommends that police agencies look to the private sector as a way to guide and facilitate this process. While the rhetoric may be evidenced in this and other policy documents and mission statements, it may well not be matched, in reality, by the actions of the police agencies themselves.

COMMUNITY POLICING AND PROVINCIAL GOVERNMENTS

A number of provinces have incorporated the community policing concept into their public safety strategies (Leighton, 1994). As mentioned above, the Ontario Police Services Act legislated community policing through six key principles and the Ontario government department responsible for policing is actively supporting the approach through training and the development of provincial standards of policing (Leighton, 1994).

In October 1989, the government of New Brunswick approved funding for a study to examine, in a comprehensive fashion, the delivery of policing service in New Brunswick. Professor Alan Grant of Osgoode Hall Law School undertook the research and, in 1992, the Solicitor General of New Brunswick released a report entitled *Policing Arrangements in New Brunswick: 2000 and Beyond*. The aim of the report was to "...examine present policing arrangements and policies in the province of New Brunswick with a view to formalizing a rational basis for the modification of the existing arrangements, if necessary, to address the policing requirements in the province into the next century" (Grant, 1992).

The final report contained 51 recommendations which fall into two categories: those which address the need to reform the structure of provincial policing and those which address institutional problems with individual police forces (Solicitor General of New Brunswick, 1993). The report endorses the community policing ideology by stating the policing philosophy of the province should emphasize community based law enforcement, in which forces would be attuned to both cultural and ethnic diversity and linguistic differences between regions, as well as reflect the make-up of the community.

The most comprehensive endorsement of community policing can be found in a recent report on policing in British Columbia. In June 1992, Colin Gabelman, the Attorney General for BC, appointed Justice Wallace Oppal to conduct an inquiry into policing for the province. In September 1994, a Commission of Inquiry into Policing in British Columbia released its 700-page report, which contained over 300 recommendations, entitled *Closing the Gap: Policing and the Community* (Oppal, 1994). The commission's terms of reference were expansive and covered virtually every issue related to policing.

The inquiry commissioned over 50 separate research projects, consulted key stakeholders (police chiefs, police unions, advocacy groups, women's groups), held 57 days of public hearings and received over 1,100 written submissions in order to inform its work. It divided the final report into nine sections: the governance of the police, community-based policing, regionalization of policing services, human resource management, use of non-police personnel, Aboriginal policing, high-risk policing, complaints and discipline and the role of the RCMP.

Just as *A Vision of the Future* firmly endorsed organizational change and community policing, so too does the Oppal report. But unlike the federal policy document, which was more of a mission statement, the Oppal report draws upon its own research findings to illustrate that neither the municipal police agencies nor the RCMP has managed to communicate the philosophy of community policing to its members, made changes in organizational structure and functions or successfully fostered closer links to the community it serves. The inquiry recommended the province amend the Police Act and identify community policing as an appropriate model for providing accountable, efficient and effective police services (Oppal, 1994).

Over 81 recommendations were made relating to human resource management. The first of these suggests that municipal police agencies adopt strategies for organizational change that include consultation with members. Although leadership, strategic planning and private sector management principles are mentioned, they are not cited to the same degree as in *A Vision of the Future*. However, in discussing leadership, the report recommends that the available literature from the private sector be adopted to meet policing needs.

In the section devoted to the RCMP, the report states the province has limited control over the RCMP. It therefore questions whether the RCMP is the most appropriate law enforcement body to fulfill the future needs of the province.

In summary, the Oppal report firmly endorses organizational change and the adoption of community policing, but is cognizant of the limitations and problems that may be encountered.

COMMUNITY POLICING PROBLEMS AND ISSUES

There are, of course, problems related to the adoption and implementation of community policing. These have been listed by a number of commentators (Leighton, 1991; Skogan, 1990; Skolnick and Bayley, 1986; Smith, 1987; Wycoff, 1989). The two basic premises of community policing: greater involvement with the community and a change in the structure of the police organization have been queried. Although benefits to the community have been outlined (Skolnick and Bayley, 1988), there are many doubts. Three broad issues can be examined, which incorporate all the concerns expressed. Firstly, the role of the community, secondly, the lack of research and, thirdly, the commitment of the police to organizational change.

Role of the community

The first issue concerns the participation of the community: how can the community be defined (Hunt and Magenau, 1993)? Supposing that it can, what evidence is there it will participate in policy decision-making (Goldstein, 1987), want to be involved (Nelken, 1985) and be prepared to tell the police its concerns (Skogan, 1990)? It is difficult, if not impossible, to form a working definition of community, because communities tend not to be homogeneous consensus bodies (Leighton, 1991). There remains, to date, no adequate working definition of community. As there is obviously no single community, it follows that there can be no single way to conduct community policing (Riechers and Roberg, 1990).

The social composition of an area is bound to influence community policing initiatives. Community policing will always be in danger of being adopted by the affluent, white middle-class areas leaving the poorer ones to traditional, reactive policing (Bayley, 1989; Skolnick and Bayley, 1988). There are problems with moving empowerment philosophies to actual programs and, in this respect, community policing often fails to penetrate the areas where it is arguably needed (Clarke, 1987; Kinsey, Lea and Young, 1986; Lea and Young, 1984). Empirical evidence of this has been collected in the study of Neighbourhood Watch in three police forces in England. This study illustrates that the schemes tended to be adopted only in white, middle-class, property-owning areas (McConnville and Shepherd, 1992). Similar findings have been revealed in the United States (Grinc, 1994). Community policing programs seem to be more readily adopted by home-owners and those who already have roots in the community (Skogan, 1990).

The nature of community policing can be influenced, not only by the social structure, but also by the size and location of the community. The fact that community is "such a different animal in rural and urban areas" (Shapland and Vagg, 1988, p. 2) has not been addressed. There exists confusion over whether the police in rural and frontier areas of Canada are already operating community policing (Wasson and Crawford, 1977) or whether they are employing what may be interpreted as conventional urban crime-control policing (Murphy, 1989). Community policing has been proposed as a panacea for all policing. Its applicability to inner-city areas may be questionable, given the social problems and the harsh realities of crime that may exist in these environments (Jones, 1983; Skogan, 1990).

The fact that some groups, neighborhoods or jurisdictions may not want community policing has not been addressed. Rather, community policing seems to have been accepted as the suitable model of policing for all areas, irrespective of the wishes of individuals living there. While there has been recognition that differing (community policing) policies and practices will be required in different areas, the fundamental question of whether the community wants community policing has not been asked.

Actually involving members of the community in crime prevention and related projects is problematic. Research undertaken in Britain on police community liaison panels, introduced in 1984 to facilitate dialogue between the police and the public, has shown them to be wanting on three accounts. Firstly, they are unrepresentative of the community—a point also demonstrated by others who have conducted research on community involvement (Lea and Young, 1984; Nelken, 1985); secondly, they have had problems attracting members; and finally, they are not politically accountable (Lea and Young, 1984; Morgan, 1987). In addition, special interest groups may be able to influence police and community perceptions of crime and disorder by attending these committees, increasing the attention given to a particular problem by their direct intervention, (Melchers, 1993). The RCMP is currently in the process of introducing similar groups in its detachment areas (Seagrave, 1993).

It would appear that even the proponents of community policing are themselves unclear about the role of the community. Should the community be seen as a consumer of police services, as a partner/co-producer, as a source of authority and influence or as an alternative (Murphy, 1989)? Although, in both Canada and the US, structures exist for public involvement in policing policy, in practice there has been little evidence of the wider public having any influence on police policy and practices (Mawby, 1990). There exists little empirical data on why this is so, but it could be conjectured that the problems faced in North America are similar to those experienced by the British police community liaison panels.

Lack of research

Although the rhetoric within police and policy fields may proclaim the success of community policing—for example, a policy document of the Toronto Police Department argued that it was based on "sound proven ideas" (Toronto Police, 1991, p. 17)—there has been little empirical evaluation of it, leading to the conclusion that community policing has traded on its philosophical and moral appeal and has failed to examine the underlying assumptions on which it is based. Evaluation studies require goals and objectives. One of the reasons for the lack of evaluation may well be that police agencies are unsure of the goals of community policing initiatives and do not know how to conduct research on community policing (Seagrave, 1992).

The lack of research has been highlighted by many (Bayley, 1991; Broderick, 1991; Clairmont, 1991; Green and Taylor, 1989; Leighton, 1991; Murphy and Muir, 1985; Murphy, 1988) and, in Canada, has led to a reliance on American literature (Murphy, 1989). The efficiency of the public as co-producers of crime prevention remains untested (Skolnick and Bayley, 1988). With few exceptions (e.g., Ministry of the Solicitor General, 1994), the community policing literature generally offers typologies, normative statements and criticisms of professional policing, rather than implementation and impact analysis

(Clairmont, 1991). The studies that have been conducted in North America have provided contradictory findings and, upon closer inspection, do not test the proposed theoretical rationale for the philosophy of community policing (Green and Taylor, 1989). The outcome of community policing policies in the US remains uncertain (Green and Mastrofski, 1989; Trojanowicz and Bucqueroux, 1990).

Likewise, in Britain, many community policing initiatives, such as community constables, neighborhood policing and Neighborhood Watch have been shown to be unsuccessful. Reiner (1992), in reviewing these initiatives, suggests that difficulties lie both in implementing the programs as intended and in measuring effectiveness, an issue also identified in North America (Rosenbaum and Lurigo, 1994). The evaluation of initiatives is contentious. As a concept, community policing is difficult to test, because its goals and objectives, which should be defined and measured as indicators of success, are unknown. If it cannot be defined operationally, it cannot be evaluated systematically (Green and Taylor, 1989; Murphy, 1989).

The research undertaken in the United States, despite receiving praise by some (Linden, 1991), has been shown to be largely descriptive. Moreover, it has been criticized for being little more than anecdotal (Mastrofski, 1989) and for revealing inconsistent results which did not test the theoretical rationale (Green and Taylor, 1989). There has been little systematic, in-depth exploration of what the police actually do in the name of community policing; likewise, there is limited information on the nature of community involvement in problem solving (Goldstein, 1990).

There is debate over both the extent and benefits of community policing in Canada. Murphy (1989) illustrates that the few studies undertaken have focused on the implementation process rather than the possibility of organizational change and, as such, have involved survey data which provide limited information on the impact, success or failure of a program. He concludes that, if community policing is to progress, police and funding agencies have to pursue more critical and methodologically sophisticated evaluation studies. Leighton (1994) states there have been only two formal published reports that provide comprehensive, rigorous impact evaluations of community policing programs. Normandeau (1993), however, adds another three to this list, and Kennedy (1991) contends that, while there may be evaluations of pilot projects, ongoing monitoring of new initiatives is virtually non-existent. Despite this bleak scenario, there have been a few notable evaluation studies (e.g., Hornick et al., 1990, 1991; Walker and Walker, 1989). The Edmonton Police Service is frequently cited as being the best example of community policing in Canada and is recognized as such by two American agencies with an interest in police research and development, the Police Executive Research Forum and the National Institute of Justice.

Implementation problems have been identified in many community policing innovations. The RCMP action plans have received criticism for their lack of clear instructions on how the organizational and operational elements of community policing programs should be addressed (Walker, 1992). Recently, the RCMP made efforts to address this criticism by initiating pilot projects in a number of detachments to assess the potential for implementing community policing policies.

The scant research mirrors the lack of theory and illustrates that community policing is a concept frequently discussed but rarely defined or analyzed in depth.

Commitment from police organizations

There are two distinct systems of internal control within police organizations: the police subculture and the formal military-bureaucratic system, comprised of a strict hierarchical chain of command and a formal organizational code (Goldsmith, 1990). The community policing philosophy argues for a more participatory management approach, a flattening of the hierarchy and the adoption of a new, proactive style of policing. It therefore advocates changing the mechanistic and centralized bureaucracy into a structure that is organic and decentralized, and recommends the input, not only of the community, but of police employees as well. It becomes apparent that major structural, managerial and personnel changes are required in police organizations before community policing can be implemented (Riechers and Roberg, 1990; Roberg, 1994).

While the benefits of this new philosophy for the organization have been described as increasing morale, enhancing career development, increasing consensus, creating job satisfaction and making the organization more professional (Greene, 1987; Skolnick and Bayley, 1988; Wycoff, 1989), these propositions are merely speculative. Research remains inconclusive. For example, Greene (1987) assessed several community policing programs in the United States and found that police officers' attitudes towards the community and police work did improve as a result of these programs. In a similar approach, Lurigo and Rosenbaum (1994) reviewed 12 studies of police officers and found that community policing had a number of positive effects on police employees. However, questions regarding the methodological soundness of these studies made them surmise it was impossible to draw firm conclusions about the effects of reform on police officers' attitudes. Skeptics have queried whether an organization such as the police can change an ideology that places such emphasis on the 'thief taking' role and the segregation of police from civilians (Baldwin and Kinsey, 1982).

As illustrated in Chapter 6, there is a wealth of literature that has shown the traditionally conservative police subculture to be resistant to change (Grimshaw and Jefferson, 1987; Goldstein, 1987; Holdaway, 1984). Commitment from the police to organizational change has been identified as a problem for community policing (Clairmont, 1991; Mastrofski, 1989; Skolnick and Bayley, 1988). This cynicism has been attributed to the police subculture, which is regarded as being unsympathetic towards the service model of policing, having little time for community policing ideals and placing a low value on community beat work (McConnville and Shepherd, 1992).

In their study of Neighbourhood Watch, McConnville and Shepherd (1992) argue most police officers at the 'sharp end' of policing regard community beat work as a sop to liberal society which, if undertaken at all, should be done by misfits or officers due for retirement. They go on to show that community policing was not attractive to most police officers, who characterized it as "drinking tea with old ladies," "visiting schools and talking to children" and attending meetings, none of which was real police work (p. 151). This observation reflects findings of an earlier US study in which police officers were noted as seeing community relations as "Mickey Mouse bullshit" (Reuss-Ianni, 1983, p. 121).

The success of community policing may depend, in part, on the police subculture, but it will also be a product of organizational structural and management reform (Murphy, 1989; Riechers and Roberg, 1990; Trojanowicz and Trojanowicz, 1975). Indeed, a key difference between a department that is experimenting and tinkering with programs and one that is striving for a comprehensive community policing strategy is to be found in the changes that have occurred within the operational and administrative systems (Moore, 1994).

Despite the enthusiasm expressed by some senior police officers for the community policing philosophy—an outlook which may well have been influenced by pressure from government and social elites (Reiner, 1992)—it is currently unknown whether the introduction of community policing has led to changes in the organizational structure of police departments. It has been suggested that community policing policies and programs have been simply incorporated into the existing bureaucracy (Murphy, 1988). Community policing has to overcome what has been termed 'organizational rigidity' (Bayley, 1991). It is the organizational environment that creates the difficulty for community policing (Fielding, 1989). Yet the organizational structure is the medium through which this new style of policing should take place; this is the area requiring more study (Green et al., 1994).

The success of any initiative may depend on the chief officers' abiding and energetic commitment to it (Brown, 1986; Deszca, 1988; Skolnick and Bayley, 1986), or, alternatively, on a few key individuals who have promoted changes and who have taken a lead in initiating structural change and innovation in service delivery (Kennedy, 1991). Any shift towards community policing will be undermined if management is uncommitted. On an extremely pessimistic note, one recent publication (Oppal, 1994) has commented that community policing requires changes that may be too complex for traditional police managers, demanding sophisticated and unusual leadership skills not normally associated with police management.

While police leaders may articulate commitment to community policing, there may be a certain strata of the police subculture that is not so positive. The literature has suggested that problems arise, particularly with members of middle management, many of whom have based their careers around traditional policing philosophies and therefore are reluctant to embrace change (Clairmont, 1991; Roberg, 1994). Community policing, if it is to produce the desired results, must be the operating philosophy of the whole department (Goldstein, 1987). In this regard, it is as much a force for organizational change as it is an attempt to change the police role in the community (Murphy, 1986).

Community policing implies not only a shift in police style, but also a substantial change in the traditional role and power of the police, which requires an expansion of both the formal and informal authority of the community (Murphy, 1988). Police organizations have been shown to be some of the most intractable of public bureaucracies (Green et al., 1994) and are highly resistant to change. The reform of policy is more complex for police organizations than for other bureaucracies (Manning, 1977). Difficulties in implementing community policing in BC have been attributed to the archaic structure of policing organizations (Oppal, 1994). The question is to what extent are the police capable of adopting new organizational principles?

> The difficulty for community policing may lie...in securing an organizational environment in which it can endure (Fielding et al, 1989, p. 62).

Green et al. (1994) have cautioned that, historically, organizational change in police agencies has met with only limited success, with the change efforts adapting to the organization, rather than the organization adapting to the intended change. This, they attribute to the culturally inward-looking police organization, which distances itself from clients and civilian oversight.

Despite this contention, it would appear that there are signs of a growing desire amongst the managerial ranks to reform the subculture of the lower ranks and implement change (Holdaway, 1989). Currently, this is just an impressionistic view readily open to challenge. Others see police agencies as all too often containing the failings of other not-for-profit bureaucracies, whose leaders lack competence, vision and the ability to change and instead are addicted to formal rules that no longer work (Punch, 1983). The successful adoption of community policing philosophy in Canada will depend on fundamental changes in the management, administration and organizational structure of police agencies.

SUMMARY

The extent to which community policing has replaced the professional crime control or bureaucratic model of policing as the dominant philosophy in many police organizations is yet to be determined. *A Vision of the Future* illustrates the federal government's commitment to the philosophy. It is not a scholarly text of policing strategies, but rather a "purposive document seeking to create the conditions for consensus on the necessity and a specific direction for change" (Melchers, 1993, p. 50). In many respects, community policing is advancing because it makes sense both fiscally and politically, not because it has been shown to work, "this is dangerous because policy making unsupported by facts is fickle" (Skolnick and Bayley, 1988, p. 69). The extent to which community policing represents organizational change in every police agency in Canada is open to debate.

This chapter has shown how community policing grew out of a reaction against the bureaucratic professional model of policing. Anomalies in the reactive, incident-driven style were recognized during the 1960s and traditional policing practices were questioned. Subsequently, community policing philosophies were deemed appropriate. Over the last twenty years, acceptance of the community policing concept has grown considerably in the United States and Canada. While its development in Canada has undoubtedly been influenced by events in the United States, there is concrete evidence that the community policing concept exists to varying degrees at every level of policing.

In discussing community policing, three areas of concern were identified: the involvement of the community, the lack of research and the commitment from the police organization to organizational change.

QUESTIONS FOR DISCUSSION

1. To what extent does community policing mirror the principles of Robert Peel's philosophy of policing?

2. Describe Kelling and Moore's three periods of policing.

3. What influences and changes led to the current demands for community policing in the United States?

4. What influences and changes led to the current demands for community policing in Canada?

5. *A Vision of the Future* argues that police agencies need to adopt private sector management principles to enhance their service delivery. How relevant do you think this idea is?

6. What evidence is there that the RCMP is moving towards the community policing model?

7. Do you think the introduction of community policing will be easier for federal, provincial or municipal police agencies? Give reasons for your answers.

8. What is incident-driven policing?

9. What is the police subculture? How and why does it resist the movement towards community policing?

10. Suggest ways in which research on community policing in Canada could be encouraged.

FURTHER READING

Green, J.R. and Mastrofski, S.D. (1989). *Community Policing: Rhetoric or Reality*. New York: Praeger. This book contains articles by a number of prolific policing scholars from the United States and discusses many key concepts such as definitions, potential, strategies, policies and concerns as they relate to the community policing philosophy.

Chacko, James and Nancoo, Stephen E. (1993). *Community Policing in Canada*. Toronto: Canadian Scholars' Press Inc. This edited text includes eighteen articles written on the subject of community policing, many of which were originally published in academic journals. The text provides a useful, comprehensive collection of the Canadian literature.

Normandeau, A. and Leighton, B. (1990). *A Vision of the Future of Policing in Canada: Police Challenge 2000—Background Document.* Ottawa: Police and Security Branch, Ministry Secretariat, Solicitor General. This document is the result of a consultation process between the Solicitor General, police agencies and academics. It outlines issues that will influence policing in Canada as the millennium dawns and advocates the adoption of community policing policies to address social and economic developments.

Murphy, C. and Muir, G. (1985). *Community Based Policing; A Review of the Critical Issues.* Ottawa: Solicitor General. This report provides a review of the literature up to 1985. It is divided into four sections that discuss community policing with reference to the changing nature of Canadian society, the role of the police, management and strategies. Chris Murphy is one of the most prolific writers on community policing in Canada.

REFERENCES

Anderson, J. (1982). "The future of policing." In T. Bennett (Ed.) *The Future of Policing.* Cambridge: Institute of Criminology.

Baldwin, R. and Kinsey, R. (1982). *Police Powers and Politics.* London: Quartet.

Bayley, D.H. (1989). "Community policing: A report from the devil's advocate." In J.R. Green and S.D. Mastrofski (Eds.) *Community Policing; Rhetoric or Reality.* New York: Praeger.

Bayley, D. (1991). *Managing the Future: Prospective Issues in Canadian Policing.* Ottawa: Solicitor General

Bittner, E. (1967). "The police on skid row: A study in peacekeeping." *American Sociological Review, 32.*

Broderick, J. (1991). "Review essay: Community policing and problem oriented policing." *American Journal of Police, X*(4).

Brown, W.J. (1986). "Organizational assessment: Determining the state of a police organization." *Journal of Police Science and Administration, 14*(4).

Cadieux, P. (1990). "Community policing: A vision of the future of policing in Canada." In D. Loree and R. Walker (Eds.) *Community Crime Prevention: Shaping the Future.* Ottawa: Royal Canadian Mounted Police.

Chacko, James and Nancoo, Stephen E. (1993). *Community Policing in Canada.* Toronto: Canadian Scholars' Press Inc.

Clairmont, D.H. (1991). "Community-based policing: Implementation and impact." *Canadian Journal of Criminology, 33*(3-4).

Clairmont, Donald (1993). "Community-based policing and organizational change." In James Chacko and Stephen E. Nancoo (Eds.) *Community Policing in Canada.* Toronto: Canadian Scholars' Press.

Clarke, M. (1987). "Citizenship, community and management of crime." *British Journal of Criminology, 27*(1).

Crank, J.P. (1994). "Watchman and the community: Myth and institutionalization in policing." *Law and Society Review, 28*(2).

Deszca, G. (1988). "The communication of ideology in police forces." *Canadian Police College Journal, 12*(4).

Fielding, N., Kemp, C. and Norris, C. (1989). "Constraints on the practice of community policing." In Rod Morgan and David Smith (Eds.) *Coming to Terms With Policing: Perspectives on Policy.* London: Routledge.

Fielding, N. (1988). *Joining Forces: Police Training, Socialization and Occupational Competence.* London: Routledge.

Friedmann, Robert R. (1992). *Community Policing: Comparative Perspectives and Prospects.* Hemel Hempstead: Harvester Wheatsheaf.

Germann, A.C. (1969). "Community policing: An assessment." *Journal of Criminal Law, Criminology and Police Science, 60*(1).

Goldstein, H. (1987). "Towards community oriented policing: Potential basic requirements and threshold questions." *Crime and Delinquency, 33*(1).

Goldstein, H. (1990). *Problem Oriented Policing.* New York: McGraw Hill.

Grant, Alan (1992). *Policing Arrangements in New Brunswick: 2000 and Beyond.* Fredericton: Department of the Solicitor General.

Green, J.R. and Taylor, R.B. (1989). "Community based policing and foot patrol: Issues of theory and evaluation." In J.R. Green and S.D. Mastrofski (Eds.) *Community Policing: Rhetoric or Reality.* New York: Praeger.

Green, J.R. and Mastrofski, S.D. (1989). *Community Policing: Rhetoric or Reality.* New York: Praeger.

Green, Jack R., Bergman, William T. and McLaughlin, Edward J. (1994). "Implementing community policing: Cultural and structural change in police organizations." In Dennis P. Rosenbaum (Ed.) *The Challenge of Community Policing: Testing the Promises.* California: Sage.

Greene, J.R. (1987). *Police-Community Relations and Officer Job Satisfaction: An Evaluation.* Paper presented at the meeting of the Academy of Criminal Justice Sciences, St. Louis: Missouri.

Grimshaw, Roger and Jefferson, Tony (1987). *Interpreting Policework: Policy and Practice in Forms of Beat Policing.* London: Allen Unwin.

Grinc, Randolph M. (1994). "'Angels in marble': Problems in stimulating community involvement in community policing." *Crime and Delinquency, 40*(3).

Holdaway, Simon (1984). *Inside the British Police: A Force at Work.* Oxford: Basil Blackwell.

Holdaway, S. (1989). "Discovering structure. Studies of the British police occupational structure." In M. Weatheritt (Ed.) *Police Research: Some Future Prospects.* Aldershot: Gower Publishing Company Ltd.

Horne, D. (1992). "Public opinion surveys: Implications for police organizations." *Canadian Police College Journal, 16*(4).

Hornick, J.P., Burrows, T.A., Tjowvold, I. and Phillips, D.M. (1990). *An Evaluation of the Neighbourhood Foot Patrol Program of the Edmonton Police Service.* Ottawa: Solicitor General of Canada.

Hornick, Joseph P., Burrows, Barbara A., Phillips, Donna M. and Leighton, Barry (1991). "An impact evaluation of the Edmonton neighbourhood foot patrol program." *The Canadian Journal of Program Evaluation, 6*(1).

Hunt, Raymond G. and Magenau, John M. (1993). *Power and the Police Chief: An Institutional and Organizational Analysis.* Newbury Park: Sage.

Jones, S. (1983). "Community policing in Devon and Cornwall: Some research findings on the relationship between the public and the police." In T. Bennett (Ed.) *The Future of Policing.* Cambridge: Institute of Criminology.

Kelling, G.L. (1986). "The changing function of urban police: The historical and political context of community policing." In D.J. Loree and C. Murphy (Eds.) *Community Policing in the 1980s: Recent Advances in Police Programs.* Ottawa: Solicitor General.

Kelling, G.L. and Moore, M.H. (1988). "From political to reform to community: The evolving strategy of police." In J.R. Green and S.D. Mastrofski (Eds.) *Community Policing; Rhetoric or Reality.* New York: Praeger.

Kennedy, L.W. (1991). "The evaluation of community based policing in Canada." *Canadian Police College Journal, 15*(4).

Kinsey, R., Lea, J. and Young, J. (1986). *Losing the Fight Against Crime.* London: Routledge.

Lambert, Leah (1988). "Police ministations in Toronto: An experience in compromise." *RCMP Gazette, 50*(6).

Lea, J. and Young, J. (1984). *What is to be Done about Law and Order?* London: Penguin.

Leighton, B.N. (1991). "Visions of community policing: Rhetoric or reality in Canada." *Canadian Journal of Criminology, 33*(3-4).

Leighton, B.N. (1994). "Community policing in Canada: An overview of experience and evaluations." In Dennis P. Rosenbaum (Ed.) *The Challenge of Community Policing: Testing the Promises.* California: Sage.

Linden, Rick. (1991). "The impact of evaluation research on policing policy in Canada and the United States." *Canadian Journal of Program Evaluation, 6*(1).

Lurigo, Arthur J. and Rosenbaum, Dennis P. (1994). "The impact of community policing on police personnel: A review of the literature." In Dennis P. Rosenbaum (Ed.) *The Challenge of Community Policing: Testing the Promises.* California: Sage.

Manning, P. (1977). *Police Work.* Cambridge, Mass.: MIT Press.

Manning, P.K. (1989). "Community policing as a drama of control." In J.R. Green and S.D. Mastrofski (Eds.) *Community Policing; Rhetoric or Reality.* New York: Praeger.

Marquis, Greg (1991). Canadian police chiefs and law reform: The historical perspective. *Canadian Journal of Criminology 33*(3-4).

Mastrofski, S.D. (1989). "Community policing as reform: A Cautionary Tale." In J.R. Green and S.D. Mastrofski (Eds.) *Community Policing; Rhetoric or Reality.* New York: Praeger.

Mawby, R.I. (1990). *Comparative Policing Issues: The British and American System in International Perspective.* London: Unwin Hyman.

McConnville, Mike and Shepherd, Dan (1992). *Watching Police Watching Communities.* London: Routledge.

Melchers, R. (1993). "A commentary on 'A vision of the future of policing in Canada: Police challenge 2000'." *Canadian Journal of Criminology, 35*(1).

Moore, Mark H. (1994). "Research synthesis and policy implications." In Dennis P. Rosenbaum (Ed.) *The Challenge of Community Policing: Testing the Promises.* California: Sage.

Morgan, R. (1987). "Police accountability: Developing the local infrastructure." *British Journal of Criminology, 27*(1).

Murphy, C. (1986). *The Social and Formal Organization of Small Town Policing. A Comparative Analysis of RCMP and Municipal Policing.* Unpublished doctoral dissertation, University of Toronto.

Murphy, C. (1988). "Community problems, problem communities and community policing in Toronto." *Journal of Research in Crime and Delinquency, 24*(4).

Murphy, C. (1989). "The development, impact and implications of community policing in Canada." In J.R. Green and S.D. Mastrofski (Eds.) *Community Policing; Rhetoric or Reality.* New York: Praeger.

Murphy, C. and Muir, G. (1985). *Community Based Policing; A Review of the Critical Issues.* Ottawa: Solicitor General.

Nelken, D. (1985). "Community involvement in crime control." *Current Legal Problems.*

Normandeau, A. (1993). "Policing in Montreal: A New Vision." *Canadian Journal of Criminology, 35*(2).

Normandeau, A. and Leighton, B. (1990). *A Vision of the Future of Policing in Canada: Police Challenge 2000—Background Document.* Ottawa: Police and Security Branch, Ministry Secretariat, Solicitor General.

Normandeau, A. and Leighton, B. (1991). "Police and Society in Canada." *Canadian Journal of Criminology, 33*(3-4).

Oettermeir, T.N. and Brown, Lee P. (1989). "Community policing." In J.R. Green and S.D. Mastrofski (Eds.) *Community Policing: Rhetoric or Reality.* New York: Praeger.

Operational Policing Review (1990). Joint Consultative Committee of the Police Staff Associations, Surbiton, Surrey: The Police Foundation.

Oppal, The Honourable Mr. Justice Wallace T. (1994). *Closing the Gap: Policing and the Community.* Commission of Inquiry Policing in British Columbia. Victoria, B.C.: Attorney General.

Peters, T. and Waterman, R. (1982). *In Search of Excellence.* New York: Warner Books.

Punch, Maurice (1983). *Control in the Police Organization.* Cambridge, Mass.: MIT Press.

Reiner, R. (1992). *The Politics of the Police* (second edition). Hemel Hempstead: Harvester Wheatsheaf.

Reuss-Ianni, Elizabeth (1983). *Two Cultures of Policing.* New Brunswick (USA): Transaction Books.

Riechers, Lisa M. and Roberg, Roy R. (1990). "Community policing: A critical review of underlying assumptions." *Journal of Police Science and Administration, 17*(2).

Roberg, Roy R. (1994). "Can today's police agencies effectively implement community policing?" In Dennis P. Rosenbaum (Ed.) *The Challenge of Community Policing: Testing the Promises.* California: Sage.

Rosenbaum, Dennis P. and Lurigo, Arthur J. (1994). "An inside look at community policing reform: Definitions, organizational changes and evaluation findings." *Crime and Delinquency, 40*(3).

Royal Canadian Mounted Police (1990). *Strategic Action Plan: Implementation of Community Based Policing in the Royal Canadian Mounted Police.* Ottawa: Ministry of Supply and Services.

Royal Canadian Mounted Police (1992). *Strategic Action Plan for Community Policing.* Ottawa: Ministry of Supply and Services.

Scarman, Lord (1982). *The Scarman Report: The Brixton Disorders 10-12 April 1981.* Harmondsworth: Penguin.

Seagrave, J. (1992). "Community policing and the need for police research skills training." *Canadian Police College Journal, 16*(3).

Seagrave, J. (1993). "Listening to what the people say: The implementation and evaluation of community consultative groups." *RCMP Gazette, 55*(11).

Seagrave, J. (1994). "Community consultative groups: Practical guidelines." *RCMP Gazette, 56*(10).

Shapland, J. and Vagg, J. (1988). *Policing by the Public.* London: Routledge.

Skogan, W.G. (1990). *Disorder and Decline: Crime and the Spiral of Decay in American Neighborhoods.* New York: The Free Press.

Skolnick, J.H. and Bayley, D.H. (1986). *The New Blue Line.* New York: The Free Press.

Skolnick, J.H. and Bayley, D.H. (1988). *Community Policing: Issues and Practices Around the World.* United States: National Institute of Justice.

Smith, D. (1987). "The Police and the idea of community." In P. Willmott (Ed.) *Policing and the Community.* London: Policy Studies Institute. Discussion Paper 16.

Solicitor General (1994). *Canadian Community Policing Series.* Ottawa: Ministry of the Solicitor General.

Solicitor General of New Brunswick (1993). *New Brunswick Policing Study: Overview.* Fredericton: Department of the Solicitor General.

Taylor, I. (1980). "The law and order issue in the British general election and the Canadian federal election of 1979." *Canadian Journal of Sociology,* 5(3).

Toronto Police (1991). *Beyond 2000. The Strategic Plan of the Metropolitan Toronto Police.* Toronto: Metropolitan Toronto Police.

Trojanowicz, R.C. and Bucqueroux, D. (1990). *Community Policing: A Contemporary Perspective.* Michigan: Anderson Publishing.

Trojanowicz, R.C. and Trojanowicz, J.M. (1975). *Community Based Crime Prevention.* Illinois: Goodyear Publishing.

Walker, C. and Walker, S.G. (1989). *The Victoria Community Police Stations: An Exercise in Innovation.* Ottawa: Supply and Services Canada.

Walker, S. (1992). *RCMP Community Policing: Blending Tradition with Innovation—Strategic Planning Document.* Ottawa: Aboriginal Policing Directorate, Solicitor General.

Wasson, D.K. and Crawford, J.D. (1979). *Community Based Preventative Policing: A Review.* Ottawa: Solicitor General.

Wycoff, M.A. (1989). "The benefits of community policing: evidence and conjecture." In J.R. Green and S.D. Mastrofski (Eds.) *Community Policing; Rhetoric or Reality.* New York: Praeger.

POLICING ABORIGINAL PEOPLES

INTRODUCTION

It has been argued that one of the most important issues for Canadian policing in the 21st century will be Aboriginal self-determination in the delivery of police services (Skoog, 1992), even though there is currently little being written on the issue of policing Aboriginal people in the political context (Harding, 1991). The aim of this chapter is to discuss some of the issues and debates identified in relation to policing Aboriginal people and to describe the various policy initiatives introduced over the recent past. This is a multidimensional topic concerning the organization and delivery of police services by federal, provincial and municipal police agencies and incorporating issues relating to self-government and self-determination (Griffiths, 1994). In order to contextualize these discussions, an account of Aboriginal people in Canada and their relationship with the criminal justice system is required.

DEMOGRAPHICS

According to the 1986 census, 711,120 individuals reported some Aboriginal ancestry, representing 3.6% of Canada's total population (Griffiths and Verdun Jones, 1994; Normandeau and Leighton, 1990). This population consists of four groups.

1. **Status Indians.** Aboriginal people who are registered under the Indian Act (1876) and who comprise 59.9% of the Aboriginal population.

2. **Non-status Indians.** Aboriginal people who identify themselves as Aboriginal but who are not registered under the Act; they comprise 15.3% of the Native population.

3. **Métis.** People of mixed Anglo-European and Aboriginal descent who make up 20% of the Aboriginal population.

4. **Inuit (Eskimo).** These peoples represent a distinct cultural group residing in the Northwest Territories, Labrador and Northern Quebec and comprise 5.2% of the Aboriginal population.

It is impossible to speak of one Aboriginal community, as Aboriginal people demonstrate considerable diversity in culture, religions, customs and language, as well as socio-economic and political development (Normandeau and Leighton, 1990). While approximately two-thirds of Status Indians reside in rural isolated areas on 2,200 reserves organized into 604 bands, most Métis and Non-status Indians reside in semi-urban and rural areas. Therefore, in discussing the policing needs of Aboriginal peoples, homogeneity cannot be presumed, as First Nations people live in both remote, sparsely-populated reserves and major population centres such as Toronto, Montreal and Vancouver.

In describing policing arrangements for Aboriginal people, two situations are apparent: policing off reserves and policing on reserves.

POLICING OFF RESERVES

There are a number of urban communities in Canada where Aboriginal people, mostly Non-status Indians and Métis, exist in significant numbers. Ten urban centres have Native populations of over 5,000 (Normandeau and Leighton, 1990). For example, in Saskatchewan, it is estimated that 50% of all Aboriginal people live in cities and towns, with over 35,000 residing in Regina alone (Harding, 1991). In these communities, issues of policing are linked to the wider issue of multiculturalism, recognized by some to be the greatest challenge currently facing police organizations (Griffiths, 1994), and to the problem of policing non-white populations. In this regard, initiatives such as the recruitment of ethnic minority police officers, cross-cultural race relations training for officers and the development of community policing policies, such as consultative groups aimed at minority communities, illustrate ways in which police organizations have attempted to be responsive to the needs of all minority groups, including Aboriginal peoples.

POLICING ON RESERVES

As will be illustrated below, policing on reserves takes many different forms. In 1990, there were approximately 700 Aboriginal officers employed in policing or 'para-policing' reserves, representing a ratio of 1:370 persons (Normandeau and Leighton, 1990). The issue of policing reserves has promoted considerable discussion during the recent past. The use of non-Native RCMP officers to administer the law on reserves and the creation of Native police forces to patrol reserves have been two issues of particular contention. It is these concerns and others relating to on-reserve and small Aboriginal community policing that will be primarily addressed in this chapter.

ABORIGINAL PEOPLE AND THE CRIMINAL JUSTICE SYSTEM

In discussing First Nations people and the administration of policing, three concerns have been recognized (Normandeau and Leighton, 1990):

- the over-representation of Aboriginal people within the criminal justice system.
- equity of treatment—the extent to which Natives are treated fairly and justly.
- equality of service—access to policing services that meet acceptable norms and standards.

It has long been recognized that Aboriginal people are over-represented at every level of the Canadian criminal justice system (Griffiths and Yerbury, 1984; Griffiths, 1988; Harding, 1991), a situation that has led Natives to question the administration of justice and the interpretation of criminal justice policies (Depew, 1986). A number of federal, provincial and independent commissions and reports have examined the relationship between the police and Aboriginal people and illustrated it as strained, leading to conflict and high rates of arrest (Hamilton and Sinclair, 1991; Sunahara, 1992). Research has shown that Aboriginal people have unfavorable attitudes towards the police, whom they blame to some extent for their over-representation in the system. Aboriginal accused offenders comprise the single largest minority group being processed through the system (Nielsen, 1992). Despite representing only 3.6% of the national population, they comprise 12% of inmates in federal correctional institutions (Correctional Services of Canada, 1994). Research from Alberta found that 78% of Indian men and 35% of Indian women in the province had a record of arrest (Cawsey, 1991).

Their over-representation in the criminal justice system has led to accusations that they have been over-policed and mis-policed (Forcese, 1992; Harding 1991) and criticism has been directed at the RCMP, provincial and municipal forces (Griffiths, 1994). This over-representation may be more a function of low socio-economic status than race (La Prarie, 1993). Research shows that socially and economically marginal groups in society use the services provided by the police more than others (Landau, 1996). This low socio-economic status, as well as the many social problems they face (poor living conditions, unemployment, alcoholism, abuse, suicide), has been attributed to the legacy of colonialism. As noted by Jobson (1993), First Nations people have, over the last two hundred years, been deprived of their lands, subjected to the breakup of their family structures, had their culture suppressed and their spiritual traditions outlawed. These federal policies were geared towards the goal of assimilation. It has only been in the last thirty years that the effects of colonalization have begun to be dealt with. One of the areas that is slowly being addressed is policing.

WESTERN POLICING PHILOSOPHIES vs. TRADITIONAL ABORIGINAL POLICING PHILOSOPHIES

Stark contrasts exist between the philosophies of crime and crime control in western and Aboriginal communities, with ethnological accounts illustrating important differences in the way the police and policing have been conceptualized by Natives and non-Natives (Depew, 1992). The organization and administration of conventional police services in Canadian society is characterized by an 'urban' criminal justice system model, designed to prosecute, punish and deter offenders. As such, police agencies operate within a crime control, adversarial environment developed from the Anglo-European model, in which their aim is to deter, apprehend and charge offenders. The police are organized hierarchically as a para-military bureaucracy; their stress is on crime fighting and law enforcement. Although this philosophy has been challenged with the advent of community policing, it still remains largely intact.

In contrast, Aboriginal communities tend to reside in remote, rural areas and are structured in such a way that responses to crime and deviance have traditionally taken the form of reciprocal constraints derived from a variety of social relationships existing within the community and shaped by that community (Depew, 1992). The culture of Aboriginal people focuses on responsibility, not individual rights. Unlike the dominant western urban crime model "...the outlook is communitarian and holistic; the process not hierarchical and adversarial but consensual and problem solving. Healing and reparation not punishment are favored outcomes" (Jobson, 1993, p. 11). Peacekeeping is viewed as the appropriate means to resolve conflicts and this peacekeeping takes place through informal community resources, often involving councils and elders.

The purpose of a justice system in Aboriginal societies is to restore harmony within the community and to reconcile the accused with the slighted party and his/her own conscience. Consequently, the role of the police officer is diminished in a social system that relies on community constraints and social arrangements to administer social control. In Native communities, there is the belief that individuals will not turn to crime and deviance, as they are regulated by conscience and their commitment to their community; they do not need to be controlled by an external force.

The colonization process and the diverse nature of the Aboriginal communities in Canada has meant that both the Anglo-European-based and Aboriginal-based criminal justice processes have been subject to changing environmental demands and pressures (Depew, 1992). For the Native peoples, these changes were most profoundly articulated when the federal government recognized their inherent right to self-government. This development grants them authority to independently implement institutions of government, including policing for their communities. As noted by Skoog (1992), "...the Aboriginal community can rightly be expected to see autonomous policing as central to the entire self government issue" (p. 2). Accordingly, policing Aboriginal communities is at the forefront of the policing agenda as the century draws to a close. To contextualize this, a brief historical review of Aboriginal policing is required.

COLONIAL HISTORY OF ABORIGINAL POLICING

The roots of Aboriginal involvement in European policing can be traced back to the 1850s, when colonial administrators new to Canada found they needed to draw on local expertise to undertake their tasks (Skoog, 1992). Gradually, as the colonists learned more about their environment, these people became expendable and it has only been within the last thirty years that the government has revisited the issue.

The Canadian constitution of 1867 assigned responsibility for Indians and lands reserved for Indians to the federal government. This meant that, for the first one hundred years after confederation, policing Aboriginal people and their communities was deemed to be a federal responsibility, despite the fact the administration of justice, including policing, had been constitutionally assigned to provincial authorities. Consequently, until the late 1960s, Aboriginal communities were policed by the federal police force, the RCMP, even in the provinces that had provincial forces (Ontario and Quebec).

As early as 1912, recommendations were made by senior RCMP members that Native people should have their own police force to administer the provisions of the Indian Act (Horrall, 1989). This recommendation was ignored in 1912, and again in 1950, when officers commanding Edmonton and Lethbridge subdivision submitted a report to the commissioner of the RCMP, in response to a growing interest by chiefs and band councils in policing on reserves (Horrall, 1989).

POLICY DEVELOPMENTS: 1960s–1970s

The 1960s have been described as a time of awakening for Aboriginal people (Silverman and Nielsen, 1992). It was during this time that band councils became increasingly vocal in wanting to manage their own affairs and demanded input into policy. Assignment of non-Aboriginal RCMP members to the policing of reserves was unpopular with both the RCMP and Native people, so in 1969, the Department of Indian Affairs published an elaborate 'Band Constable Program' recommending that band constables be recruited by band councils to administer band by-laws. Band council police were appointed by bands under Section 81 of the Indian Act, which states that band councils can pass laws on matters such as regulation of traffic, observation of law and order and the prevention of disorderly conduct and nuisances (Jobson, 1993). While band constables were employed by the bands themselves, they required provincial approval. In 1971, the program was expanded so that, in addition to enforcing band by-laws, band constables were able to supplement the senior police forces at a local level, but could not supplant them (Canada, 1973).

In 1974, The Task Force Report on Policing in Ontario (Ontario, 1974) argued that provincial jurisdiction ought to prevail on reserves for criminal law excluding federal statute. This resulted in the RCMP withdrawing its provision of provincial and municipal police services in Ontario and Quebec. Policing services were assumed by the Ontario Provincial Police and Quebec Provincial Police. In all other provinces, the RCMP retained responsibility for policing Aboriginal communities as an extension of their federal contracts.

The 1970s also saw the publication of a federal report commissioned by the Department of Indian and Native Affairs, entitled *Task Force on Policing on Reserves* (Canada, 1973). This report recommended three options for Aboriginal policing: band council policing, municipal policing and provincial policing.

The proposal for band council policing contained three options for constables employed by the band to enforce three different levels of law, ranging from by-law enforcement to enforcement of all federal and provincial laws and criminal and civil by-laws.

The second option discussed municipal policing and suggested that police services could be secured from an existing adjacent municipality, or from the municipality in which the reserve was located. Alternatively, the band could create its own police force if it undertook the necessary legal steps to become a municipality.

The third alternative concerned provincial policing and recommended two possibilities. The first was that a separate Native Provincial Police Force be established to operate on its own, under the authority of the provincial attorney general, with its own form of police commission. The second option stated that Native policing could be conducted under the direction and control of existing provincial police arrangements, but would use Native people as special constables. This became known as 'Option 3b', receiving the greatest attention from policy makers and police agencies.

ABORIGINAL POLICE OFFICERS

'Option 3b' found its clearest articulation in the RCMP Native Special Constable Program. Here, trainees spent 16 weeks at the RCMP training headquarters in Regina and then were posted to their home areas. They had peace officer status and served as adjuncts to the RCMP (Skoog, 1992). The program had the following objectives (Statistics Canada, 1990).

- To create a system whereby Aboriginal people policed Aboriginal people and became involved in law enforcement.

- To provide a policing system flexible enough to accommodate the unique policing needs of Aboriginal communities, while at the same time ensuring services were generally equal to those received by other Canadians.

- To enhance non-Aboriginal RCMP members' awareness of the culture, customs and rights of First Nations people.

- To encourage the creation of crime prevention programs.
- To decrease the number of First Nations people coming into contact with the law.

The program was criticized for a number of reasons. It lacked Aboriginal input, failed to adequately define the role of RCMP members and offered lower salaries and less training than was received by regular members. There was also a reluctance by Natives to become involved due to community hostility and social isolation (Griffiths and Yerbury, 1984). It has been argued that the 3b program was not distinguishable from other police agencies' programs to recruit Aboriginal officers, which seek to increase Native presence but not Native control (Skoog, 1992).

In 1990, the RCMP eliminated the Native Special Constable Program and replaced it with the Aboriginal Constable Development Program, designed to increase the number of Aboriginal people eligible to become regular RCMP members (Jars, 1992). This initiative is intended for Aboriginal individuals who desire a career in law enforcement, but who may not possess the necessary basic entrance requirements. The program encourages participants to obtain the skills required to be accepted into the force and compete on an equal basis with other members of the force.

The Ontario Special Constable Program was established in 1975 by the OPP and reflects the 3b policy. The main difference between it and the RCMP program was that special constables were hired by the bands themselves and trained by the OPP. Recruits were approved by the OPP and the Ontario Police Commission (Skoog, 1992). In 1992, control was transferred from the OPP to Aboriginal agencies under a self-government agreement (Griffiths, 1994).

ABORIGINAL POLICE FORCES

The 1970s saw the introduction of the first Aboriginal police forces, characterized by a somewhat haphazard development attributed to the federal government's reluctance to grant authority to all reserve-based groups (Griffiths, 1994). These police forces, often referred to as tribal police, are employed by and accountable to the communities they serve. They differ from band constables because they have the full powers and jurisdiction of peacekeeping. Harding (1991) suggests these police officers are "...as much human service and community development workers, and play a role as conflict resolvers, as they are classical peace officers" (p. 372). The tribal police constables are usually appointed as special constables under the RCMP Act (see Appendix A) or relevant Police Act and trained through agreements between the band council and federal and provincial governments (Jobson, 1993). The jurisdiction and powers of tribal police vary depending upon their terms of appointment; consequently, many have been seen to be limited in their authority. According to some Aboriginal leaders, they do not possess the authority to adequately police in their communities because serious criminal matters are still referred to the RCMP (Skoog, 1992). Despite this concern, by assuming local control of one of the most significant components of the criminal justice system, these forces represent the closest form of autonomous policing.

The Louis Bull Police Service provides an example of an autonomous Aboriginal police force. It was granted authority on 1 May 1987 by the Solicitor General of Alberta to provide a full policing service for the Louis Bull First Nations, 70 kilometres south-east of Edmonton, with a population of approximately 900. There are eight sworn police officers, seven paid staff and two volunteers, who provide a 24-hour service on the reserve. Officers are employed to enforce the Criminal Code, other federal and provincial statutes and band by-laws. They receive training from the Solicitor General, Edmonton and Calgary police and the RCMP. Since the creation of the service, crime—particularly vandalism and alcohol-related driving offenses—has decreased (Jars, 1992). The Blood Tribal Police is another example of a tribal police force. It was established in 1979 in Alberta to serve the Blood reserve. Officers are trained for 16 weeks at the provincial police training academy and take a six-month field recruit training program administered by the RCMP. They have full peace officer powers, granted by the Alberta Police Act (Statistics Canada, 1990).

The introduction and development of Aboriginal-controlled police forces has met with a number of problems. For example, there would appear to be a lack of consensus on the appropriate action to prevent and control crime (Benson, 1991). In addition, political influence—in which Aboriginal-controlled police forces are caught between the aspirations of the band and federal and provincial legislation—has been identified as a problem. Questions have also been raised regarding the extent to which community-based criminal justice initiatives can protect individuals vulnerable to victimization. Aboriginal women have questioned whether local justice will provide assistance and protection to victims of violence and abuse, as, in the past, there has been a tendency for members of a community to avoid involvement in issues deemed to be private (Griffiths, 1994). Notwithstanding these observations, the introduction of Aboriginal police forces represents a significant development in Aboriginal people regaining ownership of their affairs.

POLICY DEVELOPMENTS: 1980s–1990s

The 1980s witnessed a number of government reports directed at the issue of First Nations policing. Concern had been voiced over ad hoc policing arrangements, differential funding formulas, escalating costs and lack of federal policy (Statistics Canada, 1990). In 1986, a federal task force—The Indian Policing Policy Review—was established to examine policing on reserves and establish a comprehensive policy framework (Oppal, 1994). The task force endorsed the concept of self-government and argued policing rights should include the power to enforce all laws—federal, provincial and band. It also stressed the need for equality in policing services and, consequently, argued for an expanded, tripartite system of policing administration involving Ottawa, the province concerned and Aboriginal representatives.

The 1986 task force is notable in that it looked only at policing on reserves and did not include representation from any First Nations people in its deliberations. In 1990, the federal government released the Indian Policing Policy Review, based on the findings of the 1986 task force. This report argued for a culturally sensitive policing service and for the active participation of Native people in policing and the administration of justice. This was followed in 1992 by a federal report entitled "First Nations Policing Policy," which articulated further the recommendations of the previous report. As consultation with Aboriginal, provincial and territorial governments did not take place, this later policy, which focuses on ten principles, was adopted neither by provincial/territorial governments nor Aboriginal people.

Jobson (1993) has argued that this spate of policies grew out of the federal government's desire to cut spending and to get the provinces and First Nations communities to take over responsibility for policing Aboriginal peoples. Despite this contention, currently, provincial governments have no constitutional authority to discuss or develop policing policy with respect to Aboriginal peoples, as distinct from the general citizens (Oppal, 1994).

In April 1992, responsibility for policing on reserves was transferred from the Department of Indian Affairs and Northern Development to the Ministry of the Solicitor General, the same ministry with responsibility for the RCMP. A few months prior to this, the Native Policing Branch of the RCMP changed its name to the Aboriginal Policing and Community Services Directorate, in recognition of the force's corporate policy to adopt community policing principles. Since 1992, there has been a movement away from bilateral (federal-First Nations) to trilateral (federal, provincial and First Nations) agreements, resulting in the creation of 36 fully independent First Nations police forces.

This retrospective account illustrates the growing attention the issue of Aboriginal policing has received over the recent past, as federal, provincial and territorial governments have been faced with considerable pressure to address the perceived inequalities in the administration of justice and delivery of services. As the chronology outlined in Table 12.1 shows, it has only been towards the end of the 20th century that the subject has been seriously discussed. On reserves today, a diversity of methods are used to satisfy policing objectives; some bands have contract arrangements with the RCMP, provincial or municipal police, while others have Aboriginal officers and, in some instances, their own tribal forces.

Due to the various policy initiatives and developments of the seventies, eighties and nineties, a number of problems have been tackled and lessons learned (Griffiths, 1994).

TABLE 12.1 Chronology of Policing Aboriginal People

1876	The Indian Act was passed.
1912	Recommendation by Superintendent Deane that Native people should have their own police force (Horrall, 1989).
1950	RCMP representatives visit Montana to discuss law enforcement on reserves with the US Office of Indian Affairs.
1960s	Band councils become more vocal in wanting to administer their own affairs.
1969	Band constable program established.
1971	Band constable program expanded, resulting in the creation of a number of independent police forces.
1973	Task force on policing reserves initiated by the federal government.
1973	Indian Special Constable Program established.
1974	The task force report on policing in Ontario (Ontario, 1974) recommends that provincial jurisdiction should dictate policing services on reserves. RCMP subsequently withdraws from Ontario and Quebec reserves.
1975	Ontario Special Constable Program established.
1978	Native Policing Branch created by RCMP to coordinate Native policing.
1986	Policing Policy Review Task Force established.
1990	Indian Policing Policy Review report.
1990	Elimination of RCMP Special Constable Program.
1990	Aboriginal Constable Development Program introduced by the RCMP.
1992	First Nations Policing Policy report.
1992	Responsibility for policing reserves transferred from the Department of Indian Affairs and Northern Development to the Solicitor General.
1992	Movement from bilateral to trilateral policing agreements.

- It is simplistic to assume the solution to problems in police-Aboriginal relations lies in the hiring of a few Aboriginal police officers. The problems are clearly more deeply rooted than this.
- Aboriginal communities should be actively involved in the development of policing policies and these should be sensitive to the diversity of the Aboriginal population itself.
- The policy of Aboriginal recruitment is limited by police forces' retention of traditional organizational structures, policies and practices alien to the Aboriginal culture.

- The police have only a limited effect on the crime and order maintenance problems that plague Aboriginal communities. Many issues require a multi-agency approach, incorporating the police, the community, social services and other criminal justice agencies, in order that they might be fully addressed.

Despite increased involvement in the delivery of police services, the relative poverty in which First Nations people find themselves will continue to contribute to the social and economic problems they face. As noted by Landau (1996), changing who wears the uniform without addressing these fundamental concerns does nothing to change the ability of the police to deal with peace and security issues. The issue of policing Aboriginal communities encompasses legal, social and economic concerns.

THE FUTURE OF ABORIGINAL POLICING

As mentioned in Chapter 3, in 1995, the RCMP had a total of 38 contracts to provide policing services to one or more Aboriginal communities, the Ontario Provincial Police provided law enforcement under one province-wide contract for 178 First Nations communities and three municipal police forces had contracts with three Aboriginal communities. In addition, there are 34 self-administered First Nations police services and 74 communities have band constables as a component of the provincial police (Aboriginal Policing Directorate, Ottawa, personal communication). Therefore, today, most policing services to First Nations communities are provided in one of three ways:

1. By regular provincial police services. It is estimated that more than 50% of the policing services to First Nations communities are provided by the RCMP, OPP or QPP (Statistics Canada, 1990).
2. By regular provincial forces that have an Aboriginal contingent. These officers perform all police functions and have powers similar to their non-Aboriginal colleagues.
3. By autonomous policing arrangements administered by the Aboriginal community.

In analyzing the potential for Aboriginal policing in the last few years of the century, Skoog (1992) has proposed three models: the crime control model, the community policing model and the political sovereignty model. He argues that, while they are conceptually distinct, the models do overlap.

Crime control model

Under this model, the goals and delivery of police services are indistinguishable from those currently existing in Canadian society. In this respect, police departments would be hierarchically structured, the maintenance of public order would be of primary importance and citizen input into policing would be limited. If Aboriginal communities adopted such a model, policing administration would be conducted by political leaders and crime control would be stressed in order to ensure social control. Police officers would be hired based on qualifications and might or might not be local residents.

Community policing model

The introduction and development of community policing has been discussed extensively in the previous two chapters. Government commentators on Aboriginal policing, such as the Manitoba Aboriginal Justice Inquiry (Hamilton and Sinclair, 1991) and the Law Reform Commission (1991), have recommended the adoption of community policing for Native people, as have academics (Depew, 1992).

Community policing is seen to be more culturally sensitive than the traditional crime control model. This factor, coupled with the emphasis on local input into police policies and practices, has made it seem applicable for the policing of Aboriginal communities. As noted by Depew (1992):

> Since its principles of organization are flexible and pragmatically oriented community based policing is more likely than the crime control approach to reflect the social, political, economic and cultural conditions of a wide range of Native communities (p. 107).

Despite this contention, the community policing philosophy is inherently tied to the traditional crime control model and has been viewed as merely enforcing the same old (white) law in a new way (Skoog, 1992). If this is the case, segments of the Aboriginal community may regard it as being too closely aligned with the established ideas of law enforcement, therefore failing to provide the necessary changes in philosophy needed if policing is to be sensitive to their cultural needs. Furthermore, political accountability for the police and police accountability to the community is an issue which, although not unique to Aboriginal communities, needs to be defined if the community policing model is to be successfully adopted (Depew, 1992). These issues, coupled with the lack of funding available for First Nations to experiment with community-based alternatives (Landau, 1996), restricts the development of this model.

Political sovereignty model

This model is the most radical of the three and awards Aboriginal people considerable autonomy over their own officers. In this model, the police would form one part of an integrated criminal justice system based, not on the adversarial approach, but on peacekeeping and community control with emphasis on mediation and reparation, not restitution. With the acceptance of the inherent right to self-government, many Aboriginal communities may, in the future, be advocating this model; however, the exact form it would take may vary among communities. Depew (1986) notes there exists no convincing evidence that indigenized police forces have reduced Aboriginal crime or deviance or improved the delivery of police services, an issue contested by others (Griffiths, 1994). While this observation could be attributed to the fact that these forces still operate within the crime control model, it illustrates that the success of the political sovereignty model in delivering police services will depend on the community itself and that community's desire to return to more culturally traditional values.

UNRESOLVED ISSUES IN ABORIGINAL POLICING

While there have been numerous developments within the field of Aboriginal policing, a number of issues remain unresolved. Griffiths (1994) draws attention to some of these.

- Who should set the standards and what should these be in the recruitment and training of Aboriginal police officers?

- What jurisdictional authority should be granted to Aboriginal police officers?

- What structures of accountability should exist for Aboriginal police officers?

- What mechanisms, if any, should be introduced to ensure that Aboriginal police forces remain free of political interference?

- What is the appropriate model for the delivery of police services by Aboriginal and non-Aboriginal police forces?

- What are the implications when Aboriginal officers police their own, small, tight-knit communities?

In evidence presented to the British Columbia Inquiry into Policing (Oppal, 1994), many bands reported that, upon attaining self-government, they would probably contract with the RCMP to deliver police services rather than encounter the problems of establishing their own police forces. The inquiry went on to note it was a misconception to state that Aboriginal people require Aboriginal police officers. Non-Aboriginal officers are acceptable if they meet the criteria for good police officers; these criteria involve becoming well acquainted with all aspects of the community. Providing a stable presence in the community has been recognized as a problem for the RCMP, which transfers officers between postings every two to three years. This practice inhibits police-community relations (Griffiths, 1994; Seagrave, 1995) and undoubtedly affects the RCMP's ability to provide culturally sensitive police services. It is one of many unresolved issues relating to Aboriginal policing.

SUMMARY

This chapter has illustrated the considerable changes that have occurred over the last thirty years in the policing of Aboriginal peoples. There has been a movement away from externally-controlled, 'foreign' policing arrangements towards a recognition of the need for culturally-specific policing practices. A trend towards the indigenization of police services on Aboriginal reserves and in Aboriginal communities is evident. Despite this movement, in all likelihood, the RCMP, provincial and municipal police forces will continue to be involved in policing Aboriginal peoples in the future.

With the inherent right to self-government, First Nations people have gained the power to exercise greater influence over the institutions that control them. This factor, coupled with attempts to reassert distinct cultural identities, ensures that considerable change can be expected in the area of Aboriginal policing during the next decade.

QUESTIONS FOR DISCUSSION

1. Why is it impossible to speak of one Aboriginal people?
2. Describe the difference between on- and off-reserve policing.
3. What is the difference between Aboriginal and European-based policing models?
4. Why are Aboriginal people over-represented in the criminal justice system?
5. Describe the options for Aboriginal policing outlined in the 1973 federal Task Force on Policing on Reserves.
6. Why was the 3b option criticized?
7. Discuss the relative advantages and disadvantages of the three models of Aboriginal policing outlined by Skoog (1992).
8. Which branch of government is currently responsible for Aboriginal policing?
9. In what way is the issue of policing related to the issue of self-government?
10. Why do you think some Aboriginal communities would prefer to be policed by the RCMP rather than establish their own policing arrangements?

FURTHER READING

Oppal, The Honourable Mr. Justice Wallace T. (1994). *Closing the Gap: Policing and the Community*. Commission of Inquiry Policing in British Columbia. Victoria, B.C.: Attorney General. This report dedicates one chapter to policing Aboriginal peoples. Although it refers only to British Columbia, it contains many of the issues pertinent to a discussion of policing Aboriginal people in Canada.

Silverman, Robert A. and Nielsen, Marianne O. (1992). *Aboriginal Peoples and the Canadian Criminal Justice System.* Toronto: Butterworths. This edited text not only provides a comprehensive analysis of Aboriginal peoples' experience with the criminal justice system but also gives details of demographic and cultural contexts, Native justice systems, and community corrections.

REFERENCES

Benson, G.F. (1991). *Developing Crime Prevention Strategies in Aboriginal Communities.* Ottawa: Solicitor General of Canada.

Canada (1973). *Task Force on Policing on Reserves.* Ottawa: Department of Indian Affairs and Northern Development.

Canada (1990). *Indian Policing Policy Review Task Force Report.* Ottawa: Indian and Northern Affairs.

Canada (1992). *First Nations Policing Policy.* Ottawa: Ministry of the Solicitor General.

Canada (1994). *Basic Facts about Corrections in Canada.* Ottawa: Ministry of Supplies and Services.

Cawsey, Mr. Justice R.A. (1991). *Justice on Trial. Report of the Task Force on the Criminal Justice System and its Impact on the Indian and Metis People of Alberta.* Main Report. Edmonton: Attorney General and Solicitor General of Canada.

Depew, R. (1986). *Native Policing in Canada: A Review of Current Issues.* Ottawa: Ministry of the Solicitor General.

Depew, R. (1992). "Policing Native communities." In Robert A. Silverman and Marianne O. Nielsen (Eds.) *Aboriginal Peoples and the Canadian Criminal Justice System.* Toronto: Butterworths.

Forcese, Dennis P. (1992). *Policing Canadian Society.* Scarborough: Prentice Hall.

Griffiths, C.T. (1988). "Native Indians and the police: The Canadian Experience." *Police Studies, 11*(4).

Griffiths, Curt T. (1994). "Policing Aboriginal Peoples." In R.C. Macleod and David Schneiderman (Eds.) *Police Powers in Canada: The Evolution and Practice of Authority.* Toronto: University of Toronto Press.

Griffiths, Curt T. and Verdun Jones, Simon N. (1994). *Canadian Criminal Justice.* Toronto: Harcourt Brace.

Griffiths, C.T. and Yerbury, J.C. (1984). "Natives and criminal justice policy: The case of Native policing." *Canadian Journal of Criminology, 26*(2).

Hamilton, Associate Chief Justice A.C. and Sinclair, Associate Chief Judge C.M. (1991). *Report of the Aboriginal Justice Inquiry of Manitoba. The Justice System and Aboriginal People.* Vol. 1. Winnipeg: Queen's Printer.

Harding, Jim (1991). "Policing and Aboriginal justice." *Canadian Journal of Criminology,* *33*(3-4).

Havemann, P. (1992). "The indigenization of social control in Canada." In Robert A. Silverman and Marianne O. Nielsen (Eds.) *Aboriginal Peoples and the Canadian Criminal Justice System.* Toronto: Butterworths.

Horrall, S.W. (1989). *Policing the Bloods. The RCMP Role 1874–1960. An historical outline.* Ottawa: RCMP.

Jars, Julie (1992). *Inventory of Aboriginal Policing Programs in Canada.* Ottawa: Ministry of the Solicitor General.

Jobson, Keith B. (1993). *First Nations Police Services: Legal Issues.* Victoria, B.C.: Ministry of the Attorney General.

La Prarie, C. (1993). *Dimensions of Aboriginal Over-Representation in Canada: Correctional Institutions and Implications for Crime Prevention.* Ottawa: Department of Justice.

Landau, Tommy (1996). "Policing and security in four remote Aboriginal communities: A challenge to coercive models of police work." *Canadian Journal of Criminology, 38*(1).

Law Reform Commission (1991). *Aboriginal People and Criminal Justice.* Ottawa: Law Reform Commission of Canada.

Normandeau, A. and Leighton, B. (1990). *A Vision of the Future of Policing in Canada: Police Challenge 2000—Background Document.* Ottawa: Police and Security Branch, Ministry Secretariat, Solicitor General.

Nielsen, M.O. (1992). "Introduction." In Robert A. Silverman and Marianne O. Nielsen (Eds.) *Aboriginal Peoples and the Canadian Criminal Justice System.* Toronto: Butterworths.

Ontario (1974). *The Police are the Public and the Public are the Police.* Toronto: Task Force on Policing in Ontario.

Oppal, The Honourable Mr. Justice Wallace T. (1994). *Closing the Gap: Policing and the Community.* Commission of Inquiry Policing in British Columbia. Victoria, B.C.: Attorney General.

Seagrave, J. (1995). *Changing the organizational culture: community policing in British Columbia.* Unpublished doctoral dissertation. Burnaby, British Columbia: Simon Fraser University.

Silverman, Robert A. and Nielsen, Marianne O. (1992). *Aboriginal Peoples and the Canadian Criminal Justice System.* Toronto: Butterworths.

Skoog, Douglas M. (1992). "Taking control: Native self-government and Native policing." *Canadian Police College Journal, 16*(1).

Statistics Canada (1990). *Policing in Canada.* Ottawa: Canadian Centre for Justice Statistics.

Sunahara, David F. (1992). "Public inquiries into policing." *Canadian Police College Journal, 16*(2).

APPENDIX A:
Royal Canadian Mounted Police Act

WARNING NOTE

Users of this consolidation are reminded that it is prepared for convenience of reference only and that, as such, it has no official sanction.

Minister of Supply and Services Canada 1993
Available in Canada through
Associated Bookstores and other booksellers

or by mail from

Canada Communication Group — Publishing
Ottawa, Canada K1A 0S9
Catalogue No. YX54–1985–R1–S19.6–93–04

CHAPTER R–10

An Act respecting the Royal Canadian Mounted Police

SHORT TITLE

Short title
1. This Act may be cited as the *Royal Canadian Mounted Police Act*. R.S., c. R–9, s. 1.

INTERPRETATION

Definitions
2. (1) In this Act,

"appropriate officer"
"appropriate officer" means, in respect of a member, such officer as is designated pursuant to subsection (3);

"child" "child" means a person who is or, in the absence of any evidence to the contrary, appears to be under the age of eighteen years;

"Code of Conduct" "Code of Conduct" means the regulations made pursuant to section 38;

"Commission" "Commission" means the Royal Canadian Mounted Police Public Complaints Commission established by section 45.29;

"Commission Chairman" "Commission Chairman" means the Chairman of the Commission;

"Commissioner" "Commissioner" means the Commissioner of the Royal Canadian Mounted Police;

"Committee" "Committee" means the Royal Canadian Mounted Police External Review Committee established by section 25;

"Committee Chairman" "Committee Chairman" means the Chairman of the Committee;

"Force" "Force" means the Royal Canadian Mounted Police;

"guardian" "guardian" means, in respect of a child, any person, other than a parent of the child, who is under a legal duty to provide for the child or who has, in law or in fact, the custody or control of the child;

"member" "member" means any person
(a) who has been appointed as an officer or other member of the Force under section 5 or paragraph 6(3)(a) or 7(1)(a), and
(b) who has not been dismissed or discharged from the Force as provided in this Act, the regulations or the Commissioner's standing orders;

"Minister" "Minister" means the Solicitor General of Canada;

"officer" "officer" means a member appointed by the Governor in Council pursuant to section 5 or paragraph 6(3)(a);

"representative" "representative" means a member who is representing or assisting another member pursuant to section 47.1.

Commissioner's standing orders (2) The rules made by the Commissioner under any provision of this Act empowering the Commissioner to make rules shall be known as Commissioner's standing orders.

Designation   (3) The Commissioner may, by rule, designate an officer to be the appropriate officer in respect of a member either for the purposes of this Act generally or for the purposes of any provision thereof in particular. R.S., 1985, c. R–10, s. 2; R.S., 1985, c. 8 (2nd Supp.), s. 1.

PART I

CONSTITUTION AND ORGANIZATION

Composition of Force

Police Force for Canada   **3.** There shall continue to be a police force for Canada, which shall consist of officers and other members and be known as the Royal Canadian Mounted Police. R.S., c. R–9, s. 3.

Employment of Force   **4.** The Force may be employed in such places within or outside Canada as the Governor in Council prescribes. R.S., c. R–9, s. 4.

Commissioner

Appointment   **5.** (1) The Governor in Council may appoint an officer, to be known as the Commissioner of the Royal Canadian Mounted Police, who, under the direction of the Minister, has the control and management of the Force and all matters connected therewith.

Delegation   (2) The Commissioner may delegate to any member any of the Commissioner's powers, duties or functions under this Act, except the power to delegate under this subsection, the power to make rules under this Act and the powers, duties or functions under section 32 (in relation to any type of grievance prescribed pursuant to subsection 33(4)), subsections 42(4) and 43(1), section 45.16, subsection 45.19(5), section 45.26 and subsections 45.46(1) and (2).
R.S., 1985, c. R–10, s. 5; R.S., 1985, c. 8 (2nd Supp.), s. 2.

Officers

Other officers   **6.** (1) The officers of the Force, in addition to the Commissioner, shall consist of
     (a) Deputy Commissioners,
     (b) Assistant Commissioners,
     (c) Chief Superintendents,
     (d) Superintendents,

(e) Inspectors,

(f) [Repealed, R.S., 1985, c. 8 (2nd Supp.), s. 3]

and such other ranks as are prescribed by the Governor in Council.

Maximum number

(2) The maximum number of officers in each rank shall be as prescribed by the Treasury Board.

Commissions

(3) The Governor in Council may

(a) appoint any person to the rank of an officer;

(b) authorize the issue of a commission under the Great Seal to an officer on the officer's first appointment to the rank of an officer;

(c) by way of promotion appoint an officer to a higher rank; and

(d) by way of demotion appoint an officer to a lower rank.

R.S., 1985, c. R–10, s. 6; R.S., 1985, c. 8 (2nd Supp.), ss. 3, 24(E).

Other Members and Supernumerary Special Constables

Appointment and designation

7. (1) The Commissioner may

(a) appoint members of the Force other than officers;

(b) by way of promotion appoint a member other than an officer to a higher rank or level for which there is a vacancy in the establishment of the Force;

(c) where the Commissioner is requested by any department of the Government of Canada or considers it necessary or in the public interest, appoint for a period not exceeding twelve months at any one time special constables supernumerary to the strength of the Force for the purpose of maintaining law and order; and

(d) designate any member, any supernumerary special constable appointed under this subsection or any temporary employee employed under subsection 10(2) as a peace officer.

Ranks and levels

(2) The ranks and levels of members other than officers and the maximum numbers of persons that may be appointed to each rank and level shall be as prescribed by the Treasury Board.

Revocation of appointment

(3) The Commissioner may at any time revoke the appointment of any supernumerary special constable appointed under subsection (1).

Certificates

(4) The Commissioner may issue

(a) a certificate to any member stating that the person to whom it is issued is a member of the Force and, if that person is also a peace officer, that the person is such an officer; and

(b) a certificate to any other person appointed or employed under the authority of this Act stating that the person to whom it is issued is a peace officer, if that person has been designated as such under subsection (1).

Evidence of appointment or designation

(5) Any document purporting to be a certificate referred to in subsection (4) is evidence in all courts and in all proceedings of the facts stated therein.

R.S., 1985, c. R–10, s. 7; R.S., 1985, c. 8 (2nd Supp.), s. 4, c. 1 (4th Supp.), s. 45(F).

Supernumerary special constables

8. Supernumerary special constables shall serve without pay and are not entitled to any pecuniary privileges or benefits under this Act. R.S., 1985, c. R-10, s. 8; R.S., 1985, c. 8 (2nd Supp.), s. 4, c. 1 (4th Supp.) s. 45(F).

Peace officer

9. Every officer and every person designated as a peace officer under subsection 7(1) is a peace officer in every part of Canada and has all the powers, authority, protection and privileges that a peace officer has by law until the officer or person is dismissed or discharged from the Force as provided in this Act, the regulations or the Commissioner's standing orders or until the appointment of the officer or person expires or is revoked.

R.S., 1985, c. R–10, s. 9; R.S., 1985, c. 8 (2nd Supp.), s. 4.

Qualifications

Qualifications

9.1 (1) Subject to subsection (2), no person shall be appointed to be a member unless that person is a Canadian citizen, is of good character and has the necessary physical qualities and, in the case of a member other than an officer, that person meets such other qualifications for appointment to the Force as the Commissioner may, by rule, prescribe.

Exception

(2) When no person who meets the qualifications described in subsection (1) is available for appointment as a member, any person who is not a Canadian citizen but meets the other qualifications described in that subsection that are applicable to that person may be appointed to be a member.

R.S., 1985, c. 8 (2nd Supp.), s. 4.

Civilian Staff

Appointment and employment

10. (1) Subject to subsection (2), the civilian employees that are necessary for carrying out the functions and duties of the Force shall be appointed or employed under the *Public Service Employment Act*.

Temporary civilian staff

(2) The Commissioner may employ such number of temporary civilian employees at such remuneration and on such other terms and conditions as are prescribed by the Treasury Board, and may at any time dismiss or discharge any such employee.

(3) [Repealed, R.S., 1985, c. 8 (2nd Supp.), s. 5]
R.S., 1985, c. R–10, s. 10; R.S., 1985, c. 8 (2nd Supp.), s. 5.

Reserve

Establishment

11. (1) The Governor in Council may make regulations providing for the establishment of a Royal Canadian Mounted Police Reserve, for the appointment of members and officers thereof and for defining their powers, duties and functions.

Application of this Part to Reserve

(2) Except as provided by the regulations made under subsection (1), this Part does not apply to members of the Royal Canadian Mounted Police Reserve. R.S., c. R–9, s. 12.

Tenure of Office of Members

Tenure of officers

12. (1) Officers of the Force hold office during the pleasure of the Governor in Council.

Other members

(2) No member other than an officer may be dismissed or discharged from the Force except as provided in this Act, the regulations or the Commissioner's standing orders.
R.S., 1985, c. R–10, s. 12; R.S., 1985, c. 8 (2nd Supp.), s. 6.

Suspension

Suspension

12.1 Every member who has contravened, is found contravening or is suspected of contravening the Code of Conduct or an Act of Parliament or of the legislature of a province may be suspended from duty by the Commissioner.
R.S., 1985, c. 8 (2nd Supp.), s. 7.

Headquarters

Headquarters

13. The headquarters of the Force and the offices of the Commissioner shall be at Ottawa.
R.S., c. R–9, s. 14.

Oaths

Oaths **14.** (1) Every member shall, before entering on the duties of the member's office, take the oath of allegiance and the oaths set out in the schedule.

Authority to administer (2) The oaths prescribed by subsection (1), and any other oath or declaration that may be necessary or required, may be taken by the Commissioner before any judge, magistrate or justice of the peace having jurisdiction in any part of Canada, and by any other member before the Commissioner or any officer or person having authority to administer oaths or take and receive affidavits.
R.S., 1985, c. R–10, s. 14; R.S., 1985, c. 8 (2nd Supp.), s. 8.

Absence of Commissioner

Authority where Commissioner absent **15.** (1) In the event that the Commissioner is absent or unable to act or the office is vacant, the senior Deputy Commissioner at the headquarters of the Force has, for the time being, the control and management of the Force and all matters connected therewith, and for such purposes the senior Deputy Commissioner may exercise all the powers of the Commissioner under this Act or any other Act.

Authority where Commissioner and Deputy Commissioners absent (2) In the event that the Commissioner and all the Deputy Commissioners are absent or unable to act or the offices are vacant, the senior Assistant Commissioner at the headquarters of the Force has, for the time being, the control and management of the Force and all matters connected therewith, and for such purposes the senior Assistant Commissioner may exercise all of the powers of the Commissioner under this Act or any other Act. R.S., c. R–9, s. 16.

16. [Repealed, R.S., 1985, c. 8 (2nd Supp.), s. 9]

17. [Repealed, R.S., 1985, c. 8 (2nd Supp.), s. 10]

Duties

Duties **18.** It is the duty of members who are peace officers, subject to the orders of the Commissioner,
(a) to perform all duties that are assigned to peace officers in relation to the preservation of the peace, the prevention of crime and of offenses against the laws of Canada and the laws in force in any province in which they may be employed, and the apprehension of criminals and offenders

and others who may be lawfully taken into custody;

(b) to execute all warrants, and perform all duties and services in relation thereto, that may, under this Act or the laws of Canada or the laws in force in any province, be lawfully executed and performed by peace officers;

(c) to perform all duties that may be lawfully performed by peace officers in relation to the escort and conveyance of convicts and other persons in custody to or from any courts, places of punishment or confinement, asylums or other places; and

(d) to perform such other duties and functions as are prescribed by the Governor in Council or the Commissioner. R.S., c. R–9, s. 18.

19. [Repealed, R.S., 1985, c. 8 (2nd Supp.), s. 11]

Arrangements with provinces

20. (1) The Minister may, with the approval of the Governor in Council, enter into an arrangement with the government of any province for the use or employment of the Force, or any portion thereof, in aiding the administration of justice in the province and in carrying into effect the laws in force therein.

Arrangements with municipalities

(2) The Minister may, with the approval of the Governor in Council and the lieutenant governor in council of any province, enter into an arrangement with any municipality in the province for the use or employment of the Force, or any portion thereof, in aiding the administration of justice in the municipality and in carrying into effect the laws in force therein.

Payment for services

(3) The Minister may, with the approval of the Treasury Board, in any arrangement made under subsection (1) or (2), agree on and determine the amount of money to be paid by the province or municipality for the services of the Force.

Taking over other police forces

(4) There may be included in any arrangement made under subsection (1) or (2) provision for the taking over by the Force of officers and other members of any provincial or municipal police force.

Report to Parliament

(5) The Minister shall cause to be laid before Parliament a copy of every arrangement made under subsection (1) or (2) within fifteen days after it is made or, if Parliament is not then sitting, on any of the first fifteen days next thereafter that either House of Parliament is sitting. R.S., c. R–9, s. 20.

Regulations and Rules

Regulations

21. (1) The Governor in Council may make regulations
(a) respecting the administrative discharge of members;
(b) for the organization, training, conduct, performance of duties, discipline, efficiency, administration or good government of the Force; and
(c) generally, for carrying the purposes and provisions of this Act into effect.

Rules

(2) Subject to this Act and the regulations, the Commissioner may make rules
(a) respecting the administrative discharge of members; and
(b) for the organization, training, conduct, performance of duties, discipline, efficiency, administration or good government of the Force.
R.S., 1985, c. R–10, s. 21; R.S., 1985, c. 8 (2nd Supp.), s. 12.

Pay and Allowances

Pay and allowances

22. (1) The Treasury Board shall establish the pay and allowances to be paid to members.

Reduction in pay where demotion

(1.1) Where, pursuant to this Act, a member is demoted, the rate of pay of that member shall be reduced to the highest rate of pay for the rank or level to which the member is demoted that does not exceed the member's rate of pay at the time of the demotion.

During imprisonment

(2) No pay or allowances shall be paid to any member in respect of any period during which the member is serving a sentence of imprisonment.

During suspension

(3) The Treasury Board may make regulations respecting the stoppage of pay and allowances of members who are suspended from duty. R.S., 1985, c. R–10, s. 22; R.S., 1985, c. 8 (2nd Supp.), s. 13.

Benefit Trust Fund

Fees, gifts, etc., payable to Fund

23. (1) All
(a) fees, costs remuneration or commissions, other than pay and allowances under section 22, and
(b) gifts, awards and bequests, if money or converted into money, other than gifts or rewards under subsection (3),

earned by or awarded, paid or granted to any member in connection with the performance of the member's duties in the

Force shall be paid to the Benefit Trust Fund maintained by the Force, unless the Minister directs otherwise.

Pay, forfeitures payable to Fund

(2) Notwithstanding any other Act, all pay forfeited under this Act and the proceeds of all forfeitures and seizures awarded or adjudged to any member in connection with the performance of the member's duties in the Force shall be paid to the Benefit Trust Fund maintained by the Force.

Purpose of Benefit Trust Fund

(3) The money paid to the Benefit Trust Fund pursuant to this section shall be used
(a) for the benefit of members and former members and their dependants;
(b) as a reward, grant or compensation to any person who assists the Force in the performance of its duties in any case where the Minister is of the opinion that the person is deserving of recognition for the service rendered;
(c) as a reward to any person appointed or employed under the authority of this Act for good conduct or meritorious service; and
(d) for such other objects for the benefit of the force as the Minister may direct.

Regulations

(4) The Governor in Council may make regulations governing the management and disposition by loan, grant or otherwise of any money paid to the Benefit Trust Fund pursuant to this section.
R.S., 1985, c. R–10, s. 23; R.S., 1985, c. 8 (2nd Supp.), s. 14.

Disposition of Property

Abandoned or lost property

24. Where it appears to the Commissioner
(a) that any personal property that has, in the Yukon Territory or the Northwest Territories, come into the hands of any member in the course of the member's duties has been abandoned by the owner thereof or the person entitled thereto, or
(b) that a reasonable attempt has been made to find the owner of or person entitled to any personal property that has, in the Yukon Territory or the Northwest Territories, come into the hands of any member in the course of the member's duties, but the owner or person cannot be found,

the Commissioner may make such disposition of the property as the Commissioner in the circumstances deems fit, but the proceeds, if any, from the sale or other disposition of the property, and any such property consisting of money, shall be paid into the Consolidated Revenue Fund.

R.S., 1985, c. R–10, s. 24; R.S., 1985, c. 8 (2nd Supp.), s. 24(E).

Boards of Inquiry

Board of Inquiry

24.1 (1) The Minister or the Commissioner may appoint such persons as the Minister or Commissioner considers appropriate as a board of inquiry to investigate and report on any matter connected with the organization, training, conduct, performance of duties, discipline, efficiency, administration or government of the Force or affecting any member or other person appointed or employed under the authority of this Act.

Matter to be investigated

(2) Where the Minister or the Commissioner appoints a board of inquiry under subsection (1), the Minister or Commissioner shall specify in writing the matter that the board is to investigate and report on.

Powers of board of inquiry

(3) A board of inquiry has, in relation to the matter before it, power

(a) to summon any person before the board and to require that person to give oral or written evidence on oath and to produce such documents and things under that person's control as the board deems requisite to the full investigation and consideration of that matter;

(b) to administer oaths;

(c) to receive and accept on oath or by affidavit such evidence and other information as the board sees fit, whether or not such evidence or information is or would be admissible in a court of law; and

(d) to make such examination of records and such inquiries as the board deems necessary.

Rights of persons interested

(4) Any person whose conduct or affairs are being investigated by a board of inquiry or who satisfies a board of inquiry that the person has a substantial and direct interest in the matter before the board shall be afforded a full and ample opportunity, in person or by counsel or a representative, to present evidence, to cross-examine witnesses and to make representations before the board.

Representation of witnesses

(5) A board of inquiry shall permit any person who gives evidence in the investigation by the board to be represented by counsel or a representative.

Restriction　(6) Notwithstanding subsection (3), a board of inquiry may not receive or accept in an investigation

(a) subject to subsection (7), any evidence or other information that would be inadmissible in a court of law by reason of any privilege under the law of evidence;

(b) any answer or statement made in response to a question described in subsection 35(8), 40(2), 45.1(11), 45.22(8) or 45.45(9);

(c) any answer or statement made in response to a question described in subsection (7) before any other board of inquiry appointed under this section; or

(d) any answer or statement made in the course of attempting to dispose of a complaint under section 45.36.

Witness not excused from testifying　(7) In an investigation by a board of inquiry, no witness shall be excused from answering any question relating to the matter before the board when required to do so by the board on the ground that the answer to the question may tend to criminate the witness or subject the witness to any proceeding or penalty.

Answer not receivable　(8) Where the witness is a member, no answer or statement made in response to a question described in subsection (7) shall be used or receivable against the witness in any hearing under section 45.1 into an allegation of contravention of the Code of Conduct by the witness, other than a hearing into an allegation that with intent to mislead the witness gave the answer or statement knowing it to be false.

Investigation and hearing in private　(9) Unless the Minister or the Commissioner directs otherwise, an investigation and any hearing by a board of inquiry appointed by the Minister or Commissioner, as the case may be, shall be conducted in private.

Exception　(10) Notwithstanding subsection (9),

(a) while a child is testifying in an investigation or at a hearing by a board of inquiry, the child's parent or guardian may be present; and

(b) when authorized by a board of inquiry, a member may attend a hearing before the board as an observer for the purpose of familiarizing the member with procedures under this section.

Return of documents, etc.　(11) Any document or thing produced pursuant to this section to a board of inquiry shall, on the request of the person producing the document or thing, be released to that person within a reasonable time after completion of the board's investigation and report.

R.S., 1985, c. 8 (2nd Supp.), s. 15.

PART II

ROYAL CANADIAN MOUNTED POLICE EXTERNAL REVIEW COMMITTEE

Establishment and Organization of Committee

Committee established

25. (1) There is hereby established a committee, to be known as the Royal Canadian Mounted Police External Review Committee, consisting of a Chairman, a Vice-Chairman and not more than three other members, to be appointed by order of the Governor in Council.

Full- or part-time

(2) The Committee Chairman is a full-time member of the Committee and the other members may be appointed as full-time or part-time members of the Committee.

Tenure of office

(3) Each member of the Committee shall be appointed to hold office during good behaviour for a term not exceeding five years but may be removed for cause at any time by order of the Governor in Council.

Re-appointment

(4) A member of the Committee is eligible for re-appointment on the expiration of the member's term of office.

Eligibility

(5) No member of the Force is eligible to be appointed or to continue as a member of the Committee.

Salary of full-time members

(6) Each full-time member of the Committee is entitled to be paid such salary in connection with the work of the Committee as may be approved by order of the Governor in Council.

Fees of part-time members

(7) Each part-time member of the Committee is entitled to be paid fees in connection with the work of the Committee as may be approved by order of the Governor in Council.

Expenses

(8) Each member of the Committee is entitled to be paid reasonable travel and living expenses incurred by the member while absent from the member's ordinary place of residence in connection with the work of the Committee.

Benefits of full-time members

(9) The full-time members of the Committee are deemed to be employed in the Public Service for the purposes of the *Public Service Superannuation Act* and to be employed in the public service of Canada for the purposes of the *Government Employees Compensation Act* and any regulations made under section 9 of the *Aeronautics Act*.

R.S., 1985, c. R–10, s. 25; R.S., 1985, c. 8 (2nd Supp.), s. 16.

Committee Chairman
26. (1) The Committee Chairman is the chief executive officer of the Committee and has supervision over and direction of the work and staff of the Committee.

Absence or incapacity
(2) In the event of the absence or incapacity of the Committee Chairman or if the office of Committee Chairman is vacant, the Minister may authorize the Vice-Chairman to exercise the powers and perform the duties and functions of the Committee Chairman.

Delegation
(3) The Committee Chairman may delegate to the Vice-Chairman any of the Committee Chairman's powers, duties or functions under this Act, except the power to delegate under this subsection and the duty under section 30.
R.S., 1985, c. R–10, s 26; R.S., 1985, c. 8 (2nd Supp.), s. 16.

Head office
27. (1) The head office of the Committee shall be at such place in Canada as the Governor in Council may, by order, designate.

Staff
(2) Such officers and employees as are necessary for the proper conduct of the work of the Committee shall be appointed in accordance with the *Public Service Employment Act.*

Idem
(3) The Committee may, with the approval of the Treasury Board,
(a) engage on a temporary basis the services of persons having technical or specialized knowledge of any matter relating to the work of the Committee to advise and assist the Committee in the exercise or performance of its powers duties and functions under this Act; and
(b) fix and pay the remuneration and expenses of persons engaged pursuant to paragraph (a).
R.S., 1985, c. R–10, s. 27; R.S., 1985, c. 8 (2nd Supp.), s. 16.

Duties

Duties of Committee
28. (1) The Committee shall carry out such functions and duties as are assigned to it by this Act.

Duties of Committee Chairman
(2) The Committee Chairman shall carry out such functions and duties as are assigned to the Committee Chairman by this Act.
R.S., 1985, c. R–10, s. 28; R.S., 1985, c. 8 (2nd Supp.), s. 16.

Rules

Rules

29. Subject to this Act, the Committee may make rules respecting

(a) the sittings of the Committee;

(b) the manner of dealing with matters and business before the Committee generally, including the practice and procedure before the Committee;

(c) the apportionment of the work of the Committee among its members and the assignment of members to review grievances or cases referred to the Committee; and

(d) the performance of the duties and functions of the Committee under this Act generally.

R.S., 1985, c. R–10, s. 29; R.S., 1985, c. 8 (2nd Supp.), s. 16.

Annual Report

Annual report

30. The Committee Chairman shall, within three months after the end of each fiscal year, submit to the Minister a report of the activities of the Committee during that year and its recommendations, if any, and the Minister shall cause a copy of the report to be laid before each House of Parliament on any of the first fifteen days on which that House is sitting after the day the Minister receives it.

R.S., 1985, c. R–10, s. 30; R.S., 1985, c. 8 (2nd Supp.), s. 16.

PART III

GRIEVANCES

Presentation of Grievances

Right of member

31. (1) Subject to subsections (2) and (3), where any member is aggrieved by any decision, act or omission in the administration of the affairs of the Force in respect of which no other process for redress is provided by this Act, the regulations or the Commissioner's standing orders, the member is entitled to present the grievance in writing at each of the levels, up to and including the final level, in the grievance process provided for by this Part.

Limitation period

(2) A grievance under this Part must be presented

(a) at the initial level in the grievance process, within thirty days after the day on which the aggrieved member knew or reasonably ought to have known of the decision, act or omission giving rise to the grievance; and

(b) at the second and any succeeding level in the grievance process, within fourteen days after the day the aggrieved member is served with the decision of the immediately preceding level in respect of the grievance.

Restriction

(3) No appointment by the Commissioner to a position prescribed pursuant to subsection (7) may be the subject of a grievance under this Part.

Access to information

(4) Subject to any limitations prescribed pursuant to paragraph 36(b), any member presenting a grievance shall be granted access to such written or documentary information under the control of the Force and relevant to the grievance as the member reasonably requires to properly present it.

No penalty for presenting grievance

(5) No member shall be disciplined or otherwise penalized in relation to employment or any term of employment in the Force for exercising the right under this Part to present a grievance.

Decision

(6) As soon as possible after the presentation and consideration of a grievance at any level in the grievance process, the member constituting the level shall render a decision in writing as to the disposition of the grievance, including reasons for the decision, and serve the member presenting the grievance and, if the grievance has been referred to the Committee pursuant to section 33, the Committee Chairman with a copy of the decision.

Excluded appointments

(7) The Governor in Council may make regulations prescribing for the purposes of subsection (3) any position in the Force that reports to the Commissioner either directly or through one other person.
R.S., 1985, c. R–10, s. 31; R.S., 1985, c. 8 (2nd Supp.), s. 16.

Final level in grievance process

32. (1) The Commissioner constitutes the final level in the grievance process and the Commissioner's decision in respect of any grievance is final and binding and, except for judicial review under the *Federal Court Act*, is not subject to appeal to or review by any court.

Commissioner not bound

(2) The Commissioner is not bound to act on any findings or recommendations set out in a report with respect to a grievance referred to the Committee under section 33, but if the Commissioner does not so act, the Commissioner shall include in the decision on the disposition of the grievance the reasons for not so acting.

Rescission or amendment of decision

(3) Notwithstanding subsection (1), the Commissioner may rescind or amend the Commissioner's decision in respect of a grievance under this Part on the presentation to the Commissioner of new facts or where, with respect to the finding of any fact or the interpretation of any law, the Commissioner determines that an error was made in reaching the decision.

R.S., 1985, c. R–10, s. 32; R.S., 1985, c. 8 (2nd Supp.), s. 16; 1990, c. 8, s. 65.

Reference to Committee

Reference to Committee

33. (1) Before the Commissioner considers a grievance of a type prescribed pursuant to subsection (4), the Commissioner shall refer the grievance to the Committee.

Idem

(2) Notwithstanding subsection (1), a member presenting a grievance to the Commissioner may request the Commissioner not to refer the grievance to the Committee and, on such a request, the Commissioner may either not refer the grievance to the Committee or, if the Commissioner considers that a reference to the Committee is appropriate notwithstanding the request, refer the grievance to the Committee.

Material to be furnished to Committee

(3) Where the Commissioner refers a grievance to the Committee pursuant to this section, the Commissioner shall furnish the Committee Chairman with a copy of
(a) the written submissions made at each level in the grievance process by the member presenting the grievance;
(b) the decisions rendered at each level in the grievance process in respect of the grievance; and
(c) the written or documentary information under the control of the Force and relevant to the grievance.

Grievances referable to Committee

(4) The Governor in Council may make regulations prescribing for the purposes of subsection (1) the types of grievances that are to be referred to the Committee.

R.S., 1985, c. R–10, s. 33; R.S., 1985, c. 8 (2nd Supp.), s. 16.

Review by Committee Chairman

34. (1) The Committee Chairman shall review every grievance referred to the Committee pursuant to section 33.

Action by Committee Chairman

(2) Where, after reviewing a grievance, the Committee Chairman is satisfied with the disposition of the grievance by the Force, the Committee Chairman shall prepare and send a report in writing to that effect to the Commissioner and the member presenting the grievance.

Idem   (3) Where, after reviewing a grievance, the Committee Chairman is not satisfied with the disposition of the grievance by the Force or considers that further inquiry is warranted, the Committee Chairman may

    (a) prepare and send to the Commissioner and the member presenting the grievance a report in writing setting out such findings and recommendations with respect to the grievance as the Committee Chairman sees fit; or

    (b) institute a hearing to inquire into the grievance.

Hearing   (4) Where the Committee Chairman decides to institute a hearing to inquire into a grievance, the Committee Chairman shall assign the member or members of the Committee to conduct the hearing and shall send a notice in writing of the decision to the Commissioner and the member presenting the grievance.

R.S., 1985, c. R–10, s. 34; R.S., 1985, c. 8 (2nd Supp.), s. 16.

Committee   **35.** (1) For the purposes of this section, the member or members conducting a hearing to inquire into a grievance are deemed to be the Committee.

Notice   (2) The Committee shall serve a notice in writing of the time and place appointed for a hearing on the parties.

Sittings of Committee   (3) Where a party wishes to appear before the Committee, the Committee shall sit at such place in Canada and at such time as may be fixed by the Committee, having regard to the convenience of the parties.

Powers of Committee   (4) The Committee has, in relation to the grievance before it, the powers conferred on a board of inquiry, in relation to the matter before it, by paragraphs 24.1(3)(a), (b) and (c).

Rights of persons interested   (5) The parties and any other person who satisfies the Committee that the person has a substantial and direct interest in a grievance before the Committee shall be afforded a full and ample opportunity, in person or by counsel or a representative, to present evidence, to cross-examine witnesses and to make representations at the hearing.

Representation of witnesses   (6) The Committee shall permit any person who gives evidence at a hearing to be represented by counsel or a representative.

Restriction

(7) Notwithstanding subsection (4) but subject to subsection (8), the Committee may not receive or accept any evidence or other information that would be inadmissible in a court of law by reason of any privilege under the law of evidence.

Witness not excused from testifying

(8) In a hearing, no witness shall be excused from answering any question relating to the grievance before the Committee when required to do so by the Committee on the ground that the answer to the question may tend to criminate the witness or subject the witness to any proceeding or penalty.

Answer not receivable

(9) Where the witness is a member, no answer or statement made in response to a question described in subsection (8) shall be used or receivable against the witness in any hearing under section 45.1 into an allegation of contravention of the Code of Conduct by the witness, other than a hearing into an allegation that with intent to mislead the witness gave the answer or statement knowing it to be false.

Hearing in private

(10) A hearing shall be held in private, except that
(a) while a child is testifying at the hearing, the child's parent or guardian may attend the hearing; and
(b) when authorized by the Committee, a member may attend the hearing as an observer for the purpose of familiarizing the member with procedures under this section.

Return of documents, etc.

(11) Any document or thing produced pursuant to this section to the Committee shall, on the request of the person producing the document or thing, be released to the person within a reasonable time after completion of the Committee's report.

Expenses

(12) Where the Committee sits at a place in Canada that is not the ordinary place of residence of a member whose grievance is before the Committee or of the member's counsel or representative, that member, counsel or representative is entitled, in the discretion of the Committee, to receive such travel and living expenses incurred by the member, counsel or representative in appearing before the Committee as may be fixed by the Treasury Board.

Report

(13) On completion of a hearing, the Committee shall prepare and send to the parties and the Commissioner a report in writing setting out such findings and recommendations with respect to the grievance as the Committee sees fit.

Definition of "parties"

(14) In this section, "parties" means the appropriate officer and the member whose grievance has been referred to the Committee pursuant to section 33.

R.S., 1985, c. R–10, s. 35; R.S., 1985, c. 8 (2nd Supp.), s. 16.

Rules

36. The Commissioner may make rules governing the presentation and consideration of grievances under this Part, including, without limiting the generality of the foregoing, rules

(a) prescribing the members or classes of members to constitute the levels in the grievance process; and

(b) specifying, for the purposes of subsection 31(4), limitations, in the interests of security or the protection of privacy of persons, on the right of a member presenting a grievance to be granted access to information relating thereto.

R.S., 1985, c. R–10, s. 36; R.S., 1985, c. 8 (2nd Supp.), s. 16.

PART IV

DISCIPLINE

Standards

Standards

37. It is incumbent on every member

(a) to respect the rights of all persons;

(b) to maintain the integrity of the law, law enforcement and the administration of justice;

(c) to perform the member's duties promptly, impartially and diligently, in accordance with the law and without abusing the member's authority;

(d) to avoid any actual, apparent or potential conflict of interests;

(e) to ensure that any improper or unlawful conduct of any member is not concealed or permitted to continue;

(f) to be incorruptible, never accepting or seeking special privilege in the performance of the member's duties or otherwise placing the member under any obligation that may prejudice the proper performance of the member's duties;

(g) to act at all times in a courteous, respectful and honourable manner; and

(h) to maintain the honour of the Force and its principles and purposes.

R.S., 1985, c. R–10, s. 37; R.S., 1985, c. 8 (2nd Supp.), s. 16.

Code of Conduct

Code of Conduct

38. The Governor in Council may make regulations, to be known as the Code of Conduct, governing the conduct of members.
R.S., 1985, c. R–10, s. 38; R.S., 1985, c. 8 (2nd Supp.), s. 16.

Contravention of
Code of Conduct

39. (1) Every member alleged to have contravened the Code of Conduct may be dealt with under this Act either in or outside Canada,

(a) whether or not the alleged contravention took place in or outside Canada; and

(b) whether or not the member has been charged with an offence constituted by, included in or otherwise related to the alleged contravention or has been tried, acquitted, discharged, convicted or sentenced by a court in respect of such an offence.

No interference
with jurisdiction of
courts

(2) Nothing in this Act affects the jurisdiction of any court to try a member for any offence triable by that court.
R.S., 1985, c. R–10, s. 39; R.S., 1985, c. 8 (2nd Supp.), s. 16.

Investigation

Investigation

40. (1) Where it appears to an officer or to a member in command of a detachment that a member under the command of the officer or member has contravened the Code of Conduct, the officer or member shall make or cause to be made such investigation as the officer or member considers necessary to enable the officer or member to determine whether that member has contravened or is contravening the Code of Conduct

Member not
excused from
answering

(2) In any investigation under subsection (1), no member shall be excused from answering any question relating to the matter being investigated when required to do so by the officer or other member conducting the investigation on the ground that the answer to the question may tend to criminate the member or subject the member to any proceeding or penalty.

Answer not
receivable

(3) No answer or statement made in response to a question described in subsection (2) shall be used or receivable in any criminal, civil or administrative proceedings, other than a hearing under section 45.1 into an allegation that with intent to mislead the member gave the answer or statement knowing it to be false.

Definition of
"detachment"

(4) In this section and section 41, "detachment" includes such other unit of the Force as the Commissioner may, by rule, specify. R.S., 1985, c. R–10, s. 40; R.S., 1985, c. 8 (2nd Supp.), s. 16.

Informal Disciplinary Action

Informal
disciplinary action

41. (1) Subject to this section, the following informal disciplinary action may be taken in respect of a contravention of the Code of Conduct, namely,

(a) counselling;

(b) recommendation for special training;

(c) recommendation for professional counselling;

(d) recommendation for transfer;

(e) direction to work under close supervision;

(f) subject to such conditions as the Commissioner may, by rule, prescribe, forfeiture of regular time off for any period not exceeding one work day; and

(g) reprimand.

Action by member
in command

(2) Where it is established to the satisfaction of a member, other than an officer, in command of a detachment that a member under the command of the member has contravened the Code of Conduct, the member in command may take any one or more of the actions referred to in paragraphs (1)(a) to (f) against that member.

Action by officer

(3) Where it is established to the satisfaction of an officer that a member, other than an officer, under the command of the officer has contravened the Code of Conduct, the officer may, if no action has been taken under subsection (2) in respect of the contravention, take any one or more of the actions referred to in paragraphs (1)(a) to (g) against that member.

Idem

(4) Where it is established to the satisfaction of an officer that an officer under the command of the officer has contravened the Code of Conduct, the officer in command may take any one or more of the actions referred to in paragraphs (1)(a) to (f) against that officer.

Action by
appropriate officer

(5) Where it is established to the satisfaction of an appropriate officer that an officer has contravened the Code of Conduct, the appropriate officer may, if no action has been taken under subsection (4) in respect of the contravention, take any one or more of the actions referred to in paragraphs (1)(a) to (g) against the officer who has contravened the Code of Conduct.

Idem   (6) Where it is not established to the satisfaction of an appropriate officer that a member against whom informal disciplinary action was taken under subsection (2), (3) or (4) has contravened the Code of Conduct, the appropriate officer may rescind that action.

Idem   (7) Where it is established to the satisfaction of an appropriate officer that a member against whom informal disciplinary action was taken under subsection (2), (3) or (4) has contravened the Code of Conduct, but the appropriate officer is of the opinion that the action so taken was inappropriate in the circumstances, the appropriate officer may vary that action by taking any one or more of the actions referred to in paragraphs (1)(a) to (g) in addition to or in substitution for that action.

Restrictions   (8) Notwithstanding subsections (2) to (7), an officer or other member may take informal disciplinary action under this section only against members of lower rank or level and only if the officer or other member is of the opinion that, having regard to the gravity of the contravention and to the surrounding circumstances, the action is sufficient.

Action not grievable or appealable   (9) Notwithstanding any provision of Part III, the informal disciplinary actions referred to in paragraphs (1)(a) to (d) may not be the subject of a grievance under that Part or be appealed under this Part.

Definition of "officer"   (10) In this section "officer", in addition to the members referred to in the definition "officer" in subsection 2(1), includes such other member or member of such class of other members as the Commissioner may, by rule, prescribe.
R.S., 1985, c. R–10, s. 41; R.S., 1985, c. 8 (2nd Supp.), s. 16.

Appeal   **42.** (1) Any member against whom informal disciplinary action referred to in any of paragraphs 41(1)(e) to (g) is taken may appeal that action at each of the levels, up to and including the final level, in the appeal process provided for by this section.

Decision on appeal   (2) Subject to subsection (3), each level in the appeal process provided for by this section may dispose of an appeal by
(a) dismissing the appeal and confirming the informal disciplinary action being appealed; or
(b) allowing the appeal and either rescinding the informal disciplinary action being appealed or varying that action by taking any one or more of the actions referred to in paragraphs 41(1)(a) to (g) in substitution for that action.

Restriction (3) On appeal under this section, the informal disciplinary action referred to in paragraph 41(1)(g) may not be taken in substitution for those referred to in paragraphs 41(1)(e) and (f).

Final level—
Deputy
Commissioner (4) The Deputy Commissioner designated by the Commissioner for the purposes of this section constitutes the final level in the appeal process with respect to appeals taken by members, other than officers, from informal disciplinary actions referred to in paragraphs 41(1)(e) and (f) and the Deputy Commissioner's decision on any such appeal is final and binding and, except for judicial review under the *Federal Court Act*, is not subject to appeal to or review by any court.

Rescission or
amendment of
decision (5) Notwithstanding subsection (4), the Deputy Commissioner referred to in that subsection may rescind or amend the Deputy Commissioner's decision on an appeal in respect of which the Deputy Commissioner constitutes the final level in the appeal process on the presentation to the Deputy Commissioner of new facts or where, with respect to the finding of any fact or the interpretation of any law, the Deputy Commissioner determines that an error was made in reaching the decision.

Final level—
Commissioner (6) The Commissioner constitutes the final level in the appeal process with respect to appeals taken by officers from informal disciplinary action referred to in any of paragraphs 41(1)(e) to (g) and with respect to appeals taken by members, other than officers, from informal disciplinary action referred to in paragraph 41(1)(g) and the Commissioner's decision on any such appeal is final and binding and, except for judicial review under the *Federal Court Act*, is not subject to appeal to or review by any court.

Rescission or
amendment of
decision (7) Notwithstanding subsection (6), the Commissioner may rescind or amend the Commissioner's decision on an appeal under this section on the presentation to the Commissioner of new facts or where, with respect to the finding of any fact or the interpretation of any law, the Commissioner determines that an error was made in reaching the decision.

Rules (8) The Commissioner may make rules governing appeals under this section, including, without restricting the generality of the foregoing, rules
(a) prescribing the levels in the appeal process;
(b) prescribing the time within which an appeal may be made at any level in the appeal process and providing for extensions thereof; and

(c) regulating the practice and procedure for appeals under this section.

Not in derogation
(9) Nothing in this section is in derogation of the power conferred by section 41 to rescind or vary informal disciplinary action.
R.S., 1985, c. R–10, s 42; R.S., 1985, c. 8 (2nd Supp.), s. 16; 1990, c. 8, s. 66.

Formal Disciplinary Action

Initiation
43. (1) Subject to subsections (7) and (8), where it appears to an appropriate officer that a member has contravened the Code of Conduct and the appropriate officer is of the opinion that, having regard to the gravity of the contravention and to the surrounding circumstances, informal disciplinary action under section 41 would not be sufficient if the contravention were established, the appropriate officer shall initiate a hearing into the alleged contravention and notify the officer designated by the Commissioner for the purposes of this section of that decision.

Adjudication board
(2) On being notified pursuant to subsection (1), the designated officer shall appoint three officers as members of an adjudication board to conduct the hearing and shall notify the appropriate officer of the appointments.

Qualifications
(3) At least one of the officers appointed as a member of an adjudication board shall be a graduate of a school of law recognized by the law society of any province.

Notice of hearing
(4) Forthwith after being notified pursuant to subsection (2), the appropriate officer shall serve the member alleged to have contravened the Code of Conduct with a notice in writing of the hearing, together with
(a) a copy of any written or documentary evidence that is intended to be produced at the hearing;
(b) a copy of any statement obtained from any person who is intended to be called as a witness at the hearing; and
(c) a list of exhibits that are intended to be entered at the hearing.

Contents of notice
(5) A notice of hearing served on a member pursuant to subsection (4) may allege more than one contravention of the Code of Conduct and shall contain
(a) a separate statement of each alleged contravention;
(b) a statement of the particulars of the act or omission constituting each alleged contravention;

(c) the names of the members of the adjudication board; and

(d) a statement of the right of the member to object to the appointment of any member of the adjudication board as provided in section 44.

Statement of particulars

(6) Every statement of particulars contained in a notice of hearing in accordance with paragraph (5)(b) shall contain sufficient details, including, where practicable, the place and date of each contravention alleged in the notice, to enable the member who is served with the notice to determine each such contravention so that the member may prepare a defence and direct it to the occasion and events indicated in the notice.

Restriction

(7) No hearing may be initiated by an appropriate officer under this section in respect of an alleged contravention of the Code of Conduct by a member if the informal disciplinary action referred to in paragraph 41(1)(g) has been taken against the member in respect of that contravention.

Limitation period

(8) No hearing may be initiated by an appropriate officer under this section in respect of an alleged contravention of the Code of Conduct by a member after the expiration of one year from the time the contravention and the identity of that member became known to the appropriate officer.

Certificate

(9) A certificate purporting to be signed by an appropriate officer as to the time an alleged contravention of the Code of Conduct by a member and the identity of that member became known to the appropriate officer is, in the absence of evidence to the contrary, proof of that time without proof of the signature or official character of the person purporting to have signed the certificate. R.S., 1985, c. R–10, s. 43; R.S., 1985, c. 8 (2nd Supp.), s. 16.

Adjudication Board

Objection to member of adjudication board

44. (1) Within seven days after the day a member is served with a notice of hearing under subsection 43(4), the member may object in writing to the designated officer referred to in subsection 43(1) to the appointment of any member of the adjudication board, and the designated officer shall on receiving the objection decide whether to reject the objection or to allow the objection and appoint a new member of the board.

Reasons for objection

(2) An objection under subsection (1) shall contain reasons for the objection.

Notice

(3) After the designated officer makes a decision under subsection (1) with respect to an objection, the designated officer shall serve the member making the objection with a notice in writing setting out the decision and the reasons therefor and, if the objection is allowed, the designated officer shall

(a) appoint a new member of the adjudication board; and

(b) set out in the notice

(i) the name of the new member, and

(ii) a statement of the right of the member to object to the appointment of the new member as provided in this section.

Objection to new member

(4) The provisions of this section apply, with such modifications as the circumstances require, with respect to the appointment of a new member under subsection (3) as though the notice setting out the name of the new member were a notice referred to in subsection (1).

Eligibility limited

(5) An officer is not eligible to be appointed as a member of an adjudication board if the officer

(a) has conducted an investigation under section 40 in respect of the conduct that is the subject of the hearing;

(b) was a member of a board of inquiry that conducted an investigation in respect of the conduct that is the subject of the hearing;

(c) is the immediate superior officer of the member whose conduct is the subject of the hearing; or

(d) is otherwise involved in the initiation or processing of the case against the member whose conduct is the subject of the hearing.

Chairman

(6) After the conclusion of all proceedings under this section, the designated officer shall designate one of the members of the adjudication board as chairman.

R.S., 1985, c. R–10, s. 44; R.S., 1985, c. 8 (2nd Supp.), s. 16.

Powers of adjudication board

45. An adjudication board has, in relation to the case before it, the powers conferred on a board of inquiry, in relation to the matter before it, by paragraphs 24.1(3)(a), (b) and (c).

R.S., 1985, c. R–10, s. 45; R.S., 1985, c. 8 (2nd Supp.), s. 16.

Hearing

Parties

45.1 (1) An appropriate officer who initiates a hearing and the member whose conduct is the subject of the hearing are parties to the hearing.

Notice of time and place of hearing

(2) An adjudication board shall set the place, date and time for a hearing and serve the parties thereto with a notice in writing of that place, date and time.

Date and time of hearing

(3) The date and time for a hearing set pursuant to subsection (2) shall not be less than seven days after the day the member whose conduct is the subject of the hearing is served with the notice under that subsection.

Allegations read

(4) At the commencement of a hearing, the chairman of the adjudication board shall read to the member whose conduct is the subject of the hearing the allegation or allegations of contravention of the Code of Conduct contained in the notice of the hearing and shall thereupon give the member an opportunity to admit or deny each such allegation or to raise, as a preliminary objection to any such allegation, the fact that the informal disciplinary action referred to in paragraph 41(1)(g) has been previously taken against the member in respect of the act or omission constituting any such allegation or that the act or omission was previously the subject of a hearing under this section, but nothing in this subsection affects the validity of a new hearing ordered under this Part.

Refusal

(5) Where a member does not admit, deny or raise a preliminary objection to an allegation read to the member pursuant to subsection (4), the member is deemed to have denied the allegation.

Dismissal where objection established

(6) Where a preliminary objection raised pursuant to subsection (4) is established to the satisfaction of the adjudication board, the board shall dismiss the allegation to which the objection is raised.

Testimony of member

(7) Notwithstanding any other provision of this Part, a member whose conduct is the subject of a hearing is not compelled to testify at the hearing, but the member may give evidence under oath and where the member does so, subsections (11) and (12) apply to the member.

Right to present evidence, etc.

(8) The parties to a hearing shall be afforded a full and ample opportunity, in person or by counsel or a representative, to present evidence, to cross-examine witnesses and to make representations at the hearing.

Representation of witnesses

(9) An adjudication board shall permit any person who gives evidence at a hearing to be represented by counsel or a representative.

Restriction

(10) Notwithstanding section 45 but subject to subsection (11), an adjudication board may not receive or accept any evidence or other information that would be inadmissible in a court of law by reason of any privilege under the law of evidence.

Witness not excused from testifying

(11) In a hearing, no witness shall be excused from answering any question relating to the case before the adjudication board when required to do so by the board on the ground that the answer to the question may tend to criminate the witness or subject the witness to any proceeding or penalty.

Answer not receivable

(12) Where the witness is a member, no answer or statement made in response to a question described in subsection (11) shall be used or receivable against the witness in any hearing under this section into an allegation of contravention of the Code of Conduct by the witness, other than a hearing into an allegation that with intent to mislead the witness gave the answer or statement knowing it to be false.

Adjournment

(13) An adjudication board may from time to time adjourn a hearing.

Hearing in private

(14) A hearing before an adjudication board shall be held in private, except that

(a) while a child is testifying at the hearing, the child's parent or guardian may attend the hearing; and

(b) when authorized by the board, a member may attend the hearing as an observer for the purpose of familiarizing the member with procedures under this Part.

Hearing to be recorded

(15) A hearing before an adjudication board shall be recorded and, if a party to the hearing makes a request under subsection 45.13(2) or the decision of the board is appealed under section 45.14, a transcript thereof shall be prepared.
R.S., 1985, c. 8 (2nd Supp.), s. 16.

Amendment of notice

45.11 (1) Where, at any time during a hearing, it appears to the adjudication board that there is a technical defect in the notice of the hearing under subsection 43(4) that does not affect the substance of the notice, the board, if it is of the opinion that the member whose conduct is the subject of the hearing will not be prejudiced in the conduct of the defence by an amendment, shall make such order for the amendment of the notice as it considers necessary to meet the circumstances of the case.

Procedure (2) Where a notice of hearing is amended pursuant to subsection (1), the adjudication board shall, if the member whose conduct is the subject of the hearing so requests, adjourn the hearing for such period as the board considers necessary to enable the member to meet the notice as so amended.

Endorsing notice (3) An order to amend a notice of hearing shall be endorsed on the notice and signed by the chairman of the adjudication board and the hearing shall proceed as if the notice had been originally drawn as amended.
R.S., 1985, c. 8 (2nd Supp.), s. 16.

Decision **45.12** (1) After considering the evidence submitted at the hearing, the adjudication board shall decide whether or not each allegation of contravention of the Code of Conduct contained in the notice of the hearing is established on a balance of probabilities.

In writing (2) A decision of an adjudication board shall be recorded in writing and shall include a statement of the findings of the board on questions of fact material to the decision, reasons for the decision and a statement of the sanction, if any, imposed under subsection (3) or the informal disciplinary action, if any, taken under subsection (4).

Sanctions (3) Where an adjudication board decides that an allegation of contravention of the Code of Conduct by a member is established, the board shall impose any one or more of the following sanctions on the member, namely,

(a) recommendation for dismissal from the Force, if the member is an officer, or dismissal from the Force, if the member is not an officer;

(b) direction to resign from the Force and, in default of resigning within fourteen days after being directed to do so, recommendation for dismissal from the Force, if the member is an officer, or dismissal from the Force, if the member is not an officer;

(c) recommendation for demotion, if the member is an officer, or demotion, if the member is not an officer; or

(d) forfeiture of pay for a period not exceeding ten work days.

Informal disciplinary action (4) In addition to or in substitution for imposing a sanction under subsection (3), an adjudication board may take any one or more of the informal disciplinary actions referred to in paragraphs 41(1)(a) to (g).

Restriction

(5) The sanction referred to in paragraph (3)(c) may not be imposed on an inspector or a constable.

Maximum forfeiture of pay

(6) Where an adjudication board decides that two or more allegations of contravention of the Code of Conduct by a member contained in one notice of hearing are established, the total period for forfeiture of pay that may be imposed on the member under subsection (3) in respect of all such allegations shall not exceed ten work days.

Copy of decision to parties when absent

(7) Where a decision of an adjudication board is rendered in the absence of a party to the hearing, the board shall serve that party with a copy of its decision.
R.S., 1985, c. 8 (2nd Supp.), s. 16.

Record

45.13 (1) An adjudication board shall compile a record of the hearing before it, which record shall include
(a) the notice of the hearing under subsection 43(4);
(b) the notice of the place, date and time of the hearing under subsection 45.1(2);
(c) a copy of all written or documentary evidence produced at the hearing;
(d) a list of any exhibits entered at the hearing; and
(e) the recording and the transcript, if any, of the hearing.

Delivery of transcript on request

(2) A party to a hearing before an adjudication board shall be furnished, without charge, with a copy of the transcript of the hearing, if the party so requests in writing within seven days after
(a) the day the decision of the board is rendered, if it is rendered in the presence of that party; or
(b) in any other case, the day notice of the decision is given to that party.
R.S., 1985, c. 8 (2nd Supp.), s. 16.

Appeal

Appeal to Commissioner

45.14 (1) Subject to this section, a party to a hearing before an adjudication board may appeal the decision of the board to the Commissioner in respect of
(a) any finding by the board that an allegation of contravention of the Code of Conduct by the member is established or not established; or
(b) any sanction imposed or action taken by the board in consequence of a finding by the board that an allegation referred to in paragraph (a) is established.

Presumption

(2) For the purposes of this section, any dismissal of an allegation by an adjudication board pursuant to subsection 45.1(6) or on any other ground without a finding by the board that the allegation is established or not established is deemed to be a finding by the board that the allegation is not established.

Grounds of appeal

(3) An appeal lies to the Commissioner on any ground of appeal, except that an appeal lies to the Commissioner by an appropriate officer in respect of a sanction or an action referred to in paragraph (1)(b) only on the ground of appeal that the sanction or action is not one provided for by this Act.

Limitation period

(4) No appeal may be instituted under this section after the expiration of fourteen days from the later of
(a) the day the decision appealed from is rendered, if it is rendered in the presence of the party appealing, or the day a copy of the decision is served on the party appealing, if it is rendered in the absence of that party, and
(b) if the party appealing requested a transcript pursuant to subsection 45.13(2), the day the party receives the transcript.

Statement of appeal

(5) An appeal to the Commissioner shall be instituted by filing with the Commissioner a statement of appeal in writing setting out the grounds on which the appeal is made and any submissions in respect thereof.

Statement served on other party

(6) A party appealing a decision of an adjudication board to the Commissioner shall forthwith serve the other party with a copy of the statement of appeal.

Submissions in reply

(7) A party who is served with a copy of the statement of appeal under subsection (6) may, within fourteen days after the day the party is served with the statement, file with the Commissioner written submissions in reply, and if the party does so, the party shall forthwith serve a copy thereof on the party appealing.
R.S., 1985, c. 8 (2nd Supp.), s. 16.

Reference to Committee

45.15 (1) Before the Commissioner considers an appeal under section 45.14, the Commissioner shall refer the case to the Committee.

Exception

(2) Subsection (1) does not apply in respect of an appeal if each allegation that is subject of the appeal was found by the adjudication board to have been established and only one or more of the informal disciplinary actions referred to in paragraphs 41(1)(a) to (g) have been taken by the board in consequence of the finding.

Request by member

(3) Notwithstanding subsection (1), the member whose case is appealed to the Commissioner may request the Commissioner not to refer the case to the Committee and, on such a request, the Commissioner may either not refer the case to the Committee or, if the Commissioner considers that a reference to the Committee is appropriate notwithstanding the request, refer the case to the Committee.

Material to be furnished to Committee

(4) Where the Commissioner refers a case to the Committee pursuant to this section, the Commissioner shall furnish the Committee Chairman with the materials referred to in paragraphs 45.16(1)(a) to (c).

Applicable provisions

(5) Sections 34 and 35 apply, with such modifications as the circumstances require, with respect to a case referred to the Committee pursuant to this section as though the case were a grievance referred to the Committee pursuant to section 33. R.S., 1985, c. 8 (2nd Supp.), s. 16.

Consideration of appeal

45.16 (1) The Commissioner shall consider an appeal under section 45.14 on the basis of
(a) the record of the hearing before the adjudication board whose decision is being appealed,
(b) the statement of appeal, and
(c) any written submissions made to the Commissioner,

and the Commissioner shall also take into consideration the findings or recommendations set out in the report, if any, of the Committee or the Committee Chairman in respect of the case.

Disposal of appeal against finding

(2) The Commissioner may dispose of an appeal in respect of a finding referred to in paragraph 45.14(1)(a) by
(a) dismissing the appeal and confirming the decision being appealed;
(b) allowing the appeal and ordering a new hearing into the allegation giving rise to the finding; or
(c) where the appeal is taken by the member who was found to have contravened the Code of Conduct, allowing the appeal and making the finding that, in the Commissioner's opinion, the adjudication board should have made.

Disposal of appeal against sanction

(3) The Commissioner may dispose of an appeal in respect of a sanction or action referred to in paragraph 45.14(1)(b) by
(a) dismissing the appeal and confirming the decision being appealed; or

(b) allowing the appeal and either varying or rescinding the sanction or action.

New hearing

(4) Where the Commissioner orders a new hearing into an allegation pursuant to subsection (2), an adjudication board shall be appointed in accordance with this Part to conduct the hearing and the new hearing shall be held in accordance with this Part as if it were the first hearing into that allegation.

Copy of decision

(5) The Commissioner shall as soon as possible render a decision in writing on an appeal, including reasons for the decision, and serve each of the parties to the hearing before the adjudication board whose decision was appealed and, if the case has been referred to the Committee pursuant to section 45.15, the Committee Chairman with a copy of the decision.

Commissioner not bound

(6) The Commissioner is not bound to act on any findings or recommendations set out in a report with respect to a case referred to the Committee under section 45.15, but if the Commissioner does not so act, the Commissioner shall include in the decision on the appeal the reasons for not so acting.

Commissioner's decision final

(7) A decision of the Commissioner on an appeal under section 45.14 is final and binding and, except for judicial review under the *Federal Court Act*, is not subject to appeal to or review by any court.

Rescission or amendment of decision

(8) Notwithstanding subsection (7), the Commissioner may rescind or amend the Commissioner's decision on an appeal under section 45.14 on the presentation to the Commissioner of new facts or where, with respect to the finding of any fact or the interpretation of any law, the Commissioner determines that an error was made in reaching the decision.
R.S., 1985, c. 8 (2nd Supp.), s. 16; 1990, c. 8, s. 67.

Stay of Execution of Decision

Stay of execution of decision

45.17 (1) Where a decision that imposes a sanction referred to in subsection 45.12(3) is rendered under section 45.12, the execution of the decision is stayed until after the expiration of the time within which an appeal may be taken under section 45.14.

Idem

(2) Where an appeal is taken under section 45.14 in relation to a decision described in subsection (1), the execution of the decision is stayed until after the appeal is disposed of.
R.S., 1985, c. 8 (2nd Supp.), s. 16.

PART V

DISCHARGE AND DEMOTION

Ground for Discharge or Demotion

Ground for discharge or demotion

45.18 (1) Any officer may be recommended for discharge or demotion and any other member may be discharged or demoted on the ground, in this Part referred to as the "ground of unsuitability", that the officer or member has repeatedly failed to perform the officer's or member's duties under this Act in a manner fitted to the requirements of the officer's or member's position, notwithstanding that the officer or member has been given reasonable assistance, guidance and supervision in an attempt to improve the performance of those duties.

Limitation

(2) No officer may be recommended for a demotion under this Part of more than one rank and no other member may be demoted under this Part by more than one rank or level.

Exceptions

(3) No inspector may be recommended for demotion under this Part and no constable may be demoted under this Part. R.S., 1985, c. 8 (2nd Supp.), s. 16.

Notice of intention

45.19 (1) Before any officer is recommended for discharge or demotion under this Part or any other member is discharged or demoted under this Part, the appropriate officer shall serve the officer or other member with a notice in writing of the intention to recommend the discharge or demotion of the officer or to discharge or demote the other member, as the case may be.

Contents of notice

(2) A notice of intention served on an officer or other member under subsection (1) shall include

(a) particulars of the acts or omissions constituting the ground of unsuitability on which it is intended to base the recommendation for discharge or demotion or the discharge or demotion, as the case may be;

(b) where the officer or other member is not a probationary member, a statement of the right of the officer or other member to request, within fourteen days after the day the notice is served, a review of the officer's or member's case by a discharge and demotion board; and

(c) where the officer or other member is a probationary member, a statement of the right of the officer or other member to make, within fourteen days after the day the notice is served, written representations to the appropriate officer.

Opportunity to examine material

(3) An officer or other member who is served with a notice under subsection (1) shall be given a full and ample opportunity to examine the material relied on in support of the recommendation for discharge or demotion or the discharge or demotion, as the case may be.

Request for review

(4) An officer or other member, except a probationary member, who is served with a notice under subsection (1) may, within fourteen days after the day the notice is served, send to the appropriate officer a request in writing for a review of the officer's or member's case by a discharge and demotion board.

Request to be forwarded to designated officer

(5) An appropriate officer shall forthwith after receiving a request under subsection (4) forward the request to the officer designated by the Commissioner for the purposes of this section.

Written representations

(6) A probationary member who is served with a notice under subsection (1) may, within fourteen days after the notice is served, make written representations to the appropriate officer.

Notice of decision

(7) Where an officer or other member, except a probationary member, who is served with a notice under subsection (1) does not request a review of the officer's or member's case by a discharge and demotion board within the time limited for doing so, the appropriate officer shall serve the officer or other member with a notice in writing of the decision to recommend discharge or demotion of the officer or to discharge or demote the member, as the case may be.

Idem

(8) Where a probationary member who is served with a notice under subsection (1) does not make written representations to the appropriate officer within the time limited for doing so, the appropriate officer shall serve the probationary member with a notice in writing of the decision to recommend discharge of the probationary member or to discharge the probationary member, as the case may be.

Consideration of written representations

(9) An appropriate officer shall forthwith after receiving written representations pursuant to subsection (6) consider the representations and either
(a) direct that the probationary member be retained in the Force; or
(b) serve the probationary member with a notice in writing of the decision to recommend discharge of the probationary member or to discharge the probationary member, as the case may be.

Effective date   (10) A member, other than an officer, who is served with a notice under subsection (7), (8) or (9) is discharged on such day as is specified in the notice or is demoted on such day and to such rank or level as is specified in the notice, as the case may be.

Definition of "probabationary member"   (11) In this section, "probationary member" means a member with less than two years of service in the Force. R.S., 1985, c. 8 (2nd Supp.), s. 16.

Review by Discharge and Demotion Board

Discharge and demotion board   **45.2** (1) Within seven days after the day a designated officer receives a request under subsection 45.19(5), the designated officer shall appoint three officers as members of a discharge and demotion board to conduct the review requested and shall serve the officer or other member requesting the review with a notice in writing setting out the names of the officers so appointed.

Qualifications   (2) At least one of the officers appointed as a member of a discharge and demotion board shall be a graduate of a school of law recognized by the law society of any province.

Applicable provisions   (3) Subsections 44(1) to (4) apply, with such modifications as the circumstances require, with respect to a notice under subsection (1) as though
(a) the designated officer serving the notice were the designated officer referred to in subsection 43(1);
(b) the notice were a notice of hearing referred to in subsection 44(1); and
(c) the discharge and demotion board were an adjudication board.

Eligibility limited   (4) An officer is not eligible to be appointed as a member of a discharge and demotion board if the officer
(a) is the immediate superior officer of the member whose case is to be reviewed by the board; or
(b) is involved in the initiation or processing of the case that is to be reviewed by the board.

Chairman   (5) After the conclusion of all proceedings under this section, the designated officer shall designate one of the members of the discharge and demotion board as chairman. R.S., 1985, c. 8 (2nd Supp.), s. 16.

Powers of discharge and demotion board

45.21 A discharge and demotion board has, in relation to the case before it, the powers conferred on a board of inquiry, in relation to the matter before it, by paragraphs 24.1(3)(a), (b) and (c). R.S., 1985, c. 8 (2nd Supp.), s. 16.

Parties

45.22 (1) An officer or other member who sends a request under subsection 45.19(4) for a review of the officer's or member's case by a discharge and demotion board and the appropriate officer to whom the request is sent are parties to the review.

Material to be provided to board

(2) A discharge and demotion board shall, prior to reviewing the case before it, be provided by the appropriate officer with the material that the officer or other member requesting the review was given an opportunity to examine pursuant to subsection 45.19(3).

Review of case

(3) A discharge and demotion board shall, after due notice to the officer or other member requesting the review, review the case before it and for that purpose shall give to the officer or other member a full and ample opportunity, in person or by counsel or a representative, to appeal before the board, to make representations to it, to present documentary evidence to it and, with leave of the board, to call witnesses.

Idem

(4) Subject to subsection (3), a discharge and demotion board may review the case before it in the absence of the officer or other member requesting the review.

Testimony of member

(5) Notwithstanding any other provision of this Part, the officer or other member who has requested a review of the officer's or member's case by a discharge and demotion board is not compelled to testify at any hearing before the board, but the officer or member may give evidence under oath and where the officer or member does so, subsections (8) and (9) apply to the officer or member.

Representation of witnesses

(6) A discharge and demotion board shall permit any person who gives evidence at any hearing before the board to be represented by counsel or a representative.

Restriction

(7) Notwithstanding section 45.21 but subject to subsection (8), a discharge and demotion board may not receive or accept any evidence or other information that would be inadmissible in a court of law by reason of any privilege under the law of evidence.

Witness not excused from testifying

(8) In a review by a discharge and demotion board, no witness shall be excused from answering any question relating to the case before the board when required to do so by the board on the ground that the answer to the question may tend to criminate the witness or subject the witness to any proceeding or penalty.

Answer not receivable

(9) Where the witness is a member, no answer or statement made in response to a question described in subsection (8) shall be used or receivable against the witness in any hearing under section 45.1 into an allegation of contravention of the Code of Conduct by the witness, other than a hearing into an allegation that with intent to mislead the witness gave the answer or statement knowing it to be false.

Adjournment

(10) A discharge and demotion board may from time to time adjourn any hearing before the board.

Hearing in private

(11) Any hearing before a discharge and demotion board shall be held in private, except that
(a) while a child is testifying at the hearing, the child's parent or guardian may attend the hearing; and
(b) when authorized by the board, a member may attend the hearing as an observer for the purpose of familiarizing the member with procedures under this Part.

Evidence and representations to be recorded

(12) All oral evidence and representations before a discharge and demotion board shall be recorded and, if a party to the review by the board makes a request under subsection 45.23(6) or the decision of the board is appealed under section 45.24, a transcript thereof shall be prepared.
R.S., 1985, c. 8 (2nd Supp.), s. 16.

Decision

45.23 (1) After reviewing the case before it, a discharge and demotion board shall decide whether or not the ground of unsuitability is established on a balance of probabilities.

In writing

(2) A decision of a discharge and demotion board shall be recorded in writing and shall include a statement of the findings of the board on questions of fact material to the decision, reasons for the decision and a statement of the action taken by the board under subsection (3) or (4).

Where ground established

(3) Where a discharge and demotion board decides that the ground of unsuitability is established, the board shall
(a) recommend that the officer be discharged or discharge the other member, as the case may be, or

(b) recommend that the officer be demoted or demote the other member, as the case may be,

but the board shall not take the action referred to in paragraph (a) if the notice of intention served on that officer or other member was a notice to recommend demotion of the officer or to demote the other member, as the case may be.

Where ground not established
(4) Where a discharge and demotion board decides the ground of unsuitability is not established, the board shall direct that the officer or other member be retained in the Force at the present rank or level of the officer or other member.

Copy of decision to parties
(5) A discharge and demotion board shall serve each of the parties to the review by the board with a copy of its decision.

Delivery of transcript on request
(6) A party to a review by a discharge and demotion board shall be furnished, without charge, with a copy of the transcript of any hearing before the board, if that party so requests in writing within seven days after the day the decision of the board is served on that party.
R.S., 1985, c. 8 (2nd Supp.), s. 16.

Appeal

Appeal to Commissioner
45.24 (1) A party to review by a discharge and demotion board may appeal the decision of the board to the Commissioner, but no appeal may be instituted under this section after the expiration of fourteen days from the later of
(a) the day the decision is served on that party, and
(b) if that party requested a transcript pursuant to subsection 45.23(6), the day that party receives the transcript.

Grounds of appeal
(2) An appeal lies to the Commissioner on any ground of appeal.

Statement of appeal
(3) An appeal to the Commissioner shall be instituted by filing with the Commissioner a statement of appeal in writing setting out the grounds on which the appeal is made and any submissions in respect thereof.

Statement served on other party
(4) A party appealing a decision of a discharge and demotion board to the Commissioner shall forthwith serve the other party with a copy of the statement of appeal.

Submissions in reply
(5) A party who is served with a copy of the statement of appeal under subsection (4) may, within fourteen days after the day the statement is served, file with the Commissioner written

submissions in reply, and if that party does so, that party shall forthwith serve a copy thereof on the party appealing.
R.S., 1985, c. 8 (2nd Supp.), s. 16.

Reference to Committee **45.25** (1) Before the Commissioner considers an appeal under section 45.24, the Commissioner shall refer the case to the Committee.

Request by member (2) Notwithstanding subsection (1), the officer or other member whose case is appealed to the Commissioner may request the Commissioner not to refer the case to the Committee and, on such a request, the Commissioner may either not refer the case to the Committee or, if the Commissioner considers that a reference to the Committee is appropriate notwithstanding the request, refer the case to the Committee.

Material to be furnished to Committee (3) Where the Commissioner refers a case to the Committee pursuant to this section, the Commissioner shall furnish the Committee Chairman with the materials referred to in paragraphs 45.26(1)(a) to (e).

Applicable provisions (4) Sections 34 and 35 apply, with such modifications as the circumstances require, with respect to a case referred to the Committee pursuant to this section as though the case were a grievance referred to the Committee pursuant to section 33.
R.S., 1985, c. 8 (2nd Supp.), s. 16.

Consideration of appeal **45.26** (1) The Commissioner shall consider an appeal under section 45.24 on the basis of
(a) the material that the officer or other member was given an opportunity to examine pursuant to subsection 45.19(3),
(b) the transcript of any hearing before the discharge and demotion board whose decision is being appealed,
(c) the statement of appeal,
(d) any written submissions made to the Commissioner, and
(e) the decision of the discharge and demotion board being appealed,

and the Commissioner shall also take into consideration the findings or recommendations set out in the report, if any, of the Committee or the Committee Chairman in respect of the case.

Decision on appeal (2) The Commissioner may dispose of an appeal under section 45.24 by
(a) dismissing the appeal and confirming the decision being appealed;

(b) allowing the appeal and ordering a new review of the case by a discharge and demotion board; or

(c) where the appeal is taken by the officer or other member whose case was reviewed by the discharge and demotion board, allowing the appeal and

(i) directing that the officer or other member be retained in the Force at the present rank or level of the officer or other member, or

(ii) recommending that the officer be demoted or demoting the other member, as the case may be.

New review
(3) Where the Commissioner orders a new review of a case by a discharge and demotion board pursuant to subsection (2), a discharge and demotion board shall be appointed in accordance with this Part and the new review shall be conducted in accordance with this Part as if it were the first review of the case.

Copy of decision
(4) The Commissioner shall as soon as possible render a decision in writing on an appeal, including reasons for the decision, and serve each of the parties to the review by the discharge and demotion board and, if the case has been referred to the Committee pursuant to section 45.25, the Committee Chairman with a copy of the decision.

Commissioner not bound
(5) The Commissioner is not bound to act on any findings or recommendations set out in a report with respect to a case referred to the Committee under section 45.25, but if the Commissioner does not so act, the Commissioner shall include in the decision on the appeal the reasons for not so acting.

Commissioner's decision final
(6) A decision of the Commissioner on an appeal under section 45.24 is final and binding and, except for judicial review under the *Federal Court Act*, is not subject to appeal to or review by any court.

Rescission or amendment of decision
(7) Notwithstanding subsection (6), the Commissioner may rescind or amend the Commissioner's decision on an appeal under section 45.24 on the presentation to the Commissioner of new facts or where, with respect to the finding of any fact or the interpretation of any law, the Commissioner determines that an error was made in reaching the decision.
R.S., 1985, c. 8 (2nd Supp.), s. 16; 1990, c. 8, s. 68.

Stay of Execution of Decision

Stay of execution of decision
45.27 (1) Where a decision to recommend that an officer be discharged or demoted or to discharge or demote any other member is rendered under section 45.23, the execution of the

decision is stayed until after the expiration of the time within which an appeal may be taken under section 45.24.

Idem

(2) Where an appeal is taken under section 45.24 in relation to a decision described in subsection (1), the execution of the decision is stayed until after the appeal is disposed of.
R.S., 1985, c. 8 (2nd Supp.), s. 16.

Resignation

Resignation from Force

45.28 Nothing in this Part shall be construed as preventing a discharge and demotion board or the Commissioner from offering a member against whom a ground of unsuitability has been established pursuant to this Part the opportunity of resigning from the Force.
R.S., 1985, c. 8 (2nd Supp.), s. 16.

PART VI

ROYAL CANADIAN MOUNTED POLICE PUBLIC COMPLAINTS COMMISSION

Establishment and Organization of Commission

Commission established

45.29 (1) There is hereby established a commission, to be known as the Royal Canadian Mounted Police Public Complaints Commission, consisting of a Chairman, a Vice-Chairman, a member for each contracting province and not more than three other members, to be appointed by order of the Governor in Council.

Consultation

(2) A member of the Commission for a contracting province shall be appointed after consultation with the Minister or other elected representative responsible for police affairs in that province.

Full- or part-time

(3) The Commission Chairman is a full-time member of the Commission and the other members may be appointed as full-time or part-time members of the Commission.

Tenure of office

(4) Each member of the Commission shall be appointed to hold office during good behaviour for a term not exceeding five years but may be removed for cause at any time by order of the Governor in Council.

Re-appointment

(5) A member of the Commission is eligible for re-appointment on the expiration of the member's term of office.

Eligibility   (6) No member of the Force is eligible to be appointed or to continue as a member of the Commission.

Alternate member   (7) The Governor in Council may, by order, appoint a person to be an alternate member for any member of the Commission, other than the Commission Chairman, and the alternate member so appointed may act as a member of the Commission in the event of the absence, incapacity or ineligibility to conduct a hearing of that member.

Idem   (8) An alternate member shall be appointed as a part-time member of the Commission and subsections (2), (4) to (6) and (10) and (11) apply, with such modifications as the circumstances require, to an alternate member as though the alternate member were a member of the Commission.

Salary of full-time members   (9) Each full-time member of the Commission is entitled to be paid such salary in connection with the work of the Commission as may be approved by order of the Governor in Council.

Fees of part-time members   (10) Each part-time member of the Commission is entitled to be paid such fees in connection with the work of the Commission as may be approved by order of the Governor in Council.

Expenses   (11) Each member of the Commission is entitled to be paid reasonable travel and living expenses incurred by the member while absent from the member's ordinary place of residence in connection with the work of the Commission.

Benefits of full-time members   (12) The full-time members of the Commission are deemed to be employed in the Public Service for the purposes of the *Public Service Superannuation Act* and to be employed in the public service of Canada for the purposes of the *Government Employees Compensation Act* and any regulations made under section 9 of the *Aeronautics Act*.

Definition of "contracting province"   (13) In this section, "contracting province" means a province the government of which has entered into an arrangement with the Minister pursuant to section 20.
R.S., 1985, c. 8 (2nd Supp.), s. 16.

Commission Chairman   **45.3** (1) The Commission Chairman is the chief executive officer of the Commission and has supervision over and direction of the work and staff of the Commission.

Absence or
incapacity

(2) In the event of the absence or incapacity of the Commission Chairman or if the office of Commission Chairman is vacant, the Minister may authorize the Vice-Chairman to exercise the powers and perform the duties and functions of the Commission Chairman.

Delegation

(3) The Commission Chairman may delegate to the Vice-Chairman any of the Commission Chairman's powers, duties or functions under this Act, except the power to delegate under this subsection and the duty under section 45.34. R.S., 1985, c. 8 (2nd Supp.), s. 16.

Head Office

45.31 (1) The head office of the Commission shall be at such place in Canada as the Governor in Council may, by order, designate.

Staff

(2) Such officers and employees as are necessary for the proper conduct of the work of the Commission shall be appointed in accordance with the *Public Service Employment Act*.

Idem

(3) The Commission may, with the approval of the Treasury Board,

(a) engage on a temporary basis the services of persons having technical or specialized knowledge of any matter relating to the work of the Commission to advise and assist the Commission in the exercise or performance of its powers, duties and functions under this Act; and

(b) fix and pay the remuneration and expenses of persons engaged pursuant to paragraph (a). R.S., 1985, c. 8 (2nd Supp.), s. 16.

Duties

Duties of
Commission

45.32 (1) The Commission shall carry out such functions and duties as are assigned to it by this Act.

Duties of
Commission
Chairman

(2) The Commission Chairman shall carry out such functions and duties as are assigned to the Commission Chairman by this Act. R.S., 1985, c. 8 (2nd Supp.), s. 16.

Rules

Rules

45.33 Subject to this Act, the Commission may make rules respecting

(a) the sittings of the Commission;

(b) the manner of dealing with matters and business before the Commission generally, including the practice and procedure before the Commission;

(c) the apportionment of the work of the Commission among its members and the assignment of members to review complaints referred to the Commission; and

(d) the performance of the duties and functions of the Commission under this Act generally.

R.S., 1985, c. 8 (2nd Supp.), s. 16.

Annual Report

Annual report   **45.34** The Commission Chairman shall, within three months after the end of each fiscal year, submit to the Minister a report of the activities of the commission during that year and its recommendations, if any, and the Minister shall cause a copy of the report to be laid before each House of Parliament on any of the first fifteen days on which that House is sitting after the day the Minister receives it.

R.S., 1985, c. 8 (2nd Supp.), s. 16.

PART VII

PUBLIC COMPLAINTS

Receipt and Investigation of Complaints

Complaints by public   **45.35** (1) Any member of the public having a complaint concerning the conduct, in the performance of any duty or function under this Act, of any member or other person appointed or employed under the authority of this Act may, whether or not that member of the public is affected by the subject-matter of the complaint, make the complaint to

(a) the Commission;

(b) any member or other person appointed or employed under the authority of this Act; or

(c) the provincial authority in the province in which the subject-matter of the complaint arose that is responsible for the receipt and investigation of complaints by the public against police.

Acknowledgement of complaint   (2) Every complaint under subsection (1) shall be acknowledged in writing, if the complaint is in writing or if the complainant requests that the complaint be so acknowledged.

Notification of Commissioner   (3) The Commissioner shall be notified of every complaint under subsection (1).

Notification of member

(4) Forthwith after being notified of a complaint under subsection (3), the Commissioner shall notify in writing the member or other person whose conduct is the subject-matter of the complaint of the substance of the complaint unless, in the Commissioner's opinion, to do so might adversely affect or hinder any investigation that is being or may be carried out in respect of the complaint.
R.S., 1985, c. 8 (2nd Supp.), s. 16.

Informal disposition

45.36 (1) The Commissioner shall consider whether a complaint under subsection 45.35(1) can be disposed of informally and, with the consent of the complainant and the member or other person whose conduct is the subject-matter of the complaint, may attempt to so dispose of the complaint.

Statements not admissible

(2) No answer or statement made, in the course of attempting to dispose of a complaint informally, by the complainant or the member or other person whose conduct is the subject-matter of the complaint shall be used or receivable in any criminal, civil or administrative proceedings other than, where the answer or statement was made by a member, a hearing under section 45.1 into an allegation that with intent to mislead the member gave the answer or statement knowing it to be false.

Record of informal disposition

(3) Where a complaint is disposed of informally, a record shall be made of the manner in which the complaint was disposed of, the complainant's agreement to the disposition shall be signified in writing by the complainant and the member or other person whose conduct is the subject-matter of the complaint shall be informed of the disposition.

Investigation

(4) Where a complaint is not disposed of informally, the complaint shall be investigated by the Force in accordance with rules made pursuant to section 45.38.

Right to refuse or terminate investigation

(5) Notwithstanding any other provision of this Part, the Commissioner may direct that no investigation of a complaint under subsection 45.35(1) be commenced or that an investigation of such a complaint be terminated if, in the Commissioner's opinion,

(a) the complaint is one that could more appropriately be dealt with, initially or completely, according to a procedure provided under any other Act of Parliament;

(b) the complaint is trivial, frivolous, vexatious or made in bad faith; or

(c) having regard to all the circumstances, investigation or further investigation is not necessary or reasonably practicable.

Notification of
complainant and
member

(6) Where the Commissioner makes a direction in respect of a complaint pursuant to subsection (5), the Commissioner shall give notice in writing to the complainant and, if the member or other person whose conduct is the subject-matter of the complaint has been notified under subsection 45.35(4), to that member or other person, of the direction and the reasons therefor and the right of the complainant to refer the complaint to the Commission for review if the complainant is not satisfied with the direction.
R.S., 1985, c. 8 (2nd Supp.), s. 16.

Complaints
initiated by
Commission
Chairman

45.37 (1) Where the Commission Chairman is satisfied that there are reasonable grounds to investigate the conduct, in the performance of any duty or function under this Act, of any member or other person appointed or employed under the authority of this Act, the Commission Chairman may initiate a complaint in relation thereto and where the Commission Chairman does so, unless the context otherwise requires, a reference hereafter in this part to a complainant includes a reference to the Commission Chairman.

Notification of
Commissioner and
Minister

(2) The Commission Chairman shall notify the Minister and the Commissioner of any complaint initiated under subsection (1).

Notification of
member

(3) Forthwith after being notified of a complaint under subsection (2), the Commissioner shall notify in writing the member or other person whose conduct is the subject-matter of the complaint of the substance of the complaint unless, in the Commissioner's opinion, to do so might adversely affect or hinder any investigation that is being or may be carried out in respect of the complaint.

Investigation

(4) A complaint under subsection (1) shall be investigated by the Force in accordance with rules made pursuant to section 45.38.
R.S., 1985, c. 8 (2nd Supp.), s. 16.

Rules

45.38 The Commissioner may make rules governing the procedures to be followed by the Force in notifying persons under this Part and in investigating, disposing of or otherwise dealing with complaints under this Part.
R.S., 1985, c. 8 (2nd Supp.), s. 16.

Interim reports

45.39 The Commissioner shall notify in writing the complainant and the member or other person whose conduct is the subject-matter of the complaint of the status of the investigation of the complaint to date not later than forty-five days after being notified of the complaint and monthly thereafter during the course of the investigation unless, in the Commissioner's opinion, to do so might adversely affect or hinder any investigation that is being or may be carried out in respect of the complaint. R.S., 1985, c. 8 (2nd Supp.), s. 16.

Final report

45.4 On completion of the investigation of a complaint, the Commissioner shall send to the complainant and the member or other person whose conduct is the subject-matter of the complaint a report setting out

(a) a summary of the complaint;

(b) the results of the investigation;

(c) a summary of any action that has been or will be taken with respect to resolution of the complaint; and

(d) in the case of a complaint under subsection 45.35(1), the right of the complainant to refer the complaint to the Commission for review if the complainant is not satisfied with the disposition of the complaint by the Force. R.S., 1985, c. 8 (2nd Supp.), s. 16.

Reference to Commission

Reference to Commission

45.41 (1) A complainant under subsection 45.35(1) who is not satisfied with the disposition of the complaint by the Force or with a direction under subsection 45.36(5) in respect of the complaint may refer the complaint in writing to the Commission for review.

Material to be furnished

(2) Where a complainant refers a complaint to the Commission pursuant to subsection (1),

(a) the Commission Chairman shall furnish the Commissioner with a copy of the complaint; and

(b) the Commissioner shall furnish the Commission Chairman with the notice under subsection 45.36(6) or the report under section 45.4 in respect of the complaint, as the case may be, and such other materials under the control of the Force as are relevant to the complaint. R.S., 1985, c. 8 (2nd Supp.), s. 16.

Review by Commission Chairman

45.42 (1) The Commission Chairman shall review every complaint referred to the Commission pursuant to subsection 45.41(1) or initiated under subsection 45.37(1) unless the Commission Chairman has previously investigated, or instituted a hearing to inquire into, the complaint under section 45.43.

Action by
Commission
Chairman

(2) Where, after reviewing a complaint, the Commission Chairman is satisfied with the disposition of the complaint by the Force, the Commission Chairman shall prepare and send a report in writing to that effect to the Minister, the Commissioner, the member or other person whose conduct is the subject-matter of the complaint and, in the case of a complaint under subsection 45.35(1), the complainant.

Idem

(3) Where, after reviewing a complaint, the Commission Chairman is not satisfied with the disposition of the complaint by the Force or considers that further inquiry is warranted, the Commission Chairman may

(a) prepare and send to the Minister and the Commissioner a report in writing setting out such findings and recommendations with respect to the complaint as the Commission Chairman sees fit;

(b) request the Commissioner to conduct a further investigation into the complaint; or

(c) investigate the complaint further or institute a hearing to inquire into the complaint.

R.S., 1985, c. 88 (2nd Supp.), s. 16.

Institution of
hearing without
Force report

45.43 (1) Where the Commission Chairman considers it advisable in the public interest, the Commission Chairman may investigate, or institute a hearing to inquire into, a complaint concerning the conduct, in the performance of any duty or function under this Act, of any member or other person appointed or employed under the authority of this Act, whether or not the complaint has been investigated, reported on or otherwise dealt with by the Force under this Part.

Force not required
to act before report

(2) Notwithstanding any other provision of this Part, where the Commission Chairman investigates, or institutes a hearing to inquire into, a complaint pursuant to subsection (1), the Force is not required to investigate, report on or otherwise deal with the complaint before the report under subsection (3) or the interim report under subsection 45.45(14) with respect to the complaint has been received by the Commissioner.

Report on
investigation

(3) On completion of an investigation under paragraph 45.42(3)(c) or subsection (1), the Commission Chairman shall prepare and send to the Minister and the Commissioner a report in writing setting out such findings and recommendations with respect to the complaint as the Commission Chairman sees fit

unless the Commission Chairman has instituted, or intends to institute, a hearing to inquire into the complaint under that paragraph or subsection.
R.S., 1985, c. 8 (2nd Supp.), s. 16.

Hearing

45.44 (1) Where the Commission Chairman decides to institute a hearing to inquire into a complaint pursuant to subsection 45.42(3) or 45.43(1) the Commission Chairman shall assign the member or members of the Commission to conduct the hearing and send a notice in writing of the decision to the Minister, the Commissioner, the member or other person whose conduct is the subject-matter of the complaint and, in the case of a complaint under subsection 45.35(1), the complainant.

Provincial representation

(2) Where a complaint that is to be the subject of a hearing concerns conduct occurring in the course of providing services pursuant to an arrangement entered into under section 20, the member of the Commission appointed for the province in which the conduct occurred shall be assigned, either alone or with other members of the Commission, to conduct the hearing.
R.S., 1985, c. 8 (2nd Supp.), s. 16.

Commission

45.45 (1) For the purposes of this section, the member or members conducting a hearing to inquire into a complaint are deemed to be the Commission.

Notice

(2) The Commission shall serve a notice in writing of the time and place appointed for a hearing on the parties.

Sittings of Commission

(3) Where a party wishes to appear before the Commission, the Commission shall sit at such place in Canada and at such time as may be fixed by the Commission, having regard to the convenience of the parties.

Powers of Commission

(4) The Commission has, in relation to the complaint before it, the powers conferred on a board of inquiry, in relation to the matter before it, by paragraphs 24.1(3)(a), (b) and (c).

Rights of persons interested

(5) The parties and any other person who satisfies the Commission that the person has a substantial and direct interest in a complaint before the Commission shall be afforded a full and ample opportunity, in person or by counsel, to present evidence, to cross-examine witnesses and to make representations at the hearing.

Representation of witnesses

(6) The Commission shall permit any person who gives evidence at a hearing to be represented by counsel.

Appropriate officer

(7) In addition to the rights conferred by subsections (5) and (6), the appropriate officer may be represented or assisted at a hearing by any other member.

Restriction

(8) Notwithstanding subsection (4), the Commission may not receive or accept

(a) subject to subsection (9), any evidence or other information that would be inadmissible in a court of law by reason of any privilege under the law of evidence;

(b) any answer or statement made in response to a question described in subsection 24.1(7), 35(8), 40(2), 45.1(11) or 45.22(8);

(c) any answer or statement made in response to a question described in subsection (9) in any hearing under this section into any other complaint; or

(d) any answer or statement made in the course of attempting to dispose of a complaint under section 45.36.

Witness not excused from testifying

(9) In a hearing, no witness shall be excused from answering any question relating to the complaint before the Commission when required to do so by the Commission on the ground that the answer to the question may tend to criminate the witness or subject the witness to any proceeding or penalty.

Answer not receivable

(10) Where the witness is a member, no answer or statement made in response to a question described in subsection (9) shall be used or receivable against the witness in any hearing under section 45.1 into an allegation of contravention of the Code of Conduct by the witness, other than a hearing into an allegation that with intent to mislead the witness gave the answer or statement knowing it to be false.

Hearing in public

(11) A hearing to inquire into a complaint shall be held in public, except that the Commission may order the hearing or any part of the hearing to be held in private if it is of the opinion that during the course of the hearing any of the following information will likely be disclosed, namely,

(a) information the disclosure of which could reasonably be expected to be injurious to the defence of Canada or any state allied or associated with Canada or the detection, prevention or suppression of subversive or hostile activities;

(b) information the disclosure of which could reasonably be expected to be injurious to law enforcement; and

(c) information respecting a person's financial or personal affairs where that person's interest outweighs the public's interest in the information.

Return of documents, etc.

(12) Any document or thing produced pursuant to this section to the Commission shall, on the request of the person producing the document or thing, be released to that person within a reasonable time after completion of the final report under subsection 45.46(3).

Expenses

(13) Where the Commission sits at a place in Canada that is not the ordinary place of residence of the member or other person whose conduct is the subject-matter of the complaint, of the complainant or of the counsel of that member or other person or that complainant, that member or other person, complainant or counsel is entitled, in the discretion of the Commission, to receive such travel and living expenses incurred by the member or other person, complainant or counsel in appearing before the Commission as may be fixed by the Treasury Board.

Interim report

(14) On completion of a hearing, the Commission shall prepare and send to the Minister and the Commissioner a report in writing setting out such findings and recommendations with respect to the complaint as the Commission sees fit.

Definition of "parties"

(15) In this section and section 45.46, "parties" means the appropriate officer, the member or other person whose conduct is the subject-matter of a complaint and, in the case of a complaint under subsection 45.35(1), the complainant. R.S., 1985, c. 8 (2nd Supp.), s. 16.

Review of complaint

45.46 (1) On receipt of a report under subsection 45.42(3), 45.43(3) or 45.45(14), the Commissioner shall review the complaint in light of the findings and recommendations set out in the report.

Decision of Commissioner

(2) After reviewing a complaint in accordance with subsection (1), the Commissioner shall notify the Minister and the Commission Chairman in writing of any further action that has been or will be taken with respect to the complaint, and where the Commissioner decides not to act on any findings or recommendations set out in the report, the Commissioner shall include in the notice the reasons for not so acting.

Final report

(3) After considering a notice under subsection (2), the Commission Chairman shall prepare and send to the Minister, the Commissioner and the parties a final report in writing setting out such findings and recommendations with respect to the complaint as the Commission Chairman sees fit. R.S., 1985, c. 8 (2nd Supp.), s. 16.

Record **45.47** The Commissioner shall

(a) establish and maintain a record of all complaints received by the Force under this Part; and

(b) on request, make available to the Commission any information contained in the record.

R.S., 1985, c. 8 (2nd Supp.), s. 16.

PART VIII

GENERAL

Miscellaneous Provisions having General Application

Definition of "board" **46.** (1) In this section and sections 47 to 47.3, "board" means

(a) a board of inquiry appointed under section 24.1,

(b) an adjudication board appointed under section 43 or 44, and

(c) a discharge and demotion board appointed under section 45.2,

and, except for the purposes of subsection (4), includes the Committee and the Commission.

Proceedings (2) All proceedings before a board shall be dealt with by the board as informally and expeditiously as the circumstances and considerations of fairness permit.

Witness fees (3) Any person, other than a member, summoned to attend at any proceeding before a board is entitled, in the discretion of the board, to receive the like fees and allowances for so attending as if summoned to attend before the Federal Court.

Rules (4) Subject to subsection (5), the Commissioner may make rules governing the proceedings, practice and procedure before a board and the performance of the duties and functions of a board under this Act.

Idem (5) The Minister may make rules governing the proceedings, practice and procedure before a board of inquiry appointed by the Minister under section 24.1 and the performance of the duties and functions of such a board under this Act or the Minister may adopt as such rules the rules or any part of the rules made under subsection (4).

R.S., 1985, c. R–10, s. 46; R.S., 1985, c. 8 (2nd Supp.), s. 18.

Immunity

47. No criminal or civil proceedings lie against any person for anything done, reported or said in good faith in any proceedings before a board.

R.S., 1985, c. R–10, s. 47; R.S., 1985, c. 8 (2nd Supp.), s. 18.

Representation

47.1 (1) Subject to any rules made pursuant to subsection (3), a member may be represented or assisted by any other member in any

(a) presentation of a grievance under Part III;

(b) proceeding before a board, other than the Commission;

(c) preparation of written representations under subsection 45.19(6); or

(d) appeal under section 42, 45.14 or 45.24.

Privilege

(2) Where a member is represented or assisted by another member pursuant to subsection (1), communications passing in confidence between the two members in relation to the grievance, proceeding, representations or appeal are, for the purposes of this Act, privileged as if they were communications passing in professional confidence between the member and the member's solicitor.

Rules

(3) The Commissioner may make rules prescribing

(a) the members or members of any class of members who may not represent or assist another member in any grievance, proceeding, preparation or appeal referred to in subsection (1); and

(b) the circumstances in which a member may not represent or assist another member in any grievance, proceeding, preparation or appeal referred to in subsection (1).

R.S., 1985, c. 8 (2nd Supp.), s. 18.

Personal service

47.2 (1) Subject to subsection (2), any notice, decision or other document required by this Act to be served by a person or a board shall be served by or on behalf of that person or board personally on the person to whom the notice, decision or document is directed.

Service by mail

(2) Any notice, decision or other document required by this Act to be served by a person or a board on the Commissioner, an appropriate officer, the Committee Chairman or the Commission Chairman is sufficiently served if it is sent by or on behalf of that person or board by prepaid first class mail addressed to the Commissioner, that appropriate officer, the Committee Chairman or the Commission Chairman, as the case may be.

Proof of personal service

(3) Where, by or pursuant to this Act, provision is made for personal service of a notice, decision or other document, a certificate purporting to be signed by a person, in this subsection referred to as the "deponent", that the notice, decision or document was served personally by the deponent on a named day on the person to whom it was directed and that the deponent identifies as an exhibit attached to the certificate a true copy of the notice, decision or document is evidence of the personal service and of the notice, decision or document, without proof of the signature of the deponent.
R.S., 1985, c. 8 (2nd Supp.), s. 18.

Legal proceedings

47.3 Section 16 of the *Canada Evidence Act* applies in respect of any proceedings before a board as though
(a) the proceeding were a legal proceeding; and
(b) the board were a judge, justice or other presiding officer.
R.S., 1985, c. 8 (2nd Supp.), s. 18.

Extensions of time limitations

47.4 (1) Where the Commissioner is satisfied that the circumstances justify an extension, the Commissioner may, on motion by the Commissioner or on application, and after giving due notice to any member affected thereby, extend the time limited by subsection 31(2), 44(1), 45.13(2), 45.14(4), 45.14(7), 45.19(4), 45.19(6), 45.23(6), 45.24(1) or 45.24(5) for the doing of any act therein described and specify terms and conditions in connection therewith.

Reference to time

(2) Where a time is extended under this section, any reference in this Act to the time shall be construed as a reference to the time as so extended.
R.S., 1985, c. 8 (2nd Supp.), s. 18.

Evidence not admissible

47.5 No evidence that informal or formal disciplinary action under Part IV or proceedings under Part V have been taken against a member shall be used or receivable against that member in any criminal proceedings.
R.S., 1985, c. 8 (2nd Supp.), s. 18.

Offences

Bribes, etc.

48. (1) Every person who
(a) [Repealed, R.S., 1985, c. 8 (2nd Supp.), s. 19]
(b) makes any agreement with any member to induce the member in any way to forego the member's duty, or
(c) concerts or connives at any act whereby any rule, order or regulation made under Part I may be evaded,

is guilty of an offence punishable on summary conviction.

(2) [Repealed, R.S., 1985, c. 8 (2nd Supp.), s. 19]

R.S., 1985, c. R–10, s 48; R.S., 1985, c. 8 (2nd Supp.), ss. 19, 24(E).

Unlawful use of name of Force

49. (1) Every person is guilty of an offence punishable on summary conviction who, without the authority of the Commissioner, uses

(a) the name of the Force or any abbreviation thereof or any words or letters likely to be mistaken therefor,

(b) any picture or other representation of a member of the Force, or

(c) any mark, badge or insignia of the Force, as all or any part of the name of any corporation, company, partnership or unincorporated association, in any advertising, for any business or trade purpose, or in such a way as to represent or imply that the Force uses or approves or endorses the use of any goods or services.

Personation of former member

(2) Every person not being a former member who, without the authority of the Commissioner, uses any clothing, equipment, badge, medal, ribbon, document or other thing in such a manner as to lead a reasonable belief that the person was a member of the Force is guilty of an offence punishable on summary conviction.

Consent to prosecution

(3) No proceedings in respect of an offence under this section shall be instituted without the consent of the Minister. R.S., 1985, c. R–10, s. 49; R.S., 1985, c. 8 (2nd Supp.), s. 20.

Attendance of witnesses, etc.

50. Every person who

(a) on being duly summoned as a witness or otherwise under Part I, III, IV, V or VII, makes default in attending,

(b) being in attendance as a witness in any proceeding under Part I, III, IV, V or VII,

(i) refuses to take an oath or solemn affirmation required of that person,

(ii) refuses to produce any document or thing under that person's control and required to be produced by that person, or

(iii) refuses to answer any question that requires an answer,

(c) at any proceeding under Part I, III, IV, V or VII, uses insulting or threatening language or causes any interference or disturbance, or

(d) prints observations or uses words likely to influence improperly a board of inquiry under Part I, the Committee under Part III, IV or V, the Commission under Part VII, an adjudication board under Part IV or a discharge and demotion board under Part V or witnesses at any proceeding under Part I, III, IV, V or VII or to bring any such proceeding into disrepute, or in any other manner whatever displays contempt of any such proceeding,

is guilty of an offence punishable on summary conviction. R.S., 1985, c. R–10, s. 50; R.S., 1985, c. 8 (2nd Supp.), s. 21.

Punishment **51.** Every person who is convicted of an offence under this part is liable to a fine of not more than five hundred dollars or to imprisonment for a term of not more than six months or to both. R.S., c. R–9, s. 51.

Limitation period **52.** Proceedings in respect of an offence under this part may be instituted at any time within but not later than two years after the time when the subject-matter of the proceedings arose. R.S., c. R–9, s. 52.

53. [Repealed, R.S., 1985, c. 8 (2nd Supp.), s. 22]

SCHEDULE

(Section 14)

OATH OF OFFICE

I, ..., solemnly swear that I will faithfully, diligently and impartially execute and perform the duties required of me as a member of the Royal Canadian Mounted Police, and will well and truly obey and perform all lawful orders and instructions that I receive as such, without fear, favour or affection of or toward any person. So help me God.

OATH OF SECRECY

I, ..., solemnly swear that I will not disclose or make known to any person not legally entitled thereto any knowledge or information obtained by me in the course of my employment with the Royal Canadian Mounted Police. So help me God. R.S., 1985, c. 8 (2nd Supp.), s. 23.

RELATED PROVISIONS

— R.S., 1985, c. 8 (2nd Supp.), s. 24(1):

"**24.** (1) Wherever the word "force" appears in the English version of the said Act or in any order, rule or regulation made thereunder, there shall in every case, unless the context otherwise requires, be substituted the word "Force"."

— R.S., 1985, c. 8 (2nd Supp.), s. 25:

Transfer of Funds   "**25.** The amount standing to the credit of the fund established by section 45 of the said Act immediately before the commencement of this Act shall be credited to the Benefit Trust Fund referred to in section 23 of the said Act as amended by this Act and shall be used in the manner and for the purposes established by or pursuant to section 23 as so amended."

APPENDIX B:
Police Services Act

Revised Statutes of Ontario, 1990, Chapter P.15

(Note: by Order in Council made February 3, 1993, the powers and duties of the Minister were transferred to the Solicitor General and Minister of Correctional Services.)

1. Declaration of principles

1. Police services shall be provided throughout Ontario in accordance with the following principles:

1. The need to ensure the safety and security of all persons and property in Ontario.
2. The importance of safeguarding the fundamental rights guaranteed by the *Canadian Charter of Rights and Freedoms* and the *Human Rights Code*.
3. The need for co-operation between the providers of police services and the communities they serve.
4. The importance of respect for victims of crime and understanding of their needs.
5. The need for sensitivity to the pluralistic, multiracial and multicultural character of Ontario society.
6. The need to ensure that police forces are representative of the communities they serve. R.S.O. 1990, c.-P.15, s.-1.

2. Declaration of principles

2. In this Act,

"association" means an association whose members belong to one police force and whose objects include the improvement of their working conditions and remuneration; ("association")

"board" means, except in Part VI, a municipal police services board; ("commission de police")

"chief of police" means a municipal chief of police or the Commissioner of the Ontario Provincial Police and includes an acting chief of police; ("chef de police")

"Commission" means the Ontario Civilian Commission on Police Services; ("Commission") "member of a police force" means a police officer, and in the case of a municipal police force includes an employee who is not a police officer; ("membre d'un corps de police")

"municipality" includes district, metropolitan and regional municipalities and the County of Oxford; ("municipalité")

"police force" means the Ontario Provincial Police or a municipal police force; ("corps de police")

"police officer" means a chief of police or any other police officer, but does not include a special constable, a First Nations Constable, a by-law enforcement officer or an auxiliary member of a police force; ("agent de police")

"prescribed" means prescribed by the regulations; ("prescrit")

"regulations" means the regulations made under this Act. ("règlements") R.S.O. 1990, c.-P.15, s.-2.

PART I   Responsibility for Police Services

SOLICITOR GENERAL

3.(1) Administration of Act

3. 3.(1) This Act, except Part VI, shall be administered by the Solicitor General.

3.(2)Duties and powers of Solicitor General

3.(2) The Solicitor General shall,

(a) monitor police forces to ensure that adequate and effective police services are provided at the municipal and provincial levels;

(b) monitor boards and police forces to ensure that they comply with prescribed standards of service;

(c) monitor the establishment and implementation of employment equity plans;

(d) develop and promote programs to enhance professional police practices, standards and training;

(e) conduct a system of inspection and review of police forces across Ontario;

(f) assist in the co-ordination of police services;

(g) consult with and advise boards, municipal chiefs of police, employers of special constables and associations on matters relating to police and police services;

(h) develop, maintain and manage programs and statistical records and conduct research studies in respect of police services and related matters;

(i) provide to boards and municipal chiefs of police information and advice respecting the management and operation of police forces, techniques in handling special problems and other information calculated to assist;

(j) issue directives and guidelines respecting policy matters;

(k) develop and promote programs for community-oriented police services;

(l) operate the Ontario Police College.

3.(3) Ontario Police College continued

3.(3) The police college known as the Ontario Police College for the training of members of police forces is continued. R.S.O. 1990, c.-P.15, s.-3.

MUNICIPALITIES

4.(1) Police services in municipalities

4. 4.(1) Every municipality to which this subsection applies shall provide adequate and effective police services in accordance with its needs.

4.(2) Application of subsection (1)

4.(2) Subsection (1) applies to,

(a) cities, towns, villages and townships (other than area municipalities within regional or metropolitan municipalities); and

(b) regional and metropolitan municipalities.

4.(3) Exception, Muskoka

4.(3) Subsection (1) does not apply to The District Municipality of Muskoka or to its area municipalities.

4.(4) Exception, Ottawa-Carleton

4.(4) Subsection (1) does not apply to The Regional Municipality of Ottawa-Carleton but does apply to its area municipalities.

Note: On January 1, 1995, subsection 4 (4) is repealed. See: 1994, c.-1, ss.-25, 28-(3).

4.(5) Exception, Oxford County

4.(5) Subsection (1) does not apply to the County of Oxford but does apply to its area municipalities.

4.(6) Exemption of towns of less than 5,000

4.(6) The Lieutenant Governor in Council may, on the Solicitor General's recommendation, exempt any town having a population of less than 5,000 according to the last enumeration taken under section 15 of the *Assessment Act* from the application of subsection (1), and the exemption continues in effect until it is revoked.

4.(7) Restriction, villages and townships

4.(7) Subsection (1) applies to a village or township only if it has been so designated by the Lieutenant Governor in Council on the Solicitor General's recommendation; the designation may relate to all or part of the village or township. R.S.O. 1990, c.-P.15, s.-4.

5. Methods of establishing municipal police forces

5. A municipality's responsibility for providing police services shall be discharged in one of the following ways:

1. The board may appoint the members of a police force under clause 31-(1)-(a), in which case the municipal council shall pay the cost of the police force.
2. The board may enter into an agreement under section 7-(sharing police services).
3. The council may enter into an agreement under section 10-(agreements for provision of police services by O.P.P.).
4. With the Commission's approval, the municipality may adopt a different method of providing police services. R.S.O. 1990, c.-P.15, s.-5.

6.(1) Amalgamation of police forces

6. 6.(1) Despite any other Act, two or more municipalities that have police forces may enter into an agreement to amalgamate them.

6.(2) Contents of amalgamation agreement

6.(2) The agreement shall deal with,

(a) the establishment and composition of a board for the amalgamated police force;
(b) the amalgamation of the police forces and the appointment or transfer of their members;
(c) the amalgamated board's use of the assets and its responsibility for the liabilities associated with the police forces;
(d) the budgeting of the cost for the operation of the amalgamated police force;
(e) any other matter that is necessary or advisable to effect the amalgamation.

6.(3) Commission's approval

6.(3) The agreement does not take effect until the Commission has approved the organization of the amalgamated police force.

6.(4) Exception, board appointments

6.(4) Appointments to a board for an amalgamated police force may be made before the agreement takes effect. R.S.O. 1990, c.-P.15, s.-6.

7. Municipal agreements for sharing police services

7. Two boards may agree that one board will provide police services to the other, on the conditions set out in the agreement. R.S.O. 1990, c.-P.15, s.-7.

8.(1) Additional municipal police forces

8. 8.(1) A municipality to which subsection 4-(1) (obligation to provide police services) does not apply may, with the Commission's approval, establish and maintain a police force.

8.(2)Transition

8.(2) An approval given or deemed to have been given under section 19 of the *Police Act*, being chapter 381 of the Revised Statutes of Ontario, 1980, in respect of a police force that was being maintained on the 30th day of December, 1990, shall be deemed to have been given under this section.

8.(3)Revocation

8.(3) The Commission may revoke an approval given or deemed to have been given under this section. R.S.O. 1990, c.-P.15, s.-8.

9.(1) Failure to provide police services

9. 9.(1) If the Commission finds that a municipality to which subsection 4-(1) applies is not providing police services, it may request that the Commissioner have the Ontario Provincial Police give assistance.

9.(2)Inadequate police services

9.(2) If the Commission finds that a municipal police force is not providing adequate and effective police services or is not complying with this Act or the regulations, it may communicate that finding to the board of the municipality and direct the board to take the measures that the Commission considers necessary.

9.(3)Idem

9.(3) If the board does not comply with the direction, the Commission may request that the Commissioner have the Ontario Provincial Police give assistance.

9.(4)Crown Attorney's request

9.(4) In any area for which a municipality is required to provide police services, the Crown Attorney may request that the Commissioner have the Ontario Provincial Police give assistance.

9.(5)Board's request

9.(5) A board may, by resolution, request that the Commissioner have the Ontario Provincial Police give assistance.

9.(6)Request of chief of police in emergency

9.(6) A municipal chief of police who is of the opinion that an emergency exists in the municipality may request that the Commissioner have the Ontario Provincial Police give assistance.

9.(7)Chief of police to advise board

9.(7) A chief of police who makes a request under subsection (6) shall advise the chair of the board of the fact as soon as possible.

9.(8)Assistance of O.P.P.

9.(8) When a request is made under this section, the Commissioner shall have the Ontario Provincial Police give such assistance as he or she considers necessary.

9.(9) Cost of services

9.(9) The Commissioner shall certify the cost of the services provided under this section by the Ontario Provincial Police and, unless the Solicitor General directs otherwise, the municipality shall pay that amount to the Treasurer of Ontario.

9.(10) Idem

9.(10) The amount may be deducted from any grant payable to the municipality out of provincial funds or may be recovered by a court action, with costs, as a debt due to Her Majesty. R.S.O. 1990, c.-P.15, s.-9.

10.(1) Municipal agreements for provision of police services by O.P.P.

10. 10.(1) The Solicitor General may enter into an agreement with the council of a municipality for the provision of police services for the municipality by the Ontario Provincial Police.

10.(2) Board's consent

10.(2) The agreement requires the board's consent.

10.(3) Collective bargaining

10.(3) No agreement shall be entered into under this section if, in the Solicitor General's opinion, the council seeks the agreement for the purpose of defeating the collective bargaining provisions of this Act.

10.(4) Duties of O.P.P.

10.(4) When the agreement comes into effect, the members of the Ontario Provincial Police assigned to the municipality shall provide police services, including by-law enforcement, for the municipality, and shall perform any other duties that are specified in the agreement.

10.(5) Payment into Consolidated Revenue Fund

10.(5) The amounts received from the municipality under the agreement shall be paid into the Consolidated Revenue Fund.

10.(6) Role of board

10.(6) If the municipality has an agreement under this section, section 31-(responsibilities of board), section 38-(municipal police force) and clause 39-(3)-(a) (estimates respecting police force) do not apply; however, the board shall advise the Solicitor General and the senior officer of the Ontario Provincial Police in the municipality with respect to police services in the municipality, and may generally determine priorities in the municipality with respect to police services, in accordance with the agreement and with provincial policies affecting the Ontario Provincial Police. R.S.O. 1990, c.-P.15, s.-10.

11.(1) Fines

11. 11.(1) This section applies if a municipality is entitled to receive fines paid as a result of prosecutions instituted by police officers of the municipal police force.

11.(2)Idem

11.(2) If the municipality does not have its own police force because of an agreement under section 7 or 10, the police officers who are assigned to the municipality under the agreement shall, for the purposes of determining entitlement to fines, be deemed to be police officers of the municipal police force. R.S.O. 1990, c.-P.15, s.-1

12.(1) Rates for cost of police services

12. 12.(1) With the Commission's approval, the costs incurred by a municipality in providing police services may be paid by levying different rates for different areas defined by the municipal council or by levying rates in some but not all areas.

12.(2)Exemption for farm lands and buildings

12.(2) With the Commission's approval, the municipal council may grant a total or partial exemption from a rate or rates levied under subsection (1) to lands and buildings used exclusively for farming purposes. R.S.O. 1990, c.-P.15, s.-12.

13.(1) Special areas

13. 13.(1) If, because of the establishment of a business or for any other reason, special circumstances or abnormal conditions in an area make it inequitable, in the Solicitor General's opinion, to impose the responsibility for police services on a municipality or on the Province, the Lieutenant Governor in Council may designate the area as a special area.

13.(2)Agreement for provision of police services by O.P.P.

13.(2) The person who operates the business or owns the special area shall enter into an agreement with the Solicitor General for the provision of police services by the Ontario Provincial Police for the special area.

13.(3)Duties of O.P.P., payment

13.(3) Subsections 10-(4) and (5) apply to the agreement with necessary modifications.

13.(4)Failure to enter into agreement

13.(4) If the person who operates the business or owns the special area does not enter into an agreement as subsection (2) requires, the Ontario Provincial Police shall provide police services for the area.

13.(5)Cost of services

13.(5) The costs of the services may be recovered from the person by a court action, with costs, as a debt due to Her Majesty. R.S.O. 1990, c.-P.15, s.-13.

14. Police services outside municipality

14. A municipality that has an interest in land outside the territory of the municipality may agree to pay all or part of the cost of providing police services for the land. R.S.O. 1990, c.-P.15, s.-14.

15.(1) Municipal by-law enforcement officers

15. 15.(1) A municipal council may appoint persons to enforce the by-laws of the municipality.

15.(2)Peace officers

15.(2) Municipal by-law enforcement officers are peace officers for the purpose of enforcing municipal by-laws. R.S.O. 1990, c.-P.15, s.-15.

16. Aid to survivors

16. A municipal council may grant financial or other assistance for the benefit of the surviving spouses and children of members of the municipal police force who die from injuries received or illnesses contracted in the discharge of their duties. R.S.O. 1990, c.-P.15, s.-16.

ONTARIO PROVINCIAL POLICE

17.(1) Commissioner

17. 17.(1) There shall be a Commissioner of the Ontario Provincial Police who shall be appointed by the Lieutenant Governor in Council.

17.(2)Functions

17.(2) Subject to the Solicitor General's direction, the Commissioner has the general control and administration of the Ontario Provincial Police and the employees connected with it.

17.(3)Employment equity plans

17.(3) The Commissioner shall prepare and implement an employment equity plan in accordance with section 48 and the regulations.

17.(4)Annual report

17.(4) After the end of each calendar year, the Commissioner shall file with the Solicitor General an annual report on the affairs of the Ontario Provincial Police. R.S.O. 1990, c.-P.15, s.-17.

18.(1) Composition of O.P.P.

18. 18.(1) The Ontario Provincial Police shall consist of the Commissioner and other police officers appointed under the *Public Service Act*.

18.(2)Ranks

18.(2) The Commissioner shall establish the ranks within the Ontario Provincial Police and shall determine the rank of each police officer.

18.(3)Commissioned officers

18.(3) The Lieutenant Governor in Council may name police officers of the Ontario Provincial Police to the rank of commissioned officers and may authorize the issue of commissions to them under the Great Seal.

18.(4)Employees

18.(4) The Commissioner may appoint such other employees as are required in connection with the Ontario Provincial Police. R.S.O. 1990, c.-P.15, s.-18.

19.(1) Responsibilities of O.P.P.

19. 19.(1) The Ontario Provincial Police have the following responsibilities:

1. Providing police services in respect of the parts of Ontario that do not have municipal police forces other than by-law enforcement officers.
2. Providing police services in respect of all navigable bodies and courses of water in Ontario, except those that lie within municipalities designated by the Solicitor General.
3. Maintaining a traffic patrol on the King's Highway, except the parts designated by the Solicitor General.
4. Maintaining a traffic patrol on the connecting links within the meaning of section 21 of the *Public Transportation and Highway Improvement Act* that are designated by the Solicitor General.
5. Maintaining investigative services to assist municipal police forces on the Solicitor General's direction or at the Crown Attorney's request.

19.(2)Municipal by-laws

19.(2) The Ontario Provincial Police have no responsibilities in connection with municipal by-laws, except under agreements made in accordance with section 10. R.S.O. 1990, c.-P.15, s.-19.

20. Aid to survivors

20. The Lieutenant Governor in Council may, out of money appropriated for that purpose by the Legislature, grant financial or other assistance for the benefit of the surviving spouses and children of members of the Ontario Provincial Police who die from injuries received or illnesses contracted in the discharge of their duties. R.S.O. 1990, c.-P.15, s.-20.

PART II   Ontario Civilian Commission on Police Services

21.(1) Commission continued

21. 21.(1) The commission known as the Ontario Police Commission is continued under the name of Ontario Civilian Commission on Police Services in English and under the name of Commission civile des services policiers de l'Ontario in French.

21.(2)Composition

21.(2) The Commission shall consist of not fewer than three and not more than nine members who shall be appointed by the Lieutenant Governor in Council.

21.(3)Chair

21.(3) The Lieutenant Governor in Council may designate one of the members of the Commission to be the chair.

21.(4)Delegation

21.(4) The chair may authorize a member of the Commission to exercise the Commission's powers and perform its duties with respect to a particular matter, but the authority conferred on the Commission by sections 23 and 24 may not be delegated.

21.(5)Quorum

21.(5) Two members of the Commission constitute a quorum.

21.(6)Proceedings open to the public

21.(6) Meetings, hearings, investigations and inquiries conducted by the Commission shall be open to the public, subject to subsection (7), and notice of them shall be published in the manner that the Commission determines.

21.(7)Exception

21.(7) The Commission may exclude the public from all or part of a meeting, hearing, investigation or inquiry if it is of the opinion that,
    (a) matters involving public security may be disclosed and, having regard to the circumstances, the desirability of avoiding their disclosure in the public interest outweighs the desirability of adhering to the principle that proceedings be open to the public; or
    (b) intimate financial or personal matters or other matters may be disclosed of such a nature, having regard to the circumstances, that the desirability of avoiding their disclosure in the interest of any person affected or in the public interest outweighs the desirability of adhering to the principle that proceedings be open to the public.

21.(8)Admissibility of documents

21.(8) A document purporting to be issued by the Commission and signed by one of its members is admissible in evidence without proof of the signature or authority of the person signing.

21.(9)Annual report

21.(9) After the end of each calendar year, the Commission shall file with the Solicitor General an annual report on its affairs.

21.(10)Expenses

21.(10) The money required for the Commission's purposes shall be paid out of the amounts appropriated by the Legislature for that purpose. R.S.O. 1990, c.-P.15, s.-2

22.(1) Powers and duties of Commission

22. 22.(1) The Commission's powers and duties include,

- (a) if the Solicitor General advises the Commission that a board or municipal police force is not complying with prescribed standards of police services,
  - (i) directing the board or police force to comply, and
  - (ii) if the Commission considers it appropriate, taking measures in accordance with subsection 23-(1);
- (b) if the Solicitor General advises the Commission that a board or municipal chief of police is not complying with the requirements of this Act and the regulations respecting employment equity plans,
  - (i) directing the board or chief of police to comply, and
  - (ii) if the Commission considers it appropriate, taking measures in accordance with subsection 23-(2);
- (c) conducting investigations with respect to municipal police matters under section 25;
- (d) conducting inquiries into matters relating to crime and law enforcement under section 26;
- (e) inquiring into any matter regarding the designation of a municipality under subsection 4-(7) (police services in villages and townships) and, after a hearing, making recommendations to the Solicitor General;
- (f) hearing and disposing of appeals by members of police forces in accordance with Part V.

22.(2)Powers of Commission in hearings, investigations and inquiries

22.(2) When the Commission conducts a hearing, investigation or inquiry, it has all the powers of a commission under Part II of the *Public Inquiries Act*, which Part applies to the proceeding as if it were an inquiry under that Act.

22.(3)Counsel

22.(3) At the Commission's request, the Solicitor General may appoint counsel to assist the Commission in a hearing, investigation or inquiry. R.S.O. 1990, c.-P.15, s.-22.

23.(1) Sanctions for failure to comply with prescribed standards of police services

23. 23.(1) If the Commission is of the opinion, after holding a hearing, that a board or municipal police force has flagrantly or repeatedly failed to comply with prescribed standards of police services, the Commission may take any of the following measures or any combination of them:

1. Suspending the chief of police, one or more members of the board, or the whole board, for a specified period.
2. Removing the chief of police, one or more members of the board, or the whole board from office.
3. Disbanding the police force and requiring the Ontario Provincial Police to provide police services for the municipality.
4. Appointing an administrator to perform specified functions with respect to police matters in the municipality for a specified period.

23.(2)Sanctions for failure to comply with requirements respecting employment equity plans

23.(2) If the Commission is of the opinion, after holding a hearing, that a board or municipal chief of police has failed to comply with the requirements of this Act and the regulations respecting employment equity plans, the Commission may take any of the following measures or any combination of them:

1. Suspending the chief of police, one or more members of the board, or the whole board, for a specified period.
2. Removing the chief of police, one or more members of the board, or the whole board from office.
3. Appointing an administrator to perform specified functions with respect to employment equity, recruitment and promotion in the police force for a specified period.

23.(3)Suspension with or without pay

23.(3) If the Commission suspends the chief of police or members of the board who are entitled to remuneration under subsection 27-(12), it shall specify whether the suspension is with or without pay.

23.(4)Defence

23.(4) The Commission shall not take measures under subsection (2) with respect to the failure of a chief of police to meet specific goals or timetables contained in the employment equity plan if the Commission finds that the chief of police has made all reasonable efforts to meet them.

23.(5)Powers of administrator

23.(5) An administrator appointed under paragraph 4 of subsection (1) or paragraph 3 of subsection (2) has all the powers necessary for the performance of his or her functions.

23.(6)Replacement of chief of police

23.(6) If the Commission suspends or removes the chief of police, it may appoint a person to replace him or her.

23.(7)Parties

23.(7) The parties to the hearing are the chief of police, the board, any member of the board that the Commission designates and, if the Commission so directs, the association or associations representing members of the police force.

23.(8)Idem

23.(8) The Commission may add parties at any stage of the hearing on the conditions it considers proper.

23.(9)Replacement of suspended or removed member

23.(9) If the Commission suspends a member of a board or removes him or her from office, the municipal council or the Lieutenant Governor in Council, as the case may be, shall appoint a person to replace the member.

23.(10)Consequences of removal and suspension

23.(10) A member who has been removed shall not subsequently be a member of any board, and a member who has been suspended shall not be reappointed during the period of suspension.

23.(11)Appeal to Divisional Court

23.(11) A party may appeal to the Divisional Court within thirty days of receiving notice of the Commission's decision.

23.(12)Grounds for appeal

23.(12) An appeal may be made on a question that is not a question of fact alone, or from a penalty, or both.

23.(13)Idem

23.(13) An appeal may also be made from a finding that a chief of police has made all reasonable efforts to meet the specific goals and timetables contained in an employment equity plan.

23.(14)Appeal by non-parties

23.(14) If the consent of the Attorney General is sought within thirty days of the Commission's decision and is given, a person who is not a party may appeal under subsection (13) as if he or she were a party. R.S.O. 1990, c.-P.15, s.-23.

24.(1) Emergency, interim order

24. 24.(1) The Commission may make an interim order under subsection 23-(1), without notice and without holding a hearing, if it is of the opinion that an emergency exists and that the interim order is necessary in the public interest.

24.(2)Restriction

24.(2) The Commission shall not remove a person from office or disband a police force by means of an interim order. R.S.O. 1990, c.-P.15, s.-24.

25.(1) Investigations into police matters

25. 25.(1) The Commission may, at the Solicitor General's request, at a municipal council's request or of its own motion, investigate, inquire into and report on,

   (a) the conduct or the performance of duties of a municipal chief of police or other municipal police officer, an auxiliary member of a municipal police force, a special constable, a by-law enforcement officer or a member of a board;
   (b) the administration of a municipal police force;
   (c) the manner in which police services are provided for a municipality;
   (d) the police needs of a municipality.

25.(2)Cost of investigation

25.(2) The cost of an investigation conducted at a council's request shall be paid by the municipality, unless the Solicitor General directs otherwise.

25.(3)Report

25.(3) The Commission shall communicate its report of an investigation under subsection (1) to the Solicitor General at his or her request and to the board or council at its request, and may communicate the report to any other person as the Commission considers advisable.

25.(4)Penalties, member of police force

25.(4) If the Commission concludes after a hearing that a member of a police force is not performing or is incapable of performing the duties of his or her position in a satisfactory manner, it may direct that the member be,

   (a) demoted as the Commission specifies, permanently or for a specified period;
   (b) dismissed; or
   (c) retired, if the member is entitled to retire.

25.(5)Penalties, member of board

25.(5) If the Commission concludes, after a hearing, that a member of a board is guilty of misconduct or is not performing or is incapable of performing the duties of his or her position in a satisfactory manner, it may remove or suspend the member.

25.(6)Appeal to Divisional Court

25.(6) A member of a police force or of a board on whom a penalty is imposed under subsection (4) or (5) may appeal to the Divisional Court within thirty days of receiving notice of the Commission's decision.

25.(7)Grounds for appeal

25.(7) An appeal may be made on a question that is not a question of fact alone, or from a penalty, or both.

25.(8)Replacement of suspended or removed member

25.(8) If the Commission suspends a member of a board or removes him or her from office, the municipal council or the Lieutenant Governor in Council, as the case may be, shall appoint a person to replace the member.

25.(9)Consequences of removal and suspension

25.(9) A member who has been removed shall not subsequently be a member of any board, and a member who has been suspended shall not be reappointed during the period of suspension. R.S.O. 1990, c.-P.15, s.-25.

26.(1) Inquiries respecting crime and law enforcement

26. 26.(1) The Lieutenant Governor in Council may direct the Commission to inquire into and report to the Lieutenant Governor in Council on any matter relating to crime or law enforcement, and shall define the scope of the inquiry in the direction.

26.(2)Public Inquiries Act applies

26.(2) Section 6 (stated case) of the *Public Inquiries Act* applies to inquiries conducted under this section.

26.(3)Rights of witnesses

26.(3) Witnesses at inquiries conducted under this section have the right to retain and instruct counsel and all the other rights of witnesses in civil courts.

26.(4)Offence

26.(4) Any person who knowingly discloses, without the Commission's consent, evidence taken in private at an inquiry conducted under this section or information likely to identify the witness is guilty of an offence and on conviction is liable to a fine of not more than $5,000. R.S.O. 1990, c.-P.15, s.-26.

PART III   MUNICIPAL POLICE SERVICES BOARDS

27.(1) Police services boards

27. 27.(1) There shall be a police services board for every municipality that maintains a police force.

27.(2)Boards of commissioners of police continued as police services boards

27.(2) Every board of commissioners of police constituted or continued under the *Police Act*, being chapter 381 of the Revised Statutes of Ontario, 1980, or any other Act and in existence on the 31st day of December, 1990, is continued as a police services board.

27.(3)Name

27.(3) A board shall be known as *(insert name of municipality)* Police Services Board and may also be known as Commission des services policiers de *(insert name of municipality)*.

27.(4)Three-member boards in smaller municipalities

27.(4) The board of a municipality whose population according to the last enumeration taken under section 15 of the *Assessment Act* does not exceed 25,000 shall consist of,

  (a) the head of the municipal council, or another council member appointed by resolution of the council; and
  (b) two persons appointed by the Lieutenant Governor in Council.

27.(5)Five-member boards in larger municipalities

27.(5) The board of a municipality, other than a regional or metropolitan municipality, whose population according to the last enumeration taken under section 15 of the *Assessment Act* exceeds 25,000 shall consist of,

  (a) the head of the municipal council, or another council member appointed by resolution of the council;
  (b) one person appointed by resolution of the council; and
  (c) three persons appointed by the Lieutenant Governor in Council.

27.(6)Smaller municipalities, option to expand board

27.(6) The council of a municipality to which subsection (4) would otherwise apply may determine, by resolution, that the composition of its board shall be as described in subsection (5).

27.(7)Transition

27.(7) A resolution passed under clause 8-(2a)-(b) of the *Police Act*, being chapter 381 of the Revised Statutes of Ontario, 1980, before the 31st day of December, 1990, shall be deemed to have been passed under subsection (6).

27.(8)Regional and metropolitan municipalities

27.(8) The board of a regional or metropolitan municipality shall consist of,

  (a) two council members appointed by resolution of the municipal council; and
  (b) three persons appointed by the Lieutenant Governor in Council.

27.(9)Seven-member boards in certain circumstances

27.(9) The council of a regional or metropolitan municipality whose population according to the last enumeration taken under section 15 of the *Assessment Act* exceeds 300,000 may apply to the Lieutenant Governor in Council for an increase in the size of its board; if the Lieutenant Governor in Council approves the application, the board shall consist of,

    (a) the head of the council, or another council member appointed by reso-
lution of the council;

    (b) two council members appointed by resolution of the council; and

    (c) four persons appointed by the Lieutenant Governor in Council.

27.(10)Vacancies

27.(10) If the position of a member appointed by the Lieutenant Governor in Council becomes vacant, the Solicitor General may appoint a replacement to act until the Lieutenant Governor in Council makes a new appointment.

27.(11)Idem

27.(11) If the position of a member who is appointed by a municipal council or holds office by virtue of being the head of a municipal council becomes vacant, the board shall notify the council, which shall forthwith appoint a replacement.

27.(12)Remuneration

27.(12) The council shall pay the members of the board who are appointed by the Lieutenant Governor in Council or Solicitor General remuneration that is at least equal to the prescribed amount.

27.(13)Judges and justices of the peace ineligible

27.(13) No judge or justice of the peace shall be appointed as a member of a board.

27.(14)Transition, judges and justices of the peace

27.(14) A judge or justice of the peace who is a member of a board on the 31st day of December, 1990, may continue to be a member until the 31st day of December, 1993.

27.(15)Transition, municipalities without boards

27.(15) In the case of a municipality that is required by subsection (1) to have a police services board and that does not, on the 31st day of December, 1990, have a board of commissioners of police, the following rules apply:

    1. Subsection (1) does not apply to the municipality until the 31st day of December, 1991.

    2. Until subsection (1) applies to the municipality, the council shall perform the duties and may exercise the powers that this Act imposes and confers on police services boards. R.S.O. 1990, c.-P.15, s.-27.

28. Election of chair

28. The members of a board shall elect a chair at the board's first meeting in each year. R.S.O. 1990, c.-P.15, s.-28.

29.(1) Protection from personal liability

29. 29.(1) No action or other proceeding for damages shall be instituted against a member of a board for any act done in good faith in the execution or intended execution of his or her duty or for any alleged neglect or default in the execution in good faith of that duty.

29.(2)Board's liability

29.(2) Subsection (1) does not relieve a board of liability for a member's acts or omissions, and the board is liable as if that subsection had not been enacted and as if the member were the board's employee. R.S.O. 1990, c.-P.15, s.-29.

30.(1) Board may contract, sue and be sued

30. 30.(1) A board may contract, sue and be sued in its own name.

30.(2)Members not liable for board's contracts

30.(2) The members of a board are not personally liable for the board's contracts. R.S.O. 1990, c.-P.15, s.-30.

31.(1) Responsibilities of boards

31. 31.(1) A board is responsible for the provision of police services and for law enforcement and crime prevention in the municipality and shall,

    (a) appoint the members of the municipal police force;

    (b) generally determine, after consultation with the chief of police, objectives and priorities with respect to police services in the municipality;

    (c) establish policies for the effective management of the police force;

    (d) recruit and appoint the chief of police and any deputy chief of police, and annually determine their remuneration and working conditions, taking their submissions into account;

    (e) direct the chief of police and monitor his or her performance;

    (f) establish an employment equity plan in accordance with section 48 and the regulations, review its implementation by the chief of police and receive regular reports from him or her on that subject;

    (g) receive regular reports from the chief of police on disclosures and decisions made under section 49 (secondary activities);

    (h) establish guidelines with respect to the indemnification of members of the police force for legal costs under section 50;

    (i) establish guidelines for the administration by the chief of police of the public complaints system under Part VI;

    (j) review the administration by the chief of police of the public complaints system and receive regular reports from him or her on that subject.

31.(2)Members of police force under board's jurisdiction

31.(2) The members of the police force, whether they were appointed by the board or not, are under the board's jurisdiction.

31.(3)Restriction

31.(3) The board may give orders and directions to the chief of police, but not to other members of the police force, and no individual member of the board shall give orders or directions to any member of the police force.

31.(4)Idem

31.(4) The board shall not direct the chief of police with respect to specific operational decisions or with respect to the day-to-day operation of the police force.

31.(5)Training of board members

31.(5) The board shall ensure that its members undergo any training that the Solicitor General may provide or require.

31.(6)Rules re management of police force

31.(6) The board may, by by-law, make rules for the effective management of the police force.

31.(7)Guidelines re secondary activities

31.(7) The board may establish guidelines consistent with section 49 for police officers' disclosure of secondary activities to the chief of police and for the decisions of the chief of police under subsection 49-(4). R.S.O. 1990, c.-P.15, s.-3.

32. Oath of office

32. Before entering on the duties of office, a member of a board shall take an oath or affirmation of office in the prescribed form. R.S.O. 1990, c.-P.15, s.-32.

33.(1) Agreement to constitute joint board

33. 33.(1) Despite any special Act, two or more municipalities whose combined population according to the last enumeration taken under section 15 of the *Assessment Act* exceeds 5,000 may enter into an agreement to constitute a joint board.

33.(2)Idem

33.(2) The agreement must be authorized by by-laws of the councils of the participating municipalities and requires the consent of their boards.

33.(3)Composition of board

33.(3) The joint board shall consist of,

    (a) the heads of the councils of the participating municipalities; and
    (b) other members appointed by the Lieutenant Governor in Council.

33.(4) Application of Act to joint boards

33.(4) The provisions of this Act that apply to boards also apply with necessary modifications to joint boards. R.S.O. 1990, c.-P.15, s.-33.

34. Delegation

34. A board may delegate to two or more of its members any authority conferred on it by this Act, except,

    (a) the authority to hear the appeals of police officers found guilty of misconduct under Part V, which must be exercised by a quorum; and

    (b) the authority to bargain under Part VIII, which the board may delegate to one or more members. R.S.O. 1990, c.-P.15, s.-34.

35.(1) Meetings

35. 35.(1) The board shall hold at least four meetings each year.

35.(2) Quorum

35.(2) A majority of the members of the board constitutes a quorum.

35.(3) Proceedings open to the public

35.(3) Meetings and hearings conducted by the board shall be open to the public, subject to subsection (4), and notice of them shall be published in the manner that the board determines.

35.(4) Exception

35.(4) The board may exclude the public from all or part of a meeting or hearing if it is of the opinion that,

    (a) matters involving public security may be disclosed and, having regard to the circumstances, the desirability of avoiding their disclosure in the public interest outweighs the desirability of adhering to the principle that proceedings be open to the public; or

    (b) intimate financial or personal matters or other matters may be disclosed of such a nature, having regard to the circumstances, that the desirability of avoiding their disclosure in the interest of any person affected or in the public interest outweighs the desirability of adhering to the principle that proceedings be open to the public. R.S.O. 1990, c.-P.15, s.-35.

36. Admissibility of documents

36. A document purporting to be a by-law of the board signed by a member or purporting to be a copy of such a by-law certified correct by a member is admissible in evidence without proof of the signature or authority of the person signing. R.S.O. 1990, c.-P.15, s.-36.

37. Power with respect to witnesses

37. In performing its duties under this Act, a board has all the powers of a commission under Part II of the *Public Inquiries Act,* which Part applies to the board as if it were conducting an inquiry under that Act. R.S.O. 1990, c.-P.15, s.-37.

38. Municipal police force

38. A municipal police force shall consist of a chief of police and such other police officers and other employees as the board considers adequate, and shall be provided with the equipment and facilities that the board considers adequate. R.S.O. 1990, c.-P.15, s.-38.

39.(1) Estimates

39. 39.(1) Each year, the board shall submit to the municipal council or to each council responsible for maintaining the police force, as the case may be, its estimates for the year.

39.(2)Time

39.(2) The estimates shall be submitted at least one month before the beginning of the fiscal year of the municipality or municipalities, as the case may be; if they are to be submitted to municipalities whose fiscal years begin on different dates, they shall be submitted to all the councils at least one month before the earliest date.

39.(3)Idem

39.(3) The estimates shall show, separately, the amounts that will be required,

    (a) to maintain the police force and provide it with equipment and facilities; and

    (b) to pay the expenses of the board's operation other than the remuneration of board members.

39.(4)Commission hearing in case of disagreement

39.(4) If the council does not approve the board's estimates or disagrees with the board on the number of members of the police force that is adequate or the equipment and facilities that are adequate, the Commission shall determine the question after a hearing. R.S.O. 1990, c.-P.15, s.-39.

40.(1) Reduction or abolition of police force

40. 40.(1) A board may terminate the employment of a member of the police force for the purpose of abolishing the police force or reducing its size if the Commission consents and if the abolition or reduction does not contravene this Act.

40.(2)Criteria for Commission's consent

40.(2) The Commission shall consent to the termination of the employment of a member of the police force under subsection (1) only if,

    (a) the member and the board have made an agreement dealing with severance pay or agreed to submit the matter to arbitration; or

(b) the Commission has made an order under subsection (3).

40.(3)Order imposing arbitration

40.(3) If the member and the board do not make an agreement dealing with severance pay and do not agree to submit the matter to arbitration, the Commission, if it is of the opinion that it would be appropriate to permit the abolition of the police force or the reduction of its size, may order the member and the board to submit the matter to arbitration and may give any necessary directions in that connection.

40.(4)Arbitration

40.(4) Section 124 applies to an arbitration referred to in this section with necessary modifications. R.S.O. 1990, c.-P.15, s.-40.

PART IV Police Officers and Other Police Staff

CHIEF OF POLICE

41.(1) Duties of chief of police

41. 41.(1) The duties of a chief of police include,
- (a) in the case of a municipal police force, administering the police force and overseeing its operation in accordance with the objectives, priorities and policies established by the board under subsection 31-(1);
- (b) ensuring that members of the police force carry out their duties in accordance with this Act and the regulations and in a manner that reflects the needs of the community, and that discipline is maintained in the police force;
- (c) ensuring that the police force provides community-oriented police services;
- (d) administering discipline in accordance with Part V;
- (e) administering the public complaints system under Part VI;
- (f) implementing the employment equity plan established under section 48 and the regulations;
- (g) in the case of a municipal police force, reporting to the board at regular intervals on public complaints and on the implementation of the employment equity plan.

41.(2)Chief of police reports to board

41.(2) The chief of police reports to the board and shall obey its lawful orders and directions. R.S.O. 1990, c.-P.15, s.-4.

POLICE OFFICERS

42.(1) Duties of police officer

42. 42.(1) The duties of a police officer include,

(a) preserving the peace;
(b) preventing crimes and other offences and providing assistance and encouragement to other persons in their prevention;
(c) assisting victims of crime;
(d) apprehending criminals and other offenders and others who may lawfully be taken into custody;
(e) laying charges, prosecuting and participating in prosecutions;
(f) executing warrants that are to be executed by police officers and performing related duties;
(g) performing the lawful duties that the chief of police assigns;
(h) in the case of a municipal police force and in the case of an agreement under section 10-(agreement for provision of police services by O.P.P.), enforcing municipal by-laws;
(i) completing the prescribed training.

42.(2)Power to act throughout Ontario

42.(2) A police officer has authority to act as such throughout Ontario.

42.(3)Powers and duties of common law constable

42.(3) A police officer has the powers and duties ascribed to a constable at common law. R.S.O. 1990, c.-P.15, s.-42.

43.(1) Criteria for hiring

43. 43.(1) No person shall be appointed as a police officer unless he or she,

(a) is a Canadian citizen or a permanent resident of Canada;
(b) is at least eighteen years of age;
(c) is physically and mentally able to perform the duties of the position, having regard to his or her own safety and the safety of members of the public;
(d) is of good moral character and habits; and
(e) has successfully completed at least four years of secondary school education or its equivalent.

43.(2)Idem

43.(2) A candidate for appointment as a police officer shall provide any relevant information or material that is lawfully requested in connection with his or her application. R.S.O. 1990, c.-P.15, s.-43.

44.(1) Probationary period

44. 44.(1) A municipal police officer's probationary period begins on the day he or she is appointed and ends on the later of,

  (a) the first anniversary of the day of appointment;
  (b) the first anniversary of the day the police officer completes an initial period of training at the Ontario Police College.

44.(2)Time for completing initial training

44.(2) The police officer shall complete the initial period of training within six months of the day of appointment.

44.(3)Termination of employment during probationary period

44.(3) A board may terminate a police officer's employment at any time during his or her probationary period but, before doing so, shall give the police officer reasonable information with respect to the reasons for the termination and an opportunity to reply, orally or in writing, as the board may determine.

44.(4)Only one probationary period

44.(4) Subsections (1), (2) and (3) do not apply to a police officer who has completed a probationary period with another municipal police force. R.S.O. 1990, c.-P.15, s.-44.

45. Oaths of office and secrecy

45. A person appointed to be a police officer shall, before entering on the duties of his or her office, take oaths or affirmations of office and secrecy in the prescribed form. R.S.O. 1990, c.-P.15, s.-45.

46. Political activity

46. No municipal police officer shall engage in political activity, except as the regulations permit. R.S.O. 1990, c.-P.15, s.-46.

MEMBERS OF POLICE FORCES

47.(1) Accommodation of needs of disabled member of municipal police force

47. 47.(1) Subject to subsection (2), if a member of a municipal police force becomes mentally or physically disabled and as a result is incapable of performing the essential duties of the position, the board shall accommodate his or her needs in accordance with the *Human Rights Code*.

47.(2)Undue hardship

47.(2) The board may discharge the member, or retire him or her if entitled to retire, if, after holding a hearing at which the evidence of two legally qualified medical practitioners is received, the board,

(a) determines, on the basis of that evidence, that the member is mentally or physically disabled and as a result incapable of performing the essential duties of the position, and what duties the member is capable of performing; and

(b) concludes that the member's needs cannot be accommodated without undue hardship on the board.

47.(3)Idem, O.P.P.

47.(3) Subject to subsection (4), if a member of the Ontario Provincial Police becomes mentally or physically disabled and as a result is incapable of performing the essential duties of the position, the Commissioner shall accommodate the member's needs in accordance with the *Human Rights Code*.

47.(4)Idem

47.(4) The member may be discharged, or retired if entitled to retire, if, after holding a hearing at which the evidence of two legally qualified medical practitioners is received, the Commissioner or a person whom he or she designates,

(a) determines, on the basis of that evidence, that the member is mentally or physically disabled and as a result incapable of performing the essential duties of the position, and what duties the member is capable of performing; and

(b) concludes that the member's needs cannot be accommodated without undue hardship on the Crown in right of Ontario.

47.(5)Appeal

47.(5) A member of a police force who is discharged or retired under subsection (2) or (4) may appeal to the Commission by serving a written notice on the Commission and on the board or the Commissioner, as the case may be, within thirty days of receiving notice of the decision.

47.(6)Powers of Commission

47.(6) The Commission may confirm, alter or revoke the decision or may require the board or Commissioner, as the case may be, to rehear the matter.

47.(7)Decision

47.(7) The Commission shall promptly give written notice of its decision, with reasons, to the appellant and to the board or Commissioner, as the case may be.

47.(8)Participation of members of Commission

47.(8) No member of the Commission shall participate in the decision unless he or she was present throughout the hearing of the appeal and, except with the consent of the appellant, no decision of the Commission shall be given unless all members who were present throughout the hearing participate in the decision. R.S.O. 1990, c.-P.15, s.-47.

48.(1) Employment equity plans

48. 48.(1) Every police force shall have an employment equity plan prepared in accordance with this section and the regulations.

48.(2)Contents of plan

48.(2) An employment equity plan shall provide for,

- (a) the elimination of systemic barriers to the recruitment and promotion of persons who are members of prescribed groups;
- (b) the implementation of positive measures with respect to the recruitment and promotion of those persons, so as to make the police force more representative of the community or communities it serves; and
- (c) specific goals and timetables with respect to the elimination of systemic barriers, the implementation of positive measures and the composition of the police force.

48.(3)Board to prepare plan for municipal police force

48.(3) In the case of a municipal police force, the board shall prepare the employment equity plan and submit it to the Solicitor General for approval.

48.(4)Commissioner to prepare plan for O.P.P.

48.(4) In the case of the Ontario Provincial Police, the Commissioner shall prepare the employment equity plan and submit it to the Solicitor General for approval.

48.(5)Solicitor General

48.(5) Before approving the employment equity plan, the Solicitor General may require that changes be made to it. R.S.O. 1990, c.-P.15, s.-48.

49.(1) Restrictions on secondary activities

49. 49.(1) A member of a police force shall not engage in any activity,

- (a) that interferes with or influences adversely the performance of his or her duties as a member of a police force, or is likely to do so;
- (b) that places him or her in a position of conflict of interest, or is likely to do so;
- (c) that would otherwise constitute full-time employment for another person; or
- (d) in which he or she has an advantage derived from employment as a member of a police force.

49.(2)Exception, paid duty

49.(2) Clause (1)-(d) does not prohibit a member of a police force from performing, in a private capacity, services that have been arranged through the police force.

49.(3)Disclosure to chief of police

49.(3) A member of a police force who proposes to undertake an activity that may contravene subsection (1) or who becomes aware that an activity that he or she has already undertaken may do so shall disclose full particulars of the situation to the chief of police.

49.(4)Decision of chief of police

49.(4) The chief of police shall decide whether the member is permitted to engage in the activity and the member shall comply with that decision. R.S.O. 1990, c.-P.15, s.-49.

50.(1) Liability for torts

50. 50.(1) The board or the Crown in right of Ontario, as the case may be, is liable in respect of torts committed by members of the police force in the course of their employment.

50.(2)Indemnification of member of municipal police force

50.(2) The board may, in accordance with the guidelines established under clause 31-(1)-(h), indemnify a member of the police force for reasonable legal costs incurred,

    (a) in the defence of a civil action, if the member is not found to be liable;
    (b) in the defence of a criminal prosecution, if the member is found not guilty;
    (c) in respect of any other proceeding in which the member's manner of execution of the duties of his or her employment was an issue, if the member is found to have acted in good faith.

50.(3)Agreement

50.(3) The police force and the board may, in an agreement made under Part VIII, provide for indemnification for the legal costs of members of the police force, except the legal costs of a member who is found guilty of a criminal offence; if such an agreement exists, the board shall indemnify members in accordance with the agreement and subsection (2) does not apply.

50.(4)Council responsible for board's liabilities

50.(4) The council is responsible for the liabilities incurred by the board under subsections (1), (2) and (3).

50.(5)Indemnification of member of O.P.P.

50.(5) The Treasurer of Ontario may indemnify, out of the Consolidated Revenue Fund, a member of the Ontario Provincial Police for reasonable legal costs incurred,

(a) in the defence of a civil action, if the member is not found to be liable;

(b) in the defence of a criminal prosecution, if the member is found not guilty;

(c) in respect of any other proceeding in which the member's manner of execution of the duties of his or her employment was an issue, if the member is found to have acted in good faith.

50.(6)Agreement

50.(6) The Ontario Provincial Police and the Crown in right of Ontario may, in an agreement made under the *Public Service Act*, provide for indemnification for the legal costs of members of the police force, except the legal costs of a member who is found guilty of a criminal offence; if such an agreement exists, the Treasurer shall indemnify members in accordance with the agreement and subsection (5) does not apply. R.S.O. 1990, c.-P.15, s.-50.

51.(1) Police cadets

51. 51.(1) With the board's approval, a municipal chief of police may appoint persons as police cadets to undergo training.

51.(2)Idem

51.(2) A police cadet is a member of the municipal police force. R.S.O. 1990, c.-P.15, s.-5

52.(1) Auxiliary members of municipal police force

52. 52.(1) With the Commission's approval, a board may appoint auxiliary members of the police force.

52.(2)Notice of suspension or termination

52.(2) If the board suspends or terminates the appointment of an auxiliary member of the police force, it shall promptly give the Commission written notice of the suspension or termination.

52.(3)Auxiliary members of O.P.P.

52.(3) The Commissioner may appoint auxiliary members of the Ontario Provincial Police.

52.(4)Authority of auxiliary members of police force

52.(4) An auxiliary member of a police force has the authority of a police officer if he or she is accompanied or supervised by a police officer and is authorized to perform police duties by the chief of police.

52.(5)Restriction

52.(5) The chief of police may authorize an auxiliary member of the police force to perform police duties only in special circumstances, including an emergency, that the police officers of the police force are not sufficiently numerous to deal with.

52.(6)Oaths of office and secrecy

52.(6) A person appointed to be an auxiliary member of a police force shall, before entering on the duties of his or her office, take oaths or affirmations of office and secrecy in the prescribed form. R.S.O. 1990, c.-P.15, s.-52.

SPECIAL CONSTABLES

53.(1) Special constables appointed by board

53. 53.(1) With the Commission's approval, a board may appoint a special constable to act for the period, area and purpose that the board considers expedient.

53.(2)Special constables appointed by Commissioner

53.(2) With the Commission's approval, the Commissioner may appoint a special constable to act for the period, area and purpose that the Commissioner considers expedient.

53.(3)Powers of police officer

53.(3) The appointment of a special constable may confer on him or her the powers of a police officer, to the extent and for the specific purpose set out in the appointment.

53.(4)Restriction

53.(4) A special constable shall not be employed by a police force to perform on a permanent basis, whether part-time or full-time, all the usual duties of a police officer.

53.(5)Idem

53.(5) Subsection (4) does not prohibit police forces from employing special constables to escort and convey persons in custody and to perform duties related to the responsibilities of boards under Part X.

53.(6)Suspension or termination of appointment

53.(6) The power to appoint a special constable includes the power to suspend or terminate the appointment, but if a board or the Commissioner suspends or terminates an appointment, written notice shall promptly be given to the Commission.

53.(7)Commission

53.(7) The Commission also has power to suspend or terminate the appointment of a special constable.

53.(8)Information and opportunity to reply

53.(8) Before a special constable's appointment is terminated, he or she shall be given reasonable information with respect to the reasons for the termination and an opportunity to reply, orally or in writing as the board, Commissioner or Commission, as the case may be, may determine.

53.(9)Oaths of office and secrecy

53.(9) A person appointed to be a special constable shall, before entering on the duties of his or her office, take oaths or affirmations of office and secrecy in the prescribed form. R.S.O. 1990, c.-P.15, s.-53.

FIRST NATIONS CONSTABLES

54.(1) First Nations Constables

54. 54.(1) With the Commission's approval, the Commissioner may appoint a First Nations Constable to perform specified duties.

54.(2)Further approval

54.(2) If the specified duties of a First Nations Constable relate to a reserve as defined in the *Indian Act* (Canada), the appointment also requires the approval of the reserve's police governing authority or band council.

54.(3)Powers of police officer

54.(3) The appointment of a First Nations Constable confers on him or her the powers of a police officer for the purpose of carrying out his or her specified duties.

54.(4)Duty to consult

54.(4) The Commissioner shall not suspend or terminate the appointment of a First Nations Constable whose specified duties relate to a reserve without first consulting with the police governing authority or band council that approved the appointment.

54.(5)Suspension or termination of appointment

54.(5) The power to appoint a First Nations Constable includes the power to suspend or terminate the appointment, but if the Commissioner suspends or terminates an appointment, written notice shall promptly be given to the Commission.

54.(6)Commission

54.(6) The Commission also has power to suspend or terminate the appointment of a First Nations Constable.

54.(7)Information and opportunity to reply

54.(7) Before a First Nations Constable's appointment is terminated, he or she shall be given reasonable information with respect to the reasons for the termination and an opportunity to reply, orally or in writing as the Commissioner or Commission, as the case may be, may determine.

54.(8)Oaths of office and secrecy

54.(8) A person appointed to be a First Nations Constable shall, before entering on the duties of his or her office, take oaths or affirmations of office and secrecy in the prescribed form. R.S.O. 1990, c.-P.15, s.-54.

EMERGENCIES

55.(1) Emergencies

55. 55.(1) In an emergency, the Solicitor General may make an agreement with the Crown in right of Canada or of another province or with any of its agencies for the provision of police services.

55.(2)Authority to act as police officers

55.(2) The agreement authorizes all peace officers to whom it relates to act as police officers in the area to which the agreement relates.

55.(3)Application

55.(3) For the purpose of the *Workers Compensation Act*, the relationship between a member of a police force and the body that employs him or her continues as if an agreement had not been made under this section.

55.(4)Expense of calling out Canadian Forces

55.(4) If the services of the Canadian Forces are provided under this section, the municipality in whose territory the services are required shall pay all the related expenses.

55.(5)Resignation during emergency prohibited

55.(5) Subject to sections 33 and 34 of the *National Defence Act* (Canada), while an agreement made under this section is in force, no member of a police force that has jurisdiction in the area to which the agreement relates shall resign without the consent of the chief of police. R.S.O. 1990, c.-P.15, s.-55.

PART V   Disciplinary Proceedings

56. Misconduct

56. A police officer is guilty of misconduct if he or she,
- (a) commits an offence described in a prescribed code of conduct;
- (b) contravenes section 46 (political activity);
- (c) engages in an activity that contravenes subsection 49-(1) (secondary activities) without the permission of his or her chief of police, being aware that the activity may contravene that subsection;
- (d) contravenes subsection 55-(5) (resignation during emergency);

(e) contravenes section 57-(inducing misconduct, withholding services);
(f) contravenes subsection 96-(4) (photography at hearing);
(g) contravenes subsection 100-(6) (obstructing Police Complaints Commissioner);
(h) contravenes subsection 108-(2) (confidentiality);
(i) contravenes section 117-(trade union membership);
(j) deals with personal property, other than money or a firearm, in a manner that is not consistent with section 132;
(k) deals with money in a manner that is not consistent with section 133;
(l) deals with a firearm in a manner that is not consistent with section 134;
(m) contravenes a regulation made under paragraph 15-(equipment), 16-(use of force), 17-(standards of dress, police uniforms) 20-(police pursuits) or 21-(records) of subsection 135-(1). R.S.O. 1990, c.-P.15, s.-56.

57.(1) Inducing misconduct

57. 57.(1) No person, including a member of a police force, shall,

(a) induce or attempt to induce a member of a police force to withhold his or her services; or
(b) induce or attempt to induce a police officer to commit misconduct.

57.(2)Withholding services

57.(2) No member of a police force shall withhold his or her services.

57.(3)Offence

57.(3) A person who contravenes subsection (1) or (2) is guilty of an offence and on conviction is liable to a fine of not more than $2,000 or to imprisonment for a term of not more than one year, or to both.

57.(4)Consent of Solicitor General

57.(4) No prosecution shall be instituted under this section without the consent of the Solicitor General. R.S.O. 1990, c.-P.15, s.-57.

58.(1) Chief to investigate misconduct

58. 58.(1) Any apparent or alleged misconduct by a police officer shall be investigated by his or her chief of police.

58.(2)Effect of complaint

58.(2) When a complaint is made under Part VI with respect to apparent or alleged misconduct by a police officer, the following rules apply:

1. The complaint shall be dealt with in accordance with Part VI, and recourse shall be had to this Part only as Part VI permits.
2. Any investigation of the matter under this Part and any hearing under section 60 are suspended as soon as the chief of police becomes aware that a complaint has been made. R.S.O. 1990, c.-P.15, s.-58.

59.(1) Procedure in case of misconduct not of serious nature

59. 59.(1) If the chief of police investigates apparent or alleged misconduct and concludes that the police officer is guilty of misconduct but that the misconduct is not of a serious nature, the following rules apply:

1. The chief of police shall provide the police officer with reasonable information concerning the matter and shall give him or her an opportunity to reply, orally or in writing.
2. The chief of police may then admonish the police officer and may cause an entry concerning the matter, the action taken and the police officer's reply to be made in his or her employment record.
3. If the police officer refuses to accept the admonition, the chief of police shall not cause particulars to be recorded without first holding a hearing.

59.(2)Expungement

59.(2) An entry made in the police officer's employment record under paragraph 2 of subsection (1) shall be expunged from the record two years after being made if during that time no other entries concerning misconduct have been made in the record under this Part or Part VI.

59.(3)Agreement

59.(3) Nothing in this section affects agreements between boards and police officers or associations that permit other penalties than admonition to be administered, if the police officer in question consents, without a hearing under section 60. R.S.O. 1990, c.-P.15, s.-59.

60.(1) Hearing

60. 60.(1) A chief of police may hold a hearing to determine whether a police officer belonging to his or her police force is guilty of misconduct.

60.(2)Prosecutor

60.(2) The chief of police shall designate to be prosecutor at the hearing,

(a) a police officer of the rank of sergeant or higher;
(b) if there is none of that rank, a police officer of a rank equal to or higher than that of the police officer who is the subject of the hearing; or
(c) a legal counsel.

60.(3)Recording of evidence

60.(3) The oral evidence given at the hearing shall be recorded and copies of transcripts shall be provided on the same terms as in the Ontario Court (General Division).

60.(4)Examination of evidence

60.(4) Before the hearing, the police officer shall be given an opportunity to examine any physical or documentary evidence that will be produced or any report whose contents will be given in evidence.

60.(5)Idem

60.(5) If the hearing is being conducted as a result of a complaint made under Part VI, the complainant shall likewise be given an opportunity to examine evidence and reports before the hearing.

60.(6)Police officer not required to give evidence

60.(6) Despite section 12 of the *Statutory Powers Procedure Act*, the police officer shall not be required to give evidence at the hearing.

60.(7)Limited admissibility of certain statements

60.(7) In the case of a hearing that is being conducted as a result of a complaint made under Part VI, no statement made by the police officer or complainant in the course of an attempt to resolve the complaint informally shall be admitted in evidence at the hearing, except with the consent of the person who made the statement.

60.(8)Person conducting hearing not to communicate in relation to subject-matter of hearing

60.(8) The person conducting the hearing shall not communicate directly or indirectly in relation to the subject-matter of the hearing with any person or person's counsel or representative, unless the police officer and the prosecutor receive notice and have an opportunity to participate.

60.(9)Exception

60.(9) However, the person conducting the hearing may seek legal advice from an adviser independent of the police officer and the prosecutor, and in that case the nature of the advice shall be communicated to them so that they may make submissions as to the law.

60.(10)Release of exhibits

60.(10) Within a reasonable time after the matter has been finally determined, documents and things put in evidence at the hearing shall, on request, be released to the person who produced them.

60.(11)Stay

60.(11) If the police officer is charged with an offence under a law of Canada or of a province or territory in connection with the alleged misconduct, the hearing shall continue unless the Crown Attorney advises the chief of police that it should be stayed until the conclusion of the court proceedings.

60.(12)Six-month limitation period, exception

60.(12) If six months have elapsed since the facts on which an allegation of misconduct is based first came to the attention of the chief of police, no notice of hearing shall be served unless the board (in the case of a municipal police officer)

or the Commissioner (in the case of a member of the Ontario Provincial Police) is of the opinion that it was reasonable, under the circumstances, to delay serving the notice of hearing. R.S.O. 1990, c.-P.15, s.-60.

61.(1) Penalties

61. 61.(1) If misconduct is proved at the hearing on clear and convincing evidence, the chief of police may,

> (a) dismiss the police officer from the police force;
> (b) direct that the police officer be dismissed in seven days unless he or she resigns before that time;
> (c) demote the police officer, specifying the manner and period of the demotion;
> (d) suspend the police officer without pay for a period not exceeding thirty days or 240 hours, as the case may be;
> (e) direct that the police officer forfeit not more than five days' or forty hours' pay, as the case may be; or
> (f) direct that the police officer forfeit not more than twenty days or 160 hours off, as the case may be.

61.(2) Calculation

61.(2) Penalties imposed under clauses (1)-(d), (e) and (f) shall be calculated in terms of days if the police officer normally works eight hours a day or less and in terms of hours if he or she normally works more than eight hours a day.

61.(3) Idem

61.(3) Instead of or in addition to a penalty described in subsection (1), the chief of police may reprimand the police officer.

61.(4) Dismissal and demotion

61.(4) The chief of police shall not impose the penalties of dismissal or demotion unless the notice of hearing or a subsequent notice served on the police officer indicated that they might be imposed if the misconduct were proved on clear and convincing evidence.

61.(5) Notice of decision

61.(5) The chief of police shall promptly give written notice of the decision, with reasons, to the police officer and, in the case of a municipal police force, to the board.

61.(6) Idem

61.(6) If the hearing was conducted as a result of a complaint made under Part VI, the chief of police shall also give notice of the decision, with reasons, to the complainant and to the Police Complaints Commissioner.

61.(7) Police officer's employment record

61.(7) No reference to the allegations of misconduct or the hearing shall be made in the police officer's employment record, and the matter shall not be taken into account for any purpose relating to his or her employment, unless,

>   (a) misconduct is proved on clear and convincing evidence; or
>   (b) the police officer resigns before the matter is finally disposed of. R.S.O. 1990, c.-P.15, s.-61.

62.(1) Misconduct by municipal chief of police

62. 62.(1) A board may hold a hearing to determine whether the chief of police is guilty of misconduct, and this Part applies with necessary modifications.

62.(2)Commission hearing

62.(2) The chief of police may, by serving a notice to that effect on the board and the Commission, require that the Commission hold the hearing instead of the board. R.S.O. 1990, c.-P.15, s.-62.

63.(1) Appeal to board

63. 63.(1) A municipal police officer on whom a penalty is imposed under section 61 may appeal to the board by serving a notice of appeal on the board and the chief of police within fifteen days of receiving notice of the decision.

63.(2)Hearing

63.(2) The board shall hear the appeal on the record, but may receive new or additional evidence as it considers just.

63.(3)Powers of board

63.(3) The board may confirm, alter or revoke the decision or may require the chief of police to rehear the matter.

63.(4)Board's decision

63.(4) The board shall promptly give written notice of its decision, with reasons, to the chief of police and the police officer.

63.(5)Participation of members

63.(5) No member of the board shall participate in the decision unless he or she was present throughout the hearing of the appeal and, except with the police officer's consent, no decision of the board shall be given unless all members who were present throughout the hearing participate in the decision.

63.(6)Members not to communicate in relation to subject-matter of appeal

63.(6) The members of the board who participate in the decision shall not communicate directly or indirectly in relation to the subject-matter of the appeal with any person or person's counsel or representative, unless the police officer and the chief of police receive notice and have an opportunity to participate.

63.(7)Exception

63.(7) However, the board may seek legal advice from an adviser independent of the police officer and the chief of police, and in that case the nature of the advice shall be communicated to them so that they may make submissions as to the law.

63.(8)Further appeal to Commission

63.(8) The police officer may appeal to the Commission from the board's decision by serving a notice of appeal on the Commission, the board and the chief of police within thirty days of receiving notice of the decision. R.S.O. 1990, c.-P.15, s.-63.

64. Hearing by Commission instead of board

64. Instead of hearing a police officer's appeal under section 63, the board may, on its own initiative or on the application of the police officer or the chief of police, require the Commission to hear the appeal. R.S.O. 1990, c.-P.15, s.-64.

65. O.P.P., appeal to Commission from Commissioner's decision

65. A member of the Ontario Provincial Police on whom a penalty is imposed under section 61 may appeal to the Commission by serving a written notice on the Commission and the Commissioner within thirty days of receiving notice of the decision. R.S.O. 1990, c.-P.15, s.-65.

66. Exception in case of public complaint

66. If the hearing was conducted as a result of a complaint made under Part VI, sections 63 and 65 do not apply and the police officer may only appeal in accordance with that Part. R.S.O. 1990, c.-P.15, s.-66.

67. Appeals to Commission

67. Subsections 63-(2) to (7) apply to appeals heard by the Commission as if references to the board were references to the Commission and, in the case of an appeal from a board's decision, as if references to the chief of police were references to the board. R.S.O. 1990, c.-P.15, s.-67.

68. Extension of time for appeals

68. The board or Commission may grant an extension of the time provided for giving it a notice of appeal, before or after the expiry of the time, and may give directions in connection with the extension. R.S.O. 1990, c.-P.15, s.-68.

69. Delegation

69. A chief of police may authorize any member of the police force to exercise any power or perform any duty of the chief of police referred to in this Part, subject to the following rules:

1. A hearing under section 60 shall be conducted by a police officer of the rank of inspector or higher.
2. A police officer from another police force who meets the requirements of paragraph 1 may conduct the hearing, with the approval of his or her chief of police.
3. The measures referred to in subsection 59-(1) (procedure in case of misconduct not of serious nature) shall be taken by a police officer of the rank of inspector or higher. R.S.O. 1990, c.-P.15, s.-69.

70.(1) Notice

70. 70.(1) A notice required to be given under this Part is sufficiently given if delivered personally or sent by prepaid registered mail addressed to the person.

70.(2)Notice by mail

70.(2) Notice that is given by mail shall be deemed to be given on the fifth day after the day of mailing, unless the person to whom the notice is to be given establishes that he or she, acting in good faith, through absence, accident, illness or other cause beyond his or her control failed to receive the notice until a later date. R.S.O. 1990, c.-P.15, s.-70.

71.(1) Suspension

71. 71.(1) If a police officer is suspected of or charged with an offence under a law of Canada or of a province or territory or is suspected of misconduct, the chief of police may suspend him or her from duty with pay.

71.(2)Revocation and reimposition of suspension

71.(2) The chief of police may revoke the suspension and later reimpose it, repeatedly if necessary, as he or she considers appropriate.

71.(3)Duration of suspension

71.(3) Unless the chief of police revokes the suspension, it shall continue until the final disposition of the proceeding in which the police officer's conduct is at issue.

71.(4)Conditions of suspension

71.(4) While suspended, the police officer shall not exercise any of the powers vested in him or her as a police officer or wear or use clothing or equipment that was issued to him or her in that capacity.

71.(5)Suspension without pay

71.(5) If a police officer is convicted of an offence and sentenced to a term of imprisonment, the chief of police may suspend him or her without pay, even if the conviction or sentence is under appeal. R.S.O. 1990, c.-P.15, s.-7.

72.(1) Earnings from other employment

72. 72.(1) If a police officer is suspended with pay, the pay for the period of suspension shall be reduced by the amount that he or she earns from other employment during that period.

72.(2)Exception

72.(2) Subsection (1) does not apply to earnings from other employment that was commenced before the period of suspension. R.S.O. 1990, c.-P.15, s.-72.

PART VI   Public Complaints

73.(1) Definitions

73. 73.(1) In this Part,

"bureau" means the public complaints investigation bureau of a police force; ("bureau")

"Commissioner" means the Police Complaints Commissioner appointed under section 99. ("commissaire")

73.(2)Police officer

73.(2) In this Part, unless the context indicates otherwise, a reference to a police officer is a reference to the police officer who is the subject of a complaint. R.S.O. 1990, c.-P.15, s.-73.

74. Attorney General

74. This Part shall be administered by the Attorney General. R.S.O. 1990, c.-P.15, s.-74.

75. Application of Part

75. Complaints by members of the public about the conduct of police officers shall be dealt with in accordance with this Part. R.S.O. 1990, c.-P.15, s.-75.

76.(1) Bureau

76. 76.(1) Every chief of police shall establish and maintain a public complaints investigation bureau.

76.(2)Staff

76.(2) The chief of police shall ensure that the bureau is supplied with sufficient staff to perform its duties effectively.

76.(3)Small police forces

76.(3) If the police force has fewer than twenty police officers, the bureau of another police force may, under an agreement made in accordance with section 7-(municipal agreements for sharing police services) or 10-(municipal agreements for provision of police services by O.P.P.), act as the first-named police force's bureau as well; in that case, subsections (1) and (2) do not apply. R.S.O. 1990, c.-P.15, s.-76.

INITIAL HANDLING OF COMPLAINT

77.(1) Complaint by member of public

77. 77.(1) A member of the public may make a complaint about the conduct of a police officer, orally or in writing,

    (a) at the bureau of the police force to which the complaint relates, or at a station or detachment of that police force; or

    (b) at an office of the Commissioner; or

    (c) at any bureau, police station or detachment.

77.(2)Recording of complaint

77.(2) The person who receives the complaint shall record it on a form provided by the Commissioner and shall give a copy of the completed form to the person who makes the complaint.

77.(3)Information

77.(3) The person who makes the complaint shall also be given a statement, in a form provided by the Commissioner, that sets out the procedures followed in dealing with a complaint and describes the rights of a complainant.

77.(4)Preservation of evidence, preliminary investigation

77.(4) The person on duty who is in charge of a place when a complaint is received shall,

    (a) take all reasonable steps to ensure that evidence that might otherwise be lost is secured immediately;

    (b) if he or she considers it appropriate, ensure that a preliminary investigation is conducted immediately; and

    (c) ensure that a report on the evidence and on the preliminary investigation, if any, is forthwith prepared and attached to the complaint.

77.(5)Copies of complaint

77.(5) The person who records the complaint shall forthwith send copies of it,

    (a) to the bureau, the chief of police and the Commissioner, in the case of a complaint made at a station or detachment of the police force to which it relates;

(b) to the chief of police and the Commissioner, in the case of a complaint made at the bureau of the police force to which it relates;

(c) to the bureau and the chief of police of the police force to which it relates, in the case of a complaint made at an office of the Commissioner;

(d) to the Commissioner, in the case of a complaint made at a bureau, station or detachment of a different police force than the one to which it relates.

77.(6)Complaint made to another police force

77.(6) If a complaint was made at a bureau, station or detachment of a different police force than the one to which it relates, the Commissioner shall forthwith send copies of the complaint and of any report prepared under subsection (4) to the appropriate bureau.

77.(7)Complaint made more than six months after incident

77.(7) A complaint that is made more than six months after the incident to which it relates shall be further dealt with under this Part only if the Commissioner so directs. R.S.O. 1990, c.-P.15, s.-77.

78.(1) Complaint by Commissioner

78. 78.(1) In exceptional circumstances, the Attorney General may direct the Commissioner to make a complaint about the conduct of a police officer.

78.(2)Recording of complaint, copies

78.(2) The Commissioner shall cause the complaint to be recorded and shall send copies to the bureau and the chief of police of the force to which it relates.

78.(3)Complainant

78.(3) The Commissioner is the complainant in the case of a complaint made under this section.

78.(4)Non-application of certain provisions

78.(4) Subsection 77-(7) and sections 80-(notice to potential complainant), 81 (classification of complaint), 82 (reclassification), 83 (informal resolution) and 85 (decision by chief of police re no further action) do not apply to complaints made under this section. R.S.O. 1990, c.-P.15, s.-78.

79.(1) Notice to police officer

79. 79.(1) When the bureau receives a complaint, the person in charge shall forthwith give the police officer notice of the substance of the complaint, unless in the person's opinion to do so might prejudice the investigation.

79.(2)Form

79.(2) The notice shall be written on a form provided by the Commissioner. R.S.O. 1990, c.-P.15, s.-79.

80.(1) Notice to potential complainant

80. 80.(1) If the complaint is made by a person who was not directly affected by the incident and did not observe it, the Commissioner shall, as soon as possible after receiving the complaint, attempt to find the person who was directly affected by the incident or who observed it and send him or her a notice.

80.(2)Idem

80.(2) The notice shall indicate that a complaint has been made, that the person is entitled to be the complainant in the matter and that the complaint will not be dealt with further unless he or she is the complainant.

80.(3)Idem

80.(3) The notice shall also include information about the procedures followed in dealing with a complaint and the rights of a complainant.

80.(4)No further action

80.(4) The complaint shall not be further dealt with under this Part if,

    (a) no person who was directly affected by the incident or who observed it can be found; or

    (b) the person to whom the Commissioner sends the notice does not, within thirty days of the date on which it is sent, file with the Commissioner a request to be the complainant in the matter.

80.(5)Disciplinary proceeding

80.(5) However, if a disciplinary proceeding is commenced against the police officer in respect of the complaint, the chief of police shall notify the Commissioner of the proceeding and of its result, and the Commissioner shall then notify the person who made the complaint.

80.(6)Reopening of matter

80.(6) If the person to whom the Commissioner sends the notice files a request to be the complainant in the matter after the thirty-day period referred to in subsection (4), the Commissioner may cause the matter to be reopened despite the late filing if he or she considers it advisable to do so. R.S.O. 1990, c.-P.15, s.-80.

81.(1) Classification of complaint

81. 81.(1) When the bureau receives a complaint, the person in charge shall consider whether it relates to possible misconduct under section 56, to other matters or to both.

81.(2)Idem

81.(2) If the person in charge is of the opinion that all or part of the complaint relates only to other matters than possible misconduct, he or she may, with the Commissioner's consent, classify the complaint or part of the complaint as an inquiry.

81.(3)Notice and investigation

81.(3) When all or part of a complaint has been classified as an inquiry, the person in charge shall forthwith notify the complainant and the police officer of the fact and may cause the inquiry to be investigated.

81.(4)Response to complainant

81.(4) Not more than sixty days after the bureau receives the original complaint, the person in charge shall send the complainant a written response to the inquiry and shall also send the Commissioner a copy of the response, together with a summary of the results of any investigation.

81.(5)Effect

81.(5) A complaint or part of a complaint that is classified as an inquiry and not reclassified as a complaint and that is the subject of a response under this section need not be dealt with further under this Part. R.S.O. 1990, c.-P.15, s.-8.

82.(1) Reclassification

82. 82.(1) During the course of the investigation of an inquiry, if the person in charge concludes that all or part of it relates to possible misconduct, he or she may reclassify the inquiry or part of the inquiry as a complaint.

82.(2)Idem

82.(2) After receiving a summary of the results of the investigation of an inquiry, the Commissioner may direct the person in charge to reclassify all or part of it as a complaint.

82.(3)Notice

82.(3) The person in charge shall forthwith notify the complainant and the police officer of the reclassification, and shall also notify the Commissioner in the case of a reclassification under subsection (1).

82.(4)Effect

82.(4) An inquiry or part of an inquiry that is reclassified as a complaint shall be dealt with as such under this Part. R.S.O. 1990, c.-P.15, s.-82.

INFORMAL RESOLUTION, WITHDRAWAL

83.(1) Informal resolution by person in charge of bureau

83. 83.(1) If the complainant and the police officer consent, the complaint may be resolved informally by the person in charge of the bureau, before the chief of police gives notice of a decision under section 90, or by the Commissioner after that time.

83.(2)Board's consent

83.(2) If a board of inquiry has begun to hear evidence or argument in respect of the complaint, its consent is also required for an informal resolution.

83.(3)Record

83.(3) When a complaint is resolved informally, the resolution shall be recorded on a form provided by the Commissioner and signed by the complainant and police officer.

83.(4)Copies

83.(4) Copies of the record shall be provided to the complainant and the police officer, and to the Commissioner if the complaint was resolved by the person in charge of the bureau.

83.(5)Commissioner's decision that complaint to continue

83.(5) If the Commissioner is of the opinion that the informal resolution is the result of a misunderstanding or a threat or other improper pressure, he or she may decide that the complaint shall continue to be dealt with under this Part despite the informal resolution.

83.(6)Notice

83.(6) The Commissioner shall give notice of the decision, with reasons, to the complainant, the police officer, the chief of police and the person in charge of the bureau. R.S.O. 1990, c.-P.15, s.-83.

84.(1) Withdrawal of complaint

84. 84.(1) The complainant may withdraw the complaint by giving a notice of withdrawal to the person in charge of the bureau, before the chief of police gives notice of a decision under section 90, or to the Commissioner after that time.

84.(2)Idem, complaint made by Commissioner

84.(2) If the complaint was made under section 78, the Commissioner may withdraw it by giving a notice of withdrawal to the chief of police and a copy to the police officer; subsection (3) applies to the withdrawal but subsections (4) to (7) do not.

84.(3)Board's consent

84.(3) If a board of inquiry has begun to hear evidence or argument in respect of the complaint, it shall not be withdrawn without the board's consent.

84.(4)Copies

84.(4) A copy of the notice of withdrawal shall be provided to the police officer, and to the Commissioner if the person in charge of the bureau received the notice.

84.(5)Form

84.(5) The notice of withdrawal shall be written on a form provided by the Commissioner.

84.(6)Commissioner's decision that complaint to continue

84.(6) If the Commissioner is of the opinion that the withdrawal is the result of a misunderstanding or a threat or other improper pressure, he or she may decide that the complaint shall continue to be dealt with under this Part despite the withdrawal.

84.(7)Notice

84.(7) The Commissioner shall give notice of the decision, with reasons, to the complainant, the police officer, the chief of police and the person in charge of the bureau. R.S.O. 1990, c.-P.15, s.-84.

POWERS OF CHIEF OF POLICE

85.(1) Decision re no further action

85. 85.(1) At any time before making a decision under section 90, the chief of police may decide that the complaint or part of it shall not be further dealt with under this Part, if he or she is of the opinion that the complaint or part is frivolous or vexatious or was made in bad faith.

85.(2)Notice

85.(2) The chief of police shall give the Commissioner, the complainant and the police officer notice of the decision. R.S.O. 1990, c.-P.15, s.-85.

86.(1) Power to commence or continue disciplinary proceeding

86. 86.(1) The chief of police may commence or continue a disciplinary proceeding against a police officer under Part V even if,

(a) the complaint is withdrawn or is resolved informally; or
(b) the complaint is not to be further dealt with under this Part because of subsection 77-(7) (complaint filed more than six months after incident) or section 80-(complaint made by person not directly affected), or because of a decision by the chief of police under section 85.

86.(2)Notice to Commissioner and complainant

86.(2) The chief of police shall give the Commissioner and the complainant notice of a decision to commence or continue a disciplinary proceeding in the circumstances described in subsection (1), and shall also give them notice of the results of the proceeding. R.S.O. 1990, c.-P.15, s.-86.

INVESTIGATION OF COMPLAINT

87.(1) Investigation

87. 87.(1) The person in charge of the bureau shall cause an investigation to be conducted into the complaint in accordance with the prescribed procedures.

87.(2)Interim reports

87.(2) During the course of the investigation, the person in charge shall send the Commissioner, the complainant and the police officer interim reports on the investigation at monthly intervals.

87.(3)Idem

87.(3) The first interim report shall be sent not more than thirty days after the bureau receives the complaint.

87.(4)Exception

87.(4) If there are no new matters to report, the person in charge may send the Commissioner, the complainant and the police officer a notice to that effect instead of an interim report.

87.(5)Idem

87.(5) The person in charge may withhold an interim report from the complainant or the police officer if, in his or her opinion, it is desirable to do so in order to avoid prejudicing the investigation, but in that case shall forthwith notify the Commissioner of the decision and the reasons for it.

87.(6)Final report

87.(6) When the investigation has been completed, the person in charge shall cause a final report to be prepared and shall send copies of it to the Commissioner, the chief of police, the complainant and the police officer.

87.(7)Contents

87.(7) The final report shall contain,

    (a) a summary of the complaint, including a description of the police officer's alleged misconduct;

    (b) a summary of the investigation, including summaries of the information obtained from the complainant, the police officer and any witnesses; and

    (c) a description and analysis of any physical evidence obtained.

87.(8)Further investigation

87.(8) After receiving a final report, the Commissioner may require the chief of police to have the complaint investigated further.

87.(9)Idem

87.(9) A summary of the results of any further investigation shall be sent to the persons who received the final report.

87.(10)Forms

87.(10) The interim reports and final report shall be written on forms provided by the Commissioner. R.S.O. 1990, c.-P.15, s.-87.

88.(1) Investigation by Commissioner

88. 88.(1) The Commissioner may conduct the investigation into the complaint, instead of the bureau,

    (a) for any reason, after receiving the first interim report or after the thirty-day period referred to in subsection 87-(3) has expired;

    (b) if the complainant has commenced a court proceeding against the police officer, the police force or the chief of police, the police services board or the municipality (in the case of a municipal police force) or the Crown in right of Ontario (in the case of the Ontario Provincial Police) in connection with the incident to which the complaint relates;

    (c) if the Commissioner has reasonable grounds to believe that undue delay or other unusual circumstances have affected the bureau's investigation or the preparation of its final report; or

    (d) if the chief of police requests that the Commissioner conduct the investigation.

88.(2)Duty of chief of police

88.(2) The chief of police, if he or she becomes aware that the complainant has commenced a court proceeding of the kind described in clause (1)-(b), shall forthwith notify the Commissioner of the fact.

88.(3)Complaints concerning more than one police force

88.(3) If the complaint concerns more than one police force, the Commissioner shall conduct the investigation.

88.(4)Notice

88.(4) When the Commissioner decides to conduct the investigation, he or she shall forthwith notify the chief of police, giving reasons in the case of a decision under clause (1)-(a) or (c).

88.(5)Effect on bureau

88.(5) When the Commissioner notifies the chief of police of a decision to conduct the investigation, the person in charge of the bureau shall forthwith end any investigation begun by the bureau and send to the Commissioner the evidence that has been gathered and the documents relating to the complaint.

88.(6)Manner of conducting investigation

88.(6) Section 87 applies to the Commissioner's investigation, with necessary modifications, except that the Commissioner shall send the first interim report not more than thirty days after giving notice of the decision to conduct the investigation. R.S.O. 1990, c.-P.15, s.-88.

89.(1) Investigation of complaint made by Commissioner

89. 89.(1) If the complaint was made under section 78, the Commissioner shall conduct the investigation in accordance with the prescribed procedures, and section 87 does not apply.

89.(2)Interim reports

89.(2) The Commissioner shall send the police officer and the chief of police interim reports on the investigation at monthly intervals.

89.(3)Idem

89.(3) The first interim report shall be sent not more than thirty days after the Commissioner makes the complaint.

89.(4)Exception

89.(4) If there are no new matters to report, the Commissioner may send the police officer and the chief of police a notice to that effect instead of an interim report.

89.(5)Idem

89.(5) The Commissioner may withhold an interim report from the police officer if, in his or her opinion, it is desirable to do so to avoid prejudicing the investigation, but in that case shall forthwith notify the chief of police of the decision and the reasons for it.

89.(6)Final report

89.(6) When the investigation has been completed, the Commissioner shall cause a final report to be prepared and shall send copies of it to the chief of police and the police officer.

89.(7)Contents

89.(7) The final report shall contain,
- (a) a summary of the complaint, including a description of the police officer's alleged misconduct;
- (b) a summary of the investigation, including summaries of the information obtained from the police officer and any witnesses; and
- (c) a description and analysis of any physical evidence obtained. R.S.O. 1990, c.-P.15, s.-89.

DECISION BY CHIEF OF POLICE

90.(1) Review of final report

90. 90.(1) The chief of police shall review the final report of the investigation of a complaint and may order further investigation if he or she considers it advisable.

90.(2)Results of further investigation

90.(2) A summary of the results of any further investigation shall be sent to the persons who received the final report, and to the Commissioner if he or she conducted the original investigation.

90.(3)Decision

90.(3) After reviewing the final report and the results of any further investigation, the chief of police shall,

  (a) decide that no further action is necessary;
  (b) admonish the police officer regarding the matter in accordance with subsection 59-(1);
  (c) hold a disciplinary hearing under section 60;
  (d) order that all or part of the complaint be the subject of a hearing by a board of inquiry; or
  (e) cause an information to be laid against the police officer and refer the matter to the Crown Attorney for prosecution.

90.(4)Idem

90.(4) If the chief of police decides to hold a disciplinary hearing under section 60 or orders a hearing by a board of inquiry, he or she may at the same time cause an information to be laid against the police officer.

90.(5)Notice

90.(5) The chief of police shall give written notice of the decision to the Commissioner, the complainant and the police officer, with reasons in the case of a decision that no further action is necessary or a decision to admonish the police officer.

90.(6)Idem

90.(6) If the chief of police orders a hearing by a board of inquiry, he or she shall also notify the chair appointed under subsection 103-(9).

90.(7)Six-month time limit

90.(7) The chief of police shall give notice of the decision within six months of receiving the final report, unless the Commissioner grants an extension.

90.(8)Deemed decision

90.(8) If the chief of police does not give notice of the decision within the six-month period and is not granted an extension, he or she shall be deemed to have decided that no further action is necessary. R.S.O. 1990, c.-P.15, s.-90.

REVIEW BY COMMISSIONER

91.(1) Review by Commissioner

91. 91.(1) The Commissioner shall review the decision of the chief of police,

   (a) at the complainant's or police officer's request, in the case of a decision under section 90 to admonish the police officer;
   (b) at the complainant's request, in the case of a decision under section 90 that no further action is necessary;
   (c) at the complainant's request, in the case of a decision under section 85 that the complaint or part of it not be further dealt with under this Part.

91.(2)Idem

91.(2) The Commissioner may, if in his or her opinion it is in the public interest to do so, review the decision of the chief of police,

   (a) in the case of a decision under section 90 to admonish the police officer;
   (b) in the case of a decision under section 90 that no further action is necessary;
   (c) in the case of a decision under section 85 that the complaint or part of it not be further dealt with under this Part.

91.(3)Idem

91.(3) The Commissioner shall, at the complainant's request, review the decision made in a disciplinary hearing under section 60 arising out of a complaint.

91.(4)Thirty-day limit

91.(4) The complainant or police officer may request a review by the Commissioner only within thirty days of receiving notice of the decision, unless the Commissioner grants an extension.

91.(5)Complaint made by Commissioner

91.(5) In the case of a complaint made under section 78, the Commissioner may review,

   (a) a decision by the chief of police to admonish the police officer;
   (b) a decision by the chief of police that no further action is necessary;
   (c) the decision made in a disciplinary hearing under section 60 arising out of the complaint.

91.(6)Commissioner's decision

91.(6) After conducting the review, the Commissioner may decide to take no further action, or may order a hearing by a board of inquiry if he or she believes it to be necessary in the public interest.

91.(7)Notice

91.(7) The Commissioner shall forthwith give written notice of his or her decision, with reasons in the case of a decision to take no further action, to the chief of police, the complainant and the police officer.

91.(8)Idem

91.(8) If the Commissioner orders a hearing by a board of inquiry, he or she shall also notify the chair appointed under subsection 103-(9). R.S.O. 1990, c.-P.15, s.-9.

HEARING BY BOARD OF INQUIRY

92.(1) Police officer's appeal to board

92. 92.(1) If a penalty is imposed on a police officer after a disciplinary hearing under section 60 that was conducted as a result of the complaint, he or she may appeal to a board of inquiry by serving a notice of appeal on the Commissioner, the chair of the panel and the chief of police within fifteen days of receiving notice of the decision.

92.(2)Notice to complainant

92.(2) The Commissioner shall forthwith notify the complainant of the appeal.

92.(3)Extension of time for appeal

92.(3) A member of the panel who was appointed on a recommendation made under subsection 103-(2) may grant an extension of the time provided for serving a notice of appeal, before or after the expiry of the time, and may give directions in connection with the extension.

92.(4)Appeal to be combined with other hearing

92.(4) The hearing of the police officer's appeal and any hearing ordered by the Commissioner under section 91 shall be combined. R.S.O. 1990, c.-P.15, s.-92.

93.(1) Constitution of board

93. 93.(1) A board of inquiry shall be constituted,
- (a) when the chief of police orders under section 90 that a matter be heard by a board of inquiry;
- (b) when the Commissioner orders a hearing under section 91; and
- (c) when a police officer appeals under section 92.

93.(2)Assignment of members to board

93.(2) The chair of the panel shall assign the following members of the panel to the board of inquiry, choosing members from the area where the complaint arose if possible:

1. As presiding officer, a member who was appointed on a recommendation made under subsection 103-(2).
2. A member who was appointed on a recommendation made under subsection 103-(3).
3. A member who was appointed on a recommendation made under subsection 103-(4).

93.(3)Complaint against chief of police

93.(3) In the case of a complaint against a chief of police, the board of inquiry shall include, instead of a member of the panel who was appointed on a recommendation made under subsection 103-(3), a person, other than a police officer or a member of the Law Society of Upper Canada, appointed to the board of inquiry by the chair of the panel on the recommendation of the Ontario Association of Chiefs of Police. R.S.O. 1990, c.-P.15, s.-93.

94.(1) New hearing, exception

94. 94.(1) The hearing before the board of inquiry shall be a new hearing, unless it follows a disciplinary hearing under section 60; in that case it shall be on the record, but the board may receive new or additional evidence as it considers just.

94.(2)Record of disciplinary hearing

94.(2) If a board is constituted following a disciplinary hearing, the chief of police shall cause a record of the hearing to be prepared, at the Commissioner's expense if the Commissioner ordered the hearing before the board.

94.(3)Idem

94.(3) The record shall include a transcript and shall be accompanied by the documents, physical evidence and exhibits considered at the disciplinary hearing. R.S.O. 1990, c.-P.15, s.-94.

95.(1) Parties

95. 95.(1) The parties to a hearing are,

(a) the complainant;
(b) the police officer;
(c) the Commissioner; and
(d) the chief of police, in the case of an appeal by the police officer.

95.(2)Idem

95.(2) The board of inquiry may add parties at any stage of the hearing on the conditions it considers proper.

95.(3)Carriage

95.(3) In the case of a hearing ordered by the chief of police or by the Commissioner, the Commissioner has carriage of the matter and, in the case of an appeal by the police officer, the police officer has carriage.

95.(4)Statement of alleged misconduct

95.(4) In the case of a hearing ordered by the chief of police or by the Commissioner, the chief of police or the Commissioner, as the case may be, shall provide the parties with a concise statement of the allegations of misconduct to be heard. R.S.O. 1990, c.-P.15, s.-95.

96.(1) Notice of hearing

96. 96.(1) The board of inquiry shall appoint a time for the hearing and notify the parties.

96.(2)Examination of evidence

96.(2) Before the hearing, the police officer and the complainant shall be given an opportunity to examine any physical or documentary evidence that will be produced or any report whose contents will be given in evidence at the hearing.

96.(3)Recording of evidence

96.(3) The oral evidence given at the hearing shall be recorded and copies of transcripts shall be provided on the same terms as in the Ontario Court (General Division).

96.(4)Application

96.(4) Section 136 of the *Courts of Justice Act* (photography at court hearing) applies with necessary modifications to the hearing.

96.(5)Police officer not required to give evidence

96.(5) Despite section 12 of the *Statutory Powers Procedure Act*, the police officer shall not be required to give evidence at the hearing.

96.(6)Limited admissibility of certain statements

96.(6) No statement made by the police officer or complainant in the course of an attempt to resolve the complaint informally shall be admitted in evidence at the hearing, except with the consent of the person who made the statement.

96.(7)Board not to communicate in relation to subject-matter of hearing

96.(7) The board of inquiry shall not communicate directly or indirectly in relation to the subject-matter of the hearing with any person or party or party's counsel or representative, unless all parties receive notice and have an opportunity to participate.

96.(8)Exception

96.(8) However, the board may seek legal advice from an adviser independent of the parties, and in that case the nature of the advice shall be communicated to the parties so that they may make submissions as to the law.

96.(9)Adjournment for view

96.(9) If it appears to be in the interests of justice, the board may direct that the board, the parties and their counsel or representatives shall have a view of any place or thing, and may adjourn the hearing for that purpose.

96.(10)Release of exhibits

96.(10) Within a reasonable time after the matter has been finally determined, documents and things put in evidence at the hearing shall, on request, be released to the person who produced them.

96.(11)Stay

96.(11) If the police officer is charged with an offence under a law of Canada or of a province or territory in connection with the misconduct or possible misconduct to which the complaint relates, the hearing shall continue unless the Crown Attorney advises the presiding officer that it should be stayed until the conclusion of the court proceedings.

96.(12)Only members at hearing to participate in decision

96.(12) No member of the board shall participate in a decision unless he or she was present throughout the hearing and heard the parties' evidence and argument; except with the parties' consent, no decision shall be given unless all the members so present participate in it.

96.(13)Decision

96.(13) The decision of a majority of the members of the board is the board's decision. R.S.O. 1990, c.-P.15, s.-96.

97.(1) Penalties

97. 97.(1) If misconduct is proved at the hearing on clear and convincing evidence, the chief of police may make submissions as to penalty and the board of inquiry may,

    (a) dismiss the police officer from the police force;
    (b) direct that the police officer be dismissed in seven days unless he or she resigns before that time;
    (c) demote the police officer, specifying the manner and period of the demotion;
    (d) suspend the police officer without pay for a period not exceeding thirty days or 240 hours, as the case may be;
    (e) direct that the police officer forfeit not more than five days' or forty hours' pay, as the case may be; or

(f) direct that the police officer forfeit not more than twenty days or 160 hours off, as the case may be.

97.(2)Calculation

97.(2) Penalties imposed under clauses (1)-(d), (e) and (f) shall be calculated in terms of days if the police officer normally works eight hours a day or less and in terms of hours if he or she normally works more than eight hours a day.

97.(3)Idem

97.(3) Instead of or in addition to a penalty described in subsection (1), the board may reprimand the police officer.

97.(4)Notice of decision

97.(4) The board shall promptly give written notice of the decision, with reasons, to the parties and the Attorney General. R.S.O. 1990, c.-P.15, s.-97.

98.(1) Appeal to Divisional Court

98. 98.(1) A party to a hearing before a board of inquiry may appeal to the Divisional Court within thirty days of receiving notice of the board's decision.

98.(2)Grounds for appeal

98.(2) An appeal may be made on a question that is not a question of fact alone, or from a penalty, or both.

98.(3)Attorney General

98.(3) The Attorney General is entitled to be heard, by counsel or otherwise, on the argument of the appeal. R.S.O. 1990, c.-P.15, s.-98.

POLICE COMPLAINTS COMMISSIONER

99.(1) Appointment of Commissioner

99. 99.(1) The Lieutenant Governor in Council shall appoint a Police Complaints Commissioner, to hold office for a term not exceeding five years.

99.(2)Reappointment

99.(2) The Commissioner may be reappointed for a further term or terms not exceeding five years in each case.

99.(3)Employees

99.(3) Such employees as are considered necessary for the purposes of this Part may be appointed under the *Public Service Act.*

99.(4)Remuneration

99.(4) The Commissioner shall be paid such remuneration and allowance for expenses as may be fixed by the Lieutenant Governor in Council.

99.(5)Records

99.(5) The Commissioner shall maintain copies of all records, reports and other materials received under this Part.

99.(6)Monitoring handling of complaints

99.(6) The Commissioner shall monitor the handling of complaints by bureaus and chiefs of police.

99.(7)Local offices

99.(7) The Commissioner may establish local offices.

99.(8)Idem

99.(8) Anything that is given to or served upon the Commissioner under this Part may be given or served at one of the local offices.

99.(9)Annual report

99.(9) The Commissioner shall report annually to the Attorney General.

99.(10)Audit

99.(10) The Commissioner's accounts shall be audited annually by the Provincial Auditor. R.S.O. 1990, c.-P.15, s.-99.

100.(1) Powers on investigation or review

100. 100.(1) For the purposes of an investigation under section 88 or 89 or a review under section 91, the Commissioner may, if he or she has reasonable grounds to believe that it is necessary to do so in furtherance of the investigation or review, enter a police station after informing the chief of police and examine there documents and things related to the complaint.

100.(2)Powers on inquiry

100.(2) For the purposes of an investigation or review, the Commissioner has the powers of a commission under Part II of the *Public Inquiries Act*, which Part applies to the investigation or review as if it were an inquiry under that Act.

100.(3)Appointment of person to make investigation or review

100.(3) The Commissioner may, in writing, appoint a person to make any investigation or review the Commissioner is authorized to make and the person has all the powers and duties of the Commissioner relating to the investigation and the review.

100.(4)Identification

100.(4) The person shall be provided with a certificate of appointment containing his or her photograph, and while exercising any powers or performing any duties in respect of the investigation or review shall produce the certificate of appointment upon request.

100.(5)Report

100.(5) The person shall report the results of the investigation or review to the Commissioner.

100.(6)Obstruction

100.(6) No person shall obstruct the Commissioner or a person appointed under subsection (3) or withhold from the Commissioner or person or conceal or destroy any documents or things related to the investigation or review.

100.(7)Search warrant

100.(7) If a justice of the peace is satisfied, on an application made without notice by the Commissioner or a person appointed under subsection (3), that there are reasonable grounds to believe that there are in any place documents or things relating to an investigation or review, the justice of the peace may make an order authorizing the applicant, together with such persons as he or she calls on for assistance, to enter the place, by force if necessary, search for the documents or things and examine them.

100.(8)Entry and search at night restricted

100.(8) The entry and search shall not be made between the hours of 9 p.m. and 6 a.m. unless the order so authorizes.

100.(9)Removal of books, etc.

100.(9) The Commissioner may, upon giving a receipt, remove any documents or things examined under subsection (1) or (7) relating to the investigation or review, shall cause them to be copied with reasonable dispatch and shall then return them promptly to the person from whom they were removed.

100.(10)Admissibility of copies

100.(10) A copy made as provided in subsection (9) and certified to be a true copy by the Commissioner is admissible in evidence in any proceeding and is proof, in the absence of evidence to the contrary, of the original document and its contents.

100.(11)Appointment of expert

100.(11) The Commissioner may appoint an expert to examine documents or things examined under subsection (1) or (7). R.S.O. 1990, c.-P.15, s.-100.

101.(1) Recommendations concerning police practices or procedures

101. 101.(1) The Commissioner may make recommendations with respect to the practices or procedures of a police force by sending the recommendations, with any supporting documents, to,

    (a) the Attorney General;
    (b) the Solicitor General;

(c) the chief of police;

(d) the association, if any; and

(e) the police services board, in the case of a municipal police force.

101.(2)Comments

101.(2) Within ninety days of receiving the recommendations, the chief of police, association and police services board shall send their comments to the Attorney General, the Solicitor General and the Commissioner. R.S.O. 1990, c.-P.15, s.-10.

102. Judicial review of Commissioner's decisions

102. The Commissioner's decisions under subsection 83-(5) (complaint to continue to be dealt with despite informal resolution), subsection 84-(6) (complaint to continue to be dealt with despite withdrawal) and clause 88-(1)-(c) (decision to conduct investigation because of undue delay) shall be deemed to be made in the exercise of a statutory power of decision. R.S.O. 1990, c.-P.15, s.-102.

BOARDS OF INQUIRY

103.(1) Panel for boards of inquiry

103. 103.(1) The Lieutenant Governor in Council shall appoint a panel of persons to act as members of boards of inquiry to conduct hearings in connection with complaints.

103.(2)Recommendations for appointment

103.(2) One-third of the members of the panel shall be members of the Law Society of Upper Canada who are recommended for appointment by the Attorney General.

103.(3)Idem

103.(3) One-third of the members of the panel shall be persons, other than police officers and members of the Law Society of Upper Canada, who are recommended for appointment by the Police Association of Ontario.

103.(4)Idem

103.(4) One-third of the members of the panel shall be persons, other than police officers and members of the Law Society of Upper Canada, who are recommended for appointment by the Association of Municipalities of Ontario.

103.(5)Failure to make recommendations

103.(5) The Attorney General may make the recommendations under subsection (3) or (4) if the Police Association of Ontario or the Association of Municipalities of Ontario, as the case may be, do not submit written recommendations to the Attorney General within the time that he or she specifies.

103.(6)Term

103.(6) Appointments to the panel shall be for a term not exceeding three years and a member may be reappointed for a further term or terms.

103.(7)Continuance in office for uncompleted assignments

103.(7) A member of the panel whose term expires without reappointment continues in office for the purpose of completing the work of a board to which he or she was assigned before the expiration of the term.

103.(8)Remuneration

103.(8) The members of the panel shall be paid such remuneration and expenses as may be fixed by the Lieutenant Governor in Council.

103.(9)Chair

103.(9) The Lieutenant Governor in Council shall appoint a person to be the chair of the panel.

103.(10)Annual summary of decisions

103.(10) The chair shall cause to be prepared and published an annual summary of the decisions of boards, with reasons. R.S.O. 1990, c.-P.15, s.-103.

GENERAL MATTERS

104. Police officer's employment record

104. No reference to a complaint, a hearing held under this Part or a disciplinary hearing conducted under section 60 as a result of the complaint shall be made in the police officer's employment record, and the matter shall not be taken into account for any purpose related to his or her employment, unless,

   (a) the police officer is convicted of an offence in connection with the incident;
   (b) misconduct is proved on clear and convincing evidence at a hearing held under this Part or at a disciplinary hearing;
   (c) the chief of police admonishes the police officer in connection with the incident, in accordance with subsection 59-(1);
   (d) the police officer admits misconduct in the course of attempts to resolve the complaint informally; or
   (e) the police officer resigns before the complaint is finally disposed of. R.S.O. 1990, c.-P.15, s.-104.

105.(1) Resignation after hearing ordered

105. 105.(1) This section applies to a police officer who resigns from the police force after a hearing is ordered under section 90 or 91.

105.(2)Idem

105.(2) If the police officer resigns before a board of inquiry is constituted under section 93, the following rules apply:

1. No board of inquiry shall be constituted unless the police officer, within twelve months of the resignation, applies for employment with a police force or is employed by a police force.
2. In that case, the board acquires jurisdiction over the police officer despite the earlier resignation.

105.(3)Idem

105.(3) If the police officer resigns after a board of inquiry is constituted, the following rules apply:

1. The board of inquiry loses jurisdiction over the police officer.
2. If the police officer, within twelve months of the resignation, applies for employment with a police force or is employed by a police force, the board's jurisdiction is revived. R.S.O. 1990, c.-P.15, s.-105.

106.(1) Notice

106. 106.(1) A notice or other document required to be given or sent under this Part is sufficiently given if delivered personally or sent by prepaid registered mail addressed to the person.

106.(2)Notice by mail

106.(2) Notice that is given by mail shall be deemed to be given on the fifth day after the day of mailing, unless the person to whom the notice is to be given establishes that he or she, acting in good faith, through absence, accident, illness or other cause beyond his or her control failed to receive the notice until a later date. R.S.O. 1990, c.-P.15, s.-106.

107.(1) Delegation by chief of police

107. 107.(1) The chief of police may authorize any police officer of the rank of inspector or higher (from another police force if there is none in the chief's own police force) to exercise any power or perform any duty of the chief of police referred to in this Part.

107.(2)Delegation by Commissioner

107.(2) The Commissioner may authorize any member of his or her staff to exercise any power or perform any duty of the Commissioner referred to in this Part. R.S.O. 1990, c.-P.15, s.-107.

108.(1) Application of section

108. 108.(1) This section applies to every person engaged in the administration of this Part, including a member of a police force.

108.(2)Confidentiality, exceptions

108.(2) A person shall preserve secrecy in respect of all information obtained in the course of his or her duties and not contained in a record as defined in the *Freedom of Information and Protection of Privacy Act,* and shall not communicate such information to any other person except,

    (a) in accordance with subsection (3);

    (b) as may be required for law enforcement purposes; or

    (c) with the consent of the person, if any, to whom the information relates.

108.(3)Permitted disclosure

108.(3) A person may communicate information obtained in the course of his or her duties,

    (a) as may be required in connection with the administration of this Act and the regulations; or

    (b) to his or her counsel.

108.(4)Non-compellability

108.(4) No person shall be required to testify in a civil proceeding with regard to information obtained in the course of his or her duties, except at a hearing held under this Part or at a disciplinary hearing held under Part V.

108.(5)Inadmissibility of documents

108.(5) No document prepared under this Part as the result of a complaint and no statement referred to in subsection 96 (6) (statements made during attempt at informal resolution) is admissible in a civil proceeding, except at a hearing held under this Part or at a disciplinary hearing held under Part V. R.S.O. 1990, c.-P.15, s.-108.

109. *Ombudsman Act* not to apply

109. The *Ombudsman Act* does not apply to anything done under this Part. R.S.O. 1990, c.-P.15, s.-109.

110. Agreement for contributions

110. The Attorney General may, with the approval of the Lieutenant Governor in Council, enter into an agreement with a municipality providing for its payment to the Treasurer of Ontario, on such conditions as may be agreed upon, of contributions in respect of the amounts required for the purposes of this Part. R.S.O. 1990, c.-P.15, s.-110.

111. Offence

111. A person who contravenes subsection 96-(4) (photography at hearing), 100-(6) (obstructing Commissioner) or 108-(2) (confidentiality) is guilty of an offence and on conviction is liable to a fine of not more than $2,000. R.S.O.

1990, c.-P.15, s.-111.

112.(1) Definition

112. 112.(1) In this section, "former Act" means the *Metropolitan Toronto Police Force Complaints Act, 1984,* being chapter 63. R.S.O. 1990, c.-P.15, s.-112-(1); 1991, c.-12, s.-1-(1).

112.(2)Transition, complaints under former Act

112.(2) Despite the repeal of the former Act, complaints made under the former Act before the 31st day of December, 1990 shall be dealt with in accordance with the former Act, except that hearings before boards of inquiry that are constituted after the 31st day of December, 1990 shall be conducted in accordance with this Part. R.S.O. 1990, c.-P.15, s.-112-(2).

112.(3)Transition, boards of inquiry

112.(3) Members of boards of inquiry constituted under the former Act before the 31st day of December, 1990 are continued in office for the purpose of completing the work of the boards to which they were assigned. 1991, c.-12, s.-1-(2).

PART VII   Special Investigations

113.(1) Special investigations unit

113. 113.(1) There shall be a special investigations unit of the Ministry of the Solicitor General.

113.(2)Composition

113.(2) The unit shall consist of a director appointed by the Lieutenant Governor in Council on the recommendation of the Solicitor General and investigators appointed under the *Public Service Act.*

113.(3)Idem

113.(3) A person who is a police officer or former police officer shall not be appointed as director, and persons who are police officers shall not be appointed as investigators.

113.(4)Peace officers

113.(4) The director and investigators are peace officers.

113.(5)Investigations

113.(5) The director may, on his or her own initiative, and shall, at the request of the Solicitor General or Attorney General, cause investigations to be conducted into the circumstances of serious injuries and deaths that may have resulted from criminal offences committed by police officers.

113.(6)Restriction

113.(6) An investigator shall not participate in an investigation that relates to members of a police force of which he or she was a member.

113.(7)Charges

113.(7) If there are reasonable grounds to do so in his or her opinion, the director shall cause informations to be laid against police officers in connection with the matters investigated and shall refer them to the Crown Attorney for prosecution.

113.(8)Report

113.(8) The director shall report the results of investigations to the Attorney General.

113.(9)Co-operation of police forces

113.(9) Members of police forces shall co-operate fully with the members of the unit in the conduct of investigations. R.S.O. 1990, c.-P.15, s.-113.

PART VIII   Labour Relations

114. Definitions

114. In this Part,

"Arbitration Commission" means the Ontario Police Arbitration Commission continued by subsection 131-(1); ("Commission d'arbitrage")

"senior officer" means a member of a police force who has the rank of inspector or higher or is employed in a supervisory or confidential capacity. ("agent supérieur") R.S.O. 1990, c.-P.15, s.-114.

115.(1) Exclusion of O.P.P.

115. 115.(1) This Part, except section 117, does not apply to the Ontario Provincial Police.

115.(2)Exclusion of chief of police and deputy

115.(2) The working conditions and remuneration of the chief of police and deputy chief of police of a police force shall be determined under clause 31-(1)-(d) (responsibilities of board) and not under this Part. R.S.O. 1990, c.-P.15, s.-115.

116.(1) Hearing re person's status

116. 116.(1) If there is a dispute as to whether a person is a member of a police force or a senior officer, any affected person may apply to the Commission to hold a hearing and decide the matter.

116.(2)Decision final

116.(2) The Commission's decision is final. R.S.O. 1990, c.-P.15, s.-116.

117. Membership in trade union prohibited, exception

117. A member of a police force shall not become or remain a member of a trade union or of an organization that is affiliated directly or indirectly with a trade union, unless the membership is required for secondary activities that do not contravene section 49 and the chief of police consents. R.S.O. 1990, c.-P.15, s.-117.

118.(1) Categories

118. 118.(1) If a majority of the members of a police force, or an association that is entitled to give notices of desire to bargain, assigns the members of the police force to different categories for the purposes of this Part, bargaining, conciliation and arbitration shall be carried on as if each category were a separate police force.

118.(2)Senior officers

118.(2) If at least 50 per cent of the senior officers of a police force belong to an association composed only of senior officers, bargaining, conciliation and arbitration shall be carried on as if the senior officers were a separate police force.

118.(3)Restriction

118.(3) Bargaining, conciliation and arbitration may be carried on with more than two categories within a police force (apart from senior officers) only if the Commission has approved the creation of the categories. R.S.O. 1990, c.-P.15, s.-118.

119.(1) Notice of desire to bargain

119. 119.(1) If no agreement exists or at any time after ninety days before an agreement would expire but for subsection 129-(1) or (2), a majority of the members of a police force may give the board notice in writing of their desire to bargain with a view to making an agreement, renewing the existing agreement, with or without modifications, or making a new agreement.

119.(2)Bargaining

119.(2) Within fifteen days after the notice of desire to bargain is given or within the longer period that the parties agree upon, the board shall meet with a bargaining committee of the members of the police force.

119.(3)Idem

119.(3) The parties shall bargain in good faith and make every reasonable effort to come to an agreement dealing with the remuneration, pensions, sick leave credit gratuities and grievance procedures of the members of the police force and, subject to section 126, their working conditions.

119.(4)Filing of agreement

119.(4) The board shall promptly file a copy of any agreement with the Arbitration Commission.

119.(5)Association

119.(5) If at least 50 per cent of the members of the police force belong to an association, it shall give the notice of desire to bargain.

119.(6)Municipal plans, notice to Minister

119.(6) If the notice of desire to bargain involves pensions under a pension plan established or to be established under the *Municipal Act*, it shall also be given to the Minister of Municipal Affairs, who may determine the maximum pension benefits that may be included in any agreement or award with respect to the pension plan. R.S.O. 1990, c.-P.15, s.-119.

120.(1) Bargaining committee

120. 120.(1) The members of the bargaining committee shall be members of the police force.

120.(2)Counsel and advisors

120.(2) One legal counsel and one other advisor for each of the bargaining committee and the board may participate in the bargaining sessions.

120.(3)Police organization

120.(3) If the notice of desire to bargain is given by an association that is affiliated with a police organization, or if at least 50 per cent of the members of the police force belong to a police organization, a member of the organization may attend the parties' bargaining sessions in an advisory capacity.

120.(4)Chief of police

120.(4) The chief of police or, if the parties consent, another person designated by the chief of police may also attend the parties' bargaining sessions in an advisory capacity. R.S.O. 1990, c.-P.15, s.-120.

121.(1) Appointment of conciliation officer

121. 121.(1) The Solicitor General shall appoint a conciliation officer, at a party's request, if a notice of desire to bargain has been given.

121.(2)Duty of conciliation officer

121.(2) The conciliation officer shall confer with the parties and endeavour to effect an agreement and shall, within fourteen days after being appointed, make a written report of the results to the Solicitor General.

121.(3)Extension of time

121.(3) The fourteen-day period may be extended if the parties agree or if the Solicitor General extends it on the advice of the conciliation officer that an agreement may be made within a reasonable time if the period is extended.

121.(4)Report

121.(4) When the conciliation officer reports to the Solicitor General that an agreement has been reached or that an agreement cannot be reached, the Solicitor General shall promptly inform the parties of the report.

121.(5)No arbitration during conciliation

121.(5) Neither party shall give a notice requiring matters in dispute to be referred to arbitration under section 122 until the Solicitor General has informed the parties of the conciliation officer's report or informed them that he or she does not consider the case appropriate for the appointment of a conciliation officer. R.S.O. 1990, c.-P.15, s.-12.

122.(1) Arbitration

122. 122.(1) If matters remain in dispute after bargaining under section 119 and conciliation, if any, under section 121, a party may give the Solicitor General and the other party a written notice referring the matters to arbitration.

122.(2)Composition of arbitration board

122.(2) The following rules apply to the composition of the arbitration board:
1. The parties shall determine whether it shall consist of one person or of three persons. If they are unable to agree on this matter, or if they agree that the arbitration board shall consist of three persons but one of the parties then fails to appoint a person in accordance with the agreement, the arbitration board shall consist of one person.
2. If the arbitration board is to consist of one person, the parties shall appoint him or her jointly. If they are unable to agree on a joint appointment, the person shall be appointed by the Solicitor General.
3. If the arbitration board is to consist of three persons, the parties shall each appoint one person and shall jointly appoint a chair. If they are unable to agree on a joint appointment, the chair shall be appointed by the Solicitor General.

122.(3)Time for arbitration

122.(3) The arbitration board shall commence the arbitration within thirty days after being appointed, in the case of a one-person board, or within thirty days after the appointment of the chair, in the case of a three-person board, and shall deliver its decision or award within sixty days after commencing the arbitration.

122.(4)Representations by council

122.(4) The municipal council may make representations before the arbitration board if it is authorized to do so by a resolution.

122.(5)Criteria

122.(5) In making an award, the arbitration board shall take into account the interest and welfare of the community served by the police force as well as any local factors affecting the community.

122.(6)Filing of award

122.(6) The arbitration board shall promptly file a copy of its decision or award with the Arbitration Commission.

122.(7)Costs and expenses

122.(7) The following rules apply with respect to the costs and expenses of the arbitration:

1. The Arbitration Commission shall pay the fees of any person the Solicitor General appoints to the arbitration board.
2. Each party shall pay its own costs incurred in the arbitration, including the fees of any person it appoints to the arbitration board.
3. The parties shall share equally the costs and expenses for matters shared in common, including the fees of any person whom they jointly appoint to the arbitration board. R.S.O. 1990, c.-P.15, s.-122.

123.(1) Dispute, appointment of conciliation officer

123. 123.(1) The Solicitor General shall appoint a conciliation officer, at a party's request, if a difference arises between the parties concerning an agreement or an arbitrator's decision or award made under this Part, or if it is alleged that an agreement or award has been violated.

123.(2)Duty of conciliation officer

123.(2) The conciliation officer shall confer with the parties and endeavour to resolve the dispute and shall, within fourteen days after being appointed, make a written report of the results to the Solicitor General.

123.(3)Extension of time

123.(3) The fourteen-day period may be extended if the parties agree or if the Solicitor General extends it on the advice of the conciliation officer that the dispute may be resolved within a reasonable time if the period is extended.

123.(4)Report

123.(4) When the conciliation officer reports to the Solicitor General that the dispute has been resolved or that it cannot be resolved by conciliation, the Solicitor General shall promptly inform the parties of the report.

123.(5)No arbitration during conciliation

123.(5) Neither party shall give a notice referring the dispute to arbitration until the Solicitor General has informed the parties of the conciliation officer's report. R.S.O. 1990, c.-P.15, s.-123.

124.(1) Arbitration after conciliation fails

124. 124.(1) If the conciliation officer reports that the dispute cannot be resolved by conciliation, either party may give the Solicitor General and the other party a written notice referring the dispute to arbitration.

124.(2)Idem

124.(2) The procedure provided by subsection (1) is available in addition to any grievance or arbitration procedure provided by the agreement, decision or award.

124.(3)Composition of arbitration board

124.(3) The following rules apply to the composition of the arbitration board:
1. The parties shall determine whether it shall consist of one person or of three persons. If they are unable to agree on this matter, or if they agree that the arbitration board shall consist of three persons but one of the parties then fails to appoint a person in accordance with the agreement, the arbitration board shall consist of one person.
2. If the arbitration board is to consist of one person, the parties shall appoint him or her jointly. If they are unable to agree on a joint appointment, the person shall be appointed by the Solicitor General.
3. If the arbitration board is to consist of three persons, the parties shall each appoint one person and shall jointly appoint a chair. If they are unable to agree on a joint appointment, the chair shall be appointed by the Solicitor General.

124.(4)Time for arbitration

124.(4) The arbitration board shall commence the arbitration within thirty days after being appointed, in the case of a one-person board, or within thirty days after the appointment of the chair, in the case of a three-person board, and shall deliver a decision within a reasonable time.

124.(5)Filing of decision

124.(5) The arbitration board shall promptly file a copy of its decision with the Arbitration Commission.

124.(6)Costs and expenses

124.(6) The following rules apply with respect to the costs and expenses of the arbitration:
1. The Arbitration Commission shall pay the fees of any person the Solicitor General appoints to the arbitration board.

2. Each party shall pay its own costs incurred in the arbitration, including the fees of any person it appoints to the arbitration board.
3. The parties shall share equally the costs and expenses for matters shared in common, including the fees of any person whom they jointly appoint to the arbitration board.

124.(7)Enforcement

124.(7) After the day that is thirty days after the delivery of the decision or after the day that the decision provides for compliance, whichever is later, the arbitration board may, of its own motion, and shall, at a party's request, file a copy of the decision, in the prescribed form, with the Ontario Court (General Division).

124.(8)Idem

124.(8) The decision shall be entered in the same way as a judgment of the Ontario Court (General Division) and may be enforced as such. R.S.O. 1990, c.-P.15, s.-124.

125. Extension of time

125. The parties may agree to extend any period of time mentioned in this Part. R.S.O. 1990, c.-P.15, s.-125.

126. Restriction

126. Agreements and awards made under this Part do not affect the working conditions of the members of the police force in so far as those working conditions are determined by sections 42 to 49, subsection 50-(3) and Parts V, VI and VII of this Act and by the regulations. R.S.O. 1990, c.-P.15, s.-126.

127. Non-application

127. The *Arbitrations Act* does not apply to arbitrations conducted under this Part. R.S.O. 1990, c.-P.15, s.-127.

128. Agreements, decisions and awards binding

128. Agreements, decisions and awards made under this Part bind the board and the members of the police force. R.S.O. 1990, c.-P.15, s.-128.

129.(1) Duration of agreements, decisions and awards

129. 129.(1) Agreements, decisions and awards remain in effect until the end of the year in which they come into effect and thereafter continue in effect until replaced.

129.(2)Longer duration if parties agree

129.(2) The parties to an agreement may provide that the agreement and any decisions or awards made with respect to it shall remain in effect until the end of the year following the year in which they come into effect and thereafter shall continue in effect until replaced. R.S.O. 1990, c.-P.15, s.-129.

130.(1) Provision for expenditures

130. 130.(1) If, when the council is adopting its annual estimates, a notice of desire to bargain has been given but there is not yet an agreement, decision or award, the council shall make such provision for the payment of expenditures that will result from the expected agreement, decision or award as it considers adequate.

130.(2)Coming into effect

130.(2) An agreement, decision or award comes into effect on the first day of the fiscal period in respect of which the municipal council may make provision for it in its estimates, whether that day is before or after the agreement, decision or award is made.

130.(3)Exception

130.(3) A provision of the agreement, decision or award that does not involve municipal expenditures may come into effect earlier than the day referred to in subsection (2). R.S.O. 1990, c.-P.15, s.-130.

131.(1) Arbitration Commission continued

131. 131.(1) The commission known as the Ontario Police Arbitration Commission is continued under the name of Ontario Police Arbitration Commission in English and the name of Commission d'arbitrage de la police de l'Ontario in French.

131.(2)Composition

131.(2) The Arbitration Commission shall be composed of the following members, appointed by the Lieutenant Governor in Council:
1. Two representatives of boards, recommended for appointment by the Municipal Police Authorities.
2. Two representatives of members of associations, recommended for appointment by the Police Association of Ontario.
3. A chair.

131.(3)Terms of office

131.(3) The representatives of boards and members of associations shall hold office for two-year terms and may be reappointed; the chair shall hold office during pleasure.

131.(4)Employees

131.(4) Such employees as are necessary for the proper conduct of the Arbitration Commission's work may be appointed under the *Public Service Act.*

131.(5)Responsibilities of Arbitration Commission

131.(5) The Arbitration Commission has the following responsibilities:

1. Maintaining a register of arbitrators who are available for appointment.
2. Assisting arbitrators by making administrative arrangements in connection with arbitrations.
3. Fixing the fees of arbitrators appointed by the Solicitor General under section 124.
4. Sponsoring the publication and distribution of information about agreements, arbitrations and awards.
5. Sponsoring research on the subject of agreements, arbitrations and awards.
6. Maintaining a file of agreements, decisions and awards made under this Part.

131.(6)Regulations

131.(6) Subject to the approval of the Lieutenant Governor in Council, the Arbitration Commission may make regulations,

(a) governing the conduct of arbitrations and prescribing procedures for them;
(b) prescribing forms and providing for their use.

131.(7)Transition

131.(7) The persons who are members of the Arbitration Commission on the 31st day of December, 1990 shall continue to hold office until their terms expire, and may be reappointed in accordance with subsection (2). R.S.O. 1990, c.-P.15, s.-13.

PART IX Regulations and Miscellaneous

132.(1) Property in possession of police force

132. 132.(1) This section applies to personal property of all kinds, except firearms and money, that comes into the possession of a police force under either of the following circumstances:

1. The property was stolen from its owner or was found abandoned in a public place, and the chief of police is unable to determine who owns it.
2. The property was seized by a member of the police force in the lawful execution of his or her duties, all legal proceedings in respect of the property have been completed, there is no court order for its disposition and there is no legal requirement, apart from this section, that it be retained or disposed of.

132.(2)Sale

132.(2) The chief of police may cause the property to be sold, and the board may use the proceeds for any purpose that it considers in the public interest.

132.(3)Perishable property

132.(3) If the property is perishable, it may be sold at any time without notice.

132.(4)Non-perishable property

132.(4) If the property is not perishable, the following rules apply to its sale:

1. The property may be sold when it has been in the possession of the police force for at least one month, in the case of a motor vehicle as defined in the *Highway Traffic Act* or a bicycle, or for at least three months, in the case of other property.
2. The sale shall be by public auction.
3. At least ten days notice of the time and place of the public auction shall be given by publication in a newspaper of general circulation in the municipality.
4. The sale may be adjourned, repeatedly if necessary, until the property is sold.

132.(5)Claim of owner of property

132.(5) If a motor vehicle, bicycle or other property has been sold before it has been in the possession of the police force for three months and if the owner makes a claim before that time, the owner is entitled to receive the proceeds, less the costs of storage, advertising and sale.

132.(6)Register of property

132.(6) The chief of police shall ensure that the police force keeps a register of property and that the following rules are followed:

1. The description and location of every item of property shall be recorded.
2. If the property is sold, full particulars shall be recorded.
3. If the property is returned to its owner, his or her name, address and telephone number shall be recorded.

132.(7)Exception

132.(7) This section does not apply to a motor vehicle that is impounded under section 220 of the *Highway Traffic Act*. R.S.O. 1990, c.-P.15, s.-132.

133.(1) Money

133. 133.(1) This section applies to money that comes into the possession of a police force under the circumstances described in paragraph 1 or 2 of subsection 132-(1).

133.(2)Accounting

133.(2) The money shall be accounted for according to the prescribed method.

133.(3)Use of money

133.(3) If three months have elapsed after the day the money came into the possession of the police force and the owner has not claimed it, the board may use it for any purpose that it considers in the public interest. R.S.O. 1990, c.-P.15, s.-133.

134.(1) Firearms

134. 134.(1) This section applies to firearms that are in the possession of a police force because they have been found, turned in or seized.

134.(2)Safe-keeping, return to owner

134.(2) The chief of police shall ensure that firearms are securely stored, and that they are returned to their owners if there is a court order or other legal requirement to that effect.

134.(3)Destruction

134.(3) If all possible court proceedings relating to a firearm have been completed or the time for them has expired and there is no court order or other legal requirement governing how the firearm is to be dealt with, the chief of police shall ensure that it is destroyed promptly, unless subsection (4) applies.

134.(4)Firearm of special interest

134.(4) If the chief of police considers the firearm unique, an antique, or of educational or historical value, he or she shall notify the Director of the Centre of Forensic Sciences.

134.(5)Idem

134.(5) If the Director indicates, within three months of receiving notice, that the firearm is required for the Centre's collection, the chief of police shall ensure that it is transferred there.

134.(6)Idem

134.(6) If the Director indicates that the firearm is not required for the Centre's collection or fails to respond within three months of receiving notice, the chief of police shall ensure that the firearm is destroyed promptly.

134.(7)Disposal otherwise than by destruction

134.(7) The chief of police may dispose of a firearm to which subsection (6) applies otherwise than by having it destroyed if he or she first obtains the Solicitor General's approval of the method of disposal.

134.(8)Register of firearms

134.(8) The chief of police shall ensure that the police force keeps a register of firearms and that the following rules are followed:

    1. Every firearm's description and location shall be recorded.

2. When a firearm ceases to be in the possession of the board or of a member of the police force, full particulars shall be recorded, including the name of the person who disposed of it and the date and method of disposal.
3. If the firearm is returned to its owner, his or her name, address and telephone number shall also be recorded.
4. On or before the 31st day of January in each year, a statement shall be filed with the Commission listing the firearms that have come into the possession of the police force during the preceding calendar year, indicating which firearms are still being retained and which have been disposed of, and giving the particulars of disposition. R.S.O. 1990, c.-P.15, s.-134.

135.(1) Regulations

135. 135.(1) The Lieutenant Governor in Council may make regulations,

1. prescribing standards for police services;
2. prescribing procedures for the inspection and review by the Solicitor General of police forces;
3. requiring municipalities to provide police detention facilities, governing those facilities and providing for their inspection;
4. providing for financial aid to police training schools;
5. prescribing the minimum amount of remuneration to be paid by municipalities to the members of boards who are appointed by the Lieutenant Governor in Council or Solicitor General;
6. prescribing the procedures to be followed by boards and the places at which their meetings shall be held;
7. prescribing the forms of oaths or affirmations of office and secrecy for the purposes of section 32-(members of boards), section 45-(police officers), subsection 52-(6) (auxiliary members of police forces), subsection 53-(9) (special constables) and subsection 54-(8) (First Nations Constables);
8. respecting the government, operation and administration of police forces;
9. governing the qualifications for the appointment of persons to police forces and for their promotion;
10. prescribing groups of persons for the purposes of subsection 48-(1) (employment equity plans);
11. prescribing matters to be contained in employment equity plans;
12. respecting the political activities in which municipal police officers are permitted to engage;
13. establishing the ranks that shall be held by members of municipal police forces;
14. prescribing the minimum salary or other remuneration and allowances to be paid to members of municipal police forces;
15. regulating or prohibiting the use of any equipment by a police force or any of its members;
16. regulating the use of force by members of police forces;
17. prescribing standards of dress for police officers on duty and prescribing requirements respecting police uniforms;

18. prescribing courses of training for members of police forces and prescribing standards in that connection;
19. governing the conduct, duties, suspension and dismissal of members of police forces;
20. describing the circumstances under which members of police forces are permitted and not permitted to pursue persons by means of motor vehicles, and prescribing procedures that shall be followed when a person is pursued in that manner;
21. prescribing the records, returns, books and accounts to be kept by police forces and their members;
22. prescribing the method of accounting for fees and costs that come into the hands of members of police forces;
23. prescribing a code of conduct in which offences constituting misconduct are described for the purposes of section 56;
24. providing for the payment of fees and expenses to witnesses at hearings conducted under Part V or VI;
25. prescribing procedures for the investigation of complaints under Part VI;
26. assigning further duties to the Police Complaints Commissioner;
27. prescribing the method of accounting for money to which section 133 applies;
28. prescribing forms and providing for their use;
29. prescribing any matter that this Act requires to be prescribed or refers to as being prescribed;
30. respecting any matter that is necessary or advisable to implement this Act effectively.

135.(2)Idem

135.(2) A regulation made under subsection (1) may be general or particular in its application. R.S.O. 1990, c.-P.15, s.-135.

136. Crown bound

136. This Act binds the Crown in right of Ontario. R.S.O. 1990, c.-P.15, s.-136.

PART X   Court Security

137.(1) Court security in municipalities with police forces

137. 137.(1) A board that is responsible for providing police services for a municipality has the following responsibilities, with respect to premises where court proceedings are conducted:

1. Ensuring the security of judges and of persons taking part in or attending proceedings.
2. During the hours when judges and members of the public are normally present, ensuring the security of the premises.

3. Ensuring the secure custody of persons in custody who are on or about the premises including persons taken into custody at proceedings.
4. Determining appropriate levels of security for the purposes of paragraphs 1, 2 and 3.

137.(2)Idem, other parts of Ontario

137.(2) The Ontario Provincial Police Force has the responsibilities set out in paragraphs 1, 2, 3 and 4 of subsection (1) in those parts of Ontario in which it has responsibility for providing police services.

137.(3)Common law replaced

137.(3) The responsibilities created by this section replace any responsibility for ensuring court security that existed at common law. R.S.O. 1990, c.-P.15, s.-137.

Bibliography

Ainslie, Mary T. (1994). *The Role, Organization and Operation of the British Columbia Police Commission.* Report submitted to the Commission of Inquiry Policing in British Columbia. Victoria, B.C.: Attorney General.

Alderson, J. (1982). The future of policing. In T. Bennett (Ed.) *The Future of Policing.* Cambridge: Institute of Criminology.

Alpert Geoffrey A. and Friddell, L. (1992). *Police Vehicles and Firearms: Instruments of Deadly Force.* Prospect Heights, Illinois: Waveland Press.

Alpert, Geoffrey A. and Dunham, Roger G. (1988). *Policing In Urban America.* Prospect Heights, Ill.: Waveland Press.

Anderson, J. (1982). The future of policing. In T. Bennett (Ed.) *The Future of Policing.* Cambridge: Institute of Criminology.

Angell, John E. (1976). Organizing police for the future: An update of the democratic model. *Criminal Justice Review, 1*(2).

Arcuri, A.F. (1976). Police pride and self esteem: Indications of future occupational changes. *Journal of Police Science and Administration, 4*(2).

Baldwin, R. and Kinsey, R. (1982). *Police Powers and Politics.* London: Quartet.

Balkin, J. (1988). Why policemen don't like policewomen. *Journal of Police Science and Administration, 16*(3).

Banton M. (1964). *The Police in the Community.* London: Tavistock.

Barker, T. and Carter, D.L. (1987). *Police Deviance.* Cincinnati: Anderson.

Baseline Market Research Ltd. (1991). *Public Attitude Survey: Crime, Safety and Policing Services in New Brunswick.* New Brunswick: Department of the Solicitor General.

Bayley, D. (1991). *Managing the Future: Prospective Issues in Canadian Policing.* Ottawa: Solicitor General.

Bayley, D.H. (1985). *Patterns of Policing: A Comparative International Analysis.* New Jersey: Rutgers University Press.

Bayley, D.H. (1989). Community policing: A report from the devil's advocate. In R.J. Green and S.D. Mastrofski (Eds.) *Community Policing: Rhetoric or Reality?* New York: Praeger.

Bayley, David H. and Mendelsohn, H. (1969). *Minorities and the Police.* New York: Basic Books.

Bayley, David H. and Bittner, Egon (1993). Learning the skills of policing. In Roger D. Dunham and Geoffrey P. Alpert (Eds.) *Critical Issues in Policing: Contemporary Readings.* Prospect Heights, Illinois: Waveland Press.

Becker, H. (1963). *Outsiders.* New York: Free Press.

Bellemare, J. (1988). *Investigation into Relations between Police Forces, Visible and Other Ethnic Minorities.* Montreal: Quebec Human Rights Commission.

Bennett, S.F. and Lavarakas, P.J. (1989). Community-based crime prevention: An assessment of the Eisenhower Foundations Neighbourhood Program. *Crime and Delinquency, 25*(2).

Benson, G.F. (1991). *Developing Crime Prevention Strategies in Aboriginal Communities.* Ottawa: Solicitor General of Canada.

Bittner, E. (1967). The police on skid row: A study in peacekeeping. *American Sociological Review, 32.*

Bittner, E. (1970). *The Functions of Police in Modern Society.* Chevy Chase, Md.: National Institute of Mental Health.

Bloch, P. and Anderson, D. (1974). *Policewomen on Patrol: Final Report.* Washington D.C.: Police Foundation.

Bonifacio, P. (1991). *The Psychological Effects of Policework.* New York: Plenum Press.

Bouza, A.V. (1990). *The Police Mystique.* New York: Plenum Press.

Boydstun, J.E., Sherry, M.E. and Moelter, N.P. (1977). *Patrol Staffing in San Diego.* Washington D.C.: Police Foundation.

Bradley, David, Walker, Neil and Wilkie, Ray (1986). *Managing the Police: Law, Organization and Democracy.* Sussex: Wheatsheaf Books.

Brake, M. (1980). *The Sociology of Youth Culture and Youth Subculture.* London: Routledge and Kegan Paul.

Brillion, Yves, Louis-Guerin, Christian and Lamarche, Marie Christine (1984). *Attitudes of the Canadian Public Toward Crime Policies.* Montreal: International Centre for Comparative Criminology, University of Montreal.

Broderick, J. (1991). Review essay: Community policing and problem oriented policing. *American Journal of Police, 10*(4).

Broderick, John J. (1987). *Police in a Time of Change.* Prospect Heights, Ill.: Waveland Press.

Brodgen, M., Jefferson, T. and Walklate, S. (1988). *Introducing Policework.* London: Unwin Hyman.

Brooks, Laurie Weber (1993). Police discretionary behavior. In Roger D. Dunham and Geoffrey P. Alpert (Eds.) *Critical Issues in Policing: Contemporary Readings.* Prospect Heights, Illinois: Waveland Press.

Brown, Jennifer M. and Campbell, Elizabeth A. (1994). *Stress and Policing: Sources and Strategies.* Chichester, West Sussex: John Wiley and Sons Ltd.

Brown, Lorne and Brown, Caroline (1978). *The Unauthorized History of the RCMP.* Toronto: Lewis and Samuel.

Brown, M. K. (1981). *Working the Street: Police Discretion.* New York: Russell Sage Foundation.

Brown, W.J. (1986). Organizational assessment: Determining the state of a police organization. *Journal of Police Science and Administration, 14*(4).

Bryett, Keith (1989). Police socialization: A reassessment. *Canadian Police College Journal, 13*(4).

Buckley, Leslie Brian (1991). Attitudes toward higher education among mid-career police officers. *Canadian Police College Journal, 15*(4).

Bunyan, T. (1981). The police against the people. *Race and Class, 23*(2-3).

Burbeck, Elizabeth and Furnham, Adrian (1985). Police officer selection: A critical review of the literature. *Journal of Police Science and Administration, 13*(1).

Burke, Ronald J. and Kirchmeyer, Catherine (1990). Initial career orientations, stress and burnout in policeworkers. *Canadian Police College Journal, 14*(2).

Cadieux, P. (1990). Community policing: A vision of the future of policing in Canada. In D. Loree and R. Walker (Eds.) *Community Crime Prevention: Shaping the Future.* Ottawa: Royal Canadian Mounted Police.

Cain, M. (1973). *Society and the Policeman's Role.* London: Routledge and Kegan Paul.

Cain, M. (1979). Trends in the sociology of policework. *International Journal of the Sociology of Law, 7*(2).

Campbell, Peter and Wright, Susan (1993). Leadership in turbulent times. In The Ministry of the Solicitor General of Canada *Canadian Community Policing Series.* Ottawa: Minister of Supplies and Services.

Canada (1973). *Task Force on Policing on Reserves.* Ottawa: Department of Indian Affairs and Northern Development.

Canada (1985). Criminal victimization of elderly Canadians. *Canadian Urban Victimization Survey Bulletin, 6*(1).

Canada (1990). *Indian Policing Policy Review Task Force Report.* Ottawa: Indian and Northern Affairs.

Canada (1992). *First Nations Policing Policy.* Ottawa: Ministry of the Solicitor General.

Canada (1994). *Basic Facts about Corrections in Canada.* Ottawa: Ministry of Supplies and Services.

Carriere, K.D. (1987). Crime stoppers critically considered. *Canadain Criminology Forum, 8.*

Cawsey, Mr. Justice R.A. (1991). *Justice on Trial. Report of the Task Force on the Criminal Justice System and its Impact on the Indian and Metis People of Alberta*. Main Report. Edmonton: Attorney General and Solicitor General of Canada.

Chacko, James and Nancoo, Stephen E. (1993). *Community Policing in Canada*. Canadian Scholars' Press Inc.: Toronto.

Chamelin, Neil C., Fox, Vernon B. and Whisenand, Paul M. (1979). *Introduction to Criminal Justice*. Englewood Cliffs, N.J.: Prentice Hall.

Chatterton, M. (1976). Police in social control. In J. King (Ed.) *Control Without Custody*. Cropwood Papers No.7. Cambridge: Institute of Criminology.

Chatterton, M.R. (1979). The supervision of patrol work under the fixed points system. In S. Holdaway (Ed.) *The British Police*. London: Edward Arnold.

Chatterton, M.R. (1983). Police work and assault charges. In M. Punch (Ed.) *Control in the Police*. Cambridge, Mass.: MIT Press.

Cherniss, C. (1980). *Professional Burnout in Human Service Organizations*. New York: Praeger.

Clairmont, D.H. (1991). Community-based policing: Implementation and impact. *Canadian Journal of Criminology, 33*(3-4).

Clairmont, Donald (1993). Community-based policing and organizational change. In James Chacko and Stephen E. Nancoo (Eds.) *Community Policing in Canada*. Toronto: Canadian Scholars' Press.

Clarke, M. (1987). Citizenship, community and management of crime. *British Journal of Criminology, 27*(1).

Cohen, A.K. (1955). *Delinquent Boys: The Culture of the Gang*. Chicago: Free Press.

Cohen, B. (1980). Leadership styles of commanders in the New York City Police Department. *Journal of Police Science and Administration, 8*.

Cohen, B. and Chaiken, J.H. (1972). *Police Background Characteristics and Performance*. Lexington Mass.: Lexington.

Coleman, A. and Gorman, L. (1982). Conservatism, dogmatism and authoritarianism in British police officers. *Sociology, 16*(1).

Cooper, H.S. (1981). The evolution of Canadian policing. In W.T. McGrath and M.P. Mitchell (Eds.) *Police Function in Canada*. Toronto: Methuen.

Cordingley, P. (1979). Psychological testing in Canadian police forces. *Canadian Police College Journal, 3*(2).

Cordner, Gary W. (1989). The police on patrol. In D.J. Kenny (Ed.) *Police and Policing*. New York: Praeger Publishers.

Cordner, Gary W. (1995). Community policing: Elements and effects. *Police Forum, 5*(3).

Couttes, Larry M. (1990). Police hiring and promotion: Methods and outcomes. *Canadian Police College Journal, 14*(2).

Crank, J.P. (1986). Cynicism among police chiefs. *Justice Quarterly, 3*(3).

Crank, J.P. (1994). Watchman and the community: Myth and institutionalization in policing. *Law and Society Review 28*(2).

Crank, J.P. and Caldero, M. (1991). The production of occupational stress in medium sized police agencies: A survey of line officers in eight municipal departments. *Journal of Criminal Justice, 19.*

Critchley, T.A. (1978). *The History of the Police in England and Wales.* London: Constable Publishers.

Dantzker, Mark L. (1995). *Understanding Today's Police.* Englewood Cliffs, N.J.: Prentice Hall.

Das, Dilip K. (1993). *Policing in Six Countries Around the World.* St Louis: The C.V. Mosby Company.

Dash, J. and Reiser, M. (1978). Suicide among police in urban law enforcement agencies. *Journal of Police Science and Administration, 6.*

Davis, K.C. (1975). *Police Discretion.* Minneapolis: West Publishing Co.

Depew, R. (1986). *Native Policing in Canada: A Review of Current Issues.* Ottawa: Ministry of the Solicitor General.

Depew, R. (1992). Policing Native communities. In Robert A. Silverman and Marianne O. Nielsen (Eds.) *Aboriginal Peoples and the Canadian Criminal Justice System.* Toronto: Butterworths.

Deszca, G. (1988). The communication of ideology in police forces. *Canadian Police College Journal, 12*(4).

Downes, D. (1966). *The Delinquent Solution: A Study of Subcultural Theory.* London: Clarendon Press.

Ellis, D. (1987). *The Wrong Stuff: An Introduction to the Sociological Study of Deviance.* Don Mills, Ontario: Collier Macmillan.

Ericson, R. (1982). *Reproducing Order: A Study of Police Patrol Work.* Toronto: University of Toronto Press.

Farmer, R.E. (1990). Clinical and managerial implications of stress research on the police. *Journal of Police Science and Administration, 17.*

Fielding, N. (1988). Competence and culture in the police. *Sociology, 22*(1).

Fielding, N. (1988). *Joining Forces: Police Training, Socialization and Occupational Competence.* London: Routledge.

Fielding, N., Kemp, C. and Norris, C. (1989). Constraints on the practice of community policing. In Rod Morgan and David Smith (Eds.) *Coming to Terms With Policing: Perspectives on Policy.* London: Routledge.

Fielding, N.G. and Fielding, J.L. (1987). A study of resignation during British police recruit training. *Journal of Police Science and Administration, 15*(1).

Forcese, Dennis (1980). Police unionism: Employee management relations in Canadian police forces. *Canadian Police College Journal, 4*(2).

Forde, D.R. (1992). *Public Attitudes Towards Crime and Police Services: Survey Findings of Winnipeg in 1989 and 1992.* Winnipeg: Department of Sociology, The University of Manitoba.

Foster, J. (1989). Two stations: An ethnographic study of policing in the inner city. In D. Downes (Ed.) *Crime and the City.* Macmillian: London.

Fox, A. (1971). *The Newfoundland Constabulary.* St.John's: Robinson Blackmore Printing and Publishing Ltd.

French, J.R.P. (1975). A comparative look at stress and strain in policemen. In W.H. Kroes and J.J. Hurrell (Eds.) *Job Stress and the Police Officer: Identifying Stress Reduction Techniques.* Washington, D.C.: Department of Health Education and Welfare.

Friedmann, Robert R. (1992). *Community Policing: Comparative Perspectives and Prospects.* Hemel Hempstead: Harvester Wheatsheaf.

Fyfe, James J. (1985). *Police Management Today.* Washington, D.C.: International City Management Association.

Gaine, Larry Keith. (1975). *An Examination of Organizational Model in Traditional and Innovative Police Departments.* Unpublished doctoral dissertation. Sam Houston State University.

Germann, A.C. (1969). Community policing: An assessment. *Journal of Criminal Law, Criminology and Police Science, 60*(1).

Goldsmith, A. (1990). Taking police culture seriously. Police discretion and the limits of the law. *Policing and Society, 1*(2).

Goldsmith, Andrew and Farson, Stuart (1987). Complaints against the police in Canada: A new approach. *Criminal Law Review 11.*

Goldsmith, Andrew J. (1988). New directions in police complaints procedures; Some conceptual and comparative departures. *Police Studies: The International Review of Police Development, 11*(2).

Goldstein, H. (1977). *Policing a Free Society.* Cambridge Mass.: Ballinger.

Goldstein, H. (1979). Improving policing: A problem-oriented approach. *Crime and Delinquency, 25*(2).

Goldstein, H. (1987). Towards community oriented policing: Potential basic require-ments and threshold questions. *Crime and Delinquency. 33*(1).

Goldstein, H. (1990). *Problem Oriented Policing.* New York: McGraw Hill.

Golembiewski, Robert T. and Kim, Byong-Seob (1990). Burnout in police work: Stressors, strain and the phase model. *Police Studies: The International Review of Police Development, 13*(2).

Goolkasian, Gail A., Geddes, Ronald W. and DeJong, William (1985). *Coping with Police Stress*. Washington D.C.: National Institute of Justice.

Graef, R. (1989). *Talking Blues*. London: Collins Harvill.

Grant, Alan (1984). *The Police: A Policy Paper*. Ottawa: Ministry of Supplies and Services.

Grant, Alan (1992). *Policing Arrangements in New Brunswick: 2000 and Beyond*. Fredericton: Department of the Solicitor General.

Grant, Alan (1992). The control of police behavior. In K.R.E. McCormick and L.A. Visano (Eds.) *Understanding Policing*. Toronto: Canadian Scholars' Press.

Green, J.R. (1987). *Police Community Relations and Officer Job Satisfaction: An Evaluation*. Paper presented at the meeting of the Academy of Criminal Justice Sciences, St. Louis, Missouri.

Green, J.R. and Mastrofski, S.D. (1989). *Community Policing: Rhetoric or Reality*. New York: Praeger.

Green, J.R. and Taylor, R.B. (1989). Community based policing and foot patrol: Issues of theory and evaluation. In J.R. Green and S. D. Mastrofski (Eds.) *Community Policing: Rhetoric or Reality?* New York: Praeger.

Green, Jack R., Bergman, William T. and McLaughlin, Edward J. (1994). Implementing community policing: Cultural and structural change in police organizations. In Dennis P. Rosenbaum (Ed.) *The Challenge of Community Policing: Testing the Promises*. California: Sage.

Greenwood, P. and Petersilia, J. (1975). *The Criminal Investigative Process*. Santa Monica: Rand.

Griffiths, C.T. (1988). Native Indians and the police: The Canadian experience. *Police Studies, 11*(4).

Griffiths, C.T. and Yerbury, J.C. (1984). Natives and criminal justice policy: The case of Native policing. *Canadian Journal of Criminology, 26*(2).

Griffiths, Curt T. (1994). Policing Aboriginal Peoples. In R.C. Macleod and David Schneiderman (Eds.) *Police Powers in Canada: The Evolution and Practice of Authority*. Toronto: University of Toronto Press.

Griffiths, Curt T. and Verdun Jones, Simon N. (1994). *Canadian Criminal Justice*. Toronto: Harcourt Brace.

Grimshaw, Roger and Jefferson, Tony (1987). *Interpreting Policework: Policy and Practice in Forms of Beat Policing*. London: Allen Unwin.

Grinc, Randolph M. (1994). "Angels in marble": Problems in stimulating community involvement in community policing. *Crime and Delinquency, 40*(3).

Guller, I.B. (1972). Higher education and policemen: Attitudinal differences between freshmen and senior police college students. *Journal of Criminal Law, Criminology and Police Science, 3*.

Guyot, D. (1977). Police departments under social science scrutiny. *Journal of Criminal Justice, 5.*

Halliday, Carol-Ann (1975). *Many Minnies Later: Development of Women Police in British Columbia.* Vancouver: Vancouver Police Department.

Hamilton, Associate Chief Justice A.C. and Sinclair, Associate Chief Judge C.M. (1991). *Report of the Aboriginal Justice Inquiry of Manitoba. The Justice System and Aboriginal People.* Vol. 1 Winnipeg: Queen's Printer.

Hann, Robert G., MacGinnis, James H., Stenning, Philip C. and Farson, Stuart A. (1985). Municipal police governance and accountability in Canada: An empirical study. *Canadian Police College Journal, 29*(1).

Hann, Robert G., McGinnis, James H., Stenning, Philip C. and Farson, Stuart A. (1985). Municipal police governance and accountability in Canada: An empirical study. *Canadian Police College Journal, 9*(1).

Harding, Jim (1991). Policing and aboriginal justice. *Canadian Journal of Criminology, 33*(3-4).

Hatherley, Mary E. (1991). *The Legal Status of the Police.* Fredericton: Department of the Solicitor General, New Brunswick.

Havemann, P. (1992). The indigenization of social control in Canada. In Robert A. Silverman and Marianne O. Nielsen (Eds.) *Aboriginal Peoples and the Canadian Criminal Justice System.* Toronto: Butterworths.

Heidensohn, Frances (1992). *Women in Control? The Role of Women in Law Enforcement.* Oxford: Clarendon Press.

Hickman, T.A. (1989). *Royal Commission on the Donald Marshall Jr. Prosecution.* Nova Scotia: Queenís Printer.

Higley, Dahn D. (1984). *OPP: The History of the Ontario Provincial Police Force.* Toronto: The Queens Printer.

Holdaway, S. (1989). Discovering structure. Studies of the British police occupational structure. In M. Weatheritt (Ed.) *Police Research: Some Future Prospects.* Aldershot: Gower Publishing Company Ltd.

Holdaway, S. (1989). Discovering structure. Studies of the British police occupational structure. In M. Weatheritt (Ed.). *Police Research: Some Future Prospects.* Aldershot: Gower Publishing Company Ltd.

Holdaway, Simon (1979). *The British Police.* London: Edward Arnold.

Holdaway, Simon (1983). *Inside the British Police: A Force at Work.* Oxford: Basil Blackwell.

Hoover, Larry T. and Madner, Edward T. (1990). Attitudes of police chiefs towards private sector management principles. *American Journal of the Police. 9*(4).

Horne, D. (1992). Public opinion surveys: Implications for police organizations. *Canadian Police College Journal, 16*(4).

Hornick, J.P., Burrows, T.A., Tjowvold, I. and Phillips, D.M. (1990). *An Evaluation of the Neighborhood Foot Patrol Program of the Edmonton Police Service.* Ottawa: Solicitor General of Canada.

Hornick, Joseph P., Burrows, Barbara A., Phillips, Donna M. and Leighton, Barry (1991). An impact evaluation of the Edmonton neighborhood foot patrol program. *The Canadian Journal of Program Evaluation, 6*(1).

Horrall, S.W. (1989). *Policing the Bloods. The RCMP Role 1874-1960. An historical outline.* Ottawa: RCMP.

Hunt, R.G., McCadden, K.S. and Mordaunt, T.J. (1983). Police roles: Context and conflict. *Journal of Police Science and Administration, 11.*

Hunt, Raymond G. and Magenau, John M. (1993). *Power and the Police Chief: An Institutional and Organizational Analysis.* Newbury Park: Sage.

Hylton, J.H. (1980). Public attitudes towards crime and the police in a prairie city. *Canadian Police College Journal, 4*(4).

Inwald, R. (1985). Administrative, legal and ethical practices in the psychological testing of law enforcement officers. *Journal of Criminal Justice, 13*(1).

Jackson R.L. (1992). *Employment Equity and Ontario Police: Problems and Perspectives.* Kingston, Ontario: Industrial Relations Centre, Queenís University.

Jackson, R. (1979). Police labor relations in Canada: A current perspective. *Canadian Police College Journal, 3*(1).

Jackson, R. (1986). Canadian police labor relations in the 1980s: New environmental concerns. *Canadian Police College Journal, 10*(2).

Jain, H.C. (1994). An assessment of strategies of recruiting visible minority police officers in Canada 1985 - 1990. In R.C. Macleod and David Schneiderman (Eds.) *Police Powers in Canada: The Evolution and Practice of Authority.* Toronto: University of Toronto Press.

Jars, Julie (1992). *Inventory of Aboriginal Policing Programs in Canada.* Ottawa: Ministry of the Solicitor General.

Jayewardene, C.H.S. and Talbot, C.K. (1990). *Police Recruitment of Ethnic Minorities.* Ottawa: Canadian Police College.

Jefferson, T. (1990). *The Case Against Para-Military Policing.* Milton Keynes: Open University Press.

Jermier, John M., Slocum, John W., Fry, Louis W. and Gaines, Jeannie (1991). Organizational cultures in a soft bureaucracy: Resistance behind the myth and facade of an official culture. *Organizational Science, 2*(2).

Jobson, Keith B. (1993). *First Nations Police Services: Legal Issues.* Victoria, B.C.: Ministry of the Attorney General.

Jones, S. (1983). Community policing in Devon and Cornwall: Some research findings on the relationship between the public and the police. In T. Bennett (Ed.) *The Future of Policing.* Cambridge: Institute of Criminology.

Jones, S. and Levi, M. (1983). The police and the majority: the neglect of the obvious. *Police Journal 56*(4).

Kania, R.R.E. (1988). Should we tell the police to say 'yes' to gratuities? *Criminal Justice Ethics, 7.*

Kean, Darrell W. (1992). *Informal and formal control mechanisms: An exploration of minor discipline within police organizations.* Unpublished master's dissertation, Simon Fraser University.

Kelling, G.L. (1986). The changing function of urban police: The historical and political context of community policing. In D.J. Loree and C. Murphy (Eds.) *Community Policing in the 1980s: Recent Advances in Police Programs.* Ottawa: Solicitor General.

Kelling, G.L. (1987). *Foot Patrol.* Washington, D.C.: National Institute of Justice.

Kelling, G.L. and Moore, M.H. (1989). From political to reform to community: The evolving strategy of police. In R.J. Green and S.D. Mastrofski (Eds.) *Community Policing; Rhetoric or Reality.* New York: Praeger.

Kelling, G.L., Pate T., Dieckman D. and Brown, C.E. (1974) *The Kansas City Preventive Patrol Experiment: A Summary Report.* Washington, D.C.: Police Foundation.

Kelly, W. and Kelly, N. (1976). *Policing in Canada.* Toronto: MacMillan.

Kennedy, L. W. (1991). The evaluation of community based policing in Canada. *Canadian Police College Journal, 15*(4).

Kessler, D.A. (1985). One or two officer cars? A perspective from Kansas City. *Journal of Criminal Justice, 13.*

Kinsey, R., Lea, J. and Young, J. (1986). *Losing the Fight Against Crime.* London: Routledge.

Kinsey, R., Lea, J. and Young, J. (1999). *Losing the Fight Against Crime.* London: Routledge.

Klockars, C.B. (1985). *The Idea of Police.* Newbury Park, California: Sage.

Klockars, C.B. (1989). The rhetoric of community policing. In R.J. Green and S.D. Mastrofski (Eds.). *Community Policing: Rhetoric or Reality.* New York: Praeger.

Koenig, Daniel J. (1992). *Secondary Employment: A Discussion Paper.* Unpublished paper for the RCMP External Review Committee. Ottawa.

Kroes, W., Margolis, B. and Hurrel, J. (1974). Job stress in policemen. *Journal of Police Science and Administration, 2.*

Kroes, W.H. (1976). *Society's Victim, the Policeman: An Analysis of Job Stress in Policing,* New York: Charles C. Thomas.

Kroes, W.H. and Hurrell, J.J. (1975). *Job Stress and the Police Officer: Identifying Stress Reduction Techniques.* Washington, D.C.: Department of Health Education and Welfare.

La Prarie, C. (1993). *Dimensions of Aboriginal Over-Representation in Canada: Correctional Institutions and Implications for Crime Prevention.* Ottawa: Department of Justice.

Labovitz, S. and Hagedorn, R. (1977). An analysis of suicide rates among occupational categories. *Sociological Inquiry, 41.*

Lambert, Leah (1988). Police ministations in Toronto: An experience in compromise. *RCMP Gazette, 50*(6).

Landau, Tommy (1996). Policing and security in four remote aboriginal communities: A challenge to coercive models of police work. *Canadian Journal of Criminology, 38*(1).

Langworthy, Robert H. (1986). *The Structure of Police Organizations.* New York: Praeger.

Law Reform Commission (1991). *Aboriginal People and Criminal Justice.* Ottawa: Law Reform Commission of Canada.

Lea, J. and Young, J. (1984). *What is to be Done about Law and Order?* London: Penguin.

Lee, J.A. (1981). Some structural aspects of police deviance in relations with minority groups. In C. Shearing (Ed.) *Organizational Police Deviance.* Toronto: Butterworths.

Leighton, B.N. (1991). Visions of community policing: Rhetoric or reality in Canada? *Canadian Journal of Criminology, 33*(3-4).

Leighton, B.N. (1994). Community policing in Canada: An overview of experience and evaluations. In Dennis P. Rosenbaum (Ed.) *The Challenge of Community Policing: Testing the Promises.* California: Sage.

Lewis, C. (1992). *The Report of the Race Relations and Policing Task Force.* Toronto: Solicitor General.

Linden, R.(1983). Women in policing: A study of Lower Mainland RCMP detachments. *Canadian Police College Journal, 7*(1).

Linden, R. (1984). *Women in Policing: A Review.* Ottawa: Solicitor General.

Linden, R. (1985). Attrition among male and female members of the RCMP. *Canadian Police College Journal, 9*(2).

Linden, Rick. (1991). The impact of evaluation research on policing policy in Canada and the United States. *Canadian Journal of Program Evaluation. 6*(1).

Logan, Matt (1995). A systems application to stress management in the RCMP. *RCMP Gazette, 57*(11-12).

Loo, R. (1985). Police development for psychological services in the Royal Canadian Mounted Police. *Journal of Police Science and Administration, 13.*

Loo, R. (1987). *Police Stress and Social Supports.* Paper presented at the 48th Annual Convention of the Canadian Psychological Association, Vancouver, B.C..

Loree, D. (1988). Innovation and change in a regional police force. *Canadian Police College Journal, 12*(4).

Lumb, Richard C. (1994). Standards of professionalization: Do the American police measure up? *Police Studies, XVII*(3)

Lundman R.J. (1980). *Police and Policing: An Introduction.* New York: Holt, Rinehart and Winston.

Lurigo, Arthur J. and Rosenbaum, Dennis P. (1994). The impact of community policing on police personnel: A review of the literature. In Dennis P. Rosenbaum (Ed.) *The Challenge of Community Policing: Testing the Promises.* California: Sage.

Luthans, F. (1985). *Organizational Behavior.* New York: McGraw-Hill.

Lynch, Ronald G. (1986). *The Police Manager: Professional Leadership Skills.* New York: Random House.

Macleod, R.C. (1994). The RCMP and the evolution of provincial policing. In R.C. Macleod and David Schneider (Eds.) *Police Powers in Canada: The Evolution and Practice of Authority.* Toronto: University of Toronto Press.

Maghan, Jess (1993). The changing face of the police officer: Occupational socialization of minority police recruits. In Roger G. Dunham and Geoffrey P. Alpert (Eds.) *Critical Issues in Policing: Contemporary Readings.* Prospect Heights, Illinois: Waveland Press.

Malloy, T.E. and Mays, G.L. (1984). The police stress hypothesis: A critical evaluation. *Criminal Justice and Behaviour, 11.*

Manning, P. (1977). *Police Work.* Cambridge, Mass.: MIT Press.

Manning, P. (1979). The social control of police work. In S. Holdaway (Ed.) *The British Police.* London: Edward Arnold.

Manning, P. K. (1971). The police mandate, strategies and appearances. In J.D. Douglas (Ed.) *Crime and Justice in American Society.* Indianapolis: Bobbs-Merrill.

Manning, P.K. (1984). Community policing. *American Journal of the Police, 3*(2).

Manning, P.K. (1989). Community policing as a drama of control. In R.J. Green and S.D. Mastrofski (Eds.) *Community Policing; Rhetoric or Reality?* New York: Praeger.

Marquis, Greg (1991). Canadian police chiefs and law reform: The historical perspective. *Canadian Journal of Criminology, 33*(3-4)

Marquis Greg (1994). Power from the street: The Canadian municipal police. In R.C. Macleod and David Schneiderman (Eds.) *Police Powers in Canada: The Evolution and Practice of Authority.* Toronto: University of Toronto Press.

Martin, Maurice A. (1995). *Urban Policing in Canada: Anatomy of an Aging Craft.* Montreal: McGill-Queens University Press.

Martin, S.E. (1990). *On the Move: The Status of Women in Policing.* Washington, D.C.: Police Foundation.

Martin, S.E. (1993). Female officers on the move? A status report on women in policing. In Roger G. Dunham and Geoffrey P. Alpert (Eds.) *Critical Issues in Policing: Contemporary Readings.* Prospect Heights, Illinois: Waveland Press.

Mastrofski, S.D. (1989). Community policing as reform: A cautionary tale. In R.J. Green and S.D. Mastrofski (Eds.) *Community Policing; Rhetoric or Reality?* New York: Praeger.

Mawby, R.I. (1990). *Comparative policing Issues: The British and American System in International Perspective.* London: Unwin Hyman.

McConnville, Mike and Shepherd, Dan. (1992). *Watching Police Watching Communities.* London: Routledge.

McDougall, Allan K. (1988). *Policing: The Evolution of a Mandate.* Ottawa: Canadian Police College.

McDowell, Charles P. (1993). *Criminal Justice in the Community.* Cincinnati, Ohio: Anderson Publishing.

McGinnis, James H. (1989). Predicting police force attrition, promotion and demographic change: A computerized simulation model. *Canadian Police College Journal, 13*(2).

Melchers, R. (1993). A commentary on 'A vision of the future of policing in Canada: Police challenge 2000'. *Canadian Journal of Criminology, 35*(1).

Miller, J. and Fry, L.J. (1978). Some evidence on the impact of higher education for law enforcement personnel. *Police Chief, 45.*

Moore, Mark H. (1994). Research synthesis and policy implications. In Dennis P. Rosenbaum (Ed.) *The Challenge of Community Policing: Testing the Promises.* California: Sage.

Morgan, E.C. (1973). The North West Mounted Police: Internal problems and public criticism, 1874-1925. *Saskatchewan History, 26.*

Morgan, G. (1986). *Images of Organization.* Newbury Park: Sage.

Morgan, R. (1987). Police accountability: Developing the local infrastructure. *British Journal of Criminology, 27*(1).

Muir, W.K. (1977). *Police: Streetcorner Politicians.* Chicago: University of Chicago Press.

Murphy, C. (1986). *The Social and Formal Organization of Small Town Policing. A Comparative Analysis of RCMP and Municipal Policing.* Unpublished doctoral dissertation, University of Toronto.

Murphy, C. (1988). Community problems, problem communities and community policing in Toronto. *Journal of Research in Crime and Delinquency, 24*(4).

Murphy, C. (1989). The development, impact and implications of community policing in Canada. In J.R. Green and S.D. Mastrofski (Eds.) *Community Policing: Rhetoric or Reality?* New York: Praeger.

Murphy, C. (1991). The future of non-urban policing in Canada: Modernization, regionalization and provincialization. *Canadian Journal of Criminology, 33*(3-4).

Murphy, C. (1992). Problem oriented policing. In Ministry of the Solicitor General of Canada *Canadian Community Policing Series.* Ottawa: Minister of Supplies and Services.

Murphy, C. (1994). Community-Based Policing: A Review of the Issues, Research and Development of a Provincial *Policy*. Report prepared for The Commission of Inquiry Policing in British Columbia. Victoria, B.C.: Attorney General.

Murphy, C. and Clairmont, D. (1990). *Rural Attitudes and Perceptions of Crime, Policing and Victimization: Preliminary Findings from a Survey of Rural Nova Scotians.* Halifax: Atlantic Institute of Criminology, Dalhousie University.

Murphy, C. and de Verteuil, J. (1986).*Metropolitan Toronto Community Policing Survey: Working Paper No. 1.* Ottawa: Solicitor General of Canada.

Murphy, C. and Lithopoulos, S. (1988). *Social Determinants of Attitudes Towards the Police: Findings from the Toronto Community Policing Survey.* Ottawa: Solicitor General of Canada.

Murphy, C. and Muir, G. (1985). *Community Based Policing; A Review of the Critical Issues.* Ottawa: Solicitor General.

Murphy, P.V. and Pate, T. (1977). *Commissioner.* New York: Simon and Schuster.

Murphy, Patrick V. and Caplan, Dean Gerald (1993). Fostering integrity. In Roger G. Dunham and Geoffrey P. Alpert (Eds.) *Critical Issues in Policing: Contemporary Readings.* Prospect Heights, Illinois: Waveland Press.

Nelken, D. (1985). Community involvement in crime control. *Current Legal Problems.*

Nelson, E.D. (1992). "Employment equity" and the Red Queen's hypothesis: Recruitment and hiring in Western Canadian municipal police departments. *Canadian Police College Journal, 16*(3).

Niederhoffer, A. (1967). *Behind the Shield: The Police in Urban Society.* New York: Doubleday.

Nielsen, M.O. (1992). Introduction. In Robert A. Silverman and Marianne O. Nielsen (Eds.) *Aboriginal Peoples and the Canadian Criminal Justice System.* Toronto: Butterworths.

Normandeau, A. (1990). The police and ethnic minorities. *Canadian Police College Journal, 14*(3).

Normandeau, A. (1993). Policing in Montreal: A New Vision. *Canadian Journal of Criminology, 35*(2).

Normandeau, A. and Leighton, B. (1990). *A Vision of the Future of Policing in Canada: Police Challenge 2000: Background Document.* Ottawa: Police and Security Branch, Ministry Secretariat, Solicitor General.

Normandeau, A. and Leighton, B. (1991). Police and Society in Canada. *Canadian Journal of Criminology, 33*(3-4).

Oettermeir, T.N. and Brown, Lee P. (1991). Community policing. In R.J. Greene and S.D. Mastrofski (Eds.) *Community Policing: Rhetoric or Reality?* New York: Praeger.

Office of Population and Census Surveys (1988). *Occupational Mortality.* Series DS No.6. London: HMSO.

Ontario (1974). *The Police are the Public and the Public are the Police.* Toronto: Task Force on Policing in Ontario.

Ontario Solicitor General (1992). *A Police Learning System For Ontario: Final Report and Recommendations.* Toronto: Ministry of the Solicitor General.

Operational Policing Review (1990). Joint Consultative Committee of the Police Staff Associations, Surbiton, Surrey: The Police Foundation.

Oppal, The Honourable Mr. Justice Wallace T. (1994). *Closing the Gap: Policing and the Community.*Commission of Inquiry Policing in British Columbia. Victoria, B.C.: Attorney General.

O'Reilly, Robert R. and Dostaler, Ann. (1983). Police managers development study. *Canadian Police College Journal,* 7(1).

Ott, J. Steven (1989). *The Organizational Culture Perspective.* Chicago, Illinois: The Dorsey Press.

Owings, Chloe (1969). *Women Police.* Montclair, N.J.: Patterson Smith.

Parizeau, Alice and Szabo, Denis (1977). *The Canadian Criminal Justice System.* Lexington, Mass.: Lexington Books.

Pate, T., Bowers, R.A., Ferrara, A. and Lorence, J. (1976). *Police Response Time: Its Determinants and Effects.* Washington, D.C.: Police Foundation.

Pennell, S., Curtis, C., Henderson, J. and Tayman, J. (1989). Guardian Angels: A unique approach to crime prevention. *Crime and Delinquency, 35*(2).

Perrier, David C. and Toner, Reginald (1984). Police stress: The hidden foe. *Canadian Police College Journal, 8*(1).

Peters, T. and Waterman, R. (1982). *In Search of Excellence.* New York: Warner Books.

Policy Studies Institute (1983). *Police and the People in London.* London: Policy Studies Institute.

Potts, Lee W. (1982). Police leadership: Challenge for the eighties. *Journal of Police Science and Administration, 10*(2).

Punch, Maurice. (1979). *Policing the Inner City: A Study of Amsterdam's Warmoesstraat.* London: Macmillian.

Punch, Maurice. (1979). The secret social service. In S. Holdaway (Ed.) *The British Police.* London: Edward Arnold.

Punch, Maurice. (1983). *Control in the Police Organization.* Cambridge, Mass.: MIT Press.

Reiner, R. (1978) *The Blue Coated Worker.* Cambridge: Cambridge University Press.

Reiner, R. (1985). *The Politics of the Police.* Brighton: Wheatsheaf Books.

Reiner, R. (1991). *Chief Constables: Bobbies, Bosses or Bureaucrats?* Oxford: Clarendon Press.

Reiner, R. (1992). *The Politics of the Police.* (second edition). Hemel Hempstead: Harvester Wheatsheaf.

Reiss, A.J. (1971). *The Police and the Public.* New Haven: Yale University Press.

Reuss-Ianni, Elizabeth. (1983). *Two Cultures of Policing.* New Brunswick (USA): Transaction Books.

Riechers, Lisa M. and Roberg, Roy R. (1990). Community policing: A critical review of underlying assumptions. *Journal of Police Science and Administration, 17*(2).

Roberg, Roy R. (1976). *The Changing Police Role.* San Jose: Justice Systems Development Inc.

Roberg, Roy R. (1994). Can today's police agencies effectively implement community policing? In Dennis P. Rosenbaum (Ed.) *The Challenge of Community Policing: Testing the Promises.* California: Sage.

Roberg, Roy R. and Kuykendall, Jack (1993). *Police and Society.* Belmont, California: Wadsworth Publishing Company.

Roberg, Roy, R. (1978). An analysis of the relationship among higher education, belief systems and job performance of patrol officers. *Journal of Police Science and Administration, 6*(2).

Roberg, Roy, R. (1979). *Police Management and Organizational Behavior: A Contingency Approach.* St.Paul, Minnesota: West Publishing Co.

Rosenbaum, D.P. (1986). *Community Crime Prevention? Does it Work?* Beverly Hills, California: Sage Publications.

Rosenbaum, D.P. (1987). The theory and research behind neighborhood watch: Is it a sound fear and crime reduction strategy? *Crime and Delinquency, 33.*

Rosenbaum, Dennis P. and Lurigo, Arthur J. (1994). An inside look at community policing reform: Definitions, organizational changes and evaluation findings. *Crime and Delinquency, 40*(3).

Rosenbaum, D.P., Lurigio, A.J. and Lavrakas, P.J. (1989). Enhancing citizen participation and solving serious crime. A national evaluation of the Crime Stoppers program. *Crime and Delinquency, 35.*

Rossi, P., Berk, R. and Eidson, B. (1974). *The Roots of Urban Discontent.* New York: Wiley.

Royal Canadian Mounted Police (1990). *Fact Sheets.* Ottawa: Ministry of Supply and Services.

Royal Canadian Mounted Police (1990). *Strategic Action Plan: Implementation of Community Based Policing in the Royal Canadian Mounted Police.* Ottawa: Ministry of Supply and Services.

Royal Canadian Mounted Police (1992). *Strategic Action Plan for Community Policing.* Ottawa: Ministry of Supply and Services.

Royal Canadian Mounted Police (1995). *Fact Sheets.* Ottawa: Ministry of Supply and Services.

Rubinstein, J. (1973). *City Police*. New York: Ballantine.

Russell, Ken (1978). *Complaints Against the Police: A Sociological View*. Leicester: Milltak Limited.

Russo, Philip A., Engel, Alan S. and Hatting, Steven H. (1983). Police and occupational stress: An empirical investigation. In Richard E. Bennett (Ed.). *Police at Work: Policy Issues and Analysis*. Beverly Hills: Sage.

Sacco, Vincent F. (1994). *Community Surveys*. Ottawa: Ministry of the Solicitor General of Canada.

Sandler, G. B. and Mintz, E. (1974). Police organizations: Their changing internal and external relationships. *Police Science and Administration, 2*.

Scarman, Lord. (1982). *The Scarman Report: The Brixton Disorders 10-12 April 1981*. Harmondsworth: Penguin.

Scorer. G. (1994). *The Royal Canadian Mounted Police Complaints and Discipline*. Report submitted to the Commission of Inquiry Policing in British Columbia. Victoria, B.C.: Attorney General.

Seagram, Belinda Crawford and Stark-Adamec, Cannie (1992). Women in Canadian urban policing: Why are they leaving? *The Police Chief.*

Seagrave, J. (1992). Community policing and the need for police research skills training. *Canadian Police College Journal, 16*(3).

Seagrave, J. (1993). Listening to what the people say: The implementation and evaluation of community consultative groups. *RCMP Gazette, 55*(11).

Seagrave, J. (1993). Obtaining information for the corporate strategy: The Vancouver Police telephone survey. *Police Studies: The International Review of Police Development, 16*(4).

Seagrave, J. (1994). Advice for those who want to be boss. *RCMP Gazette, 56*(2).

Seagrave, J. (1994). Community consultative groups: Practical guidelines. *RCMP Gazette, 56*(10).

Seagrave, J. (1995). *Changing the organizational culture: Community Policing in British Columbia*. Unpublished doctoral dissertation. Burnaby, B.C.: Simon Fraser University.

Seagrave, J. (1996). Defining community policing: Interpretations from the literature, police leaders and police officers. *American Journal of Police.*

Selye, H. (1956). *The Stress of Life*. New York: McGraw Hill.

Selye, H. (1974). *Stress Without Distress*. Philadelphia: Lippincott.

Sewell, John (1985). *Police: Urban Policing in Canada*. Toronto: James Lorimer.

Shaftritz, J.M. and Ott, J.S. (1987). *Classics of Organizational Theory*. Chicago: The Dorsey Press.

Shapland J. and Vagg, J. (1988). *Policing by the Public*. London: Routledge.

Shaw, Clifford R. and Mckay, Henry D. (1942). *Juvenile Delinquency in Urban Areas.* Chicago: University of Chicago Press.

Shearing, C. (1981). *Organizational Police Deviance: Its Structure and Control.* Toronto: Butterworths.

Shearing, C.D. (1984). *Dial-a-Cop: A Study of Police Mobilization.* Toronto: Centre of Criminology, University of Toronto.

Shearing, Clifford D. and Leon, Jeffrey S. (1992). Reconsidering the police role: A challenge to a challenge of a popular conception. In K.R.E. McCormick and L.A. Visano (Eds.) *Understanding Policing.* Toronto: Canadian Scholars' Press.

Shearing, Clifford D. and Stenning, Philip C. (1987). *Private Policing.* Newbury Park, California: Sage.

Sherman, L.J. (1973). A psychological view of women in policing. *Journal of Police Science and Administration, 1.*

Sherman, L.J. (1975). Evaluation of policewomen on patrol in a suburban police department. *Journal of Police Science and Administration, 3.*

Sherman, L.W. (1978). *The Quality of Police Education: A Critical Review with Recommendations for Improving Programs in Higher Education.* San Francisco: Jossey-Bass.

Sherman, L.W., Milton, C.H. and Kelley, T.V. (1973). *Team Policing: Seven Case Studies.* Washington, D.C.: The Police Foundation.

Sherman, Lawrence W. (1974). *Police Corruption: A Sociological Perspective.* Garden City, New York: Anchor Books.

Shiner, Roger A. (1994). Citizensí rights and police powers. In R.C. Macleod and David Schneiderman (Eds.) *Police Powers in Canada: The Evolution and Practice of Authority.* Toronto: University of Toronto Press.

Silverman, Robert A. and Nielsen, Marianne O. (1992). *Aboriginal Peoples and the Canadian Criminal Justice System.* Toronto: Butterworths.

Skogan, W.G. (1990). *Disorder and Decline: Crime and the Spiral of Decay in American Neighborhoods.* New York: The Free Press.

Skolnick, J. (1966). *Justice Without Trial.* New York: Wiley.

Skolnick, J.H. and Bayley, D. H. (1986). *The New Blue Line.* New York: The Free Press.

Skolnick, J.H. and Bayley, D.H. (1988). *Community Policing: Issues and Practices Around the World.* United States: National Institute of Justice.

Skoog, Douglas M. (1992). Taking control: Native self-government and Native policing. *Canadian Police College Journal, 16*(1).

Smith, B. (1960). *Police Systems in the United States.* 2nd revised edition. New York: Harper Row.

Smith, D. (1987). The police and the idea of community. In P. Willmott (Ed.) *Policing and the Community.* London: Policy Studies Institute. Discussion Paper 16.

Solicitor General (1994). *Canadian Community Policing Series.* Ottawa: Ministry of the Solicitor General.

Solicitor General of New Brunswick (1993). *New Brunswick Policing Study : Overview.* Fredericton: Department of the Solicitor General.

Somodevilla, S.A. (1978). The psychologists role in the police department. *Police Chief, 39.*

Spelman, W. and Brown, D.K. (1982). *Calling the Police.* Washington, D.C.: Police Executive Research Forum.

Stansfield, Ronald T. (1996). *Issues in Policing: A Canadian Perspective.* Toronto: Thompson Educational Publishing.

Statistics Canada (1990). *Policing in Canada.* Ottawa: Canadian Centre for Justice Statistics.

Statistics Canada (1991).Public perceptions of crime and criminal justice. *Juristat, 11*(1).

Statistics Canada (1995). Homicide in Canada: 1994. *Juristat, 15*(11).

Statistics Canada (1995). Police personnel and expenditure in Canada 1993. *Juristat, 15*(8).

Statistics Canada (1996). Police personnel and expenditure in Canada 1994. *Juristat, 16*(1).

Stenning, Philip C. (1981). *Police Commissions and Boards in Canada.* Toronto: Centre for Criminology, University of Toronto.

Stenning, Philip C. (1989). Private police and public police: Towards a redefinition of the police role. In Donald J. Loree (Ed.) *Future Issues in Policing: Symposium Proceedings.* Ottawa: Canadian Police College.

Stenning, Philip C. (1992). The role of police boards and commissions as institutions of municipal police governance. In K.R.E. McCormick and L.A. Visano (Eds.) *Understanding Policing.* Toronto: Canadian Scholars' Press.

Stenning, Philip C. and Cornish, M. (1975). *The Legal Regulation and Control of Private Police in Canada.* Toronto: Centre for Criminology, University of Toronto.

Stonier-Newman, Lynne (1991). *Policing A Pioneer Province: The B.C. Provincial Police 1858-1950.* Madeira Park B.C.: Harbour Publishing.

Sunahara, David F. (1992). Public inquiries into policing. *Canadian Police College Journal, 16*(2).

Suriya, Senaka K. (1993). The representation of visible minorities in Canadian police: Employment equity beyond rhetoric. *Police Studies, 16*(2).

Swanson, Charles R., Territo, Leonard and Taylor, Robert W. (1988). *Police Administration.* New York: Macmillan.

Swanson, Charles R., Territo, Leonard and Taylor, Robert W. (1993) *Police Administration: Administration, Processes and Behavior.* New York: Macmillan Publishing.

Talarico, Sussette M. and Swanson, Charles R. (1982). An analysis of police perceptions of supervisory and administrative support. *Police Studies, 5(1).*

Talbot, C.K., Jayewardene, C.H.S. and Juliani, T.J. (1986). *Canada's Constables: The Historical Development of Policing in Canada.* Ottawa: Crimecare Inc.

Taylor, Frederick, W. (1947). The principles of scientific management. *Scientific Management.*

Taylor, I. (1980). The law and order issue in the British general election and the Canadian federal election of 1979. *Canadian Journal of Sociology, 5(3).*

Taylor, I. (1981). *Law and Order: Arguments for Socialism.* London: MacMillan Press.

Territo, L. and Vetter, H.J. (1981). *Stress and Police Personnel.* Boston, Mass.: Allyn and Bacon.

Terry, W.C. (1981). Police stress: The empirical evidence. *Journal of Police Science and Administration, 9.*

Thibault, E.A. Lynch, L.M. and McBride, R.B. (1990). *Proactive Police Management.* Engelwood Cliffs, N.J.: Prentice Hall.

Toronto Police. (1991). *Beyond 2000. The Strategic Plan of the Metropolitan Toronto Police.* Toronto: Metropolitan Toronto Police.

Trojanowicz, R.C. (1990). Community policing is not police community relations. *FBI Law Enforcement Bulletin.*

Trojanowicz, R.C. and Banas D.W. (1985). *Perceptions of Safety: A Comparison of foot patrol versus motor patrol officers.* Michigan: National Foot Patrol Centre, Michigan State University.

Trojanowicz, R.C. and Bucqueroux, D. (1990). *Community Policing: A Contemporary Perspective.* Michigan: Anderson Publishing.

Trojanowicz, R.C. and Trojanowicz, J.M. (1975). *Community Based Crime Prevention.* Illinois: Goodyear Publishing.

Uchida, Craig D. (1993). The development of the American police: An historical overview. In Roger G. Dunham and Geoffrey P. Alpert (Eds.) *Critical Issues in Policing.* Illinois: Prospect Heights.

Van Andel, H. (1989). Crime prevention that works: The case of public transportation in the Netherlands. *British Journal of Criminology, 29(3).*

Van Maanen, J. (1973). Observations on the making of policemen. *Human Organization, 32.*

Van Maanen, J. (1986). Power in the bottle. Informal interaction and formal authority. In S. Srivasta (Ed.) *Executive Power.* San Francisco: Jossey-Bell.

Van Wormer, K. (1981). Are males suited to police patrol work? *Police Studies. 3(2).*

Vincent, C. (1990). *Police Officer.* Ottawa: Carlton University Press.

Wagner, Allen E. and Decker, Scott H. (1993). Evaluating citizens' complaints against the police. In Roger G. Dunham and Geoffrey P. Alpert (Eds.) *Critical Issues in Policing: Contemporary Readings.* Prospect Heights, Illinois: Waveland Press.

Wagner, M. and Brzeczek, R.J. (1983). Alcohol and suicide: A fatal connection. *FBI Law Enforcement Bulletin.* August.

Waldon, K. (1982). *Visions of Order: The Canadian Mounties in Symbol and Myth.* Toronto: Butterworths.

Walker, C. and Walker, S.G. (1989). *The Victoria Community Police Stations: An Exercise in Innovation.* Ottawa: Supply and Services Canada.

Walker, S. Gail (1992). *RCMP Community Policing: Blending Tradition with Innovation - Strategic Planning Document.* Ottawa: Aboriginal Policing Directorate, Solicitor General.

Walker, S. Gail (1993). *The Status of Women in Canadian Policing: 1993.* Ottawa: Solicitor General of Canada.

Wasson, D.K. and Crawford, J.D. (1979). *Community Based Preventive Policing: A Review.* Ottawa: Solicitor General.

Watt, Susan (1991). The future of civilian oversight of policing. *Canadian Journal of Criminology, 33* (3-4).

Weatheritt, M. (1986). *Innovations in Policing.* London: Croom Hall.

Weatheritt, M. (1987). Community policing now. In P. Willmott (Ed.) *Policing and the Community.* London: Policy Studies Institute. Discussion Paper 16.

Webb, S.D. and Smith, D.L. (1980). Police stress: A conceptual overview. *Journal of Criminal Justice, 8.*

Weiner, Norman (1974). The effect of education on police attitudes. *Journal of Criminal Justice, 2.*

Westley, W. (1970). *Violence and the Police: A Sociological Study of Law, Custom and Morality.* Cambridge Mass.: MIT Press.

Wexler J.G. and Logan, D.D. (1983). Sources of stress among women police officers. *Journal of Police Science and Administration, 11.*

Whisenand, Paul M. and Ferguson, Frederick R. (1973). *The Managing of Police Organizations.* Englewood Cliffs, N.J.: Prentice Hall.

Wilkinson, Deanna L. and Rosenbaum, Dennis P. (1994). The effects of organizational structure on community policing: A comparison of two cities. In Dennis P. Rosenbaum (Ed.) *The Challenge of Community Policing: Testing the Promises.* California: Sage.

Wilson, James Q. (1968). *Varieties of Police Behavior: The Management of Law and Order in Eight Communities.* Cambridge, Mass.: Harvard University Press.

Wilson, O.W. (1977). *Police Administration.* New York: McGraw Hill.

Woods, Gerald (1984). Costs of municipal police services. *Impact, 2:* 13-22.

Wrobleski, Henry M. and Hess, Karen M. (1976). *Introduction to Law Enforcement and Criminal Justice.* New York: West Publishing Company.

Wycoff, M.A. (1989). The benefits of community policing: Evidence and conjecture. In J.R. Green and S.D. Mastrofski (Eds.) *Community Policing; Rhetoric or Reality.* New York: Praeger.

Yarmey, A. Daniel (1988). Victims and witnesses to deadly force. *Canadian Police College Journal, 12*(2).

Yarmey, A.D. (1991). Retrospective perceptions of police following victimization. *Canadian Police College Journal, 15*(2).

Young, Malcolm (1991). *An Inside Job: Policing and Police Culture in Britain.* Oxford: Clarendon Press.

Index